THE LETTERS OF WILLIAM AND DOROTHY WORDSWORTH

———

VIII

A Supplement of New Letters

EDITED BY

ALAN G. HILL

CLARENDON PRESS · OXFORD

1993

Oxford University Press, Walton Street, Oxford OX2 6DP
Oxford New York Toronto
Delhi Bombay Calcutta Madras Karachi
Kuala Lumpur Singapore Hong Kong Tokyo
Nairobi Dar es Salaam Cape Town
Melbourne Auckland Madrid
and associated companies in
Berlin Ibadan

Oxford is a trade mark of Oxford University Press

Published in the United States
by Oxford University Press Inc., New York

British Library Cataloguing in Publication Data
Data available

Library of Congress Cataloging in Publication Data
(Revised for volume 8)
Wordsworth, William, 1770–1850.
The letters of William and Dorothy Wordsworth;
arranged and edited by the late Ernest de Selincourt.
Includes indexes.
Contents: 1. The early years, 1787–1805, revised by
Chester L. Shaver. – 2. The middle years: pt. I. 1806–
1811, revised by Mary Moorman. – [etc.] – 8. A
supplement of new letters.
1. Wordsworth, Wiliam, 1770–1850 – Correspondence.
2. Wordsworth, Dorothy, 1771–1855 – Correspondence.
3. Poets, English – 19th century – Correspondence.
I. Wordsworth, Dorothy, 1771–1855. II. De Sélincourt,
Ernest, 1870–1943, ed. III. Shaver, Chester L.
IV. Hill, Alan G. V. Title.
PR5881.A48 1967 821¢.7 67–89058
ISBN 0–19–818523–5

Typeset by Hope Services (Abingdon) Ltd.
Printed in Great Britain
on acid-free paper by
Biddles Ltd.,
Guildford and King's Lynn

PREFACE

The present volume completes the new revised edition of *The Letters of William and Dorothy Wordsworth*, which was published in seven volumes between 1967 and 1988. A supplementary volume became necessary when a missing portion of the Wordsworth family papers came to light in a Carlisle attic some years after the two parts of *The Middle Years* had appeared and the series had moved on into *The Later Years*. It is unclear how these papers became separated from the main family archive which was passed down to the poet's grandson Gordon Graham Wordsworth and bequeathed by him to the Dove Cottage Trust, but the newly-discovered manuscripts have now been reunited with the other family papers at Dove Cottage, where they clearly belong, and I am grateful to my fellow Trustees for permission to make use of them in the present volume.

The most striking part of the fresh material—the tender and fervent letters that passed between the poet and his wife Mary during brief periods of separation in 1810 and 1812[1]—belongs to the poet's middle years; but the opportunity has been taken to include a few early letters from other collections, which have come to light since Chester L. Shaver edited the *Early Years* in 1967, and a much larger group belonging to the later years, which came to hand too late for me to include them in Volumes IV–VII of the series. All-in-all, this new volume brings together over a hundred and fifty additional letters which are indispensable for understanding the poet and his circle, from the revolutionary period of the 1790s to his later years at Rydal Mount as a presiding Power over the early Victorian scene.

The additional letters from the middle years have already revolutionized the commonly-held view of the poet's marriage and the dynamics of the Wordsworth family circle. If the relationship between William and Mary after nearly ten years of marriage was as passionate as these letters reveal, we must surely revise our sense of Mary's role as the wife and mother. While Wordsworth's sister Dorothy will undoubtedly remain a

---

[1] Both sides of this correspondence were edited by Beth Darlington in *The Love Letters of William and Mary Wordsworth*, 1982, but in all cases the texts have been re-established and corrected from the manuscripts.

v

paramount influence on his creative processes and an enigmatic presence in his poems, Mary's role can no longer be regarded as marginal to his imaginative life. Indeed, her private letters to William proclaim an unexpected understanding of his deepest preoccupations which Dorothy's only imply.

But these letters are not really 'love letters' in the accepted sense of the term. They also chronicle Wordsworth's daily activities in London in 1812, his numerous contacts (many of them previously unknown), and his efforts, largely successful, to heal the breach with Coleridge. The intimate communion between the poet and his wife, who was parted from him at Hindwell, is constantly interrupted by the world outside—most tragically when the news arrived of the sudden death of their daughter Catharine, who had been left behind at Grasmere in Dorothy's care. Nevertheless, the note of passion in these letters does not easily square with the hitherto accepted picture of Wordsworth. It is as unexpected as the satirical tone of his comments on the London scene, and his humorous banter with Charles Lamb in a letter of 1816. Taken together, the letters do much to dispel the idea that Wordsworth was always a reluctant and reserved letter-writer, who thought that too much attention had been given to such ephemeral productions. He later said as much to Basil Montagu in 1844. These letters, on the other hand, written solely for Mary's eyes, were (he had told her) to be preserved in the family for his descendants.

Another important undercurrent that surfaces from time to time in this volume is the poet's continuing relationship with Annette Vallon and his 'French' daughter Caroline after their affair was brought to an abrupt end during the Revolution and long after the poet's marriage to Mary Hutchinson in 1802. Annette never married, evidently regarding herself as married to the poet, in name if not in fact; and it is now clear that there was more regular contact between the two families than has hitherto been thought. There are for the first time revealing glimpses of how the French side saw Wordsworth's obligations under French law[1] to support his daughter before and after her marriage to Jean Baptiste Baudouin in 1816. The problem of Wordsworth's marriage settlement on Caroline and its continuation when his own financial circumstances became difficult later on, continued to

---

[1] This matter was elucidated by Robert Gittings and Jo Manton, *Dorothy Wordsworth*, 1985.

trouble the poet in later life, and there were even repercussions after his death (see Appendix III). An anguished letter from Annette to Dorothy in 1835, which has only recently come to light, and which is printed in Appendix II, poignantly illustrates the depth of misunderstanding which had grown up between the two families.

Other issues which are further clarified in these letters include Wordsworth's relations with Byron, Hazlitt and (later) Harriet Martineau; his contacts with William Godwin, author of *Political Justice*, and other radicals, emancipationists and non-conformists; his own political stance in response to party realignments in the final years of the Napoleonic Wars; and his later influence on the broad-church movement at Cambridge. His part in the West-morland Election of 1818 was fully set out in the second part of *The Middle Years* and there is little further to add here; but I have included in Appendix I the two newspaper articles entitled *Deception Exposed* that were there attributed to him, as it is now more widely accepted that they are probably Wordsworth's. Further letters illustrate his abiding love for Scotland and its history and literature, some later literary projects, and his anxieties about the well-being of his own beloved Lake District; but his mind also circled back to the French Revolution over fifty years earlier, and an important letter, probably to J. H. Muirhead, throws a curious half-light on the extent of his involvement in it.

The editorial procedures of previous volumes have again been followed here, but this time the letters have not been numbered. While they may be read as a separate series, they gain much more by being seen as part of the whole sequence, and the aim of the annotation has been to 'place' them in such a way that their wider reference may be appreciated. Among the numerous schol-arly enterprises that have appeared since the original volumes appeared, three particularly deserve mention: Mark Reed's *Chronology of the Middle Years, 1800–1815* (Cambridge, Mass., 1975); C. L. and A. C. Shaver's *Wordsworth's Library, A Catalogue* (New York and London, 1979); and the relevant volumes of the *Cornell Wordsworth*.

My thanks are due to the following for kindly permitting me to publish the Wordsworth letters and related manuscripts in their possession: Lord Abinger, J. Robert Barth, S.J., Mr. R. L. Bayne-Powell, Mr. J. F. Chance, Miss Lisa Jean Duncan, Mr. Sherman R. Emery, Dr. D. P. Gange, Mrs. Greenwood, Mrs. Alvin Lewis, The Earl of Lonsdale, Mrs. M. de Meza, The Marquess of

Northampton, Mr. W. Hugh Peal, Dr. Mark L. Reed, Mr. J. H. F. Spedding, Mr. W. N. Tolfree, Mr. Jonathan Wordsworth.

I gratefully acknowledge the courtesy of the Librarians and Trustees of the following institutions in making available to me the Wordsworth letters and related manuscripts in their collections: Arizona State University Library; the Armit Library, Ambleside; Baker Library, Dartmouth College; the Bodleian Library, Oxford; Brown University Library; Cornell University Library; the Cumberland Record Office, Carlisle; the Ella Strong Denison Library, Scripps College; Lambeth Palace Library; the Harold B. Lee Library, Brigham Young University; the Lilly Library, Indiana University; the Archives of the Longman Group; the Massachusetts Historical Society; the Mitchell Library, Glasgow; the Mugar Memorial Library, Boston University; the National Library of Scotland; the New York Public Library (Rare Books and Manuscripts Division); the Pierpont Morgan Library (and the Gordon Ray Collection); Princeton University Library (and the Robert H. Taylor Collection); the Public Record Office; Smith College, Northampton, Mass.; the Kenneth Spencer Research Library, University of Kansas; the Miriam Lutcher Stark Library, University of Texas; Stanford University Library; Washington University Library, St. Louis; Wesleyan University Library, Middletown, Conn.; the Robert W. Woodruff Library, Emory University; the Wordsworth Centre, Lancaster University; the Wordsworth Library, Grasmere; and Yale University Library.

In addition to the acknowledgments made in previous volumes, I should like to record my thanks to the following for assistance of various kinds during the preparation of this new volume: Dr. Paul Betz, Professor Richard Brantley, Dr. James A. Butler, Mr. Ulrick Funk, Dr. Stephen Gill, the late Robert Gittings, Dr. Keith Hanley, the late Carl H. Ketcham, Miss Jo Manton, Professor Kathleen Tillotson, the Proprietors of the *Westmorland Gazette*, Mr. N. Whistler, Dr. Robert S. Woof.

I am particularly grateful to Professor J. H. Höltgen for generously making available to me Wordsworth's letters to Lord Northampton, in advance of his own more extended treatment of them in a forthcoming article, and to Dr. Jared Curtis for drawing my attention to a number of items in American collections. I have been much indebted over the years to the staff of the Wordsworth Library, Grasmere, especially to the late Peter Laver and Mr. Jeff Cowton, the present Librarian; and to past and present members of the staff of the Oxford University Press, particularly Mr. John Bell, Miss Kim Scott Walwyn and Miss Frances Whistler. My greatest debt of all is to my wife Margaret, my co-worker throughout.

ALAN G. HILL

October 1992.

CONTENTS

ABBREVIATIONS

Morley	*Correspondence of Henry Crabb Robinson with the Wordsworth Circle*, edited by Edith J. Morley, 2 vols., Oxford, 1927.
MP	*Modern Philology.*
MW	*The Letters of Mary Wordsworth*, edited by Mary E. Burton, Oxford, 1958.
MY	*The Letters of William and Dorothy Wordsworth*, edited by the late Ernest de Selincourt, second edition, *The Middle Years*: Part I, 1806–11, revised by Mary Moorman, Part II, 1812–20, revised by Mary Moorman and Alan G. Hill, Oxford, 1969–70.
NQ	*Notes and Queries.*
Prel.	*Wordsworth's Prelude*, edited by Ernest de Selincourt: second edition, revised by Helen Darbishire, Oxford, 1959.
Prose Works	*The Prose Works of William Wordsworth*, edited by W. J. B. Owen and Jane Worthington Smyser, 3 vols., Oxford, 1974.
PW	*The Poetical Works of William Wordsworth*, edited by Ernest de Selincourt and Helen Darbishire, 5 vols., Oxford, 1940–9, and revised issues, 1952–9.
Reed	*Wordsworth, The Chronology of the Middle Years, 1800–1815*, by Mark L. Reed, Cambridge, Mass., 1975.
R.M.Cat.	*Catalogue of the Varied and Valuable Historical, Poetical, Theological, and Miscellaneous Library of the late venerated Poet-Laureate, William Wordsworth* . . . Preston, 1859; reprinted in *Transactions of the Wordsworth Society*, Edinburgh [1882–7], and in *Sale Catalogues of Libraries of Eminent Persons*, vol. ix, ed. Roy Park, 1974.
RMVB	*Rydal Mount Visitors Book*, Wordsworth Library, Grasmere.
Sadler	*Diary, Reminiscences and Correspondence of Henry Crabb Robinson*, edited by Thomas Sadler, 3 vols., 1869.
SH	*The Letters of Sara Hutchinson*, edited by Kathleen Coburn, 1954.
Southey	*Life and Correspondence of Robert Southey*, edited by C. C. Southey, 6 vols., 1849–50.
WL	The Wordsworth Library, Grasmere.

LIST OF LETTERS

PART VIII

List of Letters

List of Letters

List of Letters

D. W. to MARY ANNE RAWSON[1]

Address: To Miss M. A. Rawson, Spring Grove, Huddersfield.
MS. Dr. D. P. Gange. Hitherto unpublished.

Saville Green 19th August [1795]

My dear young Friend,

On Saturday afternoon Mrs Wm Rawson drank tea with us at Ovenden,[2] and brought the intelligence—(to me very mortifying—) that you had paid your promised farewell visit to Halifax—and that of course I should not see you or your Mama, or Sisters again. I had, as it appears without any good grounds for such a conclusion, satisfied myself that Saturday being a market-day, would not be the day of your choice, and that we should certainly see you on Monday, therefore I was greatly disappointed. I was also very sorry to hear of Catherine's (I cannot call her Miss Rawson), of Catherine's continued indisposition which I hope, however, will have left her before your departure, and that she may be in good plight to take upon herself the duties and cares of housekeeping: indeed if she be not so I shall be truly sorry for her as her spirits must needs be a little flat when she has lost Delia a second time, and you also, her constant companion at home. Mrs Rawson told me the history of your hurried visit and of your doings at Halifax; but the beautiful work-bag I suppose she had reserved for an agreeable surprize after my disappointment; for she said nothing about it, and I found the two parcels for me on the table at my return to Saville Green on Saturday evening. Both furnished me with something of a surprize, for I had really forgotten Catherine's debt and was at first puzzled to make out the meaning of the three shillings and four pence. As to the Bag, you can hardly imagine how much I value it as a keep-sake from you, and as a proof, among many others which I have noticed during the short time I have had the pleasure of being with you, of your kind and obliging disposition.

As you were probably informed by your aunt W^m, next Monday

---

[1] Niece of Mrs. William Rawson (D. W.'s 'Aunt' Threlkeld). Her parents, sisters and brother are also referred to below. D. W. had spent this summer at Halifax, attending the wedding of Jane Pollard to John Marshall on 5 Aug., before rejoining W. W. at Bristol *en route* for Racedown in late Sept. after his withdrawal from revolutionary politics. This letter follows *EY*, L. 49.

[2] A mansion outside Halifax, rented by the Pollards.

is fixed for our departure[1] therefore I can have no opportunity of hearing of you again till after M^r and Mrs Rawson's return to Spring Grove, when, through my Halifax Friends I shall be informed whether you have actually been left at school, or not, and all other particulars concerning you and all the Family which they well know will be very interesting to me.

When I took up the pen to write to you I had intended satisfying myself with a message to your sister; but on second thoughts, will enclose a note to herself. Herein, I am somewhat selfish, wishing to insure a few lines from her after your departure.

Pray give my best regards to M^r and Mrs Rawson and your Brother—and my Love to Delia and Emma; and with sincerest wishes for the health and happiness of all the Family

Believe me my dear Mary Anne,
Your obliged and affectionate Fr[iend]
D. Wordsworth

W. W. to UNKNOWN CORRESPONDENT[2]

MS. National Library of Scotland transcript. Hitherto unpublished.

Grasmere, near Ambleside
January 14th 1801.

Sir,

I feel as if I were exerting some degree of courage in thus offering the accompanying Volumes to you, our local residences, and of course, the objects presented to us must necessarily have produced a certain difference in our modes of contemplating society, and in our notions respecting the means of affecting it pleasurably. Yet I am assured, that by a mind so acute as yours in

---

[1] But according to L. 50, D. W. was still with Mrs. William Rawson at Mill House on 3 Sept.

[2] 'Letter of Wm Wordsworth evidently to some Editor of a Review (say Jeffrey?) *penes* (Nov. 29. 1865) Mr Wm Paterson, Bookseller, 74 Princes St, who allowed me to copy it.' (Note by Adam White, the Scottish naturalist, in whose album this letter is preserved). It is clearly one of the seven or eight letters sent, at S.T.C.'s suggestion, to 'persons of eminence' with complimentary copies of the 2nd edn. of *Lyrical Ballads* (see *EY*, L. 152; Griggs, ii. 665); but Francis Jeffrey would hardly have qualified for that description as early as 1801, a year before the *Edinburgh Review* first appeared. Professor Mark Reed has suggested that the addressee was possibly Monk Lewis (see Reed, pp. 108–9). The letter follows *EY*, L. 152.

the detection of the ludicrous and the faulty it cannot have remained unnoticed with what alarming rapidity our written language has been receding from the real language of life and that from the encreasing circulation of books this practice must act powerfully towards adulterating our moral feelings and of necessity the language of real life itself, this poisoning our future literature in its best and most sacred source. I claim therefore with confidence from you those favourable predispositions in the perusal of these volumes which are perhaps his due who has sincerely wished

'Respicere exemplar vitae . . . et veras hinc ducere voces'[1] At all events you will receive these volumes as a mark of respect. I have the honor to be,

your most obed[t] humble serv[t]
William Wordsworth

W. W. to WILLIAM CALVERT[2]

Address: W[m] Calvert Esq.
MS. WL (Moorsom Papers).

Grasmere Wednesday Ev:
[late Mar. 1801]

Dear Calvert,

I know that you do not set a high value on the labours of the Muses; I cannot, however, refuse myself the pleasure of requesting your acceptance of these Volumes,[3] which I offer to you from the sincere affection which I bear you, and from grateful remembrance of your Brothers.

W. Wordsworth

My Brother Christopher is come but he lodges at Ambleside being violently in love with Mr Lloyd's Sister,[4] so of course we see so little of him, that it will not be worth your while to come

---

[1] See Horace, *Ars Poetica*, ll. 317–18 (misquoted).

[2] W. W.'s school-friend, elder brother of Raisley Calvert (see *EY*, Ls. 31, 42–5). This letter follows *EY*, L. 156.

[3] The 2nd edn. of *Lyrical Ballads*.

[4] C. W. had been engaged to Charles Lloyd's sister Priscilla, a Quaker, since 1799 (see L. 123), against the wishes of her parents. They were finally married in Oct. 1804.

over to Grasmere on his account. But my Sister and I shall both be heartily glad to see you at any and at all times.

W. W. to RICHARD SHARP[1]

Address: Richard Sharpe Esqre, N°. 17 Mark Lane, London. *Single Sheet.*
Postmark: 4 Dec. 1804.
Stamp: Keswick.
MS. Miriam Lutcher Stark Library, University of Texas.
EY, L. 234(–). F. G. Stoddard, 'Two Autograph Letters of William Wordsworth', MP lxix (1971), 140.

Grasmere November 30th 1804

My dear Sir,

I ought to have written long ago to thank you for your kind exertions in my Brothers behalf[2] and for the Letter you wrote me upon this business some time since.—My Brother has spoken in his Letter to us with great satisfaction of the kindness you had shewn to him and of Mr Boddington's good wishes towards him. It gave us great pleasure to learn that he had gotten a better Voyage; poor Fellow! I suppose he was in wretched spirits about his prospects before.—

I don't know that we should have a chance of getting the Watch in any other way more speedily than by your keeping it in your own possession. However I should rather that you sent it to my Brother,[3] partly because it *is possible* he may find some method of having it conveyed to us safely in a short time, and also because I wish you should have no further trouble about it.—I had about [a] year ago a new Watch down from London by the Waggon in a box with other things and it has never gone right; I have been obliged to have it put three times into [the] hands of the Watch-mender or Marrer where it now lies.—

From the tenor of your last Letter I hope we shall have the pleasure of seeing you next summer at Grasmere; but if not next

---

[1] 'Conversation' Sharp, business partner of Samuel Boddington, friend of Samuel Rogers, and Whig M.P. for Castle Rising (1806–12), Portarlington (1816, 1818–19), and Ilchester (1826–7). See *EY*, L. 214. Part of this letter was published as L. 234.

[2] W. W.'s brother John was shortly to set off on his fifth (and last) voyage in the *Abergavenny* (see L. 232).

[3] i.e. R. W.

summer never again I am afraid here, as I am grown too great for my little tenement; not in the sense in which one of Elizabeth's ministers, I think, was it not Burleigh?[1] told her he was grown too great for his, viz. by encrease of wealth and honours through her Majesty's gracious bounty, but through the favours of Dame Nature who has made the birds too numerous for the nest.— John[2] my first born has lost much of his beauty, but he is in strength, size and manly appearance allow'd by all to be one of the first children they have seen. My younger is a girl[3] and very pretty and thriving; and great pleasure shall I have in your seeing them both and their Mother who was much disappointed in not being at home when you were last with us. She is well; my Sister is unfortunately plagued with a cough which she had had, off and on, several months; it neither affects her looks nor strength but I am not quite easy about it. She and Mrs W both begg'd their kindest remembrances to you.

As to myself I have nothing to say on that subject further than that not long after my last letter to you, I fell again to work in earnest at the Poem[4] on my own earlier life and have dispatch'd 1,600 or 1,700 lines of it since that time. With Gods blessing I shall have finished it long before next summer.—Farewell with sincerest thanks for all your kindness to my Brother and myself.

And believe me dear Sir your affectionate Friend
W. Wordsworth

[1] William Cecil (1520–98), created Lord Burghley in 1571: Lord High Treasurer, 1572–98, and Queen Elizabeth's chief minister.
[2] John W., b. 1803.
[3] Dora W., b. the previous August.
[4] *The Prelude*. For the later stages of its composition, see Reed, pp. 652–4.

W. W. to LORD HOLLAND[1]

Address: To The Right Honble Lord Holland, Holland House, Kensington.
Postmark: 22 Aug. 1806.
Stamp: Kirby Lonsdale.
MS. Princeton University Library.
Princeton University Library Chronicle, xxii (1971), 153.

Grasmere near Kendal
August 19th 1806

My dear Lord,

I felt myself greatly honourd in receiving (through the hands of Mr Longman) the Copy of your Life of Lope de Vega,[2] sent me at your Lordship's request. I was from home when it arrived, or I should have been earlier in expressing my thanks. I have read the Book with much interest; it is indeed a marvellous story. The translations seem to me to be executed with great happiness; if I might point out one that I was particularly delighted with I should fix upon that of the character of Thedoro[3] which is excellently conceived by Lope, and most admirably improved upon in the translation.

'But how can I the rules of *art* impart'[4] is wounding to my ear. I have taken the liberty of mentioning these two passages, as, considering the work as a composition they were what most pleased and displeased me.

---

[1] Henry Richard Vassall Fox, 3rd Baron Holland (see also *MY* pt. ii, L. 398), nephew of Charles James Fox, presided with his wife Elizabeth, Lady Holland, over the Whig circle at the newly-restored Holland House, Kensington. He was Lord Privy Seal, 1806–7, and much later, Chancellor of the Duchy of Lancaster under Grey and Melbourne. W.W. seems to have met Lord and Lady Holland in London in May 1806 (see Reed, p. 323), and they were to meet again at Low Wood in Aug. 1807 (ibid., p. 361). For W.W.'s other contacts in London this spring, particularly meetings with Godwin, Joseph Farington, and other artists, see Reed, pp. 316 ff. This letter follows *MY* pt. i, L. 40.

[2] Publ. 1806. Lope de Vega Carpio (1562–1635), the most prolific dramatist of the Spanish Golden Age, is credited with well over 300 plays.

[3] In Lope de Vega's *El perro del hortelano* (1613–15), the Countess of Belflor is in love with her secretary Teodoro, but declines to marry him until, by a series of deceptions, her aristocratic suitors are tricked into believing he is a Count.

[4] W.W. is referring to the discussion of Lope de Vega's *Arte nuevo de hacer Comedias*, a verse treatise on the 'new art of writing plays', written in opposition to the prevailing Aristotelian procedures. Lord Holland's translation included the couplet: For how can I the rules of art impart,/Who for myself ne'er dreamt of rule or art?

I cannot conclude without begging to be respecfully remembered to Lady Holland,[1] and adding a fervent prayer for the Restoration of the Health of your honoured Kinsman.[2]

I am,

my Lord,

With many thanks,

and the highest respect and esteem,

Your Lordships

Most obedient Servant

William Wordsworth

W. W. to JOSIAH WEDGWOOD[3]

MS. untraced.

R.B. Litchfield, Tom Wedgwood: The First Photographer, 1903, p. 127.

[Sept. 1806]

. . . When your brother entered the room where I am now writing, about four years ago,[4] I was quite heart-stricken; he was deplorably changed, which was painful to see; but his calm and dignified manner, united with his tall person and beautiful face,

[1] Elizabeth Vassall Fox, Lady Holland (1770–1845), the Whig hostess, married Lord Holland as her second husband in 1797. For an account of her meeting with W.W. at Low Wood, see *MY* pt. i, Ls. 118, 127; and *Lord Granville Leveson Gower, Private Correspondence, 1781–1821*, ed. Castalia, Lady Granville, 2 vols., 1916, ii. 280.

[2] Charles James Fox, Foreign Secretary under Grenville, died of dropsy at Chiswick House on 13 Sept. 1806, aged 57. He had been ailing for some time and his last important parliamentary act was to move for the abolition of the slave trade on 10 June, a few days before he gave up attending Parliament.

[3] See *EY*, L. 85. This fragment, which perhaps follows *MY* pt. i, L. 44, is quoted in a short account of Tom Wedgwood's life drawn up for the information of James Macintosh (see *MY* pt. ii, L. 259), who was to edit his philosophical speculations. The plan, together with Coleridge's proposed memoir, was abandoned, but S. T. C. later paid tribute to 'my munificent co-patron . . . the benefactor of my intellect' in *The Friend*. See Griggs, iii. 20, and *The Friend (Collected Works of S. T. Coleridge)*, ed. Barbara E. Rooke, 1969, i. 146–7.

[4] The visit referred to here was on Christmas Eve 1802, when S. T. C. brought Tom Wedgwood to Dove Cottage (see *EY*, L. 180). W. W. had not seen him since he came to Alfoxden in Sept. 1797 with his optimistic scheme for educating the genius of the future (see Moorman, i. 332–5).

produced in me an impression of sublimity beyond what I ever experienced from the appearance of any other human being . . .

W. W. to WILLIAM GODWIN[1]

MS. Bodleian Library. Hitherto unpublished.

Tuesday noon [21 Apr. 1807]
36 lower Thornhaugh Street[2]

Dear Sir,

First let me thank you for your kindness in calling upon me. In answer to your very friendly invitation of Mrs Wordsworth and her Sister to dine with you and Mrs Godwyn[3] on Thursday I am sorry to say, that M^rs W– and Miss Hutchinson, who are greatly obliged to you, must decline the pleasure of waiting upon you as they have laid down a general rule, which they do not in any instance mean to break through, of not going out *any where* except to old and particular Friends to dinner, or for the Evening, they having come up to town for a very short time merely to see a little of the outside of this huge City. For myself I regret that I am engaged on that day; but I mean to do myself the pleasure of calling on you very soon, and then we can I hope fix upon a day which will suit us both.[4] I am with great regret, yours most truly

Wm Wordsworth

[1] This letter follows *MY* pt. i, L. 71. The author of *Political Justice* was now running a publishing business in London, and was later to seek W.W.'s help with his *Juvenile Library* (see L. 218).

[2] Having spent the previous winter at Coleorton, the Wordsworths were staying with Basil Montagu in London, before returning to Grasmere by way of Coleorton and Halifax. For W.W.'s meetings with Scott, Joseph Farington, and possibly John Constable, see Reed, pp. 351–4.

[3] Godwin's first wife Mary Wollstonecraft had died in 1797 (see *EY*, L. 84). In 1801 he had married Mary Clairmont, mother of Claire Clairmont (1798–1879), Byron's mistress and friend of the Shelleys.

[4] W.W. and S.T.C. dined with Godwin on the 29th. In spite of their political differences, W.W. regularly called on Godwin when he was in London. Godwin's MS. Diary (*Bodleian Library MSS.*) records meetings in 1806, 1807, 1808, 1817, 1820, 1823, 1828, 1831, and 1835; and Godwin stayed the night at Rydal Mount on 28 Apr. 1816, though according to H.C.R. he left W.W. 'with very bitter and hostile feelings'. But H.C.R. added: 'I believe political feelings alone kept them aloof.' (*HCR* i. 183). See Moorman, ii. 293. Godwin's views

W. W. to JOHN TAYLOR[1]

Endorsed: To John Taylor, Editor of the 'Sun'.
MS. Mark Reed. Hitherto unpublished.

Colerton near Ashby de la Zouche
Leicestershire
May 27th [1807]

My dear Sir,

I was very sorry to leave Town without seeing you again.

Mr Coleridge had procured Tickets for the Opera that Evening;[2] so that I availed myself of yours to accomodate a Friend, under a strict charge that he should restore it according to your instructions, which I shall be most grievously sorry if he has neglected to do.

The Person in question is a careful Reader of the Evening Mail, and the service you were so kind as to offer would at least produce to us some innocent entertainment; the puff please to observe must be in plain prose, as the good man never reads verse.[3]—

Our stay here will not be more than a fortnight, we then move northward, shall be detained 3 weeks in Yorkshire, and then take up our abode quietly at Grasmere;[4] where we should be very happy to see you if you ever stroll so far. I say that not in the way of compliment, but seriously and sincerely. If you could leave the throng of business for a short while the sight of our scenery might do you good.—

Do not fail to let us hear from you soon; I shall be happy to learn that your mind is easier; be assured I take a most true and

---

were to take a conservative turn under the influence of Coleridge; in 1820 he published a study *Of Population*, in answer to Malthus, and turned to play-writing, with support from Shelley, who had finally married Mary Godwin in 1816; but he eventually (1833) accepted a sinecure in the gift of Lord Grey, as yeoman usher of the exchequer.

[1] See *EY*, Ls. 158–9. This letter follows *MY* pt. i, L. 75.

[2] S. T. C. had brought his son Hartley to London and was introducing him to the theatres and other sights. See *Poems of Hartley Coleridge*, ed. Derwent Coleridge, 2 vols., 1851, i, xxxi–v, cxcix–cciii.

[3] *Poems in Two Volumes* (1807) had just appeared, and were to be savaged by the critics later in the year. See Elsie M. Smith, *An Estimate of William Wordsworth By His Contemporaries*, 1932, pp. 69–107.

[4] Allan Bank was being made ready for the Wordsworths, though they did not move in until the following year.

lively interest in your welfare.—M^{rs} W begs to be remembered to you and believe me ever yours

Wm Wordsworth

W. W. to BASIL MONTAGU[1]

MS. Cornell. Hitherto unpublished.

Friday Morning
[?18 Mar. 1808]

Dear Montagu,

I hope Mrs Skepper[2] is better; I want some money both for my self and to send home. To morrow, about noon, I go to Dunmow, but would you be so kind as either yourself to call, or send by some trusty Person to me at the Courier off,[3] as much cash as you can spare;. let this be done either today or to morrow morning—

most affectionately your's
W Wordsworth

Do not forget to give my best Love to Mrs Skepper.

---

[1] This letter probably follows *MY* pt. i, L. 99. It was clearly written before Basil Montagu married his housekeeper, Mrs. Skepper in 1808, and probably belongs to the spring of that year, when W.W. went to London to look after Coleridge and to try to arrange publication of *The White Doe of Rylstone*, in order to defray some of his increasing expenses at home (see L. 102). The suggested date is established by reference to his visit to Dunmow (see Ls. 100, 101, 103), the residence of the Dowager Lady Beaumont, in Essex.

[2] See L. 34. She was the daughter of a York wine merchant, and widow of a lawyer, and had known Burns in her younger days.

[3] i.e. care of Daniel Stuart, at the *Courier* office in the Strand, above which Coleridge's lodgings were situated.

W. W. to D. W.[1]

Address: Miss Wordsworth, Grasmere, Kendal.
Franked: London March twenty sixth 1808 Holland.[2]
Postmark: 26 Mar. 1808.
MS. WL. Hitherto unpublished.

Sat: morn [25 Mar. 1808]

Dearest Loves,

I have just received Dorothy's Letter; and am happy to hear an account of you all upon the whole so favorable. I returned from Dunmow yesterday having been there a week save for one day. I left them all well: and was greatly pleased with old Lady Beaumont,[3] who is a very venerable Lady.—

But to speak of my return.—I hope to leave London on Wednesday at the latest—I am most anxious to be gone as in truth I am overwrought. I find Coleridge I cannot say better—he means to continue his Lectures[4] and I earnestly wish that he was fairly through them.—Tomorrow I shall go to Christopher's.[5]—

Thus far I wrote at Lord Holland's in Pall Mall, when I have called today for the first time. I have since been to call on Tuffin[6] for the 2nd time but found him not—met Boddington[7] in the street, and am to breakfast with him tomorrow to meet Sharp—I have not yet seen Longman about the Poem[8] as he expects a sight of the Manuscript and I do not chuse to send it to be thumbed by his criticasters. I do not think it likely I shall publish it all— indeed I am so thoroughly disgusted with the wretched and stupid Public, that though my wish to *write* for the sake of the People is not abated yet my loathing at the thought of publication is almost insupportable.—Therefore trouble yourselves no more about it.—

I did not find my residence at Dunmow agree with me. I was too much exhausted when I went, and was too little alone when I was there. I cannot stand a day's company much less conversation. Yesterday I saw Mrs Clarkson. There was a public dinner on the slave Trade Business and Mr C. attending Mrs C. came to

---

[1] This letter follows *MY* pt. i, L. 100.   [2] i.e. Lord Holland.
[3] The Dowager Lady Beaumont (see *EY*, L. 288).
[4] On literature, at the Royal Institution.   [5] i.e. to the rectory, Lambeth.
[6] J. F. Tuffin (see *MY* pt. i, Ls. 27 and 103).
[7] Samuel Boddington, Richard Sharp's business partner.
[8] *The White Doe of Rylstone.*

pass the day with the Lambs[1]—she looks better than when I saw her.—I write a most stupid and disjointed Letter—but thinking so fondly as I do of home and of returning to it, I scarcely know what to say—Coleridge has just had a long Letter, in which is related the fate of Sally's parents.[2] It has much affected me, and we must do for Sally what we can.—Joanna[3] I hope is much better. I cannot say I am quite satisfied with the account of Sara's[4] Health, and do earnestly entreat her to take care of herself. I should have been happy to hear that Mary was fatter. Mr Carr[5] of Bolton Abbey whom I had the pleasure of meeting in the street today tells me I am fatter than when he saw me at Bolton—I mention this as I think it will please you to hear it.—But I have certainly been troubled with a strange weakness about my heart, from (I hope) exhaustion—I know not what to do about the shawls: nor about John Monkhouse's[6] business—I shall tomorrow consult Sharp and I have already called upon him twice with that view, and have not found him at home: but it is altogether a blind business for me, as I have no acquaintance whatever in the mercantile world, save Sharp and Boddington.—Old Henry[7] I understand from a Letter of Jack to [? Sarah][8] is better, I am glad of it, when a man's death is gaped

---

[1] W. W. had been invited to breakfast at the Lambs on 15 Mar. to meet H. C. R. for the first time, and they met again the following day at Mr. Hardcastle's, Mrs. Clarkson's Deptford friend. H. C. R. subsequently sent his impressions of W. W. to his brother: 'he is a sloven and his manners are not prepossessing, his features are large and coarse; his voice is not attractive, his manners tho' not arrogant yet indicate a sense of his own worth—he is not attentive to others and speaks with decision his own opinions. He does not spare those he opposes, he has no respect for great names and avows his contempt for popular persons as well as favorite books which must often give offence. Yet with all this, I sho^d have a bad opinion of that person's discernm^t who sho^d be long in his company witht contract^g an high respect, if not a love for him. Moral purity and dignity and elevation of Sentim^t are the characteristics of his mind and muse.' (Morley, i. 52–3).

[2] George and Sarah Green of Blentarn Ghyll, who had perished on the Langdale fells. Their daughter Sally was in service with the Wordsworths.

[3] Joanna Hutchinson.   [4] S. H.

[5] The Revd. William Carr (see *MY* pt. ii, L. 419 and *LY* pt. ii, L. 706), whom W. W. had met the previous July.

[6] M. W.'s cousin, later farming at Hindwell.

[7] Henry Hutchinson (1734–1811), of Stockton, M. W.'s 'rich and selfish' bachelor uncle (see *MY* pt. i, L. 101).

[8] *MS. obscure.* 'Jack' is S. H.'s eldest brother John.

for, I always wish him to live, and live and live on. Lady Beaumont and her Sister[1] liked my Poem,[2] it did not much interest Sir George nor can I say that I have the least hope or thought that it would produce any impression—Lord Holland told me today that the Marmion he thought a very pretty story, much better than the Lay etc[3] but that the Poetry was not so good.—Southey did not like it—Southey leaves town on Monday but I shall be at home sometime before him—I hope—Whom should I see in the street today but Parson Jackson[4] our vicar—he is in Town with Lady Di—polite. Coleridge, I find, begins to lecture next Wednesday, so that I think I ought in conscience to stay to hear him once, for the sake of you all—but tomorrow I shall procure a frank from Sharp either for Monday or Tuesday and by that Letter you shall know precisely when to expect me—

Dearest Mary thanks many thanks [for] your [? addition][5] to Dorothy's Letter—I should [not have] been sorry to see a word or two from [Sarah] but I excuse her as an Invalid—Do you Dorothy contrive to preserve your health and good looks, as I hear no more about the deafness I am afraid it is no better.—Mr Clarkson's B[r][6] has lost one of his Twins by the Scarlet Fever, and there is reason to fear that a little Boy of his will die of it also. I do dread that disease, for heavens sake if it even comes near us, let us take every possible precaution, to keep from it—it is a terrible malady among children—I saw James Tobin[7] today, he looks deplorably thin and ill; he has no cough, but I think if he does not mend soon in his looks he will not be long for this world—I shall write again on Monday or Tuesday at latest, telling when you may expect me. God in heaven bless you all.

Most affectionately yours—W. W.

[? Kisses to the children][8]

---

[1] Mrs. Frances Fermor (see *EY*, L. 224).

[2] *The White Doe of Rylstone.*

[3] Scott's *Lay of the Last Minstrel* (1805) had been followed earlier this year by *Marmion.*

[4] The Revd. Thomas Jackson (see *MY* pt. i, L. 193), agent to Lady Diana le Fleming (d.1816) at Rydal Hall.

[5] *MS. torn.*   [6] John Clarkson (see *EY*, L. 240).

[7] See *EY*, L. 84.   [8] *MS. illegible.*

W. W. to FRANCIS WRANGHAM[1]

MS. untraced.
Bookseller's Catalogue.

Elleray near Troutbeck
Windermere
[Oct. 1808]

My dear Wrangham,

I have a moment to say that I have received your Letter and the enclosed Bill £41.16—which I have paid into the hands of the Treasurer for the benefit of the orphan Greens with many thanks for your kind exertions in this cause I remain affectionately,

Yours
W. Wordsworth

I am writing from the room of a sick friend[2] who is under the influence of a violent convulsion and has been so many days,—let me hear from you at your leisure.

W. W. to THOMAS DE QUINCEY[3]

Address: Thomas de Quincey Esqre No 82 Great Titchfield S^t, Cavendish Square, London. Single Sheet.
MS. WL. Hitherto unpublished.

[c. 10 Mar. 1809]

My dear Friend

I am very sorry that I must [? trepass][4] upon your patience for two days more—I had miserable head-ache yesterday and was occupied with visitors great part of the day before.

You filled up the gap with the proper word.[5]

---

[1] This letter probably follows MY pt. i, L. 127, and acknowledges receipt of a further donation from Wrangham for the orphans of George and Sarah Green of Blentarn Ghyll (see Ls. 100 and 118).

[2] John Wilson, 'Christopher North', whose new house at Elleray, below Orrest Head, was nearing completion (see L. 122).

[3] This letter, from Allan Bank, written on a sheet of the manuscript of *The Convention of Cintra*, follows MY pt. i, L. 140.   [4] MS. obscure.

[5] In his letter of 5 Mar. De Quincey, who was now in London supervising the printing of W. W.'s pamphlet, had pointed out a 'lacuna' in the latest batch of sheets from Grasmere. See L. 143, Jordan, pp. 96 ff., and *Prose Works*, i. 303.

Many thanks for your very interesting Letter which was a great delight to us all.[1]

[unsigned]

[*M. W. adds*]

You will find the interlined passage which may be difficult to read plainly written at the end of the *last* Sheet. God bless you!

M. W. and D. W. to JOHN MONKHOUSE[2]

Address: Mr John Monkhouse, Penrith.
Stamp: Keswick.
MS. WL.
MW, p. 5.

Grasmere March 16th [1809]

My dear John,

One more kind service I am going to require of you before we lose you[3]—indeed I know not what we shall do when you are gone. But first I must tell you that I have been and am most cruelly anxious about Sarah's health,[4] not having heard from her since the day after she arrived at Appleby.—If she is still at Penrith, (I think it probable she may be upon her road home), tell her to write immediately. I enclosed her a £5 note addressed to Penrith which I hope she has received. We are too, uneasily uncertain about Coleridge, who set out from Lloyd's towards Penrith or Appleby 10 days ago—in bad health, and of him we have not heard since that time[5]—the purpose of his journey was about 'The Friend'—I wish we could have some information that would set us at ease on these accounts. But the main purpose of my writing to you now is to tell you that it is our intention to

---

[1] De Quincey's lively letter from London included an account of the new *Quarterly Review*, founded in opposition to the *Edinburgh* ('To be sure, the public may not fare much the better for exchanging one imbecile dictator for another; but, from all I hear of Gifford, I cannot think him so depraved a coxcomb as Mr Jeffray . . .'), and a graphic description of the fire at the Drury Lane Theatre.

[2] This letter, written from Allan Bank, precedes *MY* pt. i, L. 141.

[3] John Monkhouse and Thomas Hutchinson, M. W.'s cousin and brother respectively, had jointly taken the farm at Hindwell, Radnor, to which they were about to move.

[4] S. H. had been ill the previous December (see *SH*, p. 11).

[5] S. T. C. had been ill at Old Brathay, but had insisted on going on to Penrith and Appleby to settle the stamp duty on the printing of *The Friend*.

pay off the Mortgage on the Patterdale Estate[1] immediately—that is as soon as may be. Will you therefore have the goodness to enquire of Mr. Ellwood[2] how long a time before-hand it is necessary to give notice that this money is to be paid in—and then you must give the old Man *due notice in full form* accordingly. The interest Money is nearly due—it would be less trouble to us and somewhat *more convenient* to pay the whole together, if it is the same to him. After you have made these enquiries, etc., you must inform us in order that we may have the money forthcoming against the time specified—but I trust we shall see you again. This business being settled, we shall be so much less dependent upon Penrith, when we have no longer an Agent there.

I hope my Aunt's Visitor[3] continues to be a good girl—we have a deal of talk about her and some longings to see her at home—but if she is any comfort and gratification to my Aunt we shall think ourselves well repaid for the want of her. The presents she promised to bring home with her are anxiously looked for, so you must tell Sarah to leave her some money if she has any; if not my Aunt must be so good as [to] advance some for her, in order that she may make her purchases. John[4] goes daily to school with great glee—and is become very anxious to be a good Scholar in order that he may be fit to be a *Printer* with his Friend Mr. de Quincey.[5] Poor Thomas is very unwell—he is about cutting some teeth and is very very feverish, irritable and cross. You will have heard that the little Joanna[6] at Stockton is dead. I had a letter from John the other day about the selling out of my Stock, when he gave me this information.

When you write, send your letter by way of Keswick to the care of Miss Crosthwaite,[7] for the Man who used to bring our letters from Ambleside has given up going—therefore as we are unable regularly to go so far as to Ambleside for them, we receive them very irregularly that way—besides it is an unsafe way at any rate, for Mr. de Q. has made out that *one* letter written to him while at G.[8] has been fairly lost.

---

[1] Broad How (see Ls. 11, 153, 207).　　　　　　　　[2] The Penrith solicitor.

[3] Dora W., who was staying with 'Aunt' Elizabeth Monkhouse at Penrith.

[4] John W.

[5] De Quincey had gone to London to superintend the printing of W. W.'s *Convention of Cintra* pamphlet, before taking up his tenancy of Dove Cottage the following Nov.

[6] Daughter of John Hutchinson by his second marriage.

[7] The Keswick draper.　　　　　　　　　　　　　　　　[8] Grasmere.

What were you doing last week within 2 miles of Keswick with 2 led horses and riding a third?—Mrs. C.[1] mentioned this circumstance in a way that has puzzled me much. How does my poor Uncle?[2]

> God bless you all for ever!
> Believe me most affly yours
> M. Wordsworth

[*D. W. writes*]

Friday afternoon 5 oclock—We are just arrived and got here very well. Sarah is quite well. We met the Poney just after we parted with J. Addison[3] and got very well here. The children have got bad colds—I hope you will write as soon as there is any change in my uncle. Mary says when my aunt chooses to part with little D. she may go to Appleby—*if* the Children are to come to Grasmere at midsummer. If Mr. C. is still at Appleby tell him here is a letter for him from Mr Wilkin.[4] God bless you. Love to my Aunt. Be sure to write.

W. W. to JOHN BROWN[5]

Address: Mr Brown, Printer, Penrith.
Stamp: Penrith.
MS. Yale University Library. Hitherto unpublished.

Grasmere Sat. June 10th [1809]

[*In M. W.'s hand*]

Sir,

The following Gentlemen wish to be placed upon the list of Subscribers to the *Friend*—they must be supplied with the first and second paper—

---

[1] Coleridge.

[2] William Monkhouse (1746–1809), brother of Elizabeth Monkhouse. He died later this year.

[3] Jane Addison, John Monkhouse's sister-in-law, and sister of R. W.'s partner Richard Addison.

[4] Distributor of Stamps for Westmorland and the Penrith district of Cumberland. W. W. succeeded him in 1813.

[5] Printer of *The Friend*. This letter, and the next, both written from Allan Bank, follow *MY* pt. i, L. 166.

W. H. Pyne Esqre, No 38 Great Argyle St London[1]
Mr Wells, York Buildings, n^r Baker S^t, D^o[2]
Timothy Holmes Esqre, Bury St Edmunds, Suffolk[3]
John Losh Esqre, Woodside, Carlisle.[4]

A package of stamped paper was forwarded from Kendal to you, last Saturday se'nnight by Mr Cookson[5]—It was something damaged, by its having been carelessly packed, before it reached Kendal. If you have not received it the neglect rests with the Kendal Carrier.

> I am etc.
> [*signed*] W. W.

W. W. to JOHN SPEDDING[6]

Address: John Spedding, Esqre.
MS. Mr. J. H. F. Spedding. Hitherto unpublished.

[early June, 1809]

Dear Spedding,

Herewith I return you your Collection of Cobbets,[7] which have been of great use to me. I have to entreat your pardon for having both soiled them and having otherwise disfigured them

---

[1] William Henry Pyne, known as Ephraim Hardcastle (1769–1843), exhibited at the R.A. (1790) and the Water-Colour Society; in 1803 he launched his *Microcosm, or a Picturesque Delineation of the Arts, Agriculture and Manufactures of Great Britain*; and subsequently he became associated with William Ackermann. Later, he turned to authorship and wrote for the *Literary Gazette* and other periodicals.

[2] William Charles Wells, F.R.S. (1757–1817), physician at St Thomas's Hospital, London, 1800–17, and author of an 'Essay on Dew' (1814). For his autobiography, published posthumously in 1818, see Griggs, iv. 950.

[3] An acquaintance of the Clarksons.

[4] John Losh (1756–1814) eldest brother of James Losh, W. W.'s early radical friend: a prominent Cumberland Whig and soda manufacturer in Newcastle.

[5] Thomas Cookson, W. W.'s Kendal friend (see L. 18).

[6] Of Mirehouse, Bassenthwaite (see *EY*, L. 38).

[7] *Cobbett's Weekly Political Register* was started in 1802; *Cobbett's Parliamentary Debates*, which was subsequently taken over by Hansard, was started a year later. William Cobbett (1762–1835) politician and agriculturalist, began to write in the radical interest from 1804.

which it was impossible for me to prevent; as in order to make use of them I was compelled to have them perpetually before me in a room black with smoke and ashes, and to mark in the margin such passages as I meant to use.

The accompanying Pamphlet[1] has cost me much labour, and I hope it may in some degree interest you. It ought to have appeared ten weeks ago—the delay has been caused by the Printer.

affectionately yours
W Wordsworth

W. W. to JOHN MILLER[2]

MS. Brown University Library.
Mark Reed, 'Wordsworth Letters, New Items', NQ ccxvii (1972), 93–6.

[4 Jan. 1810]

. . . I remain dear Sir
Yours with great truth
W. Wordsworth

Mr de Quincey has taken a cottage at Grasmere and has been here nearly three months. I am at best a wretched penman and a most impatient letter-writer. So you must pardon this scrawl.

---

[1] *The Convention of Cintra.*

[2] The missing postscript of *MY* pt. i, L. 180, which Susan Wordsworth omitted to copy, erasing the first words to indicate her cut-off point. The Revd. John Miller, younger brother of Joseph Kirkham Miller (see *LY* pt. ii, L. 658), was Fellow of Worcester College, Oxford, 1810–23, and published sermons, guides to Christian principles, and his Bampton Lectures on *The Divine Authority of Holy Scripture Asserted* (1817). He is reputed to have been the first to use the expression 'The Christian Year', which later became the title of Keble's poem. W.W. had in his library Miller's later book *Things After Death; Three Chapters on the Intermediate State . . .*, anon., 1848 (*R.M. Cat.*, no. 355), which suggests that there was some renewed contact between them in later years.

W. W. to JOSEPH WILKINSON[1]

Address: To the Revd Joseph Wilkinson, Thetford, Norfolk. *Single Sheet.*
Stamp: Kendal.
MS. WL.
Prose Works, ii. 141.

[*c.* Mar. 1810]

My dear Sir,

Herewith is matter for two more numbers; I shall send for two additional ones in a couple of days.—You will probably judge best to print matter for two numbers with each month as [you]^2 have only six months before you, and your numbers are 12.

Yours most truly

W. W.

My B^r Dr Wordsworth seeing by chance a specimen of your work put down his name then as a Subscriber, being so much pleased with it. Pray let a copy of as good impressions as you can command be sent for him to the Palace at Lambeth immediate[ly] if [ ] not been forwarded elsewhere [ ] received there.^3

[*unsigned*]

---

^1 Illustrator of *Select Views in Cumberland, Westmoreland and Lancashire* (see *EY*, L.172, and *MY* pt. i, L.176), for which W. W. had agreed to supply prose descriptions. This letter is written on a manuscript draft in S. H.'s hand of 'Section II' of *Select Views*, and may have been added when S. H. completed her copying some time before she left Grasmere for Hindwell in mid-Mar. 1810, or subsequently, when W. W. judged the moment right to send Wilkinson more copy. The letter perhaps follows *MY* pt. i, L. 187, therefore. For a full discussion of the composition and dating of 'Section II', see *Prose Works*, ii. 125–7, 139–41.

^2 *Word dropped out.*

^3 *MS. torn.*

W. W. to M. W.[1]

Addresss: Mrs Wordsworth, Grasmere, near Kendal, Westmoreland.
Stamps: Ashby de la Zouch.
MS. WL.
LL, p. 34.

[Coleorton]
[22 July 1810]
Sunday Morning

D–[2] is gone to church at Ashby with the ladies, and I seize with eagerness this opportunity to write to my dearest Love.—You will guess that I have been much agitated by your late letters, and the account of the vexations you have under gone; above all I was so much affected by the manner in which you spoke of dear little Catharine[3] and her lameness; that I had great difficulty in preventing myself from setting off immediately to see you both, and to be assured that she was not so lame as my Imagination pictured to me. The other vexation I hope will be soon over, as there is nothing formidable in the complaint if taken in time. When I recollect, however, what Thomas[4] suffered from the hooping-cough I can not but have many alarms for little W^m.[5] and I do earnestly wish that it might please God to preserve him from that complaint till the time of teething was past.—We travelled from Manchester with a little Babe, in the hooping Cough, and it was quite grievous to see how much it had been reduced and what it suffered.—Your good sense would enable you to tolerate the ill conduct of the servants; which, I confess, is very mortifying; but if one reflects, nothing different can be expected from persons so educated. To Mrs C–[6] such conduct would have been insupportable. Fail not to remember what was desired about your mouth, as I do earnestly pray that you may be relieved from that uncomfortable feeling, which at the same time can not but be injurious to your health.—And I am confident that it is a complaint within the reach of medicine:–

---

[1] This letter follows *MY* pt. i, L. 201. W. W. and D. W. had left Grasmere at the end of June for a visit to Sir George and Lady Beaumont at Coleorton, leaving M. W. behind at Allan Bank with the children.   [2] D. W.

[3] Catharine W.(b.1808), W. W.'s younger daughter, who had suffered a mild stroke the previous Apr., which had left her lame (see Ls. 188, 192–3, 200).

[4] Thomas W.(b.1806), W. W.'s younger son.

[5] W. W.'s youngest child, born the previous May.

[6] Probably Mrs. Clarkson.

We have now been here a fortnight and every thing has been done which kindness could do to make us happy; and certainly we have enjoyed ourselves much especially D– who is grown very fat and looks better than she has done, since she had that complaint at Racedown:[1] Her throat and neck are quite filled up; and if it were not for her teeth she would really look quite young. I never saw a more rapid and striking improvement in the health and appearance of any one. She has a most excellent appetite, as good a digestion and is never tired. For my own part though I should feel it a disgrace to be discont[ent]ed to any oppressive degree, with so much affectionateness, and tranquil and innocent pleasure about me, yet I do feel, that to no place where I am stationary some time can I ever be perfectly reconciled, even for a short time. When I am moving about I am not so strongly reminded of my home, and you and our little ones and the places which I love. Therefore I must say though not without regret do I say it, that I cannot help being anxious that I were gone, as when I move I shall feel myself moving towards you; though by a long circuit. O my beloved how my heart swells at the thought; and how dearly should I have enjoyed being alone with you so long!—But I must go hence into Wales;[2] surely, sweet love, this is very unlucky. Nor could I reconcile myself to it, did I not think that you regretted the necessity as much as I do.—This journey will be the greatest proof of my regard to your Sister Sara that it has ever been in my power to give her, or perhaps ever will be; and I should not be sorry that she could to a certain degree feel it as such; I say, to a degree for thoroughly to comprehend the extent and depth of the sacrifice is utterly impossible. S– has a tender heart and a loving spirit, but she is neither a wife nor a mother; nor can know any thing how I have longed to be with you—as I might be now.—Do not think, Darling, that I repine, no, I have much pleasure in making this sacrifice both for her sake and yours—You often laugh at me about Duty, but this [is] a pure march of duty, at vast expence of inclination if ever one was made by man.—

But I will leave this subject to say a word about our manner of spending our time. We are down to breakfast between half past eight and nine; from eleven to half past two I mostly ride with Sir G.—at three we dine: between six and seven have tea, and

---

[1] i.e. in 1795–7.

[2] To Hindwell, where S. H. had been staying with her brother Thomas since March.

walk till nine; once or twice we have had a little reading in the afternoon. There are several pleasant walks about this place, 'most if not all of which we have been together;[1] but, of course this is a country that is much improved by summer. Yesterday evening we peeped into a cottage where sate, by a shining fire, an old blind Man, one of the tenants. D– asked him if [he] had had much pain when he lost his sight—he replied, "no, that it declined gradually away as the sun goes down at night: a very beautiful expression! Many of the Cottages are very neat and the gardens of almost all are well tended: we entered another beside which stood a sycamore tree, the age of which the man begged me to guess—it was six and thirty years old, and had been planted by himself; of course it takes up a great space of his little garden, but he said, "he would not part with his tree on any account; he was fond of trees and it sheltered his house". This man was getting into years and a Widower; he had [a] daughter in the house with him the rest of his family (six in number) were gotten from him: this daughter was eighteen and he said "My Wife died of her." I dont know whether the expression be common but it struck me as a moving one; and I blessed God inwardly at the thought how often you had passed safely through that danger, and were still a flourishing mother. Indeed I am never instructed, never delighted, never touchd by a tender feeling but my heart instinctively turns to you. I never see a flower that pleases me but I wish for you.—

How happy should I be could I make this letter more dear and acceptable to you by giving you good news about my eye; but really it has made no progress these ten days. Nor is it any worse. The inflammation is certainly much less, than it once was; but it is still very large; though attended with no pain. I am sure it is retarded by the cause I mentioned, for which I never suffered half so much as during this absence from you, which I attribute in a great degree to our long previous separation; which really has left me nearly in the same state as I was when you were at Middleham and Gallow hill;[2] with a thousand tender thoughts intermingled, and consciousnesses of realized bliss and happiness, to render separation from you heavier and more uneasy. Our

---

[1] W. W. is thinking particularly of their stay at Coleorton in the winter of 1806–7.

[2] Before her marriage, M. W. had kept house for her brother, Thomas Hutchinson, at Gallow Hill, Yorks., and had also stayed with her brother George at Bishop Middleham, near Durham. W. W. had visited her at both places.

Friends here look forward to a repetition of this visit next year; but I cannot think of any thing of the kind; nor will I ever, except from a principle of duty, part from you again, to stay any where more than one week. I cannot bear it. I feel the shortness and uncertainty of life; I feel that we must separate finally so soon, even if our lives be lengthened, that it seems criminal to me in a high degree, to part from you except from a strong call of unquestionable moral obligation.—

Where are you now; certainly, I think, not a[t] Church—It wants 20 minutes of twelve—you are not sewing; for it is Sunday; the Children, are perhaps at Church, as I hope you have been able to keep them clear from the contagion. And yet it would perhaps be unseemly to send them to a place of public resort till the house was rid of the complaint—What then can you be all doing? strange that I should be at a loss, and yet I am; are you sitting in the front room? or strolling in the garden? I can not answer this question to my satisfaction—never mind—I can see your faces one by one, above all yours, my joy, my repose, my hope, and my support in every good thought or profitable feeling that enters into my spirit:—

How can I contrive the sooner to receive a Letter from you, in [? which you] may pour out your heart and soul to me? should I say direct to me [? at the] post office Birmingham or Ludlow, but I am not sure that I [? shall go] by Ludlow, and a Letter directed to Birmingham might possibly be carried to Lloyds.[1] If I had heard from Mr Blair,[2] I should request you to direct to me at his house; but he must have written and his letter is miscarried. However if I do hear from [him] in time; I shall request that you will write to me at his house; and again that I may have another Letter from you immediately on my arrival in Wales; a Letter for myself and of which I need only read parts to the rest of the family—I know that S–[3] will take no offense at this: for my soul demands such Letters, they seem to unite me to you person and spirit body and soul, in the privacy of sacred retirement, spite of the distance that separates us. O Dear and honoured Woman how blessed has been my lot! and how could I either long to live or lay down my life for thee even as it should please God to

[1] Charles Lloyd, snr., the Birmingham banker (see *EY*, L. 90). The text is damaged at this point by the seal.

[2] Alexander Blair (see L. 206), whom W. W. had fallen in with on his journey to Coleorton. He lived at Castle Bromwich.

[3] S. H.

appoint!—But I must turn from these awful thoughts, to things external, and more fit to be trusted to this frail paper.—

At the utmost I shall only stay here a fortnight more, I hope not more than eleven or twelve days; but I have not heard from Sara, and I do not like the thought (for my health's sake) of walking thirty or forty miles at the end of my journey; after a fortnight in Wales I hope to set my face towards home, oh with what joy. In the mean time write to me not less than twice a week on any account; and as soon as I leave this place I shall write to thee my love at least as often; so take care to have people sent over to the office—By the by let somebody be employed in cleaning the quick-set Hedge for Mr Crump[1]— I foresee we shall have much trouble about the parsonage—. I must not forget to tell thee that Sir G— has made me a present of a small and neat watch (a gold one I believe) but what is of more consequence he says it goes very well. This will be to me a great accommodation, and I shall wear it with much pleasure for the givers sake. I have read nothing at all since I came here, nor had any inclination to read; but I am somewhat grieved that my eye has benefited so little by this long holiday. D— has been so good as to abridge the sheets I wrote for Wilkinson[2] for my own part I have no longer any interest in the thing; so he must make what he can of them; as I can not do the thing in my own way I shall merely task myself with getting through it with the least trouble.

I must now prepare to bid you farewell—kiss all the children for me, and remember me to the servants. I hope you will have no visitors to disturb you; and that you will get through the hay and your other troubles and hindrances speedily, and without injury. Kiss little Catharine for me ten times over, and little William in the loneliness and peace of the night for his dear Fathers sake; and above all things take care of your own precious health. I could write on till the end of time but I must yield to the necessities of things. How do I long to tread for the first time the road that will bring me in sight of Grasmere, to pant up the hill of Allan bank to cross the threshold to see to touc[h] you to speak to you and hear you spea[k] [ta]ke care—farewell

Fail not to write to me with out reserve; never have I been able to receive such a Letter from you, let me not then be disappointed, but give me your heart that I may kiss the words a thousand times!—

[1] Owner of Allan Bank.   [2] Joseph Wilkinson.

I must bid you again farewell with a thousand kisses, on this side the paper. W. W xx

W. W. to M. W.[1]

Address: Mrs Wordsworth, Grasmere, near Kendal, Westmoreland.
Stamp: Radnor.
MS. WL.
LL, p. 59. Letters of William Wordsworth, ed. Alan G. Hill, 1984, p. 128.

Hindwell—Saturday August 11th [1810]

I arrived here at 10 this morning; where I found all well, Sara wonderfully improved in look and Joanna[2] quite fat, Sara indeed also. The House is comfortable, and its situation beside the pool, and the pool itself quite charming, and far beyond my expectation. Having said this, let me turn at once to thee my love of loves and to thy dearest of Letters which I found here, and read with a beating heart. O my blessing, how happy was I in learning that my Letter had moved thee so deeply, and thy delight in reading had if possible been more exquisite than mine in writing.[3] You seem to have been surprized at the receipt of my Letter, and surely it is odd that I did not mention to you I should avail myself of some opportunity, and as strange that you did not take for granted that I should. My Letter had been written three or four days before I could find the means of sending it off, which was the reason of its arriving so late: you would notice also that it was somewhat worn, for I had carried it about with me in my pocket.—I was sure that you would be most happy in receiving from me such a gift from the whole undivided heart for your whole and sole possession; and the Letter in answer which I have received from you today I will entrust to your keeping

[1] This letter follows *MY* pt. i, L. 202. [2] Joanna Hutchinson.

[3] In her letter of 1–3 Aug., M. W. had written: 'O My William! it is not in my power to tell thee how I have been affected by this dearest of all letters—it was so unexpected—so new a thing to see the breathing of thy inmost heart upon paper that I was quite overpowered, and now that I sit down to answer thee in the loneliness and depth of that love which unites us and which cannot be felt but by ourselves, I am so agitated and my eyes are so bedimmed that I scarcely know how to proceed—I have brought my paper, after having laid my baby upon thy sacred pillow, into my own, into THY own room—and write from Sara's little Table, retired from the window which looks upon the lasses strewing out the hay to an uncertain Sun.—(*WL MSS.*).

when I return, and they shall be deposited side by side as a bequest for the survivor of us. Every day every hour every moment makes me feel more deeply how blessed we are in each other, how purely how faithfully how ardently, and how tenderly we love each other; I put this last word last because, though I am persuaded that a deep affection is not uncommon in married life, yet I am confident that a lively, gushing, thought-employing, spirit-stirring, passion of love, is very rare even among good people. I will say more upon this when we meet, grounded upon recent observation of the condition of others. We have been parted my sweet Mary too long, but we have not been parted in vain, for wherever I go I am admonished how blessed, and almost peculiar a lot mine is.—

You praised the penmanship of my last;[1] I could wish that this should be legible also, but I fear I shall wish in vain; for I must write in a great hurry having only an hour allotted to me. Let me then first communicate the facts in which you may be interested, relating to my journey etc otherwise if I give way to the emotions of my heart first you will hear nothing of these.—On Monday morn: at 9 o'clock Sir G. B. and I left Ashby in a chaise. Sir G— had a wish to see the Leasowes[2] with me; I had never been there and he had not seen the place these thirty years; I reserve the detail of this journey till we meet. We slept the first night at Hagley[3] returned to Birmingham next day at 4 afternoon, went together to the play, and the next morning walked about the Town, and I accompanied Sir G. back on his way as far as four miles which brought me to within 2 miles a ½ of Castle Bromwich, Mr Blairs. At Mr Blairs, I found a note from my B^r Chris^r who had accidentally heard of my intention of being at Mr Blairs. I was greatly surprized at this, as I had confidently concluded that he was either gone from Birm: or had never come thither from his not having answered the Letter inviting him to Coleorton. On Thursday he came over to Mr Blairs, dined with us, and I returned with him, and supped at Lloyds, where I found Priscilla looking I thought not very well. The children[4] were

---

[1] M. W. had written: 'I look upon thy letter and I marvel how thou hast managed to write it so legibly, for there is not a word in it, that I could have a doubt about.'

[2] Shenstone's estate in Worcestershire (see L. 202).   [3] See L. 227.

[4] John Wordsworth (b. 1805), later Fellow of Trinity College, Cambridge; Charles Wordsworth (b. 1806), later Bishop of St. Andrews; and Christopher Wordsworth jnr. (b. 1807), later Bishop of Lincoln.

gone to bed and asleep so of course I can have no accurate image of them: their faces were heated and they seemed bloomed, but their natural complexions, are sallow. The eldest is the handsomest, much, the 2nd the stoutest, and the third the plainest; so it appeared as they slept and so, I was told, it is; Christopher looked uncommonly; but I am sorry to say that he is likely to have great trouble, at least I fear so) from the state of his wifes health and the nature of her malady; great expense also which at present he can ill bear,—for his living[1] has entangled him in two law suits; and you will grieve to hear that he has been much deceived as the income of it; it is some hundreds lower than he had reason to expect, so that he will be not a little pinched, unless it should please God to take the Bishop.[2] But not a word of these particulars to any body.

On friday Morning, I was called a little after three, having had two hours feverish sleep, got on the top of the Coach, it began to rain before we were out of Birming: and rained for two hours and a half; my umbrella and coat however protected me pretty well; when we were half way to Worcester the weather cleared up and I had a pleasant ride through a fine Country to that City, which stands charmingly upon the Severn, at no great distance from the Malvern hills. These hills which are a fine object brought Joseph Cottle[3] to my mind, and dearest Dorothy, who had travelled this way when she came from Newcastle to meet me at Bristol whence we journeyd to Racedown; but though much endeared to me on this latter account, I looked at them with a trembling which I cannot describe when I thought that *you* had not seen them, but *might* have seen, if you had but taken the road through Bristol when you left Racedown;[4] in which case I should certainly have accompanied you as far as Bristol; or further, perhaps: and then I thought, that you would not have taken the coach at Bristol, but that you would have walked on Northwards with me at your side, till unable to part from each other we might have come in sight of those hills which skirt the

[1] C. W. had been Dean of Bocking, Essex, since 1808.

[2] At this period the living fell within the diocese of London, the Bishop of which was John Randolph (1749–1813), previously Bishop of Oxford (1799) and then of Bangor (1807). His tenure of London was brief and undistinguished.

[3] Publisher of *Lyrical Ballads* (see *EY*, L. 57) and author of *Malvern Hills: A Poem*, 1798.

[4] M. W. had stayed with W. W. and D. W. at Racedown, late Nov. 1796-early June 1797, returning north by way of London.

road for so many miles, and thus continuing our journey (for we should have moved on at small expense) I fancied that we should have seen so deeply into each others hearts, and been so fondly locked in each others arms, that we should have braved the worst and parted no more. Under that tree, I thought as I passed along we might have rested, of that stream might have drank, in that thicket we might have hidden ourselves from the sun, and from the eyes of the passenger; and thus did I feed on the thought of bliss that might have been, which would have [been][1] intolerable from the force of regret had I not felt the happiness which waits me when I see you again. O Mary I love you with a passion of love which grows till I tremble to think of its strength; your children and the care which they require must fortunately steal between you and the solitude and the longings of absence—when I am moving about in travelling I am less unhappy than when stationary, but then I am at every moment, I will not say reminded of you, for you never I think are out of my mind 3 minutes together however I am engaged, but I am every moment seized with a longing wish that you might see the objects which interest me as I pass along, and not having you at my side my pleasure is so imperfect that after a short look I had rather not see the objects at all. But I must return to my journey. I left Worcester at half past ten, reached Leominster at 5, and there was 20 miles to Hindwell, without coach—Luckily two other persons were going part of the same way; so we took chaise for 14 miles, I slept at Presteigne 5 miles from hence, hired a guide who bore my luggage, and I arrived here before eleven.

I have read to Sara the parts of your Letter intended for her,[2] and all the rest which I could read; she will reply to these of course herself. How happy am I [to][3] learn that thou art so well, and untormented with that cruel pain in thy mouth! May it never return! if it does fail not to apply to Dr Dicks[4] remedies: for my account for really I have suffered much in this cruel complaint of thine—I have thought of it ten thousand times since we parted and sometimes I have fancied that I was caressing thee, and thou couldst not meet me with kindred delight and rapture

---

[1] *Word dropped out.*

[2] In her letter M. W. had reported on the efforts of her eldest brother John Hutchinson of Stockton-on-Tees (see *EY*, L. 83), to arrange suitable care for their handicapped sister Betsy.

[3] *Word dropped out.*   [4] Richard Scambler, the Grasmere medical man.

from the interruption[1] of this distressing pain. But far oftener for less selfish reasons has it employed my mind with an anxiety which I cannot describe; for every thing about you that is indicative of weakness or derangement of health affects me when I [am][2] absent from you, and cannot see how you look, beyond what it is in the power of words to describe. O take care of yourself for all our sakes—but I cannot bear to look that way, and I know you will do nothing to hurt yourself for my sake.—

My stomach failed about a fortnight since from too much talking, or rather from not being sufficiently alone—before I left C–[3] by taking more care I brought it about; and except in my eyelids I look well, and am well; but certainly though not weak far from being so strong as I should have been but for my old enemy: that has troubled me more than ever.—I agree with you that it was unreasonable in the B's[4] to expect me to go to C– again next summer; be assured, I shall not do it on any account nor will I go any where without thee. I cannot but think knowing how the little ones would be taken care of but that we might be happy supremely happy together in a tour of a few weeks if our circumstances would allow; but this will never, I fear be the case, nor am I anxious about this; but I never will part from you for more than a week or a *fort*night at the very utmost, unless when I [am][5] compelled by a sense of duty that leaves no choice—I can not and ought not; if I could lay in a stock of health and strength to enable me to work more vigorously when I return there might be some plea for this but the contrary is the case; for my longing day and night to see you again is more powerful far, as I said before than[6] when you were at Middleham; and when I am away from you I seem to have heart for nothing and no body else— But this theme is endless; I must content myself with your Letters for a short time; and oh most dearly shall I prize them, till I consign them to your care to be preserved whatever else we lose.

I have not yet said a word about the time I purpose to stay here; but I came with a resolution not to extend it beyond a fortnight, for a hundred reasons which will crowd in upon your mind. At all events I shall move heaven and earth to be with you by this day three weeks. I shall not stop a moment at Liverpool more than I can help, if I go that way. You may guess how eager

---

[1] *Written* interrupted.   [2] *Word dropped out.*

[3] Coleorton.   [4] Beaumonts.   [5] *Word dropped out.*

[6] *Written* that.

I am to be at home, when I tell you that Christophers entreaties and my own wishes, could not prevail upon me to stay half a day at Birmingham.—Certainly I parted from him with great regret, as he and I are likely to be so much divided. I will satisfy Sara's claim upon me and let me add a little too for Joanna and Mary Monkhouse[1] especially, and then I shall take wing and oh for the sight of dear Grasmere, and how I shall pant up the hill, and then for dear little W. and his beloved Mother, and how shall we pour out hearts together in the lonely house, and in the lonely and to *us* thrice dear Season.

Thank you for your pretty tales of Dorothy and strin[g]loving Thomas;[2] bless [him][3] he shall be contented if possible, I will bring him string from his Godmother, string for his Uncle, for Mr Addison[4] and for myself. Adieu adieu adieu, for I am told I have not a moment to lose, and that the post will be lost—this must not be again and again farewell—a thousand kisses for you all, yourself first, John Dorothy, Thomas, Catharine, W[m]. dear little Catharine I have not mentioned her, but she has often been here in my thoughts[5] again and again farewell—I fear for her Take care.

---

[1] M. W.'s cousin, who married Thomas Hutchinson in 1812.

[2] M. W. had described Thomas's obsession with string: 'He is grown more ravenous after string than ever, he now *sneaks* up-stairs into our drawers and be it tapes, stays laces or any thing in the likeness of string he has no mercy upon it.'

[3] *Word dropped out.*

[4] Henry Addison, brother of R. W.'s partner, now farming in Wales. Two years later, he seems to have been planning to return to Cumberland (see *SH*, p. 43).

[5] M. W. had written: 'Catharine I do not think has improved much this week but she has not been so well attended—I having the little one constantly, she poor thing is obliged to follow at my skirts and this makes her fretful—it is easy to know before night by her looks and by her lameness how she has been tended thro' the day—she is however perfectly well and the *arrantest* Mischief that ever lived—as soon as she enters a room she looks round to see which is the greatest mischief she can do and off she goes to accomplish it—this is no sooner done, or prevented—but away she goes to another and so on till she is weary or till I am obliged to whip her which has often been the case for she looks at you and proceeds in her wickedness undaunted, till you are obliged either to yield to her or *force* her to obedience—I do wish she may not grow tired of making curtseys before you see her, for she does this so prettily and looks so modest withal that you would be delighted with her I think you will not find her so lame as you imagine she is—the account I sent of her lameness was quite accurate, but it *looked* far worse upon paper than in her person—'

W. W. to M. W.[1]

Address: Mrs Wordsworth, Grasmere, near Kendal, Westmoreland. *Single.*
Stamp: Radnor.
MS. WL.
LL, p. 85.

[19 Aug. 1810]

My dearest Love,

Yesterday brought me your 2nd Letter[2] and one from dear Dorothy, informing me of her arrival at Bury[3] after a not unpleasant journey—I was most happy in the sight of both these Letters, particularly of yours as I had not expected quite so confidently, and had been not a little mortified by a sentence in your Letter to Sara in which you had said that you did not intend to write to me till you heard of my arrival here; which expression sadly clouded my prospect of hearing from you twice a week during my stay at Hindwell, as I had desired, and fearlessly expected.—

I will begin with noticing the news part of your last. I need not say how much I am mortified at the folly of the girls[4] leaving you particularly Sara's—Fanny I could have excused. But I hope we shall be able to suit ourselves as well, and that Dorothy need not return home sooner on account of any uncertainty on this Head. For, I believe I did not tell you, that I suggested to her the idea of staying longer, on Mrs Montagu's[5] account; whom I so exceedingly despise that I did not wish that D– who has never seen her, should have that disagreeable business to encounter. I talked with D– on this head and she was in sympathy with me. To Montagu I shall behave most kindly as my mind will prompt, but to his partner with nothing more than civility. In fact the Creature is utterly odious to me. I have, however, the satisfaction of foreseeing that we shall not be troubled long with their company as she will be for jaunting off to Keswick to see Southey etc, and C–[6] who I hope will not be returned.—I cannot say my Love with what fondness I feed on the thought of our being together without interruption day or night. I am indeed, on

---

[1] This letter follows *MY* pt. i, L. 204. [2] Of 14 Aug. (*WL MSS.*).

[3] D. W. had gone to stay with the Clarksons at Bury St. Edmunds.

[4] Sarah Youdell and Fanny Turner, servants at Allan Bank, were threatening to leave; but they thought better of it.

[5] Basil Montagu's third wife, formerly Mrs Skepper. [6] Coleridge.

many accounts sorely vexed at this visit from the M's, but far above all as it will interfere with our solitudes, so happily given, and so long and often desired.—But my heart is leading me aside when I meant only to speak for a while of matters of fact.—I do not like Gawens[1] conduct about the School, but I shall not be in a hurry to interfere; at all events we must come to some resolution about John. As to the parsonage[2] there are doubtless many and great objections, and we shall decide upon it within a week after my return at latest, as we will not be trifled with.— Yesterday Tom[3] had a Letter from Jack[4] 3 days later date than that to you in which he says that your Uncle[5] is weak, and that he has lately remade his will, and, as he told Jack in the best disposition to *you* all. Jack adds, that he has left you a piece of land. So I suppose he knows thoroughly how things are disposed of.—

The weather since I came here saving these two last days has been rainy and uncomfortable; so that we have only made very short excursions in the neighborhood—. It is a Country of many Vales, this in which Hindwell stands, the longest and widest; but the narrowest vales and the narrow parts of the wide ones are the most pleasing portions of the country. Hindwell House stands very pleasantly however, on account of the Pool in front, and the Hill opposite crowned by old Radnor church, a much more picturesque building than[6] that upon Breadon Hill not far from Coleorton; I have said that Hindwell stands pleasantly *however*, because it stands in a part where the Vale is more than three miles

---

[1] Gawen Mackereth, the elderly Grasmere schoolmaster, was reluctant to hand over his teaching duties to the new curate, the Revd. William Johnson (see *MY* pt. i, L. 223; *LY* pt. i, L. 1). In her letter of 1–3 Aug., M. W. had complained of being put out by the latter's 'vulgar presbyterian look', but the Wordsworths soon overcame their initial prejudice, and maintained their friendship with him when he moved to London two years later. See *SH*, p. 44; *MY* pt. ii, Ls. 234a and 236a.

[2] The Wordsworths were anxious to move from Allan Bank, and the Old Vicarage in Grasmere was now vacant. Another possible, and more desirable, place of residence was Butterlip How, as M. W. reported in her letter of 15–19 Aug. (which W. W. had not yet received).

[3] Thomas Hutchinson.   [4] John Hutchinson.

[5] Henry, the Hutchinsons' bachelor uncle, who died the following year (see *MY* pt. i, Ls. 215–7). His unequal distribution of his estate of some £50,000 between his nephews and nieces caused some heart-searching in the family. M. W. and her sister Joanna were jointly left a farm near Stockton which let for £100 per annum.

[6] *Written* that.

across and comparatively naked, large fields and poor Hedgerows; but the view from the windows is truly delightful, and shews beautifully the great importance of still water in Landscape. By moonlight and in the evening this Pool of three acres, seen from the window with its reflection is little less interesting than[1] one of our Lakes. I have been but a remiss Angler in it but yesterday I caught a very nice fry, eleven, several of them more than half a Pound a piece. I had only tried twice before, and not more than a few minutes, without success.—

The day before yesterday Mary Monkhouse Sara and I rode to Kington after dinner, Sara was seized with a sickness at Kington, and they were obliged to return in a post chaise.—This sickness was caused by a little precipitation in setting off at a time when S– ought to have attended leisurely to a call of Nature—I mention this awkward cause in order that the fact which I could not conceal, might not appear more alarming than it need. She was however, very ill at the time; as to complexion etc as bad as Dorothy in one of her worst fits—She is at present quite well, and I think her complexion is now as good as it was before. Yester evening Mary M– and Joanna H. Addison[2] and I walked and I was very sorry to find that the walking up hill brought a pain into M. M's side. She is by no means strong, and requires being treated with care. Long and laborious walks ought to be avoided by all means. Her digestion is bad and she is very thin; but it is a most favorable circumstance that she will here have every advantage for taking Horse exercise, the best thing in the world for her—Joanna and she and John M–[3] are ridden out (this Afternoon (Sunday) to drink tea at one of the Stephens's[4] (not the Lover) two miles and a half off.—To Morrow I go with Tom and a Mr Donaldson[5] who is here to view a Farm 12 miles off, towards Leominster, which Mr D– has some thoughts of taking. Mr D– was formerly a Barrister, a Friend of W. Taylors,[6] with whom and at St Helens he has been 3 years to learn the craft of a Farmer—He is a mild good natured little man, of humble desires, but I much fear that humble as his desires are he will not find it easy to gratify them in the farming line; which as far as profit is

---

[1] *Written* that.   [2] Henry Addison.   [3] John Monkhouse.

[4] Neighbours at Hindwell, connected with the Stephens family of Llananno, Radnorshire.

[5] Francis Donaldson, whom W. W. met from time to time in later years when he visited the Hutchinsons, was about to take a farm in the district.

[6] A farmer friend of the Hutchinsons.

concerned seems but a poor speculation. Mr D– was yesterday with Tom to look at a farm upon the Wye, belonging to James Watt[1] of Birmingham. It is small, about 120 acres, and enchantingly situated in both which particulars it would suit Mr D– but I do not think there is much likelihood of its being let reasonably.——

I shall attempt during the course of the next week to make a short tour upon the Wye with some part of the family Sara if possible. If you will look at the Map you will see the course I purpose to take: from Radnor new or old to the Hay upon the Wye, thence to Bualth, in which road long ago I met the original of Peter Bell,[2] thence up the Wye to Rhaiader, I doubt whether I spell right, and then across the country again to Radnor which is two miles from this place. This excursion with the peeps into the valleys on the side of the Wye, I mean tributary to it will take from three to 4 days. I have not yet spoken to Sara of the length of my intended stay here but I am sure she will be very good in letting me take my departure, as she knows and cannot but feel for your loneliness, and knows also though she cannot feel that how my Beloved longs for my return. Your last Letter I gave her to read both for her own gratification and that she might be awakened in some degree by it to a sense of this longing. Your former Letter I kept to my self and only read her such parts as related to matter of fact. The general strain of it was too sacred and too intensely connubial for any eye but my own——

And now my sweet and dearest love I am brought to the point where I may allow my heart to flow over a little, and but a little. But first let me tell the news about my eye which will tend to brighten what I have to say of love and hope and joy, it is, indeed at last considerably better, though still liable to derangement upon slight causes, and the swelling is far from being abated, though the inflammation is; but in fact after the inflammation is gone a relaxation is left behind which is very slow to disappear, and which I am inclined to think never goes away wholly. The

---

[1] James Watt, the Scottish engineer (see *LY* pt. ii, L. 408), in partnership with Matthew Boulton at Birmingham for the construction of steam engines, 1775–1800, lived thereafter at Heathfield Hall, just outside the city. He began buying land in Wales some years earlier, building up an extensive estate on the banks of the Wye and the Ithon in Brecon and Radnorshire, between Rhayader and Newbridge, and spent holidays on his farm at Doldowlod. See J. P. Muirhead, *Life of James Watt*, 1858, p. 484.

[2] In summer 1793. See also I. F. Note, *PW* ii. 527.

eyelid, however, is not now, strikingly unsightly, which it was from the size of the inflammation, all the while I was at Coleorton—. I am thankful that it is better, as I am sure it would have been some time before but for the cause I mentioned, which has always intervened till lately to throw it back. But the prospect of seeing my Beloved again so soon makes me more tranquil both day and night, at least enables me better to bear my longings, and to keep more genially and comfortably. My darling, I hope, we shall not part again speedily! What happiness did that part of thy Letter give me in which thou speaks of the Compliments received upon thy good looks—[1] Let me here exact a promise from thee, that when thou hast reason to expect me, thou wilt not fail to put on that Cap in which by thy own confession thou lookest best; in order that I may see thee with as much promise of health and comeliness and long life Upon thy sweet countenance as heaven will allow. I have some other promises to exact from thee but these I reserve till we meet, though I will let thee into them so far as not to leave it unsaid that they are of the same kind. And here let me not forget to add that I will bring thee a Bonnet from Liverpool; a Gypsey one Joanna recommends, and such it shall be if I can please myself, or rather if I think I can please thee, but I have not forgotten the Penrith gown; this remembrance, however, shall not cause me to despair, but only rouze me to a more careful and deliberate choice.—By the bye, who are the fine folks at the Church

---

[1] From Charles Lloyd, jnr., who had called at Allan Bank with Southey's brother Thomas. M. W. had written on 14 Aug.: 'Lloyd has pleased me by telling me, what I rather wish I had heard from some one more to be depended upon, that he never "saw me look so well in his life"—I should not wonder if this is true, for he spoke it as if it was a thing that flashed upon him when we were talking nothing about it and T. S. echoed his words—To be sure I had popped on my laced cap before I went down to them which might make a change in my appearance or I have myself fancied I was become like nobody in my looks and appearance'. And she wrote again about her state of health in her letter of 15–19 Aug.: 'I am at this moment as well, and to my own feelings have as much Life, spirit and activity about me as when I was 20 years of age—tis true I am losing my teeth and my hair is becoming grey—these, the two great ornaments my Youth had to boast of, (my hair especially I prized, because thou once ventured to speak in admiration of it) I must own are *upon the wain*—else I think I am as good as ever—and every body now begins to tell me how well I look— and I believe in my own heart that this improvement began in me on the day that I received thy letter . . .' (*WL MSS.*).

stile?[1]—who presume to look insolently upon thee with our little
William in thy arms?—Sara and M. M. have been busy in making frocks for little Catharine and D– so that with what I shall
bring and Mrs Fermors, I hope, they will be provided for sometime.

I have but a little space on this private side of the sheet to sigh
for thee and tell thee, that I am giddy at the thought of seeing
thee once more, to tell thee also that those parts of my day are in
my thoughts a thanksgiving to God for having blessed an unworthy Creature as I am with such a treasure, as thy gentle, thy loving, thy faithful thy pure spirit; for having united us by the sacred
bond of husband and wife, and for having bound us still more
closely together by those sweet darlings whose images pass and
repass across my mind all day long like the clouds in the
firmament.[2] Above all dear little Catharine I think of most for
her infirmity's sake, and her little pretty ways—Kiss her for her
fathers sake, and kiss them all—What shall I bring them, what
shall I bring John, has puzzled me most. If my promise should be
fulfilled, the promise I mean I have made to my self I shall be
home this day fortnight; and yet I think it is scarcely possible,
when I bear in mind that I must be at least 4 days on the road. Be
assured however that I shall do my utmost, and if any thing takes
place to prevent me, you shall be apprized. I dare scarcely

[1] Mr Astley of Duckinfield, near Manchester, a sporting friend of John
Wilson's, had leased Dale End, on the road from Grasmere to Langdale, in 1809
(see *MY* pt. i, L. 177), and this summer the vale became 'infested by a horde of
the Astley tribe' (L. 205), some of whom lodged in Robert Newton's cottage at
the church stile. 'I believe', M. W. had written on the 14th, 'the fine folks . . .
fancy as I pass with the Baby in my Arms that I am a shabby Nurse Maid at the
great house—for they brush or gallop past me without ever such a thought
seeming to enter their heads, as, that I am a Gentleman's wife.' The reference
seems to be to Francis Dukinfield Astley (1782–1832), Unitarian layman and
hymn-writer.

[2] In her letter of 15–19 Aug., in reply to W. W.'s of the 11th, M. W. wrote:
'O William! I really am too happy to move about on this earth, it *is well* indeed
that my employments keep me active about other things or I should not be able
to contain my felicity—Good Heavens! that I should be adored in this manner
by thee thou first and best of Men, is a lot so far beyond, not only all my hopes
but all my desires and the blessing is so weighty it is so *solemnly great* that it
would be even *painful* were I left to brood much upon the thought of it. I therefore feel a comfort in those salutary interruptions that will only admit of that
delightful, happy chearing thought of thee which I can communicate to the children and which they can in part enter into.'

promise it now, that the time is so much nearer; but it will partly depend upon the length of this little Tour (which I think will leave a more lively remembrance of my having been here on Sara's mind than any thing else) and upon the time when we set off upon it: be assured that I will do my utmost to be with you, consistently with what I owe to others; and, knowing this, expect me with chearfulness and if you can with tranquillity.—I am rather hurt, on Mr Wilsons[1] account that he has not been able to find time to pay you a moments visit, but he is a strange irregular Creature.—

I have written the greatest part of this Letter by Candlelight,[2] and I do not feel that my eyes have suffered, but I expect to be called every moment to supper, so that I am pleased to have got so far before I was interrupted. I do not expect to hear from you to morrow, nor from Dorothy and therefore I am little anxious about the post; and should not be in the smallest degree so if I were quite assured, which I never can be that I shall hear from neither of you. Your B^r Tom seems a good deal pleased with H. Addison and thinks it likely that he will prove an attentive Farmer: indeed he seems a[3] very obliging and amiable young Man, of moderate desires, and likely to be as happy as a man whose life is not intellectual can be; I mean if his health should prove good. I have left no room for Sara, or any Body; S— seems upon very good reasons determined against Miss Weir[4] for Betsy, but no doubt in a day or two she will write herself—I have not read this Letter so excuse all blunders and fill up omissions by your own ingenuity. farewell, my dear Wife, and beloved Mary.

W W.

I must again bid thee farewell on this side of the Paper with a thousand kisses 1000.

Try, Love, to guess my Enigma about promises connected with the subject of dress, it was often entreated, by me but I could

---

[1] John Wilson of Elleray. In her letter of 15–19 Aug., M. W. records a visit by Wilson, his mother, two sisters and Jane Penny, his future wife. They all subsequently repaired to Dove Cottage, lent them by De Quincey, 'where we had a neat little supper, some of Quince's wine and a snug fire in the Parlour.'

[2] *Written* candlenight.   [3] *Written* an.

[4] Miss Weir kept a boarding school at Appleby, attended at various times by the Wordsworth, Hutchinson, and Monkhouse children.

never prevail upon thee) to accord me that indulgence.—again farewell.[1]

D. W. to W. W.[2]

Address: Mr Wordsworth, at Mr Hutchinsons, Hindwell, near New Radnor, Radnorshire.
Postmark: 21 Aug. 1810.
Stamp: Bury St. Edmunds.
MS. WL. Hitherto unpublished.

Sunday 19th August. [1810]

I received your letter in bed this morning, my dearest William. I am on the Sofa dressed ready to go to Mrs Capel Lofts[3] to dinner, but I hope I shall be able to say all that is necessary before the carriage comes for, dearest William, I am anxious to write to thee again and to know that my letter is on its way to thee—but if the carriage comes I must leave off the moment, for you know Mr C. I have had a pain in my bowels and I think I do not look so

---

[1] W.W.'s letter crossed with M. W.'s of 15–19 Aug. She wrote again, on 24–25 Aug., in answer to this letter to enquire about the date of his return from Hindwell and to send news of the children, now threatened by an outbreak of smallpox in Grasmere. She concluded: 'Farewell my best beloved, above all be good to thyself—and this is the best thou canst do for us all who love thee . . . if you are out to day I hope you will have a perfect enjoyment of all you see and feel, for it is a day made on purpose for you—oh would I were travelling by your side—next Summer if we are richer we must manage something of this sort and I think our journey must be into Wales, for I am sure I shall grow most restless to see Tom and Joanna before next Summer is over and dear Mary M. also—and I have not heard of any one thing in Scotland that I have such a desire to see, as I have to travel along the banks of the Wye—God eternally bless you all! and thee my Love may he send to me safely and well, then shall I be the most happy and blessed Wife in the World.' (*WL MSS.*).

[2] D. W. was now staying with the Clarksons at Bury St. Edmunds. This letter precedes *MY* pt. i, L. 205.

[3] Capell Lofft, snr. (1751–1824), Classical scholar, poet and political activist, lived on the family estates at Troston Hall, near Bury St. Edmunds. He was an admirer of Fox and Napoleon (see *SH*, p. 82) and knew H. C. R., Clarkson, Wilberforce, Godwin and Hazlitt. In 1798, he helped to secure the publication of Robert Bloomfield's *Farmer's Boy*: his own publications included translations of Virgil and Petrarch. His first marriage was to a daughter of Henry Emlyn, the Windsor architect: his second wife, referred to here, was Sarah Watson, the poetess and mother of Capell Lofft, jnr. (see *LY* pt. iii, L.1135).

well as when I came—but it will be over in a few days. I am as
happy and comfortable here as quiet and kindness can make
me—yet I miss the sweet freedom of the country. The groves of
Coleorton tended greatly to banish home longings. Mrs C. is
well today but she has never before been quite well since I came.
Yet she is far stronger than when we saw her last. Yesterday I was
in court, and though the trials were not of an interesting kind I
was well amused for a time by the gruff smartness of the Lawyers.
But I stayed over-long and fell asleep. It was a beautiful day and
Mrs C. and I spent a pleasant hour in the evening in Mr Buck's[1]
garden—a very pretty quiet place—and there was a glorious sunset. He and I intend to go together to view the abbey gate-way
and ruins[2] and to persuade the guide to leave us to ourselves for
an hour at least. This we shall do tomorrow if the evening be
fine—but it rains today though yesterday from the rising of the
weather-glass we hoped for settled weather. Mrs C. has rode out
every day but one since I came: yesterday she went when I was
in court; but at all other times I have walked by her side. I went
to see the Ruins with Mr Clarkson and another gentleman and I
longed to have them at the door to wander amongst. The Ruins
are very interesting—the gate-way one of the finest things I ever
saw, and the gardens retired and beautiful, with dry gravel walks
and fine views of the ruin. The town of Bury is cleanly and
pretty—like so many villages—and not being paved the streets
are pleasant to walk in. With respect to my visit to Bocking, I
have written to Priscilla directing to Bocking; for, as she talked so
much of Christ[r][s] impatience to be at his living, I concluded,
though you said nothing about the time of their leaving
Birmingham that surely they would not stay there much longer.
As however they have not told me their address I must wait till I
hear from them. My plan was to stay here 5 weeks—ie a month
from this time, then go to Bocking for a fortnight, and then proceed to Stockton. This would bring me at home about the
beginning of the 2nd week of October which will be soon
enough if the Montagus go to Grasmere; for Mary says if I do
not reach home before they arrive she should wish me not to go
till they are gone. I shall certainly not go to Windsor.[3] What
could I see of Christ and his family there?—besides the expence

[1] C. C.'s father.

[2] The fine 14th century gateway and abbey ruins, adjoining Angel Hill.

[3] i.e. to stay with her uncle Canon William Cookson. But she did go after all,
and stayed with the Cooksons at nearby Binfield (see *MY* pt. i, L.208).

of it. There is a coach daily from this place to Bocking, 30 miles. I suspect that Priscilla would not let Chris^t go to see us at Coleorton, and I suspect also that she lingers out her stay at Birmingham for fear of the trouble of home, where she has new servants to hire, and further that perhaps, even if she were at home she would not wish to see me there unless they were comfortably settled—but of this last my suspicions may be quite groundless—of the first I think they are not, for Mrs Clarkson gives me awful accounts of her helplessness and the wretched management of the house. I have a great desire to see them there; and I think I may be of some use. If they seem to be as much imposed upon and as uncomfortable with their servants as when Mrs C. was there I shall advise Chris^t, as the cheapest and best plan for his wife's comfort and his own to have a regular housekeeper—no matter what wages they pay her, if they can meet with one who understands house keeping and is honest—for by Mrs C'^s account they have been in a wretched way. Now it is Chris^{t's} place to write to me, and I hope for his sake he will, wherever he be. My proposal contained in my letter addressed to Bocking was to stay a fortnight there, after I had paid my visit here. Of course they are not got to Bocking as I have had no answer. Tell me what you would have me do, and what their plans were—but there is no dependence to be placed on any plan of Priscilla's. I could not bring myself to mentioned the deficiency of the one pound note to Lady B, and she did not remember the 2/- which she borrowed of you, nor the 2/6 which she borrowed of me, so we are 4/6 out of pocket, besides washing and letters which is a great deal—and I have not had nearly enough of money to carry me home so I must either borrow or have some sent. Monday morning—the carriage came before I had done my letter. We had a pleasant visit enough. I liked poor Mr Loft very well, and they are at a nice old-fashioned place—but as to his wife, she is so full of theatrical airs and graces, that I, simple Rustic, could hardly talk to her at all. There was, however, no need that I should put myself forward for there were two Lawyers from the circuit and she was well-satisfied with their attentions. The country about Bury is very flat, and though the cottages and houses are exceedingly chearful and neat, there are so few of them that the country in general is insipid. Compared with the neighbourhood of Coleorton it is quite a desart. Yet as I said, the cottages and houses are comfortable, and it is always a pleasure to meet with one of them. We had a fine afternoon and evening and this morning is bright and sunny. I hope for your sake as well as for the harvest that we shall have fine weather, and that dear Sara will have many a nice ride with you. I am rejoiced indeed to hear that she looks so well. Oh that we could keep a house for her when she comes into the North. Mary wishes me very much to go to Stockton, and I do not see, (unless Joanna has another situation for Betsy) why I may not be of as much use as she could be. I could at least form a notion whether she was likely to be well used or not, and if she *is* well used and happy, her sisters might be at ease till another situation is found; but when you see Mary this may be decided upon. At all events Jack,[1] from whom I have had a letter, wishes very much to see me. Hartley[2] wrote to Lady B.—the penmanship Hartley's and probably the first simple Ideas—the rest all his Father's. Derwent poor lad! had broken his arm just above the wrist—he is getting well again. Tom Clarkson[3] goes to School again next Monday—his mother will be very glad. I am sorry to say he is a wearisome unpleasant Boy. Mr Clarkson is just come up to ask me if I can walk to the Farm to Tea. This I shall gladly do, so we are to set off directly after dinner, Mrs C. on horseback. Tell Sara I am writing in my own Room and the sun is shining upon the tall poplar Tree and the two green-roofed thatched cottages. The tree is steady and erect as a spire and this little peep very sweet. Do write often—though it is double expence you being in Wales and Mary at home. I must have letters or my spirits will fail. I had a letter from Mary on Saturday with delightful accounts of her own health and strength—

God bless you my dearest William and Sara! Kindest love to all. I will write next to Sara.

[unsigned]

I am going to warm myself with a walk in the streets.—I have hardly seen the Town yet. I am reading Malkin's Gil Blas[4]—and it is a beautiful Book as to printing etc but I think the Translation vulgar.

Do write soon, often, and at length—

I have had no letter from Coleorton.—

---

[1] M. W.'s brother.

[2] Hartley and Derwent, Coleridge's sons, now aged respectively 14 and 9.

[3] C. C.'s son.

[4] Benjamin Heath Malkin (see L. 174) published his translation of Le Sage's *Gil Blas* in 1809.

W. W. to D. W.[1]

Address: Miss Wordsworth, Grasmere, near Kendal [*readdressed to*] Hirdwell, Radnor.
Postmark: 24 Apr. 1812. *Stamp*: Kendal Penny Post.
MS. WL. Hitherto unpublished.

Windsor Castle, Thursday Morn [24 Apr. 1812]

My dear Friends,

Mary will no doubt have told you how we sped till the time of our parting[2] at Chester on Saturday afternoon. That evening I passed with Mrs Ireland[3] (the Husband who is a most worthy fellow was engaged) and was released from her eternal clack partly by music and still more by looking over a very small part of a magnificent collection of prints which were bequeathed to her by her former Husband. Mary would tell you how much we were pleased with Chester. On Sunday morning I mounted the Coach at four o'clock. The frost was very severe but the birds were chaunting their love songs careless the while, and the sun rose in splendour. About 10 miles from Chester, the Road ascends a High hill from which looking back I had a grand view of the plain I had crossed as far and far beyond the City of Chester with the Welsh hills skirting the plain to the left. We passed Whitchurch where are 200 french upon parole; I learned that some of them recently arrived report that Bonaparte's Life has been twice attempted lately. Their opinion is, as I was told by the same authority, that he will make a bold attempt to invade this Country, and if he fails will let us have peace upon any terms.[4] This is a foolish notion, but I report it. They allow that the English Soldiers are better than the French, but contend that their officers far surpass ours.—

---

[1] This letter follows *MY* pt. ii, L. 237. W.W. was bound for London to try to heal the breach with Coleridge (see *MY* pt. i, L. 223), which had been fuelled by Basil Montagu's indiscretion.

[2] M. W., with Thomas, was bound for Hindwell, escorted by Thomas Hutchinson, who met her at Chester.

[3] Widow of Samuel Ireland (d.1800), the engraver, who issued *Graphic Illustrations of Hogarth* (2 vols., 1794, 1799) from pictures and prints in his own collection; *A Picturesque Tour through Holland, Brabant, and part of France* (1790); and a series of *Picturesque Views* of the Thames, the Medway and the Severn, from his own drawings. His son William Henry Ireland was the forger of Shakespeare manuscripts (see *MY* pt. ii, L.341).

[4] Napoleon was now on the eve of his Russian campaign.

The Country between Chester and Wolverhampton has little variety of surface and upon the whole is very uninteresting. At Wolverhampton you enter the manufacturing Region, and the whole space between W. and Birmingham is scattered over with towns villages and factories of one kind or another. Twenty years ago I passed over this same tract,[1] and could then see in it nothing but disgusting objects; now it appeared to me (considered merely as a spectacle for the eye) very grand and interesting. The immense quantity of building spread over every side suggested the idea of Rocky Country, or an endless City shattered and laid waste by conflagration. The afternoon Sun played nobly upon the huge columns, and on the bodies of smoke that every where magnified or half obscured the various objects of the scene. In some spots also from very lofty Pipes like those of glass houses, flames of lively colour licked the air, as restless as the tongues of Dogs, when they are spent with Heat and hard running.—

We reached Birm: before six, and I resolved to go no farther that night as I was a good deal tired, and the Coach, I was told would not reach Oxford till 6 in the morning. I ordered a Bed and walked up to old Lloyd's;[2] found Olivia[3] there and an old Lady whose name I could not learn. In about an Hour appeared old Lloyd and his wife; and then daughter;[4] the old gentleman is and looks better than ever I saw, the wife is a good deal failed, and very deaf; the daughter poorly.—James Lloyd[5] I did not see, but was told he is much better; his wife was there; she seems somewhat broken in health but has an interesting Countenance. Olivia's Husband Mr Paul Sands was there, he is a pleasing well-behaved young Man; and pressed me much to stop and see the School upon the Lancastrian plan.[6] I should have liked the sight,

[1] W. W. was in France throughout 1792. He must be referring to his journey from Wales to Cambridge in the autumn of 1791.

[2] Charles Lloyd, snr., of Bingley Hall.

[3] Olivia Lloyd (1783–1854), Charles Lloyd's second daughter, married Paul Moon James (d.1854) of Wake Green, a Birmingham banker. W. W. seems to have misheard her married name, from his remarks further on.

[4] It is not clear which of Lloyd's other daughters is referred to here; but it is probably either Mary, the third, or Anna, the fourth, who had married, respectively, George and Isaac Braithwaite (see *LY* pt. i, L. 159; pt. ii, L. 531). Another daughter, Caroline (1790–1811) had died the previous autumn.

[5] James Lloyd, the second son, joined the army in 1794 and was engaged for a time to Betsy Gurney (Elizabeth Fry), but settled down later as a partner in the family bank, and succeeded his father in 1828.

[6] See *MY* pt. i, L. 133.

but thought the price of a day too much for it.—They insisted on my taking a bed in their House; I did so, and had a comfortable cup of chocolate there at half past six on Monday morn: and took my departure on the top of the Coach for Oxford at Seven.—

Ten miles from Birm: the driver pointed out to me a place where three or four days ago the Axle tree of a Coach had snapped; and one person had had his thigh broken in two places and another his leg broken.—Breakfasted at Stratford upon Avon, a respectable River, with a handsome Church and the surrounding country very pleasing, flat immediately about the place but with hills in the distance, towards the West. A little beyond Stratford some charming meadows, fine trees, a stream and a rich and beautiful country, so that as far as relates to natural objects Shakespear was fortunate in his birthplace. At Woodstock I had a peep through the gates at Blenheim; time would allow no more, reached Oxford about six.—

Called on Jackson[1] found him looking very well: he walked with me about the place and I learned from my Uncle's Letter that W. Cookson[2] was at Brazen Nose; I found him indisposed with a cold and cough, supped with him, he is like his Sister Mary, and his father, and our Chris—but has a much better complexion. Next day got up before seven and walked by my self for an hour and a half about the University and its gardens; then went to breakfast with Jackson, who conducted me to the Curiosities and by the Schools when I had the pleasure to hear one of the Coleridges,[3] Son of the Colonel, pass a most excellent examination. He does not bear any resemblance that I could discover to our Coleridges; but he is a very well-looking man of good stature, genteel appearance, and a delightful modesty of

[1] William Jackson (see *LY* pt. i, L. 9), son of the Revd. Thomas Jackson: at this time an undergraduate at Queen's.

[2] Canon Cookson's younger son William (see *MY* pt. i, Ls. 25 and 208), whom D. W. had known as a baby at Forncett. He had gone up from Eton to Oxford the previous year, and eventually became vicar of Hungerford, Berks. (1818), and of Broad Hinton, Wilts. (1835).

[3] John, later Sir John, Taylor Coleridge (see *MY* pt. ii, L. 364), scholar of Corpus Christi College, Oxford, from 1809; Fellow of Exeter, 1812–18; thereafter a barrister and contributor to the *Quarterly*, and eventually Justice of the King's Bench, 1835–58. He was the second son of S. T. C.'s elder brother, Col. James Coleridge, of the Chanter's House, Ottery St. Mary (see also *LY* pt. ii, L. 564).

manner. He was thoroughly master of his subjects and much admired by every one; and I must say I have seldom, I think never, seen a young man, in so interesting a situation. I read the other day of a Lady of fortune who fell in Love with a Corporal, and let him know her mind,—and was shewn a little on this side of Oxford a House in which dwelt a Dame of large fortune who had been fascinated by the charm of a mountebank and made an offer of her person and fortune which was accepted, now these ha[ve] rather the appearance of [?unfortunate][1] proceedings; but I really could excuse a young Lady's being smitten by a man like Coleridge, demeaning himself with the modesty and the ability which he displayed, while so many eyes were upon him. I dwell now upon these recommendations of a delicate and subdued manner, because I was told that his Cousin[2] (Son I suppose of George Coleridge) a man also of great abilities and attainments spoiled every thing by an over-laboured and ostentatious display of himself.—Both these young men have the passion of worldly ambition I am told strong upon them, and design to follow the law.—Oxford is an enchanting place, and I should have much liked to pass there another day. I left nothing of note unseen but the museum.[3]

I dined and drank tea with Jackson; and at eight oclock went to William Cookson (who was confined with his Cold) where I stayed till twelve. A friend of his was there, an Etonian, and we talked about the University etc. At eight next morning i.e. Wednesday took the top of the Coach for Slough, and arrived here by two; found all well and my aunt[4] though thin in excellent health many [?days] better than when I saw her last. So that I hope dear Mary[5] nothwithstanding her leanness may yet live to be an old Woman.—My uncle is this morning gone on business to Binfield,[6] and I am glad of the opportunity to write this; I shall

[1] *MS.* torn.

[2] The reference seems to be to William Hart Coleridge (see *MY* pt. ii, L. 586), only son of Luke Coleridge (1765–90) S. T. C.'s elder brother, who was a Student of Christ Church, 1808–24. George May Coleridge (1798–1847), only son of another of S. T. C.'s brothers, George (1764–1828), Master of the King's School at Ottery, did not go up to Oxford until 1816.

[3] i.e. the old Ashmolean, founded by Elias Ashmole (1617–92).

[4] Mrs. Dorothy Cookson.

[5] Her eldest daughter, later Mrs. John Fisher (see *LY* pt. iii, Ls. 1185 and 1323).

[6] His parish in Berkshire.

stay here over to morrow perhaps another day, as they seem to expect it. George Cookson[1] has I think a more intellectual face than W.—the girls are very pretty and interesting young women.[2] Farewell, forward this dry Letter immediately to Mary. I am a good deal [?jaded][3] with travelling, and my stomach has not recovered its tone; today though I eat only a malt roll at Breakfast it was more than I could digest, and I have been constantly oppressed in that region this long time.

Most affectionately yours
W. Wordsworth

Pray tell Thomas[4] we want to know when he will come back. God bless thee for ever my dearest Sister—

[*D. W. writes*][5]

Dearest Mary, your letter rejoices me much. I wish William's stomach had been better. I fear this will cling to him while he is away. Fanny[6] recovers very fast. Sarah[7] is much against her venturing so soon. She went today.

Hewitson[8] is coming to the garden we can get nobody else.

---

[1] The youngest son, educated at Eton and St. John's College, Cambridge: rector of St. Paul's, Deptford (1819), and incumbent of Writhlington (with Powerstock), Somerset, 1832–48.

[2] Apart from Mary, mentioned above, there were two other daughters, Anna (1796–1804), who had died, and Elizabeth, later Mrs. William Fisher.

[3] *MS. obscure.*

[4] i.e. Thomas Hutchinson.

[5] Before sending the letter on to M. W.

[6] The housemaid, recovering from illness.

[7] S.H., who adds a postscript of her own to this letter.

[8] A local handyman.

Address: To Mrs Wordsworth, at Mr Hutchinson's, Radnor. S. W.
Franked: London April thirty 1812 E Phipps.[2]
Postmark: 30 Apr. 1812.
MS. WL.
LL, p. 108.

Grosvenor
Wednesday April 29th [1812]

My beloved Mary, a Letter which about this time you will have received, will have informed you how I fared till Thursday last. My stay at Windsor was longer than I intended, viz, two days; the one, Saturday, I gave as an act of generosity, and the other as I was obliged to give, as it would have been indecent to have left a Clergymans House on a Sunday, without necessity. On Monday at 3 oclock in the afternoon I left Windsor, and reached this place, before 7; and had my Coffee immediately, sitting alone till past 11 when the Beaumonts arrived; both well and looking well.—Nothing could be kinder than the Cooksons; Mary is a sensible Girl; and I think has full as much intellect as any of the brood. Christopher,[3] now gone to India, appears to have been most foolishly extravagant. I wish, dearest Love, you had as good an appetite as Mrs Cookson; she is deplorably thin, but in good health and spirits. My Uncle wears uncommonly well.—

I was most happy to find here a Letter from you and one from Dorothy.[4] How ill the poor Lasses[5] have been! I half fear that bog behind and about the Parsonage must be [a] very unwholesome thing and wish we were in another House. Glad am I [to] find you had so pleasant [a] journey; I am sorry that I did not go with you as far as Oswestry; both for the beauty of the scenery, and because I have since heard from my French Friend.[6] He declines

---

[1] This letter follows *MY* pt. ii, L. 238. W. W. was now staying with the Beaumonts in Grosvenor Square.

[2] Gen. Edmund Phipps (1760–1837), Lord Mulgrave's younger brother: M. P. for Scarborough.

[3] Christopher Cookson, Canon Cookson's eldest son, had left Cambridge without taking his degree, and had joined the Indian Army. He married in 1821, and went to live at Wellington, Somerset.

[4] M. W. had written on 23 Apr., describing her journey to Hindwell and giving news of the family there (*WL MSS.*). D. W.'s letter is *MY* pt. ii, L. 237.

[5] The housemaids.

[6] Eustace Baudouin, a French army officer captured in Catalonia in 1811 and now a prisoner of war at Oswestry, where M. W. had tried to identify him. He

at *present* any pecuniary aid; but begs that I would exert myself
for his release; with little hope however of success. Yesterday I
went to Lambeth; but found that Chris[r] was gone into the
Country. He was expected home to day. Pris:[1] has been in the
Country 3 weeks; not however I believe at Bocking. Is not this
strange? with whom are her Children all this while?—They are a
crazy set, those Ll[ds].—I then went to M's[2] Chambers, and finding
him not at home proceeded to his House. found them both
well—there I dined and spent the evening. I did not break in
upon C's[3] business as immediately after dinner M– was sum-
moned to attend a consultation.—I have this morning written to
C Lamb begging he would let me know when I shall find him at
home and alone; as I wish to have the business sifted to the bottom, and will take his opinion how it may be done in the most
unexceptionable manner.—

Time turns to little account in London. I spent all Yesterday
morning in my excursion to Lambeth, perspiring about Westminster Hall seeing Wilkies pictures,[4] and another Exhibition,
and hunting out Montagu. I have seen nobody else. To day
wrote to George.[5] Your account about T. and M–[6] does not
surprize me; and should her health be reestablished it will be I
think a very desirable Thing. I am pretty confident you have
little satisfaction from the application to Jack.—Coleridge called
here yesterday at 4 oclock.—I find he has wished to tell his story
to the B's[7] with plentiful abuse of me to which they would not

had apparently become an intermediary between the Wordsworths and Annette
Vallon, and later (in 1816) his elder brother Jean Baptiste Martin Baudouin married W. W.'s 'French' daughter Caroline. (See Émile Legouis, *William
Wordsworth and Annette Vallon*, rev. edn. 1967, pp. 94 ff.; Moorman, ii. 330–1;
and Robert Gittings and Jo Manton, *Dorothy Wordsworth*, 1985, p. 205).

[1] Priscilla.   [2] Montagu's.   [3] Coleridge's.

[4] W. W. had known David Wilkie and his paintings for some time (see *MY*
pt. i, Ls. 43, 52, and 91). He had been elected to the Royal Academy the previous year, and in spring 1812 he exhibited 29 of his pictures and sketches in Pall
Mall, where his *Village Festival* was first shown to the public; but the exhibition
was unsuccessful and failed to cover his expenses, and his mode of advertising it
was deplored by other artists. See *Diary of Joseph Farington*, ed. Kenneth Garlick,
Angus Macintyre and Kathryn Cave, 14 vols., 1978–84, xi. 4213.

[5] George Hutchinson, M. W.'s brother, was seeking a new position as land
agent or farmer, having left similar employment in Lincolnshire with Mr.
Champion Dymoke (see *MY* pt. ii, L. 496).

[6] Thoms Hutchinson and Mary Monkhouse were planning to marry.

[7] Beaumonts.

listen. This is scandalous conduct on his part, and most ungrateful. Coleridge and Alston[1] dined lately here. Sir G— does not appear to think so highly of the only one of Alstons pictures which he has seen, as I expected.—As to his conversation Lady B— says C— will let nobody talk but himself—I heard an Artist mention Alston yesterday, he says that he thinks he paints too timidly, and would much improve by a continued residence in this Country—

Montagu is superbly lodged, and certainly and wisely denies himself no rational gratification that Money can give. Every accommodation is there in the highest style; and assuredly as far as comfort and liberty go it is impossible to be better than a Man would find himself in their House. Dr Parr[2] is there a pleasant good-humoured old Man; and it will be very convenient and agreeable for me, to call in there when I am not otherwise engaged, even before I take up my residence in the House—I saw their eldest boy, Charles,[3] a fine and engaging Child. Anne Skepper was there also—Alfred is sent to Bury; and William in order to break the impetuosity of his temper, to a Quaker school; where he is to continue a year or two—a droll Idea this, and truly finical.—

Now, My Love, omit nothing to procure an appetite; for if that be formed, I am sure health and strength will follow. Do not over fatigue thyself.—I am considerably better in health than when I wrote last, but my stomach has not yet recovered its tone if I exceed in eating however little, especially at breakfast, I am oppressed the whole of the day. My misfortune is that my appetite or inclination is no guide for what I ought to eat.—I had no inconvenience from the top of Coach; on the contrary; but still I was more fatigued with my journeys short as they were than I ever remember to have been.—The first night here I slept ill; but last night I made amends.—

[1] Washington Allston (see *MY* pt. i, L. 232; pt. ii, L. 520), 'a man of genius and the best painter yet produced by America,' according to S.T.C., who introduced him to Sir George Beaumont. The picture referred to here is either the lost *Cupid and Psyche* described in a later letter, or *Dead Man Restored to Life by Touching the Bones of the Prophet Elisha*, begun soon after he settled in London in 1811. See W. H. Gerdts and T. E. Stebbins, jnr., '*A Man of Genius*', *The Art of Washington Allston (1779–1843)*, Boston, 1979, p. 65.

[2] Dr. Samuel Parr (see *MY* pt. ii, L. 341; *LY* pt. ii, Ls. 427 and 443), the Whig controversialist.

[3] The three boys referred to here were Basil Montagu's sons by his second marriage. Anne Skepper was Mrs. Montagu's daughter by her first marriage.

I have infinite pleasure in the thought of seeing thee again in Wales; and travelling with thee.—I long for the day. Love me and think of me and wish for me, and be assured that I am repaying thee in the same coin.—It is not to be wondered that Tom's mind is unsettled as to his Book, and that he misses his Companions. Try to encourage him; he is a sweet Boy and will be universally beloved wherever he goes. Write to me frequently and the longest Letters possible; never mind whether you have facts or no to communicate; fill your paper with the breathings of your heart most tenderly your friend and Husband W. W. Love to every one.

Sir G. tells me this affair with Taylor[1] will cost him a thousand Pounds. What a shocking thing besides all the vexation!—Dr Cookson talks of going down into the North with Mary in the summer time; but I think that he will scarcely accomplish it Richard[2] I shall not see; he is at Sockbridge. I shall speak to Montagu about the Money for Luff.[3] Now mind and write frequent and very very long Letters. Adieu again adieu. W. W.—I shall call on Sharp for Franks—

Of course this Letter does not go to Grasmere I shall write thither to morrow.

W. W. to M. W.[4]

MS. WL.
LL, p. 122.

[2 May 1812]
Saturday Morning before breakfast

I am looking for a Letter from thee my dearest Love; I hope thou hast duly received mine:—first let me speak of C's affair. Upon this I have seen Montagu and Charles Lamb. Montagu is very willing to be confronted with Coleridge, but he insists that this should be in the presence of some conscientious and serious person. I have therefore begged of Lamb to communicate my sentiments to Coleridge; and to tell him that I insist upon such

---

[1] Sir George Beaumont's agent at Coleorton, whom he had dismissed.

[2] R. W. who owned an estate at Sockbridge, near Penrith.

[3] Capt. Charles Luff (see *MY* pt. i, L. 6), who had set out for Mauritius, had asked W. W. for a loan.

[4] This letter follows *MY* pt. ii, L. 239.

meeting taking place; both on my own account and his; in order that nothing may be said by [him] of my conduct towards him but what has been established by all the concurring evidence which the case admits, and that if I am to suffer in his good opinion he may precisely know to what degree I[1] ought to suffer. Would you believe it. I have seen a Letter[2] in which without naming me, though clearly meaning no other Person he calls me his bitterest Calumniator, describes the agony he has suffered in consequence of the behaviour of one (meaning me the same person) who had been in his heart of hearts; and states that his late journey to Keswick had convinced him that he had not been deluded—and accordingly being now certain of that he has recovered his tranquillity, and his very appearance is improved in consequence, etc—I was permitted to transcribe the passage which [will] be copied for you, by Dorothy; I would have given you myself the very words now, but I destroyed the slip of paper yesterday, after I had copied in a very short Letter which I wrote to Grasmere. This conduct is insufferable and I am determined to put an end to it. I am not at liberty to say to whom this letter was addressed, on account of some other business contained in it. I also know that he has spoken to the valued friends under whose roof I am in a manner which almost calls upon me to put an end to all intercourse with him for ever—

The trouble of hunting out Charles Lamb and settling the business with Montagu some engagements I have had beside, have prevented me from touching yet in many affairs but to day I purpose to take steps for having the 100£ paid in to Woodriffs[3] hands. On thursday night I was at the play,[4] the Lycaeum, where I saw some good comic acting, and last night at the House of

---

[1] *Written* to.

[2] S. T. C.'s letter to Richard Sharp of 24 Apr. (Griggs, iii. 388), which Sharp had shown to W. W. During his recent visit to Keswick, Coleridge had omitted to call on W. W. as he passed through Grasmere. 'He is offended with William, or fancies himself so—and expected W^m to make some advances to him which as he did not he was miserable the whole time he was in Keswick, and Mrs C. was right glad to get him off again, for she had no satisfaction in him—and would have given the world, I dare say, to have had him well again with W^m.' (*SH*, pp. 45–6).

[3] On Capt. Luff's behalf. Thomas Woodruff was a colleague of Lamb's at the East India House.

[4] *The Sons of Erin* by Mrs. Alicia Le Fanu (1753–1817), sister of R. B. Sheridan. Her eldest son was father of Joseph Sheridan Le Fanu, the novelist.

Commons, where I was a good deal entertained by a debate Upon the subject of Barracks. Sir Francis Burdett[1] made a most intemperate and injudicious speech and was ably replied to by Perceval.[2] Sir Francis however as far as words go speaks very elegantly and well. The Question was whether Barracks should be built at Liverpool, Bristol, and in Mary-Bone in London. This was objected to by the Opposition on the ground of Expense, and the extravagant plan on which it was proposed to raise these Buildings; and on these points the Opposition were so strong that they I think could of carried the question had it not been for the Indiscretion of Sir F. B., who drew off the attention of the House from the point of unnecessary expence, and opposing the proposition upon the ground that these barracks were part of a system to enslave the people by the means of the army, made use of such offensive expressions, and conducting his whole argument so like a factious demagogue, that several of those who meant to resist the erection of these Barracks, voted for them, very absurdly no doubt, lest by their opposition they should seem to participate or sanction the arguments and opinions of this ill-judging Sir Francis.

I breakfasted with Sharp on Thursday, he will supply me plenteously with Franks, and has kindly allowed me to have my Letters directed to him, which he will forward by the Penny Post. Therefore, Sweet Love, write often and long; and tell me every thing you do and feel. How I long to see you again! The Debate continued till near 12 Last night, and I was not in bed till One; but I contrived to rise this Morning before eight to write to thee my Darling; and I am happy to tell thee that upon the whole my health is much better; though yesterday I felt my Stomach much burthened and disordered by the indigestion which I felt in course of my conversation with Lamb upon the subject of Coleridge.—I do not know that I ever was more rouzed in my Life; and I feel the effects in my stomach at this moment.—

Sharp gave me the Order which admitted me into the Gallery of the House, and was so very kind as to come and sit near me

---

[1] Sir Francis Burdett (see L. 398), radical M.P. for Westminster, 1807–37, who specialised in denouncing abuses in the army and corruptions in parliament. In the last years of his life, he crossed to the Conservative benches as M. P. for N. Wilts. from 1837, and W. W. was on visiting terms with him and his daughter, the Baroness Burdett-Coutts (1814–1906). See *WL MSS.*

[2] Spencer Perceval (1762–1812), the Prime Minister, assassinated later this month.

twice or thrice for some time, to point out to me the different Members and give me every information which I required. He also during an uninteresting period of the Debate introduced me to the coffee room of the House where I had a comfortable and refreshing cup of Tea. A little before twelve, when the business was over, and I was waiting in the Lobby till Sharp came out, I noticed a person also waiting there whose face I was sure I had seen before, but who it was I could not make out. When Sharp appeared he accosted this Person and he turned out to be Josiah Wedgewood.[1] He did not recollect me, but had noticed me and took me for a Member of the House; He says I am a much thinner Man than I was when he knew me.—Sharp's attentions were really most obliging, and I can tell you a circumstance in regard to Coleridge most highly to his Credit; so that with all his foibles he really has a world of merit.—Montagu wishes that Josiah Wedgewood should be chosen as Arbiter in the affair of C– and myself.—

I am happy to say that Miss Lamb is something better, and Charles seems to think the dawn of her recovery is at hand.[2] I called on Tuffin in the City whither he is now driven in consequence of an endangerment of his property to the amount of twenty thousand pounds but 18.000 of it Sharp thinks he will recover. His Letter was very kind and expressed great regret that I was not under his roof. Montagu's present appartments are most sumptuous; and assuredly nothing would there have been wanting to my comfort. De Quincey is out of Town I guess at Oxford. Johnsy, I called upon the day before yesterday. I found him in a nasty Dirty place the temporary School. He seems quite pleased; but he finds Dr Bell[3] in some respects a troublesome Man to deal with.—The confirmed change of circumstance etc had decayed Jonsy's health, and he described himself as having been extremely ill; but he has now gone through the seasoning.—I hope to have two or three pleasant interviews with him; but it is astonishing how little one's time turns to account in this huge City, especially when one lives as I now do at one extremity of it. Richard[4] is in the north. Observe I mention things just as they pop into my head. I have had a brief Letter from Luff,

---

[1] S. T. C.'s and W. W.'s early benefactor.
[2] Mary Lamb had been taken ill again in late Feb.
[3] Andrew Bell the educationalist, founder of the Madras system.
[4] R. W.

transmitted by Miss Dowling[1] but she did not say when I am to call upon her. I shall call on Lord Holland, and indeed upon every Body.—

On Tuesday the 12th Instant Coleridge is to commence a course of six Lectures,[2] One guinea the course upon the Drama. This is a most odious way of picking up money, and scattering about his own and his friend's thoughts. Lady B– has taken 30 tickets, which she will have to force upon her friends and where she cannot succeed must abide by the Loss; in this way the whole probably of the expense of the Rooms Advertisements etc will be covered, and the rest the Lecturer will put into his pocket.

Did I tell you that I have written to George? I will also see Mr Curwen[3] if possible.—But success in these things must depend upon Chance. Taylor still continues to teaze Sir George; who calculates that with the Lawsuit which was to have been tried at Leicester, and all other losses he will suffer by this Man's folly and madness to the amount of 1,000£ an enormous loss!—What is T. Monkhouse's[4] address, if any occasion should lead me into the City, I should like to call upon him—I will try also to find out Captain Pasley[5] who was in Town lately.—In short I will see every thing and person I can—And I hope that by rising early I shall find opportunity to write to Grasmere, and to thee my darling long Letters.—

I wish I could make this entertaining. But so much space will be taken up as merely saying where I can go and what I do that, I am afraid that I shall scarcely be able to give those details which would embellish the subject. You will smile at this wish; as if I had forgotten that every thing relating to me, however dull in itself, must be interesting to you. How I long my darling to see thy face again; and little Thomas I am happy that his good Friends are pleased with him. How rich should I be if I had nobody in the world to love but you two; but blessed be God I am most rich in other treasures; and when I think of Grasmere too my heart overflows with joy.—

---

[1] Ann Dowling, governess in Lord Galloway's family, later ran a school in Ambleside attended by Dora W.

[2] See Griggs, iii. 390.

[3] J. C. Curwen, the Cumberland landowner and M. P. (see *MY* pt. i, L. 147).

[4] Thomas Monkhouse, M. W.'s cousin (see *MY* pt. i, L. 215).

[5] Charles William Pasley (see *MY* pt. i, Ls. 174 and 221).

This morning I must devote two hours to the reading of a tragedy to be offered for representation, the Author that indefatigable Scribbler in Verse, Sotheby[1]—One act Sir George L. B.,[2] and I have sate in judgement on. Thus far it seems well enough contrived for the stage, but the diction is intolerable for poverty and bad taste. Sotheby has called on me, and I have an invitation from his Wife, but I have not found time to return his call yet.—He is a good and honest Creature but a provoking Poet—a mock Poet of whom this Age produces such swarms. Sir James Mackintosh[3] is returned, and as he took the trouble of sending me his recantation from India, I shall not avoid him. Philips[4] is in Town, now possessed by the death of his Father of a large fortune, he is coming into parliament; and no doubt, as he is rather a soft headed Man, Sharp will have with the party the credit of every vote that his friend George gives.—

I hope Darling that thou wilt have no more dreams about my teeth dropping out; but that thy waking and sleeping thoughts of me will be of a more agreeable nature—I had many anxious fears about the Gig and was most happy to hear of your safe arrival; I know how careful Tom[5] was, but I could not pacify my mind, as the conveyance is so dangerous, and as the Horse was new to the business—At 12 to day I call on Rogers with whom I was indeed to have breakfasted,—and we are now going to the tragedy[6] so that I may possibly not have an opportunity of adding to this Letter; but be assured I shall write as often as I can, but not so often as if I had not to write to Grasmere likewise.—I cannot bring myself to write to thee a too naked Letter stripped of those tender expressions which are only for thy own eyes. I cannot do it, and oh how much have I to say that I am not able and how much that I am unwilling to trust to paper. Remember our being together at Liverpool on Wednesday that day week how sad did I feel that you[7] were so far from me. Adieu Adieu

---

[1] William Sotheby (see *MY* pt. i, L. 4), translator of Virgil's *Georgics* (1800).

[2] Lady Beaumont.   [3] See *MY* pt. i, L. 124; and *LY* pt. i, L. 195.

[4] George Philips, business partner of Richard Sharp and Samuel Boddington: M.P. for Ivelchester (i.e. Ilchester) from 1812.

[5] Thomas Hutchinson.

[6] Perhaps *The Grecian Daughter* (1772) by Arthur Murphy (1727–1805), his best known tragedy, now playing at the Covent Garden theatre. The author was a commissioner of bankrupts, edited Fielding's works (1762), and wrote an essay on Samuel Johnson (1792) and a Life of Garrick (1801).

[7] *Written* I.

Address: To Mrs Wordsworth, at Mr Hutchinson's, Radnor.
Franked: London May nine 1812 E. Phipps.
MS. WL.
LL, p. 133.

[7–9 May 1812]
Thursday afternoon, two [o]clock

I received thy dear Letter yesterday morning;[2] have just finished a Letter to Grasmere; and did not mean to sit down to write to thee, till to morrow, but I have taken up the pen, partly from the pleasure of writing to thee and partly because I dine to day with Dr Stoddart[3] at Doctor's commons, and, though I have several calls which I wish to make, yet I do not like to set out upon such business, and have to return here to dress; I shall therefore dress before I go out, and content myself with making two or three calls on my way eastward.—I am sorry to say also that I am partly a Prisoner by force of my old Enemy, who has plagued me cruelly since I came to town; from my having been so much heated in running about, and perhaps also from drinking some little wine; which I cannot find out does me any good, and therefore I think, in spite of thy advice of leaving it off altogether. I have suffered also from another cause which I need not mention.—

How happy my sweetest Darling am I [to][4] hear of thy excellent appetite; strength will be recovered rapidly I doubt not if this continues.—I entirely approve of thy resolution not to put off seeing things till I come; do not this on any account, for the reasons you mention. As to the mistake about the Wye and the Dee[5] I am sorry I missed it, as it would have entertained me; but my Eyes were guilty of a lapse on their part for I read Dee—I should have smiled at the blunder and rallied thee in thought with a thousand Kisses to justify and repay my cruelty.—I love

---

[1] This letter, and the next three, follow *MY* pt. ii, L. 241.

[2] M. W.'s letter of 2–4 May (*WL MSS.*) was full of family news and of her visits around Hindwell: 'I am writing in the sunshine, the pool dancing before me—what would I not give to wander with thee in the opposite meadow that looks so green and so beautiful—the trees by the pool and the one in the court are ready to burst into leaf, but there is not a *green* leaf to be seen, except upon the goose berry trees and here and there upon a shy hawthorn that has been in compleat shelter—nothing here is more forward than at Grasmere.'

[3] John Stoddart the lawyer.

[4] *Word dropped out.*

[5] In her letter of 23 Apr., M. W. had confused the Wye with the Dee.

thee so deeply and tenderly and constantly, and with such perfect satisfaction delight and happiness to my soul, that I scarcely can bring my pen to write of any thing else.—How blest was I to hear of those sweet thoughts of me which had flowed along thy dreams;[1] sleeping and waking my Love let me be with thee as thou art with me!—But I must tear myself from this.—

Coleridge has declined[2] to meet Montagu, and I think upon sufficient reasons: they are so hostile to each other that nothing good could proceed from bringing them together. He proposes instead to send me a statement begun some time since to be transmitted to Sara; but discontinued upon hearing that she had decided against him.—But no more upon this irksome subject in two or 3 days it shall be brought to a close and you shall hear the whole.—

I should have risen this morning at 7 to write to you, but I was in such pain from my old enemy, that I thought it better keep my horizontal and easy position in bed—This is a cruel hampering for me: I think I am worse to day on account of over fatigue yesterday. My Stomach upon the whole is stronger than it was; but I am dreadfully bound in my body.—I hope that less fatigue, and more care, will bring me ease.—I have seen Dr Bell, Alston. They both dined here on Wednesday.—Alston is slim and somewhat lank and delicate in appearance, seeming taller than he is with jet-black hair, and a complection out of which the colour appears to have been taken by a hot and relaxing climate. But his features though small are animated and intelligent. My old Friend Taylor[3] was of the Party and Alston did not talk much, but seemed to enjoy greatly what was said. He was elegantly dressed, his clothes perfectly well made and well chosen, so that as I have told Sara she would have been quite satisfied with him in this respect.—

Sat. Morning. Here I was interrupted. I should have sent you off a short Letter before—but I do not find it easy to procure Franks.—It seems to be looked on in London as a considerable

---

[1] In her letter of 2–4 May, M. W. had written about Thomas and herself: '. . . he and I often have nice talk about thee and I had sweet thoughts of thee in my dreams last night: dearest William how I do love thee! I hope I shall be no more anxious—in any other way than by those yearnings that I would not wish should be supressed, till we meet again—let me hear from thee often very often and tell me all.'

[2] Through Charles Lamb. For S.T.C.'s 'statement', see Griggs, iii. 397.

[3] John Taylor, of the *Sun*.

favor.—I am surprized and rather alarmed that I hear nothing from Grasmere.—I have now two Letters from Coleridge unopened. The last which I found on my return yester evening, but that I had determined in consequence of a conversation with Dr Bell, and with Henry Robinson upon the subject (to both of whom Coleridge had previously introduced it), not to call upon C– for this Statement as if he asserts therein what I know he has asserted elsewhere, Montagu and he must give each other lie. I therefore gave to Henry Robinson[1] a commission yesterday to wait on Coleridge which I think will bring the business to a close and in my next to be written I hope soon, you shall have the results.—I shall breakfast again with Dr Bell on Tuesday when I meet Johnsy.—I was much pleased with his good sense yesterday, and the knowledge of human Nature that he showed. I had also a long conversation with H. Robinson, not a little interesting. He seemed to apprehend that there was in Coleridge's mind a lurking literary jealousy of me. I totally rejected that supposition, and told him that I believe in my soul that envy and jealousy of that kind were faults of which Coleridge was utterly free, and that if he had not chimed in with my praises it was because he was in ill-humour with me, and not because he was uneasy at any comparison between my intellectual Powers and his. Robinson is a very clever man, and seemed sorry that he had dropped this suggestion, as I should be most sorry to think that there were any good grounds for believing it.—

I sate near an hour with Alston whom I found in his painting Room; his pictures are all left in Italy except one, the Cupid and Psyche.[2] I will describe it to you. Imagine to yourself, for the size of the Picture, the back of good large folio, in the centre of this place standing rested two naked figures a male and female human in every thing but their wings, their naked bodies fronting you but their faces inclined with an expression of enthusiastic love towards each; the figures are erect but rest against each other; the flesh is beautiful painted white and almost luminous and shaded off on the outline of the form; they stand upon the edge of a bluish brook, that plainly reflects their forms, and in the arbor of

---

[1] See *HCR* i. 74–81. The final reconciliation was largely engineered by H.C.R.: 'I flatter myself, therefore, that my pains will not have been lost, and that through the interchange of statements, which but for me would probably never have been made, a reconciliation will have taken place most desirable and salutary.'

[2] Completed in 1808, since lost. S.T.C. compared its colouring to Titian's.

a dark green grove, whither they are supposed to have retired after a shower, the ground being yet moistened and freshened with the rain drops. Cupid, not represented as commonly·like a boy, but a tall young Man has wings tipped with purple like those of an angel, and Psyche as tall for a female as he for a male, has short wings something like those of a butterfly. The figures appear to be about a span long, and are beautifully painted. I did not presume to give any *opinion* to Alston upon this Picture, but I begged he would permit me to mention the impression it made upon me.[1] The pleasure, I said, which I have received would have been greater if my *surprize* had been less. I had much pleasure but it did not unite smoothly or instinctively with my mind.—This effect I attribute to two causes, partly the style of colouring not resembling any Painter or school of Painters whose works I am acquainted with and which might in some degrees have *prepared* me for the sight of this picture, and still more from a cause which is possibly a defect in the picture itself, viz; the too strong contrast between the body of white in the two naked figures and the gloom of the groves behind them and in which they are standing. Could not I continued, this defect if defect it be, have been avoided by treating the subject differently; viz; by diffusing a luminousness from the two supernatural figures that should have died away gradually among the surrounding objects. He was struck with these observations, and said that he thought that a[2] better picture might have been constructed upon that plan; which he would attempt if he ever repainted the subject.—I think Alston both as a Man and a Painter is likely to answer the commendations bestowed upon him by Coleridge.—

Yesterday at a route I saw Davy[3] and his new Bride; she is any thing but handsome—and full of affectation; never letting her features alone. Davy looks well.—Sir James Mackintosh was of the same party and his Lady—I have seen no new Man that has interested me but Alston, and no female except a Mrs Maling, a daughter of Dr Darwin.[4] She is only about 20, but a sweet and delightful woman, lively, with talents, and wholly without affectation.—I could not conceive how with such a father, she could become so engagingly simple and natural a Creature; but

---

[1] *Written* it.   [2] *Written* he.

[3] Humphry Davy, recently knighted, had married on 11 Apr. Mrs. Jane Apreece, a wealthy widow, daughter and heiress of Charles Kerr of Kelso.

[4] Erasmus Darwin (1731–1802), poet and botanist: author of *The Botanic Garden* (1791), *Zoonomia* (1794–6), etc.

was told afterwards that the Doctor never interfered with the management of his daughters—a happy omission for them! This is the only woman I have met whom I could like you to see, in order that you might be pleased and know too what I admire.

Having an opportunity of getting this Letter franked I must close it this moment. Adieu you shall hear from me again I hope in three days at farthest.

W. W. to M. W.

MS. WL.
LL, p. 141. Letters of William Wordsworth, ed. Alan G. Hill, 1984, p. 153.

[9–13 May 1812]
Saturday night 10 oclock.

My dearest Love,

I have just returned from a walk of an hour and a half, for it has taken that time to go to and come from Baldwyns gardens,[1] whither I went with the intention of sitting an hour with Johnsy, had I found him at home. My way back led me by the end of Newman street where the Montagu's live, and I had an hour and a half of the night to spare, but I preferred coming home, where I knew I should be alone, in order to write to thee, which is the most grateful of my occupations. To day I have sent off a hasty Letter to thee, abruptly closed; and have also received one with which I find no fault but that it is too short.[2] But is it[3] not strange that I hear nothing from Grasmere? Surely a Letter must have miscarried; I wrote to them last Thursday. I hope all is well, but if I do not hear soon I shall begin to be alarmed.—

Do not put Thomas his flannel on again; I understand that every body who has worn a flannel in the night, perspires for some time after they leave it off, the same as when they wore it. That is the habit of perspiration continues: It is not however unlikely considering how weak Tom is that he may continue to perspire, during the greatest part of the summer; but I am sure that he would be much worse if he wore flannel.—I will call on Thom Monkhouse about the beginning of the ensuing week, and also upon the Addison's.[4]—I wish to hear again from Annette[5]

---

[1] Where the Central School was situated.
[2] M. W.'s letter of 6–7 May (*WL MSS.*).
[3] *Written* it is.
[4] R. W.'s partner.
[5] Annette Vallon.

before I attempt to send her any money.—I am less tormented by my old enemy than when I wrote last, though not free from inconvenience, and my stomach is I think some thing stronger. How happy should I hear that thou hast grown a little fatter with this exercise and improvement of appetite. Oh could I but see thee again in this respect which thou wert when thou came down the Lane to meet at Gallow Hill on my return with D– from france.[1] Never shall I forget thy, rich and flourishing and genial mien and appearance. Nature had dressed thee out as if expressly that I might receive thee to my arms in the full blow of health and happiness. I remind thee of that time in order that thou mayst try to put thyself into the same train as produced those delightful and cheering effects. Then thou hadst only me and D– to think of, now thou hast Me to think of, little Thomas to behold, and all our dear ones at Grasmere to play before thy memory, with our sweet little William, and all his pretty looks and harmonious tones to entertain and soothe and support and nourish and cherish thee. Tell me thou my love that thou dost some credit to my picture. Thou sayst that thou art the blessedest of Women and surely I am the most blessed of Men. The life which is led by the fashionable world in this great city is miserable; there is neither dignity nor content nor love nor quiet to be found in it. If it was not [for][2] the pleasure I find under this roof,[3] and that I am collecting something to think about; I should be unable to resist my inclination to set off to morrow, to walk with thee by the woody side of that quiet pool, near which thy days and nights are passed. O. my Mary, what a heavenly thing is pure and ever growing Love; such do I feel for thee, and D– and S– and all our dear family.—Write thou to me long and tenderly, thy next letter, may be under cover to Sharp, and the next after to Lambe, to whom I shall say that I have desired thee to direct for me.—His Sister, he writes me, is returned, but much weakened by her long and sharp illness.

Sunday Morning. Here I was interrupted last night by the arrival of the Beaumont's. I waked this morning before 7, and lay half an hour in bed thinking of thee and Grasmere; I then rose, washed myself from head to foot in cold water, shaved etc, and now, the above occupations having employed me near an hour I

---

[1] W. W. and D. W. had spent Aug. 1802 in Calais with Annette and Caroline, before returning to Gallow Hill on 24 Sept. for W. W.'s marriage to M. W. on 4 Oct.

[2] *Word dropped out.*   [3] Sir George Beaumont's.

sit down to continue my Letter to thee.—I find, that the hours in London agree with me better than those we keep in the country. I rise as you see something earlier breakfast between 9 and ten, have a luncheon, as it may happen from 12 to 3, dine as may happen between 5 and half past six, take a cup of tea or Coffee after but never any supper, so that if I do not chance to overeat myself at breakfast, my stomach is never over-burthened. I am still very costive, but in other respects I am considerably better, and look I think better.—

I hear nothing of interest in politics, except that [it][1] is apprehended that these riots may still become more general. It was feared, by government that a kind of general rising would have taken place in the manufacturing districts upon the 4th Ins^t. but it has been prevented. I suppose by this time that the number of troops quartered in the discontented parts is very considerable.— But I hear little of politics; and therefore cannot write any thing which would prove generally interesting in that way.—Henry Robinson, tells me with regret, that the number of Spaniards serving in Bonapartes armies in Spain is considerable; not he believes voluntarily but frightened and forced by the French to bear arms against their Country men.—He gives a most favorable account of the state of North Germany, and does not doubt that if our troops had gone thither instead of that miserable expedition to Walcheren[2] the whole Country would have appeared in open insurrection against the french.—I shall go to the House of Commons some other day to hear Canning,[3] and some others. De Quincey is in town as I learn from Mrs M–[4]—I wonder he has not found me out. Mrs M– says that he took fire at some thing that you said to him about the possession of the house, and retired from their House in great Indignation. He is quite mad with pride. Mrs M– says he looks very ill.—

I shall now lay down the pen for breakfast, when I again take it up I hope to tell you that I have seen Coleridge; as I expect

[1] *Word dropped out.* The outbreaks of industrial unrest and violence were centred on Nottinghamshire, and the government had introduced a Bill against Frame-breaking.

[2] During the Walcheren expedition (1809), the ministerial plan to attack Antwerp was abandoned by the field commander, Lord Chatham, who was subsequently forced to resign.

[3] Canning had been Foreign Secretary in the Portland administration but had resigned in 1809 following his duel with Castlereagh, and he had declined to serve under Perceval.   [4] Mrs. Montagu.

Robinson this morning. Ever tenderly yours. Kiss little Totts for me; I will try to find out Mr Curwen perhaps Sharp will be able to tell me. I saw Tuffin yesterday, he has a trifle for me for the Greens.[1]

My dear Love, it is now 9 o clock Wednesday Morning; I have been in Berner's street to call on C– : but he was gone down to the Courier Off: to assist Stuart in writing upon the late most dreadful event the Assassination of Mr Perceval in the Lobby of the House of Commons.[2] He was shot dead there on Monday last about five in the afternoon, by a man named Bellingham, formerly a Merchant of Liverpool.—

The business between C– and me is settled by a Letter. He stated, which I will send to you some future day an account of what Montagu said, Part of which I denied utterly, that is the most material part, and the rest though I allowed it had something of the form, I utterly denied that it had any of the spirit of Truth. But you shall have the correspondence. I hope to see Coleridge to day; his lectures are put off, on account of this event which has struck all London as I hope it would the whole Island with horror; that is all except a few of the lowest rabble—for they I am shocked to say are rejoiced. Last night I was at the play with Miss Lamb and her Brother. To day I dine at Ruffs[3] with Christopher.

I have already seen Christopher, who is, and looks well. I breakfasted with Dr Bell and Johnsy yesterday morning; Johnsy will have a good deal of vexation in his new situation, but I hope in the end it will answer. Dr Bell changes his mind, I fear, often, and has something of a plaguey manner, but he is a most excellent Creature.—I have heard nothing yet from Grasmere, and therefore am sure that some letters must have miscarried. I am very uneasy upon this subject. I shall write a brief note to day to them; I should much oftener but I only procure franks by chance, though Sharp made me so kind an offer, yet I do not like to abuse his kindness. Do you however address to him still.—Tell me if Thomas's difficulty in making water continues—and I shall speak to some medical person. I am considerably better myself in health, but when I have made a conquest of my old complaint

---

[1] i.e. for the fund to support the orphans of George and Sarah Green.

[2] Spencer Perceval, who had succeeded the Duke of Portland as Prime Minister, was assassinated on 11 May 1812 by one John Bellingham, a bankrupt with a grievance against the government.

[3] William Rough, a lawyer friend of C. W.'s.

some of those injurious accidents occur and throw me back. I am now doing well, but I fear a relapse from the same cause—I have undertaken a disagreeable employment for Dr Bell; viz to select and compose with Mr Johnson's assistance 20 pages of monosyllabic lessons for Children.—[1]

Montagu tells me that the Policy left by Luff as a security for the £100 is not worth a straw for me. Of course I cannot think of advancing the money; I called yesterday on Woodriff—to carry him to Montagus that he might hear this opinion; he Woodriff[2] was not at home, and I waited in vain upwards of an hour for his arrival—I am now writing in the gesso rooms where I have breakfasted with Bowles[3] the Poet who is just gone: he is a man of simple undisguised manners, but of mean appearance, and no strength in his conversation but it is impossible not to be pleased with his frank and ingenuous manner. This Letter will be franked by Lord Byron,[4] a Man who is now the rage in London, in consequence of his Late Poem Childe Haroldes pilgrimage. He wrote a satire some time since in which Coleridge and I were abused, but these are little thought of; and the other day I met him here and indeed it was from his mouth that Rogers first heard, and in his presence told us, the murder of Perceval.—

I wish I could make my Letters more entertaining, but I have such a number of disconnected particulars in my mind, that it is impossible to treat any of them with grace or interest. Besides, I feel as if every word, my Darling was thrown away, unless it mention some intelligence of importance relating to Friends, or unless it be employed in giving vent to the feelings of my heart towards thee. oh my Joy and my comfort, my hope and my repose, what awful thoughts passed through my mind of thee and Dorothy and home soon after I heard, first or almost in the moment in which I heard, of Mr Perceval's death. I saw him only ten short days before his death upon the floor of the house of Commons, and admired the spirit and animation with which

---

[1] These projected exercises, if completed, have not survived.

[2] *Written above the line.*   [3] William Lisle Bowles (see *EY*, L. 74).

[4] The franked address sheet has not survived. Lord Byron had just published the first two Cantos of *Childe Harold's Pilgrimage*. His earlier satire *English Bards and Scotch Reviewers* (1809) had poked fun at W. W., S. T. C., and other contemporaries, but had praised Rogers who was shortly afterwards to become his close friend. On 27 Feb., Byron had spoken in the House of Lords against the Bill for suppressing the rioting of Nottinghamshire frameworkers. See *Lord Byron. The Complete Miscellaneous Prose*, ed. Andrew Nicholson, 1991, pp. 22–7, 283–4.

he suppressed and chastized that most dangerous and foolish Demogogue Sir Francis Burdett. It is most probable that the murderer on that very day was about the House of Commons, for he has been lurking there for more than a fortnight, watching an opportunity to perpetrate the execrable Deed. The debate which I heard on that day, must have had no inconsiderable influence upon the mind of this detestable fanatic; and the lower orders of the People in London cry out Burdett for ever in the Pot houses, deeming him their champion and the Man who is rid them of all their sufferings real and imaginary. The country is no doubt in a most alarming situation; and if much firmness be not displayed by the government confusion and havoc and murder will break out and spread terribly. I am glad that I am in London at this crisis, I shall see and hear all I can; but I am melancholy in finding how one's time slips away in going after people whom one cannot find; besides this ugly affair of Coleridge which I hope may now be considered as settled, has hampered me grievously; and defrauded me of many days and hours of days.—

My sweet Love how I long to see thee; think of me, wish for me, pray for me, pronounce my name when thou art alone, and upon thy pillow; and dream of me happily and sweetly.—I am the blessedest of Men, the happiest of husbands—How often does that passage of Milton come to my mind; "I chiefly who enjoy so far the happier lot, enjoying thee, preeminent. etc[1] apologize for me to Mary Monkhouse and John for not having seen their Brother, but I have been really run off my Legs or a Prisoner in the House by appointments. On Sunday Morning Josiah Wedgewood called and sate above an hour with me; he has not had any communication with Coleridge for seven years, He spoke very kindly of him, and offered himself as a mediator, disagreeable as it was, the subject having been mentioned to him by Mrs M– [2]. I will not quarrel with Mrs M– but such has been her conduct in this case and others, and towards us all, that I must find some excuse for not placing myself under her roof. More of this when we meet. Tell me frankly can you puzzle out this wretched writing; if not do say so and I will write better; there is nothing which I would not do to give you pleasure, I would sit up all night, I would rise at midnight, nay any thing could I bring myself to without difficulty, which you would not

[1] *Paradise Lost*, iv. 445–7.   [2] Mrs. Montagu.

condemn as injurious to me. My soul is all day long full of tenderness to you and my dear Grasmere friends.—

Miss Lamb looks far better than could be expected and enjoyed herself much at the play; a stupid opera, called "the Devils Bridge,"[1] but the Farce "High Life below Stairs"[2] was very entertaining; it is an excellent Piece. It is now half past 12 and at two I must be in Grosvenor Square[3] to meet Johnsy, upon the subject of those monosyllabic books. At a quarter after three I must start for Ruffs, where I dine at four. I now proceed to write to Grasmere; how uneasy I am in never hearing from them, what can be the cause I sometimes fear a relapse of this frightful [?complaint].[4] I shall write again I hope on Saturday; and as often as ever I can. a thousand tender kisses, do write long and often Love to every body. Kiss Thomas. W. W.—

D. W. to W. W., M. W. and THOMAS W.

Address: Wm Wordsworth Esqre, at Sir George Beaumont's Bart, Grosvenor Square.
Postmark: May 13 1812.
MS. WL. Hitherto unpublished.

[11 May 1812]

Dear Thomas,

do not forget Aunt who makes your breeches, and loves you dearly—I hope after all that you[5] will bring him home again with you, but I ever may rejoice that you have him; for I do think without him you would have already begun to pine after home. I hope before we next write that we shall have tried the

---

[1] By Samuel James Arnold (1774–1852), who produced successful musical plays at the Haymarket, Drury Lane, the Lyceum, etc., and collaborated with Henry James Pye (1745–1813), the Poet Laureate, whose daughter he married.

[2] By James Townley (1714–78), headmaster of Merchant Taylor's School from 1760 and a beneficed clergyman at Hendon and in the City: brother of Sir Charles Townley, the collector of Classical antiquities. The farce referred to here was first produced at Drury Lane in 1759, and was immensely popular.

[3] This part of the letter seems to have been written at Rogers's, where W. W. had met Byron. See also *LY* pt. iv, L. 2034.

[4] *Word miswritten.*

[5] i.e. M. W.: W. W. was to forward the letter to Hindwell. The first part is missing.

electricity[1]—You have not yet gained much weight—I hope that before you leave Hindwell you will have added at least another half stone to your Body. Pray take care of yourself and be quite easy about us. If I could but give you a notion how well and lively Catharine is, I am sure you would be quite easy; for all else seem to be safe. Yet God knows how soon I may have a different tale to tell, well as every thing goes at present. I had a note from Sara on Saturday night, She has not at all tired of her Walk, and very well; but I am sorry to say she grows thinner. I see it very plainly, and she looks much worn in the face for it though I think better every where else. It is very strange that she should grow thin, for her spirits are good and she eats heartily enough, and sleeps well. I hope I have her at home again by next Thursday or Friday at the latest, when the washing will be over—I shall send this to Keswick to be forwarded by Sara as it will be as soon as if it goes by Ambleside and she may add something to it. God bless you both for ever [ ][2] that we shall hear that you have shewn M.[3] the [? matter] will not submit to delay and that all is over one [way] or another. If he[4] retains his resentment, no doubt a day will arrive unless death comes in between, when he will repent of his folly, and will be glad that he should be beloved by us for what he is, rather than for what he would now wish to be beloved for—what he can make himself *appear* to be.—If it was not for the injury he is doing you my dearest William, God knows that at this moment I have far more sorrow for his weakness—nay pity for it—than indignation against him—Give my kindest love to every member of the House of Hindwell.

Evermore your affectionate D W.

Pray make my kindest remembrances to Sir G and Lady B. I cannot read over this Scrawl. Mary, what is it Miles Holmes[5] owes us? You left no memorandum of that. Might not we direct Single Letters to M[r] Lambe?

Monday afternoon.

[S. H. adds a note][6]

[1] The Wordsworths had been persuaded to try a course of electrotherapy to cure Catharine's lameness, but in the event the machine was not used.

[2] *Seal.*   [3] Montagu.   [4] S. T. C.   [5] A farmer in Easedale.

[6] 'I have nothing to say but that I love you dearly; am well; and sadly grieved that this ugly affair should make your stay in London so uncomfortable. C's say-

W. W. to D. W.

MS. WL.
LL, p. 139 (—).

Wednesday morn [13 May 1812]

My dearest Dorothy,

How comes it? What can be the reason that I do not hear from you; if nothing ill has happened I am sure there must have been a miscarriage of letters. I have only received from Grasmere, the Letter which I found here, and one written over that of Mr de Quincey.[1] I hoped to day to have sate quietly down to a long letter to you, but unexpected engagements have intervened. I am now writing this short note at Rogers's where I have breakfasted in company with Bowles the Poet. Before half past 8 I called in Berners Street at Coleridges by appointment; but found a note telling me that he had been obliged to go down to the Courier off. to assist Street[2] in writing something appropriate upon the late horrid event, the Assassination of Mr Perceval who no doubt you will have heard was shot dead on monday Evening in the Lobby of the House of Commons.—I may possibly see Coleridge today in Grosvenor Square between the hours of 1 and 2 the business is settled by a Letter; but I have not seen him yet.—At four I dine at Ruffs with Christopher, whom I saw on monday morning looking admirably well.—On the other side I will transcribe my answer to Coleridge's statement,[3] his previous Letter[4] I do not like to part with, and have not time to transcribe. But you shall either have it or a Copy very soon.

My answer was as follows:-

I solemnly deny that I gave M—[5] commission to say any thing whatever from me to C–. All that I did say had reference merely

---

ing that he *learned* that *I* had given him up is just of a piece with the rest of his fancies . . . M^rs C and I have many a battle—but we do not quarrel. She wonders how I could love any one of whom I think so *ill*; and thinks he ought to know what I *do* think of him—why I say every thing that I say to you *have I said to himself*—and all that I believe of him now I believed formerly (except that he should ever have behaved as he has done to you or believed that you could have said these things but in the spirit of love) . . . She is sure that we think far worse of him than ever she did and is now on his side *quite*.'

[1] D. W.'s letter of 23 Apr. (*MY* pt. ii, L. 237) was written over De Quincey's letter to W. W. of 16 Apr. (Jordan, p. 260).

[2] T. G. Street, joint proprietor of the *Courier*. [3] See Griggs, iii. 397.

[4] Of 4 May (Griggs, iii. 397–402). [5] Montagu.

to an apprehended Connection between himself and M— which I was convinced must prove injurious to both; nor did it ever enter my mind that by any possibility what of this pertained could any way affect the friendship and *intimacy* between [him] and me. Of course, and [?conclusively], and to meet C's statement in detail I solemnly deny that I commissioned M to say to C that I had no hopes of him. I also solemnly deny that I said C— was in *the habit of* running into debt at little Pot-houses for gin. I also affirm as sacredly that though in some of the particulars enumerated by C. as having wounded his feelings there is something of the *form* of truth there is *absolutely nothing of the Spirit* in any of them. As for instance, that I asserted that C— had been an absolute Nuisance in my family. It is little less than morally impossible that I should have used these Words, but it is absolutely impossible that either by these words, if used, or by [any] resembling them I could mean to express the impression of my mind and heart concerning C. or the feelings of my family in respect to him. So that in every sense in which the particulars enumerated by C and the whole of them originally could, as evidences of unworthy behaviour on my part give pain to C, if he knew what I said under what circumstances I[1] spoke, with what Motive and in what spirit, I do give a most *solemn denial to the whole*.—

I have with the utmost severity of self examination looked into my own heart and soul upon this occasion and stand acquitted before my conscience of all blame except that I freely acknowledge an error of judgement in having suffered myself from any Motive however kind to the parties, and however pure to speak to a man upon so delicate [a] subject whose conduct is so little governed by the universally admitted laws of friendship and regulations of society in similar cases.

Hoping to receive from C an assurance of his entire and absolute faith in this my disavowal I have to add that I fully believe in the truth of his Statement as an expression of his conviction that M— did say all he has ascribed to him. But whether the agitation in which C represents himself to have been from the first moment M— touched upon the business may not have occasioned him to mistake M— in some important points or whether M— may not have mistaken me; or how the misapprehension which actually subsists originated—these are points into which I do not deem it necessary to enter. The

---

[1] *Written* is.

love and affection which I entertain for C— and which I trust he entertains for me do not require a solution of these difficulties.

If however C's mind still is troubled by doubts and misgivings as to the sincerity simplicity and integrity of the disavowal I have herein made I must then in satisfaction of my own honour require his consent to the first proposed interview between M— and ourselves; though aware that this would of necessity lead to an opening of the points in differences between himself and M which I think in itself very inadvisable.

Should this measure be rendered necessary by the state of C's feelings I beg that no farther steps may be taken till C— has closed the Lectures which he is on the point of commencing.—

The above was the Statement to which I received an immediate answer, stating that this had satisfied C—.[1] I will Continue to send you the whole correspondence. If you can find time do transcribe the above for Mary. I can write no more. Sir George is in the room and Mr Johnson. Of course I am writing in Grosvenor Square. You shall have a Letter at Ambleside on Monday to you both. Dearest love. Affectionate love to Sara. Kiss the children.

W. W. to D. W.[2]

MS. WL. *Hitherto unpublished.*

Friday afternoon half past four
[15 May 1812]

My dearest Dorothy,

Your Letter which I received about noon to day has relieved me from a very painful anxiety. It is little short of three weeks since I heard from you; and I was disturbed by unconquerable apprehensions that this frightful dysentery had either returned upon you or seized Sarah or some one or more of the children. Do write to me oftener, addressing your Letters alternately to Sharp and Mr Lambe; this you may venture to do, I am sure, though I have not apprized Lambe of it. I called on Coleridge yesterday, and sate with him some time; I think he looks well,

---

[1] See Griggs, iii. 403–8.

[2] This letter, which follows *MY* pt. ii, L. 242, is extensively damaged and sometimes illegible.

though considerably too fat. I felt no awkwardness at the meeting, nor was he much agitated. I saw also the Morgans,[1] and Miss Brent.[2] Mr Morgan is a little slender man of very mean appearance and seemingly in weak or bad health. His features oversmall and his complexion pallid, and his person wasted or shrunk. Mrs Morgan is a pretty interesting woman of good Stature with a fair complection, dark eyes, and a lively expressive countenance. The other, her Sister, is a little person, and slender without any thing about [her] that impressed me. But I shall speak of them more particularly when I have had a better opportunity of observing them minutely. The day before I dined at Sargeant Ruffs or Rough's to meet Christopher and Henry Robinson.[3] When we arrived at the door we found that Mrs R— had the first pains of labour upon her, so that we dined with the Doctor in attendance. H. Robinson, much against my mind, persuaded me to go and see Mrs Charles Aiken[4] in the City, that evening. Her I had told I wished to see. She is the daughter of Gilbert Wakefield, and I had often heard [her] described as an amiable woman with nothing Aikenish about her. But knowing that there was to be a party I was very unwilling to go. I found a whole gang of them with Mrs Barbauld,[5] an old snake, at their head. Mrs Charles fully answered my expectations, but for the

[1] John James Morgan, businessman, lawyer, and friend of S. T. C. since his Bristol days, had married Mary Brent and moved to Hammersmith. S. T. C. stayed with the Morgans for long periods at various times.

[2] Charlotte Brent, Mary's sister, who lived with the Morgans.

[3] For W. W.'s remarks on some of his contemporaries, see *HCR* i. 82–3. 'Wordsworth talked at his ease, having confidence in his audience. He spoke with respect of Landor's power . . . In walking afterwards, Wordsworth spoke with great contempt of Scott . . .'

[4] Anne Wakefield, daughter of Gilbert Wakefield (1756–1801), Classical scholar and controversialist, had married Dr. Charles Rochemont Aikin (1775–1847), medical writer and joint author with his brother of a *Dictionary of Chemistry and Mineralogy* (1807–14). Also present on this occasion, according to H. C. R., were his brother Arthur Aikin (1773–1854), the chemist, and his sister Lucy Aikin (1781–1864), historical writer, correspondent of Channing, and author of *Epistles on Women* (1810).

[5] Charles Aikin's aunt, Anna Letitia Barbauld (1743–1825), the poetess and dissenter, who had recently published her controversial poem *Eighteen Hundred and Eleven*: 'She does not content herself with expressing her fears lest England should perish in the present struggle,' H. C. R. wrote: 'she speaks with the confidence of a prophet of the fall of the country as if she had seen in a vision the very process of its ruin.' (*HCR* i. 63–4).

rest they were odious to me. A son of Roscoe's of Liverpool[1] was there, and [?he] forced upon me a dispute concerning Sir Francis Burdett, in which the opinions displayed by himself and the rest of the party disgusted me so much, that what with talking and what with disgust from the ignorant folly and madness which I was compelled to hear, I was made quite ill; or rather let me say that my stomach which had before to recover itself was no longer much improved, that I have been unable to support the subsequent fatigues of talking, and am more troubled with pain and constant flatulence ever since. It was for me a most unlucky and disagreeable Visit and very injurious because I cannot make a holiday to recruit my weak and sore stomach. I was also getting somewhat better of my old enemy which has thus been brought back upon me. A plague on them all!—

I have just now returned from calling with Sir George upon Coleridge; intending to proceed thence with C. and Sir G. to sit a while with Alston; but A— was not at home; for this I am sorry, as perhaps Sir G. might have said to him some thing useful upon his own art.—We then went to Mr West's[2] where we saw some interesting things. Yesterday I dined here with Lord Dunstanville,[3] Lord Harewood,[4] Lord Ashburnham,[5] Dance the Architect,[6] and Mr Jekyll,[7] the celebrated Wit of whom no doubt

---

[1] Probably Thomas Roscoe (1791–1871), fifth son of William Roscoe, the Liverpool banker and historian: translator of Benvenuto Cellini's *Memoirs*, Silvio Pellico's *Esther of Engaddi* (*R. M. Cat.*, no. 632), and other works. According to H. C. R., he was supported in the ensuing argument by his friend Yates of Liverpool, one of several brothers from the prominent Unitarian family of that name who were involved in radical causes: most probably John Ashton Yates (1781–1863), M. P. for Carlow and author of pamphlets on trade and slavery.

[2] Benjamin West (1738–1820), historical painter of American Quaker ancestry, succeeded Reynolds as President of the Royal Academy in 1792. The reference here is perhaps to some of his religious pictures, which included *Christ Healing the Sick in the Temple*, now in the National Gallery, and *Christ Rejected* (exhibited 1814).

[3] The Cornish peer, industrialist, and patron of the arts: formerly Recorder and M. P. for Penryn (1779). See also *LY* pt. i, L. 203.

[4] Edward Lascelles, 1st Earl of Harewood (1739–1820), of Harewood House, Yorks.: M. P. for Northallerton, 1761–74 and 1790–6.

[5] George Ashburnham, 3rd Earl of Ashburnham (1760–1830), had recently succeeded his father in the title, and like him was an assiduous courtier.

[6] George Dance, the younger, architect for the City of London and rebuilder of Coleorton Hall.

[7] Joseph Jekyll (d. 1837), lawyer, wit and journalist: M.P. for Calne,

you have heard; and a most ingenious and entertaining man he is, one that makes the time slip away as imperceptibly as any body need wish, while one is sitting round a table. Lord Harewood is stiff and stupid, but the two other Lords in their several ways were both interesting men. Lady Crew[1] was also of the party, a person to whom Charles Fox 30 or 40 years ago wrote verses which may be found if you think it worth while to seek for them in that miscellany of Poems[2] printed at Carlisle which I gave Mary. It contains the Minstrel etc. This morning Mr Price[3] the Picturesque called in, and we went to see some pictures of Lord Dunstanville's: among others some very accurate copies of some of the most celebrated Works of Raphael in the Vatican.—I forgot to mention that Mr Montgomery[4] the Poet was at the Aikens party; he seem to be in delicate Health and went away very soon; there is nothing favourable in his appearance and in his manner, he is just about as much of a Gentleman as Edwards of Derby.[5]—

I am now writing with my left hand upon my stomach, where I have scarcely even been able to keep one hand or the other since that unfortunate visit; and before it I believe my hand had not been upon my stomach for several days nor had I the least flatulence. How vexatious this relapse from such a cause.—You cannot conceive [how] much time is lost, when one has any business to settle, and in calling upon people without finding them at home. I mention this as an excuse for not having yet seen the Addisons, the Twinings,[6] nor T. Monkhouse nor George Mackareth's Son.[7] Pray tell me his address and also send

1787–1816, Master in Chancery, and restorer and historian (1811) of the Temple Church.

[1] She was Frances, daughter of Fulke Greville of Wilbury, Wilts., and she married (1766) John Crewe, 1st Baron Crewe (1742–1829), Whig M. P. for Stafford, 1765–8 and Cheshire, 1768–1806. Her circle included Fox, Burke, and Sheridan, who dedicated *The School for Scandal* to her.

[2] Fox's verses were first printed at the Strawberry Hill Press in 1775. For Beattie's *Minstrel*, see *MY* pt. ii, L.348.

[3] Uvedale Price, writer on 'the picturesque'.

[4] James Montgomery, Evangelical poet and hymn-writer, editor and proprietor of the *Sheffield Iris*.   [5] John Edwards, the Derby poet.

[6] Richard Twining (1749–1824), director of the East India Company and tea merchant in the Strand, married (1771) Mary Aldred of Norwich. Their eldest son Richard (1772–1857) had already joined the family firm. See also *RMVB*, 1841.

[7] Son of the parish clerk of Grasmere.

me a letter from Mr Green[1] of Ambleside to introduce Sir George and myself to that Gentleman's collection of Pictures in the City of which he spoke so highly. I have yet only been at the exhibition once for about three Quarters of an hour.—My letters I feel [are][2] not worth being sent to Mary, nor those to her worth being sent to you; I am not sure also but I add to their dullness by telling you things twice over; and do not know well what I omit, nor what I wrote to you and what to her. I live in such a bustle and hurry, I am however very glad to have got the business with C– over, and if I can bring my stomach about, I hope shall do well enough.—I could wish to have time to send more.—"Thinks I to myself was exceedingly admired by Dr Cookson Mrs Cookson and their two Daughters; it was irresistibly laughable they thought, and excellently done; and certainly (but, this between ourselves) I have seen no woman's bosom married or single less concealed than Mary C's was. So that it seems as if they who live in the world, think feel and act as it is done in the world. This young man I apprehend will [ ][3] than has most of the family.

But this I said before. Your account of Catharine upon the whole is very welcome. I hope she will go on: but I am much concerned with what you say of dearest Sara. There must be some removable cause for her losing flesh; pray do let her look to it, don't you sit up too late in the night. Dear Sara, all that I said about Cs getting Gin from public Houses, was said in the most friendly and tender spirit. I absolutely denied that he drank almost any spirit with us; and insisted upon this as a thing to his honour. But only said that if he were put at once upon the severe regimen proposed by Carlisle[4] and were unable to support it, I feared he would not have courage to avow that opinion and that he would in his weakness be tempted to deceive them if what I knew took M [ ]: he and Carlisle were too [?][5] in tales and to forgive what started as a proof of the probable apprehension of him that he had confirmed to us [he] had a small but very small supply of spirit from the Public House. So that if M. said that I stated that C was in the habit of going to Pot Houses for Gin, he stated an absolute and wretched falsehood; for I said directly the contrary. But no more on the subject, when I can find leisure I

[1] William Green, the Ambleside artist (see *MY* pt. i, L. 96).

[2] *Word dropped out.*

[3] *Several illegible words.* The whole drift of the passage is obscure.

[4] Anthony Carlisle, S. T. C.'s physician.   [5] *MS. illegible.*

will transcribe for your his representation of what M said; I cannot part with the original, because I may have occasion for it in my dealings with Montagu. Not that I shall not carefully avoid the subject with M; but M may conduct himself so as to render it necessary for me to produce this paper. I hope not.—

It now wants only a quarter of six and I must lay down my pen to dress for dinner. Most tenderly and affectionately yours my dearest Dorothy and Sara. Your letter will go to Henry tomorrow.—

Saturday afternoon half past 2

Yesterday we had at dinner a considerable party, two of the Phipps's,[1] a Mr [?Locker],[2] an elegant, but somewhat insipid fine Gentleman, Mess[rs] West and Owen,[3] Painters, Bowles the Poet, etc. Bowles I like, a [?lot][4] he is a simple, frank, unaffected Man, negligent of his person, and old fashioned or rustic in his appearance, his face has formerly been pretty good. This morning I had a call from Stuart; I am sorry to say that he has been extremely ill and is much reduced, and though he has been some time in a course of strict management, he looks ten years older than when I saw him last. His complaint broke out upon him all at once with a violent discharge of blood downwards, and reduced him in three days so much that he could scarcely stand with loss of flesh, in proportion. He says that his complaint was caused by overloading his stomach with food, and he told me how he was tempted to do so. He never drank well, but more than he ought to have done; but for 3 or 4 months before his attack he had lived very temperately in every respect; but he says that the complaint must have been laying its foundations for several years before, as he was admonished by giddiness in his head last

[*two thirds of sheet torn away*]

. . . from that quarter of [ ] extremely hurried.

This letter has already proved considerably longer than I thought I should have found time to make it; but it is incoherent

---

[1] Lord Mulgrave's brothers, Edmund Phipps, mentioned earlier, and Augustus Phipps, F.R.S. (1762–1826), Commissioner of Excise. See also *RMVB*, 1836, 1839.

[2] Probably Edward Hawke Locker, F.R.S. (1777–1849), secretary to Lord Exmouth in the East Indies, 1804–9, and in the Mediterranean, 1811–14, and Commissioner of Greenwich Hospital, 1824–44. He was a friend of Southey and Scott.

[3] William Owen, R. A. (1769–1825), portrait-painter.   [4] *Written* well.

stuff which you must excuse. Dearest Dorothy I am afraid you are very thin, after having had so bad a cold before you had well recovered of the Dysentery. Do take [care][1] of yourself, and avoid the occasions of taking these dreadful colds—but you my dearest Sara, how are you: do not overwalk yourself, and do not sit up late with D. nor let her sit up late reading foolish and stupid novels, and if little W[m's] face be not extremely scabbed, as I know you are so delicate . . .

[*two thirds of sheet torn away*]

. . . are besotted to speak of Sir George in that manner; and [ ][2] as I have had proof and as Serjeant Rough told me (but be cautious of mentioning his name) who saw the whole of the correspondence. Adieu again adieu my dearest Dorothy and Sara: it is now 20 minutes past 7, and I must insist that T. M.[3] leave his personal engagement and go directly with me to Sharp. I shall not probably have an opportunity of adding now to this letter [?][4] farewell very loving regards to you both

W. W.

W. W. to M. W.[5]

Address: M[rs] Wordsworth, M[r] Hutchinson's, Radnor.
Franked: London May sixteenth 1812 W. Sturges Bourne.[6]
Postmark: 16 May 1812.
MS. WL.
LL, p. 156.

[16 May 1812]

Darling,

    The accompanying which I received yesterday, has relieved me from much anxiety. I have a frank for Monday, for you and hope

---

[1] *Word dropped out.*

[2] *Illegible passage*: perhaps referring to Sir George Beaumont's difficulties with Taylor, the agent whom he had dismissed.

[3] M. W.'s cousin, Thomas Monkhouse.   [4] *MS. obscure.*

[5] This letter precedes *MY* pt. ii, L. 243. It was begun on D. W.'s and S. H.'s letter to M. W. of 11 May, which W. W. was forwarding to M. W. at Hindwell, and continued on a new sheet and franked on the 16th.

[6] William Sturges-Bourne (1769–1845), M.P. for Christchurch, 1802–12, and 1818–26, for some time a Lord of the Treasury and Commissioner for Indian affairs, and then Home Secretary for a few months (1827) under his friend

to write at some length on that day, therefore I have less regret in now saying so little.—I have just finished a pretty long Letter to Grasmere. Lord Lonsdale[1] will be in Town next week, and I shall make a point of seeing him; and then I shall deem my *business* in London *done* and shall be most impatient to get away to thy arms, where alone I can be happy; unless when *Duty* calls me elsewhere. And I am sure that no obligation of duty will then exist to divide us. For as to amusement etc unless I felt that it contributed to[2] my health etc, you shall know how the sentence went on but first let me tell you what a blunder I have made and this moment discovered, viz, that the rest intended for you has been written, by mistake on the cover, directed, *Miss W–* for Grasmere. A most unlucky oversight! for unfortunately there are some tender and overflowing expressions of Love which were meant for no eyes but thine, and which if I cannot erase, I must not send the Cover; for example I feel that every thing I had written[3] in the way of amusements appears worthless and insipid when I think of one sweet smile of thy face, that I absolutely pant to behold it again. Of course this must not go, and how to get rid of it I know not.—I have crossed and recrossed the Frank and part of it I fear will still be legible; at all events the very attempt to hide, will I fear give offense.—I have now blotted the sheet so that it is impossible to make out the obnoxious expressions—so let it pass; for I know not how (now that [it] is so late), to procure another frank, and I promised to write, against Monday.—

This morning Stuart called on me; he has been ill, is much reduced, and looks, I think, ten years older than when I saw him last. The complaint originated in a disorder of the Stomach which he ascribes to having often over eat himself, particularly when exhausted. He says that for some years he has had intima-

Canning before resigning his office to Lord Lansdowne and becoming Commissioner of Woods and Forests. He remained in Parliament till 1831.

[1] W. W. had approached Lord Lonsdale on 6 Feb. (L. 236) about several impending vacancies, but the latter had replied on the 25th that he was unable to forward W. W.'s wishes at this time, 'but I hope to be more fortunate on some future occasion.' 'Whatever might have been the mode you had adopted to make your wishes known to me, you may be assured it would have had the effect of claiming that attention which my respect for your Talents and character would prompt me to shew you.' (*WL MSS.*).

[2] Contributed to *written twice*. W. W. takes a new cover at this point.

[3] *Written* I had written every thing.

tions that things were not going on well, in his constitution such as giddiness in his head, languor occasionally, and falling asleep after dinner.—He had a discharge of blood and slime which brought him to the edge of the grave in a few days.—He is a most able Man. His good sense and knowledge of things are consummate. I wish that the ministers would take his advice for there is a sad want of knowledge and of firmness and the Country is in a most awful state. The Monster[1] is to be executed on Monday Morning I hope to procure, by means of the Poet Bowles a stand upon The top of Westminster Abbey whence I may see the Execution without risk or danger. It takes place on Monday Morning. I long to be with you for this London life does not agree—with me because If I am ever thrown out I cannot find leisure to recover.—

Did I tell you that Mr Henry Robinson took me to Mrs Charles Aikens, Daughter of Gilbert Wakefield. She is a most natural and pleasing Character but there unluckily I met the whole Gang among the rest the old Snake Letitia Barbauld. I had an altercation with Roscoes son upon Francis Burdett, and was so disgusted with the whole Gang save the Hostess that I was made ill. I had further to run a couple of miles to prevent my being locked out here, as I gave a general order that they were not to be sat up for me after 12.—I think of consulting some Physician upon the costiveness I feel and the great quantity of thin mucous which is involuntarily discharged from my bowels. It certainly implies that the stomach and bowels are in a most disordered State. Tell me how you are mind if you gather flesh.

Adieu. Best love to every body; I will walk into the city soon or perhaps to see Monkhouse. I have been obliged to get a new suit of Clothes with a new hat and silk stockings.

I cannot take leave of thee my beloved wife, on the other side of the Sheet. oh love me! and take care of thyself.

---

[1] John Bellingham, Perceval's assassin, had been tried at the Old Bailey the previous day and was to be publicly hanged on 18 May, not in Palace Yard (as W. W. expected) but before Newgate.

W. W. to M. W.[1]

Address: Mrs Wordsworth, Mr Hutchinson's, Radnor.
Franked: London May eighteen 1812 R^d Sharp.
Postmark: May 18.
MS. WL.
LL, p. 160.

[17–18 May 1812]
Sunday Morning half past 11.

My dearest Love,

It is a wet morning, at least it drizzles. Sir G. and Lady B. are gone to church, and I sit down to write a few words to thee on the cover of this frank which will go tomorrow.—Yesterday I dined alone with Lady B.—and we read Lord Byrons new poem[2] which is not destitute of merit; though ill-planned, and often unpleasing in the sentiments, and almost always perplexed in the construction. At half past nine I dressed for a party at Mrs Philips[3] (the Philips of Manchester) there I found a number, nay a multitude of people, chiefly of the connections of the opposition.—It is not worth while to mention their names; I did not stay above three quarters of an hour; for I am quite tired of these things; If you happen to fall into conversation with a person at all interesting, on an interesting subject, it is impossible to prosecute it; for either some body comes in between; or inclination of variety prompts or an obligation of civility enjoins, an attention to some other individual, and the conversation is immediately broken off. I have already neglected several invitations of this kind, and shall in future attend to still fewer; so that I believe that I should soon slip into as deep a solitude in London as in Grasmere. Lamb tells me that his Sister is well and that you may address to him as many Letters as you like; therefore Let there be at least two to him for one to Sharp—And do, my sweet Love, write to me often while I am here, and as long Letters as ever thou canst, even if they contain nothing but repetitions of tenderness and love.—

---

[1] This letter, and the next two, follow *MY* pt. ii, L. 243.

[2] *Childe Harold's Pilgrimage*. 'We talked of Lord Byron', H.C.R. recorded on the 24th. 'Wordsworth allowed him power, but denied his style to be English. Of his moral qualities we think the same. . . . I read Wordsworth some of Blake's poems; he was pleased with some of them, and considered Blake as having the elements of poetry a thousand times more than either Byron or Scott . . .' (*HCR* i. 85).

[3] Wife of Richard Sharp's business partner.

Coleridge dines here to day with Alston and Wilkie; I purpose this morning to call upon the Addison's, it is late but better than never—I hope to see thee much sooner than I thought of; for the Beaumonts are so alarmed by the state of the Country about Nottingham that I should not be surprized, if they do not go to Coleorton at all this summer; in which case I shall be able to join thee a full fortnight or three weeks sooner than[1] I before could venture to flatter myself; add to this consideration that I draw little benefit either for body or mind, from what I see here, and therefore upon the whole I think it far most likely that I shall not be very long before I find my way into Wales.—

Do not omit any opportunity of seeing all you can before I come; it will be enough for me to walk with thee by the side of that pretty Pool and to fish with thee beside me, and to see thee under the roof at thy good Friends.—Stuart will learn for me what can be done in the cause of the French Prisoner,[2] I have not yet settled Woodriffs business, but of course I shall not advance the money if the salary be of no value. Farewell, my darling, I am going to call on the Addison's. Again adieu.—I am invited to Montagus this evening to meet Mr Montgomery the Poet but I do not think that I shall be able to go, as it is not likely, that the Party here will break up in time. again farewell.

Monday Morning. when I had gotten some way from this house yester afternoon I found that I had made a mistake, supposing that the Addisons lived in Berner street the same street Coleridge is in whereas I believe they live in Barnard street, in consequence of this mistake I did not accomplish my intended call but turned in upon Coleridge, and walked with him and Mr Morgan to call upon Alston; from whose house we returned to Morgan's where I eat a biscuit, and we thence took a walk in the Park.—Coleridge Alston and Wilkie dined here; and we had upon the whole a pleasant evening; Alstone I like much, and will tell you more of him when we meet. Wilkie is not particularly interesting in conversation.—Today Christop[r] and Coleridge dine here; and I hope Stuart; from whom we shall perhaps hear some interesting facts.—

The Assassin[3] has not been executed in Palace Yard as was first proposed; had that been the place I should this morning have been a Spectator in safety, from the top of Westminster Abbey:

---

[1] *Written* that.

[2] Eustace Baudouin had asked the Wordsworths to help to effect his release.

[3] Bellingham.

but he suffered before Newgate; and I did not think myself justified, for the sake of curiosity in running any risk.—I should have been miserable if I had brought my life or limbs into any hazard upon such an occasion.—We have not yet heard what passed at the Execution. The man is unquestionably not of a sound mind; but it is not a madness of the nature which ought to exempt him from public justice.—His case seems in one point of view very much to resemble Antony Harrisons.[1] viz, that he had brooded so long upon a particular train of ideas, as to have been crazed upon that subject. But he is justly amenable to a criminal tribunal on this account; that he did not withstand as his reason would have enabled him to do the earlier impulses of these crazy and vindictive passions, which have risen at last by indulgence on his part to such a height that they appear in reference to this action to have overset his reason. In that he is clearly liable to the utmost severity of criminal justice, by having wilfully suffered his passions to dethrone his reason: for what is his case but an unexampled excess of those vindictive feelings, of that revenge, or (as Ld Bacon calls revenge)[2] wild kind of Justice, which in the shape of anger malignity pride cruelty and intense and cowardly selfishness, produces so much misery in the world. Would it not be a horrible thing, that the extreme of a Man's guilt, should be pleaded as a reason, why he should be exempted from punishment; because, forsooth, his crime was so atrocious that no Man in his senses could have committed it? All guilt is a deviation from reason. And had such an Assassin as this been acquitted upon the ground of insanity, the verdict would have held out an encouragement to all wicked Men, to transcend the known bounds of Wickedness, with a hope of finding security from law in the very enormity of their crimes.—I perhaps have said too much of this; but do read the trial carefully, and you will find I think manifest marks of an insanity of that species into which by little and little A Harrison was brought, though from feelings quite the reverse of this Man's; viz a delicate apprehension that he had here an instrument of doing wrong to others.—I know that A. H. had resolved at one time to shoot Robinson the Attorney of Ulverston; and certainly his mind in respect to that Man was in a state of phrenzy.—Tell me if you coincide with my view of this subject.—

[1] The Penrith solicitor and poet (see *EY*, L. 140).
[2] In his essay 'Of Revenge'.

And now my darling let me turn to thee, and to my longing to be with thee. Last night, and this morning in particular[1] I had dream after dream concerning thee; from which I woke and slipped again immediately into the same course.—I do hope and trust that it will not be long before we meet: Coleridge begins his Lectures[2] to morrow, which I shall not be sorry to hear. I do not think, they will bring him much profit. He has a world of bitter enemies, and is deplorably unpopular.—Besides people of rank are very shabby for the most part, and will never pay down their five shillings when they can avoid it. The Room will probably be crowded to morrow because subscribers may bring as many of their friends without pay as they like. The next day, will I fear present a great falling off: and I am pretty confident that by the fair gains of his lectures he will be a loser. Lady B. took 25 Tickets which she has disposed of and received the money.—But you cannot form a notion to what degree Coleridge is disliked or despised notwithstanding his great talents, his genius and vast attainments. He rises every day between 8 and 9 or earlier, this I think a great conquest. But his actions in other respects seem as little under his own power as at any period of his life. for example Lord Thurlow[3] a young Man lately sent him a volume of Poems which he has published, superbly Bound. The Poems have great merit far beyond any thing usually published. Coleridge never looked into the Book nor took any notice of this mark of attention, of course the Young Lord must be bitterly wounded in mind.

adieu most tenderly thy Husband and friend.

I will send thee another copy of Bells longer work.[4]

---

[1] *Written* particularly.

[2] H.C.R.'s brief notes (*HCR.* i. 84 ff.) are the only surviving record of these lectures.

[3] Edward Thurlow, 2nd Baron Thurlow (1781–1829), minor poet, published *Verses on Several Occasions*, 1812, an ode to the Prince Regent, and translations from Anacreon and Horace.

[4] Andrew Bell's original pamphlet on the Madras system of education came out in 1797, and was enlarged in 1808 with an account of the application of the system to English schools.

W. W. to D. W.

MS. WL. *Hitherto unpublished.*

Thursday morning half past eight
[21 May 1812]

My dearest Dorothy,

Yesterday morning I received your short note. You will have already learned that I had received several of your Letters: in fact they have all reached [me] save one long one which you say was sent under cover to Sharp to be forwarded by Mary. One of that character and with that destination I have received, but you speak of another which unfortunately has not yet reached me, and I fear never will. You may direct your Letters to Mr Lambe, and they probably will be more sure of coming to me—I know not what to say about John,[1] you will do what you and Sara think best, but if it be not absolutely necessary I would rather that he remained at Grasmere till my return.—Mary asks me what I think of your taking the 2 children (when Sara goes [on] her visit to Kendal) to the Sand side,[2] with one of the Servants, leaving the other at home, etc, no doubt she has proposed the plan to you, the Suttons[3] to have our house during your absence; and of course to pay for their accommodation.—Now as Sara does not go to Kendal for more than a week it seems unnecessary to stay home before this unless She were desirous to go with you to the sand-side. In which case you will do what you like. But as Catharine appears to me so well, one of the chief motives for incurring the trouble and expense seems done away. I cannot well say when we may be expected at Grasmere; because the Beaumonts seem doubtful whether they shall go to Coleorton, partly on account of the disturbed state of that Country, and partly, but do not on any account hint at this to any Body, on account of the ungovernable temper and very bad conduct of Taylor, who though ejected out of Sir G.'s House is still resident in the neighbourhood on the other side of Ashby. He seems to be driven by his own fierce passions; and has behaved to Sir G— in a most infamous manner. He sent Sir G. the other day a Letter full of falsehoods and impertinent and insolent in the extreme. Of course if they do not go to Coleorton I shall be at liberty sooner,

---

[1] D. W. was suggesting that John W. should move school.

[2] A village on the Duddon Sands.

[3] George Sutton (d.1817), a wealthy uncle of the second Mrs. John Hutchinson of Stockton, was proposing to visit Grasmere.

and I hope in about three weeks from this time at latest I shall be able to go down to Bocking thence to Bury and back to London, thence to Worcester, where Thomas will meet me, and my stay in Wales need not be long.—

This morning I breakfast with Davy and his Bride. She seems a very good natured woman, but of most affected manner; as he himself is, and She is very plain I think. They have a House in Berkeley Square, and are likely to live in a high style—he looks well in health. Yesterday I called a little after 7 on Johnsy, I found him in excellent health, hope, and Spirits; I sate with him till near ten, and we then walked leisurely about the town by moonlight, and called at Quinceys lodgings who five weeks ago went out of Town, as he told his Dame for one week but has not yet found his way back. Among other ways of amusing ourselves Jonsy and I took our stations for some time at the door of one [of] the largest Houses of Grosvenor Square, where a knot of people was formed to see the gay Ladies and gentlemen alight from their carriages in full dress, for a grand assembly. It was amusing, and had a particular zest to us when we thought of Grasmere, of the address a Lady [?][1] so employed. He is a shrewd and good creature and really I have a great affection for him; and I am almost confident that his new situation will answer for him in every respect, in fact he may consider his future as made.—

I attended C's first Lecture; it did his talents great honour, and contained admirable stuff; but I am sorry to say that a great part of it was wholly unfit for the audience, far too metaphisical and abstract. Nor was it generally at all liked, on this account: it was not understood. The subscribers are but few, and the profit, I think will be small; scarcely worth the trouble; and by no means a recompense for the disagreeable things to be encountered upon such an occasion: in fact it appears to me one of the least eligible ways of making money to which a man can profitably turn himself. I called on C– yesterday but did not find him at Home, meaning to state the absolute necessity of confining himself in his future Lectures to what is intelligible without effort. The audience was chiefly ladies; and the gentlemen there understood as little as They.—Adieu I cannot send off this till to morrow—

Friday noon. I am just come in from breakfasting with Sir Humphry and Lady Davy; she is a good natured clever Woman,

[1] *MS. obscure.* The reference seems to be to Lady le Fleming of Rydal Hall, and her daughter, whom W. W. had apparently called on at their London address soon after his arrival in the capital (see *LL*, pp. 131, 191).

with very inelegant manners, that have now become natural: to her now but that originated (3 oclock) While I was writing this last word Dr Stoddart was announced and after exhausting myself 3 Hours in talking with Davies I have had two hours more of Dr S– and you know that though a [?] Man he is terrible for lowering the Spirits; I was going to write originated in affectation. As I came along the street just now I heard a woman bawling out for sale the life of Bellingham. There was a group of people near her and a little Boy looked suspiciously at the paper. It was manifest that the woman could not read but She pointed to the title of her penny book and said see there 'Life, is not it life? Aye and life he had for his heart leapt about six hours after his body was dead; this the Surgeons say and you may see in the newspaper today— And he did a good deed.' Yesterday I dined at Boddingtons, Sharp and Horner[1] were prevented from attending by House of Commons business, present, Sir James and Lady Mackintosh, the Davies, Lady Cork,[2] Mr and Mrs Scarlet,[3] and Miss Boddington[4]—

[1] Francis Horner, of the *Edinburgh Review*, at this time M. P. for Wendover, Bucks.

[2] Mary Monckton (1746–1840), a vivacious 'bluestocking' who was very much admired in her youth by Dr. Johnson, was the daughter of the 1st Viscount Galway and married (1786) Edmund Boyle, 7th Earl of Cork and Orrery (d.1798). Her circle included Sheridan, Canning, Rogers, Byron, and Scott. W. W. seems to have met her on several occasions. At a later period than this, perhaps during his London visit of 1836, she sent him a warm invitation to her house, 'when you would find all your particular friends. Come either early or late . . . I am drawing towards an hundred and should be very sorry to go off the stage before I assure you in person how much I am, your very sincere Admirer . . .' (*WL MSS.*).

[3] James Scarlett, later 1st Baron Abinger, the lawyer (see also *LY* pt. i, L. 236). His wife was Louise, third daughter of Peter Campbell of Kilmory, Argyllshire.

[4] Samuel Boddington's daughter.

W. W. to M. W.

MS. WL.
LL, p. 172 (—).

May 23^d [1812]

My dereast Mary

I am most unlucky in regard to Letters. Yester day I received from thee through Lamb a short one,[1] in which mention is made of one sent off the day before and which I ought to have received through the same hand, but Lamb has never had it. I called on him yesterday after I had received the other and he tells me that no such Letter has reached him. By whom did you send it to the Office. I am heartily concerned at this; for your last is mortifying for its shortness. Indeed the whole of the Letters which I have received from you amounting to 4, dated April 23^d, another May 6th, May 13th, and the last May 20th, would not together make one *Long* Letter. I do not mention this by way of reproach but tender the language of regret to express my sense of the value of your Letters to Me. How unfortunate this last should have been lost, or delayed, I fear lost forever. And there can be no doubt but that a long one from Dorothy to Sharp is irrecoverably gone. The one from D– which I sent to day arrived yester day and you will read it with much pleasure.

As to Quincey I know not where he is; I have called twice at his lodgings, the last time a few days ago and was told by the Mistress of the House that he left Town five weeks ago with an assurance that he should return in a week: so of course I cannot consult him about his House.[2] I have written to D– my sentiments about letting ours to the Sutton's, leaving it to her own choice. But I do not my self wish it; Catharine seems to be so well that change does not appear to be necessary; and one would not like to be kept out of our House, if we should either wish or be obliged by sickness or any other cause to return to it.—In fact I do not at all like [the]³ thing, as far as I am concerned, but as I said before they may do as they think proper. Depend upon it my dearest Love I shall make all possible haste to get to you, which I certainly shall be able to accomplish sooner if the

---

¹ Of 20 May (*WL MSS.*). Her previous letter of 18 May (*WL MSS.*) had not yet arrived.

² Dove Cottage, a possible lodging for the Suttons, when they came to Grasmere.

³ *Word dropped out.*

Beaumonts do not go to Coleorton.—Chris^r is so much engaged that I am not likely to see any thing of him here, and he goes down to Bocking next week, to return when he takes his final departure I know not; but if it does not happen to suit with my plans I shall make no delay on his account, but will simply take a peep at Bocking, that is at Priscilla and her Children on my way to Mrs Clarksons. I am afraid she will be for detaining me at least a week; but if I stay any time at Bocking I can not afford so much.—

This Letter will probably reach you on Monday morning, and on Tuesday you set off on your Tour;[1] I hope not on horseback, I am sure it would fatigue you and do your health no good— fatigue is sadly injurious to invalids and to those who are not strong. Do find time to write to me, you cannot think how dear your Letters are how precious they are to me.

Surely by taking a little pocket book You may have a Letter going forward and may finish it by snatches, at those intervals when you are resting. I was half hurt when you said that you would '*write if you can*'. Can there be a doubt that you may.—I was not hurt at this if, as indicating a languor of affection on your part, I know you love me as much and as deeply as it is possible for woman to love man, or Wife to hold dear her husband; but it seems to me an indication and almost a proof that you were not aware of the delight and happiness with which the sight of a Letter from you filled my heart.—O Sylvan Wye thou Wanderer through the Woods how often has my Spirit turned to thee![2]—I shall now have a thousand added reasons to think of this Stream with tenderness when I know that you are pacing its banks.—

As you cannot receive my Letters I shall not write again till towards the close of the next week; in the meanwhile let me tell you that in respect to my old enemy I am much better; but my costiveness still continues; and I am feverish and turn and perspire a good deal in the night. In fact this Style of living does not upon the whole agree with me; I mean when I dine out, as the dinners are so very late never till 7 or after, and being asked to drink

---

[1] To the Wye. 'My heart dances', M. W. had written, 'to think that we shall meet sooner than I had hoped would be the case—next Tuesday if the Weather suits (and this day promises admirably) we set out as I told you yesterday to the Wye—we shall be absent probably a Week—in that time I can have none of these sweet letters from thee—but I will write: if I can, and O how I shall think of thee and *feel* for thee—when I am tracing this blessed river—'

[2] *Tintern Abbey*, ll. 56–7.

wine, I don't like to refuse. But above all too much talking
fatigues me, something I suffer too from hurrying about the
Streets.—Will you be interested in hearing that the new
Ministers have given in their resignation,[1] so that of course Lord
Wellesley and Canning will come in I hope without any of the
opposition. The Country is in a deplorably distracted state; and
for my own part I have no confidence in any public man or set
of men; I mean I have no confidence in their Knowledge and
Talents; and as to integrity the Marquis of W— is a desperate
profligate, and Canning is a man whose character does not stand
very high—Coleridge gives another Lecture to day; I hope it will
be more popular than the last which was much complained of for
its obscurity.

I have breakfasted twice with Sir Humphrey and Lady Davy;
she is a good natured woman with considerable cleverness but
her Manners are bad, she never lets her features alone, and gestic-
ulates and dances and bends like Mrs Jordan[2] acting the Spoilt
child. All this has originated in affectation, but she now does
without knowing what she is doing, it has become natural to her.
She is a plain woman, thin and tallish, very dark complexion, and
a wretchedly bad skin [?not] tawny but black, that is the blackest
I ever [?saw] on any english Woman. She rouges her cheeks very
high; but assuredly uses no white paint for her neck and breast.
She would wear out my [?patience with][3] her unquiet manners;
but I think Davy may [?live] [hap]py with her, fond as she is of
admiration, [?and she] has an infinite fund of Kindness and good
nature. On Monday I was to have gone with them in their
Barouche upon a fishing Excursion to some little stream about 10
miles from London, but most unluckily I found myself engaged
to dine at Lord Mulgraves[4] an engagement of full three weeks

---

[1] Marquess Wellesley, Foreign Secretary under Perceval, was unsuccessful in
forming a coalition ministry. After a vote of no confidence in the government in
the Commons on 21 May, Lord Liverpool became Prime Minister. Canning
refused to serve under him as Foreign Secretary.

[2] Mrs. Dorothea Jordan (1762–1816), the comic actress, reputed author of the
farce *The Spoiled Child*, in which she played Little Pickle, a schoolboy, was cur-
rently performing at Covent Garden. She was for long the mistress of the Duke
of Clarence, later William IV.

[3] *MS. damaged.*

[4] Henry Phipps, 1st Earl of Mulgrave and Viscount Normanby (1755–1831),
had been First Lord of the Admiralty in the Portland and Perceval administra-
tions, but was now Master General of the Ordnance, with a seat in the Cabinet.

standing. I am truly sorry for this; as I am sure that I should have enjoyed the day much and it would greatly have refreshed me. Davy will let me have a rod and some tackle to bring to Hindwell, he says he will lend it me I hope he will give it; in about two months or less they are to be at Lanterdine[1] (do I spell right?) I mean the place on the Teem near Knighton, and if I am not gone into the North we are to have a meeting. Davy appears to have attained wonderful skill in Angling; and I should like him to try his strength in Hindwell pool, but he says that the finest fishing is in the preserved Brooks near London, that there [are] many spots of this kind where he can pull as many Trout as he likes from 3 to 5 pounds weight, and that in some they make a point of throwing back into the stream every fish under two pounds and a half. His wife must either be very rich or very extravagant; for they live in an elegant house, in Berkeley square in the first style of fashion; but too much I fear on this subject. There is one disadvantage in this twofold duty of writing letters to you and Grasmere that I write so much which scarcely appears worth the trouble of expressing twice, and still less do my Letters seem worthy of being sent from one place to the other, even where no expressions of tenderness have slipped from me that are unfit for any eyes but those for which they were intended.—

Yester day evening I drank tea with Mrs Morgan Miss Brent and C— he seemed in good health and spirits,—but his face looks far too broad and full for complete health, though in other respects

See Dorothy's letter[2]

(this sheet last part of the Letter)

I sate the other day at Sothebys. I like Miss Bailey[3] much, her manners are those of an excellent English Gentlewoman; totally free from all affectation, and with a frankness that is most engaging and becoming.—I mentioned to her the late Edinborough Review in which I understood her last Publication had been most uncandidly dealt with, she said, that she could not deny but she was some what mortified, yet nothing like so much so as if the case had been less in the extreme. What I should have liked best,

---

[1] Leintwardine, near the confluence of the rivers Teme and Clun.

[2] i.e. the letter which had arrived the previous day and which W. W. was now forwarding.

[3] Joanna Baillie (see *MY* pt. ii, L. 246), had just published the third series of her *Plays on the Passions*.

said she, would have been a favorable Review but as I could not have that, they have given me the next best thing, one in which they deny me all merit. Now the middle course would have hurt me most, and therefore I have some reason to be thankful. Mr Wilson is reviewed,[1] and Miss B– who by the bye is no Witch in Poetry spoke highly of an Extract from the Poem which we had in Mss, to the sleeping Child and which is but an Attenuation of my ode to the Highland Girl.[2]—I took no notice of this obligation, but simply said that some time since I had seen those verses in Mss, and thought that they were not without merit, but that as a whole they were very languid and diffuse. I learn from H– Robinson, that Mr Wilson is represented as my Scholar, but one who has surpassed his Master. I am sorry for this; and that it is so expressed or insinuated I have no doubt, as Lamb told me the same, I am sorry for it on W–s account as it cannot but be painful to him and most probably will some day or other draw upon him a severe retribution from some of my Admirers, of whom I have more than you or I are aware of; and those who are so are devoted to me enthusiastically.—

My love, and dearest darling, am not I good in writing to thee such frequent and long Letters, Let me praise myself,—here has the morning Newspaper been lying an hour and a half beside me untouched, containing as I have heard most interesting Letters from Lord Wellesley and other great personages upon their conduct at this most interesting crisis. Yesterdays Newspaper also, containing the account of the debate, upon the Motion the result of which act was the resignation of ministers I have not read, having been engaged in writing to Grasmere.—

Before I had finished this last Sentence I was called down stairs to a conference with Sir George and Mr Wade his Attorney, and have had from him a Comment upon a Letter which Taylor has written to Sir George. Taylor's conduct has been most infamous and desperate—What is to become of him and his family I know not.—I will tell you more of this when we meet.—I am glad to hear so good an account of George;[3] I have not yet seen Curwen, and scarely know where I shall find him, nor do I hear of any person who is in want of an Agent, though I have made several Inquiries.—I will find Curwen if I can, Sharp would be the most likely perhaps to know his address, and him I expected

---

[1] John Wilson's *Isle of Palms* had just appeared. He described Jeffrey's review in the *Edinburgh* as 'beggarly'.

[2] See *PW* iii. 73.

[3] George Hutchinson.

to meet day before yesterday at Boddington's but was disappointed.—

Let me tell you an Incident.—As I was walking in South Audley Street I came to a Woman who with a small bundle of Papers in her hand was crying out—Here is the life of Bellingham who etc—There was a small group of people about her, and a little Boy among the number, who seemed to doubt if the ballad-like Papers she was offering for Sale, were really the Thing they purported to be. Yes says the Woman emphatically pointing to their title which was in Large Letters, 'life, and life he had, for his heart stirred about six hours after his Body was dead. This the Surgeons have declared, and you may read in the Newspaper of this *day*, and, so going off triumphantly she exclaimed, and a good deed he did.' Nothing can be more deplorably ferocious and savage than the lowest orders in London, and I am sorry to say that tens of thousands of the Middle class and even respectable Shop-keepers rejoice in this detestable murther, and approve of it. People talk of the national character being changed: in fact it has been changing for these thirty or 40 years during the growth of the manufacturing and trading system the Malady has been forming its self, and the eruption has now begun, but where it will end heaven knows— Depend upon it I shall keep out of the way of riots, I love you my dear wife and my Grasmere friends far too well to trust myself in the way of them.—

I received a few days ago a very kind Letter from Captain Pasley now I believe Major, in which he expresses his regret at not being able to see me in London; and expresses also his thanks for my interesting Letter;[1] which he says, he often reads, and upon which more frequently still he meditates. He would have replied to it long ago, and took up the pen, but was unable to do justice to his ideas. This gave me great satisfaction. He is at present superintending a Military Establishment at Chatham for the purpose of qualifying Officers, and also a body of common men, to conduct sieges; In which department of service our Army is yet considerably inferior to the French but he hopes to make it as much superior. He invites me down to Chatham, and if I can go I will, and return upon the 2nd.

Both my time and paper admonish me that I must lay down

---

[1] See *MY* pt. ii, L. 244. W. W.'s 'interesting letter' was his long discussion of military policy, *MY* pt. i, L. 221.

the pen; the Carriage in a few Minutes will be at the Door to take us to C–s Lecture. Adieu my darling Love—I shall see T. Monkhouse and Bessy Hutchinson;[1] and the distance is so great or I should have seen M– long since. Love me and think of me and kiss little Thomas for me, and no account fail to write to me while upon your Tour, Best Love to every body—how ardently do I long to be with you. I half hoped that your missing Letter would have found its way to me this morning—but alas it is now ½ past two and no sight of it. Farewell and take Care thy most loving Husband W. W.

N. B. I have been obliged to cut off the other half sheet finding the Letter above weight.

W. W. to M. W.[2]

Address: Mʳˢ Wordsworth, Mʳ Hutchinson's, Radnor.
Franked: London May thirtieth 1812 Byron.
Postmark: 30 May 1812.
MS. WL.
LL, p. 200.

[30 May 1812]
Saturday morning

Dearest Mary

I send you the conclusion of my last Letter.[3]—I rose this morning at 7 to write to thee my beloved. Yesterday, I walked from the Lecture[4] with the Morgans and dined and supped with them by previous invitation. On returning home I found a Letter from thee[5] with the Enclosure from Sara both of which I read before I went to bed with infinite pleasure. How unlucky that you now wish to start on Tuesday, as you will not be able to receive this Letter; nor can hear from me at all now for a week or ten days. I had provided a frank for to day calculating that it would reach Hindwell on Monday which would be six days after you set off on your Tour and perhaps two days before your return; but then to welcome you on your return, I had provided

---

[1] M. W.'s niece (d. 1827), eldest daughter of John Hutchinson of Stockton.

[2] This letter, and the next two, follow *MY* pt. ii, L. 244.

[3] i.e. the last half sheet of his letter of 23 May, removed as the package was overweight.

[4] Coleridge's fourth lecture, on Comedy.   [5] M. W.'s letter of 18 May.

another frank for Monday, to be received by my Darling on Wednesday; and all this pretty arrangement is rendered fruitless; so that my Letters will lose 3 4^{ths} of their value by being put into your hands, like a *bundle* of old newspapers. Where as had you set off at[1] the fixed time there was one provided to greet you on your return, if your Tour had lasted *less* than a week; and another if a day more. Well my sweet Love will regard this as a mark of my Ardor and ever loving thoughts of her. Oh my Mary! my own Darling, one thought one wish, one longing for thee such as now pervades my Soul and every particle of my Frame, turns human existence with all its cares and fears into a heaven of heavens. I am as a Husband, and a Father, and a Brother, the blessedest of men!—

I am now writing before breakfast, because this day I go to Hampstead to dine with Miss Baillie, and she requested that I would be with her early to take a walk before dinner. Accordingly I purpose to call on Coleridge about 12, and part of the time after breakfast (we begin breakfast about a quarter past nine) I shall have to spend with the Beaumont's.—But now let me tell thee that I do not go to Coleorton; joyful knowledge for me as it will be happy news for thee. In fact the B's are not likely to be there before six week's, perhaps two months are gone; so I am wholly relieved and *handsomely* released from that obligation; and therefore at liberty to be so much sooner with thee, to take so much the earlier a flight into thy blessed arms.—Ten days at the *utmost* will, I hope, suffice, for Bocking and for Mrs Clarkson; and within a month of this day I hope to have a kiss from thy lips, and to see Hindwell and you all. But then come the Wheelwrights[2] surely they will not interfere with us. After this piece of good news let me tell thee that thy missing Letter has reached me; the Gentleman, by the bye those Gentlemen ought never to be trusted with letters between Friends that love as we do nor with any Letters of importance) the Gentleman must no doubt have forgotten his Charge. Furthermore; I find that I did thee wrong in the formal enumeration made in my last of thy Letters; I have since discovered that I omitted one and considerably the longest; and for this omission I beg pardon.—I thought in truth that there was another in existence, and sought for it carefully, but as I keep my Letters among my Linen, I had overlooked this one, which had contrived to slip itself into the folds

---

[1] *Written* and.   [2] Thomas Monkhouse's business partner and his wife.

of a shirt. By the Bye did I tell thee that I have been obliged to lay out a deal of money in clothes, a new black suit, £6.15, a Hat 28s. a pair of silk stockings with cotton tops etc 9—and I am afraid they will scarcely prove worth the money. I was obliged to pay half a crown for having my hair cut, and the price of the hat is very high, being bought in this neighbourhood but the Man guaranteed [it] to be a good one, and my other is as brown as if it had been worn ten years.—But to return to Letters; none now are missing but the long one intended by Dorothy for us both.— I am glad of this—I think Sharp's Clerk must have neglected to put it into the twopenny off.[1]—Next Wednesday I shall see him and will enquire.

Now let me continue my story, from the point where it ends in the half sheet which ought to have gone yesterday week, viz Friday. That day I dined with C. and the Morgans, and before ten hurried off to Lamb's where I read the Waggoner,[2] to L— his Sister, and young Burney,[3] a nephew of the celebrated Miss Burney. If time had allowed I should have read Peter Bell[4] in preference. I am pleased to say that they were all extremely gratified; and sorry am I to add that constant engagements since have not permitted me to see them; though I believe that Lamb has been out of Town, otherwise he would have been at Morgans last night. I do not remember how I spent last Saturday Morning but in the evening I called upon Jonsy who was delighted to see me: and yet I am not sure but that here I am making a mistake: nay I believe I surely am mistaken, and it was the Wednesday preceding that I called on Jonsy of which I have already given you an account.—

Well from Sunday I have a distinct recollection of things,—and will give you a slight sketch. On that morn at[5] eleven H. Robinson and I left the stones of London Streets at eleven and proceeded through the fields, and through the intended Prince Regents Park[6] at Mary bone, and over Primrose Hill to Hampstead. It was a cloudy morning with a cool fanning breeze,

---

[1] The office for local mail within London.

[2] Composed 1806 and published 1819 with dedication to Lamb.

[3] Martin Charles Burney, son of Admiral James Burney (1750-1821), and nephew of Fanny Burney (1752–1840), the novelist. Lamb dedicated the second volume of his *Collected Works*, 1818, to him.

[4] Written 1798, published 1819.   [5] *Written* and.

[6] Now under construction by John Nash (1752–1835), architect of the Brighton Pavilion, at the northern limit of Regent Street.

and we had a most refreshing and agreeable walk, on our way to the Churchyard of Hampstead a Q^r of an hour before the people came out of church. We amused ourselves in reading the Epitaphs; waiting till the Congregation appeared, among whom I did not doubt that I should find Miss Baillie, who had requested me to call upon her having learned from me at dinner at Sothebys in the course of the preceding week that I should dine at Hampstead on that day. The situation of Hampstead Church is quite pleasing, looking from among and over trees towards and far beyond the great City. Miss Baillie appeared, and we walked with her to her House; and upon entering there whom should I meet but my old Acquaintance Mr Carr[1] formerly a Lawyer and now holding a high situation in the Excise; and memorable at Grasmere, on account of the very bad dinner which he had the misfortune of receiving, or rather dearest Dorothy and I had the vexation of giving him in our Little Cottage at Grasmere, before you and I, my Love were married. With Miss Baillie and this Gentleman we conversed nearly an hour upon politics and alarmed each other not a little by the mutual communication of thoughts and observations.—

Carr is [a] very respectable Man whose office and connections give him an opportunity of seeing much; and his report is in some respects, especially as far as relates to the Country encouraging. But the state of parties among the upper classes, and the want of principle, and above all of a decisive character, in the Prince Regent, not to speak of other deficiencies in him, still more to be deplored, these endanger every thing.

—The Prince's conduct is described to be capricious and unprincipled in the extreme; and he does not appear to have the slightest strain of common human feelings. Before you receive this Letter you will have learned from other sources who are to be Ministers. It is now confidently talked that the Grenvilles and Greys (plague take this one to come in!) with that profligate Man Lord Wellesley, and Canning.[2]—

From Miss B's we walked with Carr to see his house and family.—He is most charmingly situated, a House, which though not many yards from the public road sees nothing of it, but looks

---

[1] Thomas William Carr, Solicitor to the Excise.

[2] William Wyndham, 1st Baron Grenville (1759–1834), head of 'All the Talents', 1806–7, and Charles Grey, 2nd Earl Grey (1764–1845) declined to form a Whig ministry or to join a coalition with the Tories. Marquess Wellesley and Canning also in the end refused to serve.

down the hill side sprinkled with trees over a scenicly rich woody Country, like one of our uncut forests, towards the smoke of London and upon the Kentish and Surrey hills far beyond. 'Green rise the Kentish Hills in chearful air.'.[1] This said I is a sweet Spot, Yes answered he and I have reason to love it with gratitude for I believe it saved my Life. He then told me that in consequence of severe application to business his health had entirely failed, a complaint having been generated the seat of which he thought was in his heart, and I came here, said he, as I believed to die.—But relaxation from business and pure air, by little and little restored me, and I am now excellently well and my children 8 in number healthy and flourishing. The seat of his disease proved to be the Liver; he is now quite well (Look for page 8) and blooming but in the lines of his face are traces rather of sickness than years. When I last saw him about ten years ago he was the most youthful and healthful looking Man of my acquaintance. From his House we went to Mr Hammond's[2]— H. R's Friend with whom we were to dine. He is a young Man, occupying with his Sister a pleasant Cottage on the top of Hampstead Hill, the front windows looking Northwards towards and beyond, the Spire of Harrow on the Hill, and the back windows looking down a little wild slack[3] or dell towards and far beyond the Metropolis. And on the left in the same view stretch the extensive woods of Lord Mansfield[4] around Caen House. This Mr Hammond has had the moderation to withdraw nearly though not I believe entirely from business, preferring leisure and retirement with a little Literature, to heaping up money amidst care and anxiety. He is a young Man of elegant and somewhat feminine appearance, much attached to rural scenery, and having paid some attention to poetry and works of Imagination. But in these things he has much to learn; I attempted to let a little light into his mind, and perhaps some things said by me may here after produce some change in his opinions. He is a passionate admirer of Miss Edgeworth[5] and knows a good deal of her family, having

[1] John Armstrong's *Art of Preserving Health*, i. 123: a favourite poem of W. W.'s (see *LY* pt. i, L. 201).

[2] Elton Hammond (see *MY* pt. ii, L. 571a). See *HCR* i. 89-90.

[3] A small valley or hollow (*N. dial.*).

[4] David William Murray, 3rd Earl of Mansfield (1777–1840), of Caen Wood (now Kenwood) Middlesex, and Scone Palace, Perthshire. Kenwood House had been reconstructed for him in 1767-8 by Robert Adam as a suburban retreat.

[5] Maria Edgeworth (see *LY* pt. ii, L. 453).

resided some time among them in Ireland. Of Miss Edgeworth I spoke as I thought; mentioning at the same time that I had read but few of [her][1] works.—He bore my observations with great good temper and upon the whole I liked the man, though I think his mind wants strength.

We had a pleasant walk home in the evening; and I should have been much improved in health by this day, but that imprudently instead of turning quietly into the House, whither H. R. accompanied along with a Lawyer[2] who had been of the Party, I must needs, finding the B's[3] not a[t] home, take a turn with them towards their quarters. And sure it is that this additional Hours walking did my stomach and head considerable harm; but how so ever the case, I have no prudence in managing myself. But here let me say that though my stomach is weakened and it feels over burthened, and though I perspire a good deal in the night from heat and hurry in the day and from the very late dinners, with more wine than does me good, yet still upon the whole my health is improved and for these last ten days I have had scarcely any thing of my old enemy; and this I ascribe much to my having been spared in sleep, and in the mornings I am always as you would wish to know that I am. I never shall forget the sweet demonstration you gave me at Liverpool, when I was unwell, that I was far better than I was willing to believe. Tell me if you have ever thought of that since we parted.—

On Monday I dined with the B's at Lord Mulgrave's, present Mr and Mrs Phipp's,[4] a Sir Abraham Hume,[5] Lord Dunstanville, a most friendly and agreeable noble man) Mr West the Painter Mr Wilkie, and Mr and Mrs Charles Long, (look for page 10) of the treasury.[6] This Man Long was the person who prevented Luff having the place[7] of Paymaster which Lord C. Somerset[8] designed for him. His Wife draws ably and is supposed to have

---

[1] *Word dropped out.*   [2] J. F. Pollock (see *MY* pt. ii, L. 571a).

[3] Beaumonts.

[4] Augustus Phipps, Lord Mulgrave's brother, and his wife Maria.

[5] Sir Abraham Hume, 2nd Bart., F.R.S. (1749–1838), connoisseur and collector: author of a Life of Titian (1829).

[6] Charles Long, 1st Baron Farnborough (1761–1838), M.P. for Hazlemere, 1806–26, Paymaster-General, 1810–26. His wife Amelia was Hume's daughter.

[7] *Written* placed.

[8] General Lord Charles Henry Somerset (1767–1831), younger son of the 5th Duke of Beaufort: Governor of the Cape of Good Hope, and M.P. for Scarborough, 1796–1802, and for Monmouth, 1802–13.

many fine accomplishments; I did not like either the one or the other of them. I sate by Mr West the Painter, and had a very interesting account of the first determination of his mind to the art of Painting, which I shall have much pleasure in repeating to you. One anecdote I will here mention. The first thing which he can remember of his performance in the art was as follows. It happened that an Aunt of his was staying with his Mother (by the bye I ought to mention that Wests parents were Quakers, and he lived and was brought up among Quakers exclusively) this Aunt had a little child with her and one day his mother going with her sister into the garden to gather flowers, left the child[1] in its cradle sleeping under little Wests Care, with a charge that he should fan away the flies from its face. Having undertaken this employment West observed upon a desk near him an inkstand with bottles of black and red ink, and pens and paper. Instead of continuing his enforced labour he turned to them and proceed[ed] to attempt a Delineation of the infant slumbering beside him. When he had made considerable progress in this effort his Mother and Aunt returned with their flowers, Espying them and fearing to be scolded for neglect of the Child he huddled up the paper, but his Mother insisted upon seeing it, she gained her wish and exclaimed this is little Jane, upon which she snatched young West up in her arms and eagerly kissed him. 'And that kiss, said the old Painter now 75 years of age, that kiss did the business.'—Well Mother if thee be so pleased with the picture of the Child I'll draw for thee the flowers also.'—He then told several other particulars of the growth of his passion for the art and his education for the practice of it, which I reserve for our meeting.—

When we went up stairs at Lord M's I found the Countess of Wellington,[2] the Wife or rather Widow bewitched of Lord Wellington the General.—She is next to the daughter of Dr Darwin[3]—whom I mentioned some time ago the most engaging Woman I have seen in London, very pretty, even handsome, and of an intelligent expression, but all will not suffice to fix [ ] [de]bauchee her husband, who has licentiou[sly conn]ected himself with a succession of other [ ] O miserable life—oh high blessing of true [and] virtuous love![4] What rapture is one soft

---

[1] *Written* children.

[2] Sir Arthur Wellesley, now Earl of Wellington, had married (1806) Catherine Pakenham (d.1831), third daughter of Edward, 2nd Lord Longford. They lived a good deal apart.

[3] Erasmus Darwin.   [4] *MS. damaged.*

smile from the heart (or rather from the soul), or a kiss from a lip of the wife and mother, even if time have somewhat impaired the freshness of her virgin beauties; what higher rapture is the consciousness that even for the pleasures of sense, the soul is triumphant through the might of sincere love, over the body; and that the mind can spread over the faded lips a more than youthful attraction, and preserve for the frame of the Beloved one an undying spirit of delight and tenderness, which the soul feels in itself, and can impart with confidence and certainty to that human being which is the Lord of its affections. O My Mary such happiness has been, and 'heaven be praised') yet is ours.

Take care of thyself my love, and above all of thy eyes and give me good accounts of thy progress towards health and strength. As I have another frank for Monday and as this cannot be read till probably 8 or ten days are gone, I will pause here, farewell my darling, love me more than I deserve to be loved; and think of me as often as it makes thee happy to think of me and dost thee good, but no more, and no oftener. Love to every body not forgetting Miss Monkhouse.[1] I was much pleased with the account of dear John[2] and will contrive to bring some thing for him.—If I thought it possible that this Letter could be received by thee before my next I should add something to it. But to morrow you must depart on account of Piercefield[3] again and again farewell.

W. W.

W. W. to M. W.

MS. WL.
LL, p. 210.

Mond June 1st. [1812]
Eleven in the morning

Last night my sweet Darling on my return from Hampstead I was greeted by the Enclosed from Dorothy and a delightful Letter

---

[1] M. W.'s aunt Elizabeth. [2] His eldest son, left in Grasmere.

[3] Valentine Morris's estate on the Wye near Chepstow (now part of the race-course), laid out *c.*1750 by Richard Owen Cambridge (1717–1802), the poet and writer on landscape, and praised for its sublime and romantic situation in Gilpin's *Observations on the River Wye*. '. . . The united talents of a Claude, a Poussin, a Vernet and a [Thomas] Smith would scarcely be able to sketch its beauties,' according to a contemporary account by Arthur Young, the agriculturalist.

from thee dated May 23ᵈ.[1] I cannot explain how these Letters have come so irregularly. I have had one of May 25ᵗʰ [2] in my possession two or three days; and in the instance before a Letter which was sent off some days before another did not come till several days after it. Never mind since they have come at last and I have at this moment lying on the table before me 8 of thy most dear Letters besides the one of Sara to Joanna, giving so interesting an account of our Son John.—

On Saturday, I sent thee a long Letter, which thou wilt receive at the same time as this; I wish this could have been otherwise.— I came in last night wet and read both the Letters in bed. Thine was the tenderest and fondest of all I have yet received from thee, and my longing to have thee in my arms was so great, and the feelings of my heart so delicious, that my whole frame was over powered with Love and longing, Well was it for me that I was stretched upon my bed, for I think I could scarcely have stood upon my feet for excess of happiness and depth of affection. I lay awake a long time longer than I have ever done except the first night since I came to London, partly from over exertion in the course of the day, and still more from the recurrence of those thoughts and wishes which used to keep sleep from me at Grasmere, in times when our hearts were in that sympathy which experience has found to be neither illusory or transient, but which every year has strengthened and exalted.—

As I said before I had yesterday viz Sunday a most interesting

[1] M. W. had written: 'I *do* long most intensely for the time when you are to join me here—I never felt this more than when we were walking through those greenest of all green fields this morning—the birds were singing, and the air was so balmy, and I seemed to have so much leisure (a thing which I seldom have at our own sweet home) to know how blessed above all blessed creatures I should be were you but here to wander with me, and enjoy the joys of this heavenly season—dearest William! the time will soon be here I trust, and long shall it be ere we part again—if this depends upon my choice.—Yet I *do* not regret that this separation has been, for it is worth no small sacrifice to be thus assured, that instead of weakening, our union has strengthened—a hundred fold strengthened those yearnings towards each other which I used so strongly to feel at Gallow Hill—and in which you sympathized with me at that time—that these feelings are mutual now, I have the fullest proof, from thy letters and from their power and the power of absence over my whole frame—Oh William I can not tell thee how I love thee, and thou must not desire it—but feel it, O feel it in the fullness of thy soul and *believe* that I am the happiest of Wives and of Mothers and of all Women the most blessed—'

[2] *WL MSS.*

day, with nothing to regret but that I was over stimulated in Conversation and that my stomach has suffered accordingly, so that at this moment I can scarcely keep my hand from it.—But I will resume my journal—On Monday as my last Letter will have informed you I dined at Lord Mulgraves. And on Tuesday at Rogers's, present the B's Mr Price Lady Caroline, Miss Price and her Brother;[1] with whom I talked about Hindwell. He complained of his Companion Sir Harford Jones,[2] an orientalist, who took no interest in farming, and who interfered much with his wishes to see some of the Management. Accordingly I ventured to invite him to ride over during my intended stay in Radnorshire; he is [a] very well looking and agreeable Young Man. Nothing could be more deplorable than the rest of the Party: Miss P— a little deformed Creature, with a most strange enunciation, sitting by Mr Jekyll[3] a celebrated Wit, and quite pert and to use a coarse word ever rampant upon him. She is, as Sir G. observed in expression of countenance and manner just like the bad Sister who does all the Mischief in a Faery tale. Lady Caroline was coquetting away with General Fitzpatrick[4] her old Paramour, who is a most melancholy object, with a complection as yellow as a frog, a tall emaciated Figure and hobbling with the gout. He creeps abroad yet, poor Man, and may fairly be said to have one foot in the grave. It was lamentable also to see poor Price overgorging himself at dinner as he did, and falling into a lethargic sleep immediately after, from which he had not power to preserve himself two minutes together. This was truly a piteous sight for Price is a man of genuine talents, and gifted by Nature with a firm Constitution which he is destroying by gluttony. He invited me to Foxley, and if you could ride so far I should be glad to go with you to shew you the place.—Jekyll I believe I mentioned before; he is a man of exquisite conversational powers but did not shine on that day, not having the needful quantity of wine, which Rogers forgot to push about. Lord

[1] The Beaumonts, Uvedale Price and his wife Lady Caroline Price, their son Robert Price (see *LY* pt. i, L. 382) and his sister.

[2] Sir Harford Jones Brydges, 1st Bart. (1764–1847), British envoy to Persia, 1807–11: author of various works on Persian affairs, and a convinced Whig.

[3] Joseph Jekyll.

[4] General Richard Fitzpatrick (see *MY* pt. i, L. 227), a lifelong friend of Fox: M. P. for Bedfordshire, 1807–12, and Secretary of War in the ministry of 'All the Talents', 1806–7.

Hampden[1] was of the party also an elderly man of the first fashion, but interesting to me only because he possesses the Estates of
the great patriot of that name, and by the female line—is of the
same family.—

On Wednesday The B⁵ had a party at home to dinner, but it
was not very interesting, several of the invited having sent
excuses, being engaged with the present occupations which the
state of parties has created. Mr Lister[2] however was there. He is
the eldest Son of Lord Ribblesdale, and if he survives his Father
will be proprietor of Gowborough Park, and Malham Tarn etc.
The former place Sara and I visited with much pleasure last summer; and the Latter is famous for fine fishing. I had a good deal of
talk with him; and he said that he should be happy to shew me a
glen near Malham and Gordale, wholly unknown to Travellers,
with which he was sure I should be highly delighted. In the
evening came in Lady Lonsdale,[3] two of her daughters,[4] and the
Lord himself, with a Star upon his breast and the Garter round
his Knee.—As several Persons were in the room besides, I had no
conversation with him. I left a card as probably I told you some
days ago, and this morning have written a Note requesting an
interview for a few minutes.—

As to Politics the old opposition seem confident they shall
come in, but nothing is yet decided. It is clear the Prince Regent
is most averse to them; but I fear they will be forced upon him.
In fact the country is in a deplorable state; and if firmness be not
shewn by the government, with descretion also, disturbances
wide and frightful are inevitable. The Prince is neither respected
nor love[d] by any class of Men. By the bye I forgot to mention

[1] Thomas Hampden-Trevor, 2nd Viscount Hampden (1746–1824), Whig
M.P. for Lewes, 1768–74, but seceded from the Whigs with Portland in 1793:
descendant of John Hampden, the seventeenth-century patriot.

[2] Thomas Lister, 2nd Baron Ribblesdale (1790–1832) of Gisburne Park,
Skipton. W. W. seems to have visited Gowbarrow Park on Ullswater in May or
July 1811 during a visit to Watermillock. It was, according to the *Guide to the
Lakes*, a place where 'the lover of Nature might linger for hours' (*Prose Works*, ii.
167), and much earlier (1802), it had been the setting for W. W.'s poem on the
daffodils, 'I wandered lonely as a cloud' (see *DWJ* i. 131). W. W. and D. W. had
visited Gordale and Malham Cove, near Settle, in 1807.

[3] Lord Lonsdale had married Augusta (1761–1838) eldest daughter of John,
9th Earl of Westmorland.

[4] Probably the two elder daughters, Lady Elizabeth Lowther (d. 1869), and
Lady Mary Lowther, later Lady Frederick Bentinck (d. 1863).

that from Lord Mulgraves we went to Lady Crewes, and there I had the honour of being introduced to the Princess Regent;[1] an empty honour, for her R. H— was at some distance from me, and I had no conversation with her. She is a fat unwieldy Woman, but has rather a handsome and pleasing Countenance, with an expression of hilarity that is not however free from Coarseness. This was a large Assembly, saw few pretty women, and many most disgusting objects; one I encountered of a tolerable face and features, but in her native bosom so huge and tremendous, that had you seen her enter a room in that condition I am sure the soul of modest womanhood in you would have shrunk almost as with horror. Her Breasts were like two great hay-cocks or rather hay stacks, protruding themselves upon the Spectator, and yet no body seemed to notice them—

But to come to something more interesting. It now wants only 20 minutes of four. Just as was concluding the last page I received a Message from Lord Lonsdale in answer to my note that he would be glad to see me at 12. I posted away immediately. He shook me by the hand and received me very kindly. I began with enquiries after his Family, then thanked him for his Letter, and for giving me this opportunity of seeing him.—I beg[ged] leave to state in addition to the unfavorable circumstances in my course of life, mentioned in my first Letter, that had appeared to me to justify the representation I had made to him, was to be reckoned a calamity which had befallen our family in the person of my Brother Captain Wordsworth,[2] who, he would recollect, had lost his life by Shipwreck. I said that My Brother had entirely sympathized with my literary pursuits, and encouraged me to give myself entirely to that way of Life, with assurance that [if][3] I stood in need of assistance, and he proved fortunate, it should ever be ready for me.—I requested also permission to supply what appeared to me deficient in my second Letter—, deficient I mean in the expression; I had thrown myself in the mere form of words more upon his Lordships recollection of me, I said, than[4] I had a right to do. I wished to give him no unnecessary trouble, and if I could procure knowledge of any thing that was likely to suit me I certainly should not be so wanting to my own interests as to omit making an immediate application. Of course all this was soon cleared. I then said that by way of giving him a general

---

[1] Caroline of Brunswick (1768–1821), the future Queen Caroline.

[2] John Wordsworth, drowned in the wreck of the Abergavenny, 1805.

[3] *Word dropped out.*   [4] *Written* that.

Idea of what might suit me I would mention the place of Distributer of Stamps, now holden by a Relative of mine[1] at Applebye; I had endeavoured to learn the emolument of it, but could not speak accurately, but I thought that place should it prove vacant would suit me,—but I adverted to it merely as a general guide for his Lordship in this service to be done to me. He then said, that I must be aware that all his influence of this kind depended upon the Government which was now in an unsettled state. To which I replied that I was sorry for the condition of the Country in this respect; but I hope such arrangements would be made, as would not exclude his Lordship from that influence which his family and character entitled him to.—He then very amicably entered into conversation on indifferent topics for at least twenty minutes, chiefly relating to Persons and things in Cumberland and Westmoreland; he leading the Conversation; and when I took my leave he shook me by the hand; and said 'I shall not be unmindful of you':—Tell me if you are satisfied with this. I am, and know not what more I could have done. His Lordship told me that he had this morning received a Letter from Mr Southey, requesting his exertion to procure him a place recently vacant by the Death of a Frenchman of the Name of Dutens.[2] It is that of Historiographer to the King, or some thing of that kind.

Having given[3] you a detail of this interview, every thing else will appear insipid. I will only add that on Thursday last I had a most pleasant day with Rogers and Sir G— at Greenwich where we walked about that Glorious Park; and I could not help thinking how happy we could have all been there. The East Indiamen were returning from an unusually short and successful voyage, three ascending the River full sail, and one of them, I believe the Ship (though I did not then know it) the unfortunate Abergavenny's Successor. I had melancholy thoughts of poor John, but upon the whole it was a most pleasant and rememberable day. On Friday C—s[4] Lecture, dined and passed the evening at Morgans. I like the two Women[5] much and will tell you more

---

[1] Mr. Wilkin.

[2] Louis Dutens (1730–1812), Historiographer Royal. Southey was unsuccessful in spite of strong support from Lord Lonsdale, Croker, and Scott, and the Prince Regent bestowed the office on one of his chaplains. See Southey, iii. 332–3, and Curry, ii. 34, 36.

[3] *Written* giving.   [4] Coleridge's last lecture of the series.

[5] Mrs. Morgan, and her sister Miss Brent.

about them; some other time. On Saturday called at Coleridge's by 12 and he walked with me as far as Hampstead; we did not part till half past three; I dined with Sergeant Rough at Miss Baillie's; the wife of Dr Baillie,[1] and a party in the evening, a pleasant day; slept at Mr Carrs, and the history of Sunday yester day would be very long; it was a most agreeable day but I was exceedingly exhausted by long talking. Sir Humphrey and Lady Davy dined with us; I sate by Joanna Baillie, and had a long chat with her. Among other topics were discussed our little Dorothy who had charmed her much[2] and Walter Scotts wife, with whom to my utter astonishment she had been much pleased. This brought out my feelings with regard to the Lady, luckily Davy was there; and he supported what I spoke to her prejudice. I did not scruple also to say that you and Dorothy and in fact all of us had received the disagreeable impression. Miss B– said she had seen her in her own House, that she appeared to admire her Husband was attentive to her Guests, had her House apparent[ly] well ordered, and her children under excellent management. Besides, said Miss B– she wore a bunch of Roses (I do [not] know if they were artificial) in front of her cap or bonnet; and I did not like her the worse for that'.

But enough adieu my darling; a thousand kisses and embraces long and tender! I have another frank for the sixth of this month; ie. next Saturday; I should write sooner if I hope[d] the Letter would reach you, but if you only begin your tour it will be impossible, as you will surely be out above 8 days.

Thy faithful Husband W. W.

---

[1] Joanna Baillie's brother Matthew Baillie (1761–1823), anatomist, physician to St. George's Hospital, 1787–99, married Sophia Denman.

[2] During her visit to Grasmere in 1808.

W. W. to M. W.

Address: Mrs Wordsworth, Mr Hutchinson's, Radnor.
Franked: London June four 1812 Rd Sharp.
Postmark: 4 June 1812.
MS. WL.
LL, p. 226.

[3–4 June 1812]
Wednesday aftern[oon][1] 2. o clock.

My dearest Mary,

Unwilling to lose a moments time I take up the pen in a place where I ought to have been long ago, viz—T. Monkhouse's Country House.[2]—

Thursday Noon. I wrote no farther than the two lines above before T. Monkhouse returned. I sate within above half an hour; he then walked with me to Dr Stoddarts in Doctors Commons, and was so kind as to accompany me to the door of Sergeant Roughs Bedford Row, where I dined; so that we were upon the whole together between 2 and three hours. He seems a most amiable and excellent Young Man; quite worthy of his Brother and Sister.[3] I did not omit to give him my sentiments upon his course of future life; and he seemed fully sensible of the justice of all I said concerning his not retiring precipitately to the Country, till he had acquired a fortune considerably above his present needs; in order to guard against future demands.—

I shall pass one day with him at Hampstead; and it is not impossible that I may see him this very day, as I have just sent him a Note by the two penny Post that the rest of this present day is at my Command, and if he can take me in his Gig to Hampstead I shall be happy to attend him.—

Yesterday I breakfasted with Sharp from whom I procured this present Frank; otherwise, if you return on Friday that is to morrow, you would have had to wait till Monday [till] you heard of me; and that would have seemed a long time, after having been so highly fed with Letters from Grasmere and from Grosvenor Square, as you have been lately. If you do not reach home till Saturday, this will make the third letter which you will find waiting for you, and as I have a frank for Saturday also, you will have another, probably however only a short Letter, on Monday. I

---

[1] *MS. torn.*   [2] At Hampstead.
[3] John Monkhouse of The Stow and Mary Hutchinson.

107

received very expeditiously your sweet Letter from Hereford;[1] That very evening, viz Tuesday, I had been reading at Lamb's the Tintern abbey, and repeated a 100 times to my self the passage 'O Sylvan Wye thou Wanderer through the woods,' thinking of past times, and Dorothy, dear Dorothy, and you my Darling. The weather has been good and therefore I trust you have had a delightful Tour[2] without any untoward accident; oh that I could have been with you. I long to be with you, I feel nightly and daily, waking and asleep the neccessity of my not prolonging our separation; and I have the happiness of saying, that I can now look forward with some confidence as to the Time.

My *residence* in London may now almost be considered as closed; for on Monday I depart with Chris^r for Bocking. He stays there a week, which time if I find it pleasant I shall pass with him; shall then move on to Mrs Clarkson, with whom I shall stay at least a week, and during the course of the third week shall find Christopher again at Bocking and perhaps may be tempted to stay with him till he returns to Town at the close of the same third week. So that on Saturday three weeks God willing I shall certainly at the latest be returned to Town, where I shall stay three or 4 days and no more, and then proceed to Worcester; where your Brother Tom will meet me in his Gig, and we will make a short excursion to Malvern Hill which I am told is very beautiful and then for Hindwell where I shall, I trust be the happiest of men—with You all and thee, my beloved.

A month!! it seems a long time to look forward! but I have wished to take in my thoughts the very utmost allowance of time I can possibly require; and perhaps I may be able to make less

---

[1] Of 29–31 May (*WL MSS.*). M. W. wrote: 'Now my best beloved! I think I shall not again take up the Pen at Hindwell till about next week at this time, therefore from this room, which is become very dear to me from the sweet feelings which have here been excited in me—by thy letters—and from the many dear thoughts, hopes and expectations that have passed through my mind upon my pillow by the side of thy little Darling, let me on this side of the Paper bid thee a tender adieu—That thy best thoughts will go with me I am well assured—and that every object which I see that gives me pleasure will be ten thousand times more dear to me for thy sake thou wilt not doubt Dearest Love I am as happy as Woman can be wanting what constitutes that happiness—yet even *wanting this* I cannot but think that in the *thoughts* of my possessions I am the most blessed of all Women.'

[2] M. W. recounted the visit to the Wye in her letter of 2–3 June (*WL MSS.*), which had not yet arrived.

serve; certainly shall if I find that a week will at all satisfy Mrs Clarkson; for then instead of staying the whole third week with Christ͏ʳ at Bocking a couple of days, in addition to the first week could be quite enough, but if Mrs C– detains me till the middle of the third week, I cannot do less than wait till the Saturday when Chris͏ʳ must return to Town—to return along with him. So that now we see our way clearly!—and I can express the satisfaction I feel; particularly as I have discharged all claim of attention my excellent Friends here have upon me. And Lad[y] B– has had the frankness to tell me, that the room I now occupy will be of use to her Sister Miss Wills; who is in a deplorable state of health, having now been several days in the House without my having seen her once, and Sir George himself as he told me, having only seen her twice. She never comes down stairs, being afraid of meeting any one; My Room is on the same floor with the one she occupies, and Lady B– has kindly told me that the range of both rooms perhaps would be amusing and therefore might be of some use to her.—This communication which I obtained to day decided me; otherwise I might perhaps though not very probably put off my journey a few days.—So that every thing is most lucky.—

How I long, (again must I say) to be with thee; every hour of absence now is a grievous loss, because we have been parted sufficiently to feel how profoundly in soul and body we love each other; and to be taught what a sublime treasure we possess in each others love.—I am happy to say that my health has been much better, and could I manage myself as to exertion, I should be strong and well, for every cause but one; which injures me, though upon the whole I never was before so well, or had so little to complain of in that respect. But I feel every day and hour that herein I shall fare worse, the fever of thought and longing and affection and desire is strengthening in me, and I am sure will be beginning to make me wakeful and to consume me. Last night I *suffered*; and this morning I tremble with sensations that almost overpower me. I think of you by the waters and under the shades of the Wye, and the visions of nature and the music of [ ]¹ raptures of love, the love I felt for thee [ ] not venture to *tell* what he felt [ ] which inspired me as an honoured and cherished [ ] and lastly as a [ ] as an expecting Bride [ ] Husband seated for ever on the [ ] as a Father, and a long tried sharer of [ ] plea-

---

¹ *MS. damaged by fire*, as M. W. later explained (see *LL*, p. 246).

sures;—each and all of these [   ] existence have passed through my mind, [   ] over again my past self, and thy past self also, participating every sentiment of thy heart and being, as far as Nature would allow what thou hast been, from the hour of our first walks near Penrith[1] till our last parting at Chester, and till thy wanderings upon Wye, and till this very moment when I am writing, and Thou most probably art thinking of me and losing all sense of the motion of the horse that bears thee, in the tenderness and strength of thy conceptions and wishes, and remembrances. Oh my beloved—but I ought not to trust myself to this senseless and visible sheet of paper; speak for me to thyself, find the evidence of what is passing within me in *thy* heart, in thy mind, in thy steps as they touch the green grass, in thy limbs as they are stretched upon the soft earth; in thy own involuntary sighs and ejaculations, in the trembling of thy hands, in the tottering of thy knees, in the blessings which thy lips pronounce, find it in thy lips themselves, and such kisses as I often give to the empty air, and in the aching of thy bosom, and let a voice speak for me in every thing within thee and without thee. Here I stop and wherefore,—Oh what an age seems it till we shall be again together under the shade of the green trees, by the rippling of the waters, and in that hour which thou lovest the most the silence the vacancy and the impenetrable gloom of night. Happy Chamber that has been so enriched with the sweet prayers of thy pure bosom; with what gratitude shall I behold it! Ah Mary I must turn my pen from this course.

I hope that Davy will let me have an Angling Rod, and I will take care to bring Isaac Walton.[2] As to George I know not what to say I do not yet see any means of serving him, but it does seem a pity that he should bury himself in a small farm. I think it would be best for me to write to Curwen, as I am not likely to see him here.—As soon as you receive this write to me at Bocking; and let me have at least 2 Letters during the week I am there; you will be able to make the calculations; as Chris[r] returns to Town on the Saturday I shall probably leave at the same day for Bury. Now my love proceed no further with this Letter, till you have read the accompan[y]ing one

[   ] Surely you will agree with me that D– [   ][3] in saying that if I were to refuse [   ] Luff; it would imply a suspicion [   ] What

---

[1] In 1788 and 1789. See also *Prel.* (1850) xii. 261 ff.
[2] i.e. *The Compleat Angler* (first publ. 1653).
[3] This refers to a letter from D. W. which has not survived.

strange reasoning: Luff is no Man of [ ] of no legal knowledge, procured this [ ] in a great hurry and distraction of mind [ ] so easy as that he should have been mistaken [ ] [?mistaken], that is, if the security be no avail, [?nor] can I consistently with what I am either to myself or to him advance the money, when he has expressly told me that he would rather die than I should lose it. Observe then what I shall do; I have called several times on Woodriff and have found him either engaged or out; I purposed to call again yesterday but was unavoidably prevented; if the security prove invalid, I shall write to Luffs Father, state the whole particulars, and lay Luff's Letters before him, I shall do this if Woodriff approves it, and beg that he would be security for the amount; and if he refuses and no other friend will do it I cannot see that either weighing Luffs feelings and situation, or looking at my own I *ought* to do it. You have read the affecting Letter from Caroline and Mother;[1] how can I be justified in throwing away or running the risk of throwing away so large a portion of our little property as 100£, those claims existing against me added to those of thee and thine. There can be nothing honourable in a conduct so opposite to the clearest dictates of nature and justice. And as to Sara—that is an after consideration—Tell me what you think of this Account from Annette and Caroline. T– Monkhouse can get Letters sent for me into France, and I have therefore given one to him for that effect. Does not Annette appear to have behaved well (and even in a dignified manner; I shall be happy if it appears so to you—

My darling you will be quite lost amid this length and magnitude of Letters that will encounter you on your return—You will have to[2] lock yourself an hour and a half in your own room before you have travelled through them it will [be] a journey, as far as relates to name, like that you have just made through the miry and rough and difficult ways of herefordshire. I have scarcely reperused a page of my Letters to you, and therefore I know that in addition to the illegible penmanship you must have had to encounter[3] the puzzling effects of innumerable omissions of words, commissions without number of wrong words making utter nonsense. But your ingenuity and patience will I hope suffice to put all to right

It is now half past one Thursday, and I am not without a fluttering hope that every knock at the door may bring me a

---

[1] Annette.   [2] *Written* to have to.   [3] *Written* encountered.

Letter from you, and yet this is foolish for you probably would not be able to send off a Letter on Tuesday, and if so I must moderate my wishes. God bless you I hope all is going on well with you; that your Horse does not stumble, and that it will not take fright. Being in the City yesterday I called on Mr Clarkson, saw him only for a couple of minutes for he was at dinner, he looks as well as usual. As soon as I have finished this half sheet, I shall write a short note to Mrs Clarkson, telling her when she may expect me, I have owed her a Letter for more than a week; but she is indulgent. indeed if she knew what a length of time I have employed in writing to you and in Letters almost as long to Grasmere, she would not be inclined to find fault with any appearance of neglect to herself.

I should have had more time if I could have risen regularly by half past six or seven; but I have lately dined out a[lmos]t[1] constantly and seldom sate down till aft[er] [ ] that my nights have been feverish from so [?late] a [ ] which acts like a heavy supper; and bein[g] [ ] from other causes I have not slept so well having heated myself in walking too much at night in the streets; for example, last night I walked from near Grays Inn (viz. Mr Rough's House) with Christopher and H. Robinson to Lambeth Palace, thence to Grosvenor Square and thence to the end of Oxford street and back again, which was too much; but I got to talking with H. R–[2] and was not sensible how tired and heated I was. We had a pleasant day at Roughs and I read the Waggoner with which they seemed much pleased. The first part hung rather heavy, but nothing else appeared to answer amiss. Rough is a very good natured Man; his Wife had not yet come down stairs from her lying in but Christ[r] and I as married men were admitted into her apartment where we sate half an hour. There was present also a Pupil of Roughs who seemed to enjoy the poem much. I have seen nothing lately of the Montagu's—and shall not see much more of Coleridge—but he dines here to morrow with Sergeant Rough and Christ[r]. He dined also here on Tuesday with Joanna Baillie. He does not talk of Keswick and Grasmere.—I shall leave this slip with a chance of a letter arriving from you or from Grasmere, before it will be necessary to seal my frank—if it does thou [?must][3] not consider this as a farewell.

W. W.

---

[1] *MS. damaged.*   [2] See *HCR* i. 93.   [3] *Word dropped out?*

I have been obliged to tear off part of D's Letter on account of the frank—the paper I have written on is very heavy.

I cannot bid thee adieu on the other side, farewell, with a fervent kiss my beloved wife

W. W.

W. W. to D. W. and S. H.[1]

MS. WL. Hitherto unpublished.

Thursday morning half past ten
[4–5 June 1812]

My dearest Friends,

At eleven this morning or before I set off with Sir G. to Rogers's, and we all intend passing the day together at Greenwich. I brought down the account of my proceedings till about last Saturday. On Sunday morning I had a most pleasant walk with Henry Robinson through the fields and over Primrose Hill to High-gate; we crossed the intended Prince Regent's Park at Mary [le] bone which will be of vast extent, but the ground has in itself no variety for it is a dead flat, but it will have agreeable views from certain parts of Hampstead and High-gate Hills.—I had met Miss Baillie at Mr Sotheby's and as I told [her] I proposed to dine at Hampstead on Sunday she requested that I would call upon her. The course of our walk brought us to Hampstead churchyard about 20 minutes before the people were likely to come out of church.[2] So we amused ourselves among the Tombstones till the people came out, not doubting that Miss B. would be of the number. In this expectation we were not disappointed. Walking down with Miss B.—whom should I meet, Dorothy, but my Old Friend Mr Carr, to whom we gave that memorably bad dinner. He has a charming House at Hampstead, which is further endeared to him by the consciousness, at least the belief, that he owes his life to it. His health failed in consequence of severe application to business and he withdrew to this spot as he supposed to die; but tranquillity and excellent air restored him; and he there is flourishing with 8 fine blooming children about him.—Miss Baillie gave me what I understand is [a] very unusual mark of regard, i.e. she invited me to dinner, and accordingly next Saturday I go over early as she requested, in

[1] This letter follows *MY* pt. ii, L. 245.   [2] *Written* churchyard.

order to take a walk with her in the morning. That night I sleep at Mr Carr's, and the next day I dine with him. Sargeant Rough is to be of the party at Miss Baillie's if his avocations will permit; and H. Robinson will be at Mr Carr's.—

Well, on the Sunday I dined at a Mr Hammond's a friend of H. R. rather an elegant young merchant, who has in part though not wholly withdrawn from business, contented with a competency. He lives with his Sister on the top of Hampstead Hill. The House commands views backwards towards and far beyond the City and in front towards and far beyond Harrow.—Nothing remarkable occurred; I attempted to beat out of his mind an excessive admiration of Miss Edgeworth, whom he knows intimately, and indeed the whole family, having visited them in Ireland. I also dropped a few notions concerning Poetry and works of Imagination, which may tend perhaps to produce at some future period some change in his opinions: that Sunday was upon the whole a pleasant day and would have been very serviceable to me, but that with a stupid imprudence not content with the walk to Hampstead and back again, I must parade the streets of London for the hour and half after my return, in consequence of which I was exhausted and tired and injured my stomach. This was most contemptible behaviour on my part.—

Friday one oclock. Thus far I had advanced and was busy in abasing myself for my folly when I was called off, and now resume the pen meaning to devote an hour and a half to writing. We had a very pleasant day yesterday at Greenwich which having mentioned I shall recur to my journal. But first let me say that the Beaumonts do not go to Coleorton till the summer will be so far advanced that I shall not accompany them. Accordingly to my great joy, I am at full liberty to go into Wales without lengthening my absence from home. I cannot forbear mentioning this as important news. I now think of leaving London in the course of the week after next for Bocking and Bury; ten days I would fain hope will do for both, and yet I fear they will think I am churlish if I do not give more. But I am resolved in some thing less than a fortnight from this time to quit London—whither I shall return, and take my place after a stay of a day or two, for Worcester when Tom H. will meet with with his gig. Such is my present plan.—Now for my journal, On Monday I dined at Lord Mulgrave's, when nothing remarkable occurred except that I sate by West the Painter, who gave me a most interesting account of the earliest recollections which he has of his bias to Painting. This

I reserve for Grasmere. From Lord M's—but by the bye, I ought to say that then I met a very interesting woman the wife of Lord Wellington; she is both pretty and clever, and what is more has a truly expressive face; but all would not fix that Debauchee her Husband, who like an immense majority of persons of his rank seems to be utterly incapable of the pleasure of virtuous love. This Lady is one of the most engaging I have seen in London. From Lord M's I went to Lady Crewe's assembly. There was an immense Route and then I had the honour of being introduced to the Princess Regent; a barren honour; for I had no conversation with her. She is enormously fat; but has I think rather an agreeable face; seemingly very good-natured, I can tell you a good deal of her. On Tuesday I went to C's Lecture which was not so well liked as the preceding though it had great merit; and that day I dined at Rogers's; present, the Beaumonts, the Prices, including Son and daughter, and General Fitzpatrick, Mr Jekyll, a most entertaining Creature, Lord Hampden, by the mother's side I believe of the great Hampden's family, and Mr West. Dear Sara Young Price is a very pleasant young man, and we talked about his visit to Hindwell. He was very unfortunate in his Companion, Sir Harford Jones fresh from Persia, and not having the skill [and] interest in farming affaires. I invited him to ride over again, when I was in the country when he might see the Farm more at leisure. He is a truly agreeable young man, but his Sister one of the most odious little creatures in the world just like the bad Sister in the faery tales both in person, and disposition. Price the elder is killing himself by overloading his stomach in eating; he becomes quite *comatose* in Mr De Quincey's word, immediately after Dinner, that is falls into a death like sleep, and I have no doubt that he is all day long terribly uncomfortable in his stomach; a warning for me and I will take it. General Fitzpatrick is dying of the Gout and a broken constitution; he has been a most debauched man, and will be little regretted.—On Wednesday we had a party at home, not so large as was intended
. . .

[*cetera desunt*]

D. W. to W. W.[1]

Address: Mr Wordsworth.
MS. WL.
LL, p. 255.

June 4th [1812]
Thursday afternoon

My dearest Brother,

Sara and John and William and I are all in perfect health, but poor Catharine died this morning at ¼ past 5 o'clock. She had been better and more cheerful than usual all yesterday, and we had fondly flattered ourselves for three or four days, in particularly noticing how much her lameness was abated, and how well she used her hand. Mr Scambler has promised us to write to you by the same post, with an account of her illness. I shall therefore say no more than that she began to be convulsed at a little before 10 last night; and died this morning at ¼ past 5.—Upon most mature deliberation we have concluded it best not to write to Mary. It would be impossible for her to be here at the Funeral; and we think that she will be better able to stand the shock when it is communicated by you.—You will be by her side to import all the consolation which can be given. May God bless and support you both. We are as well as we can be after so sudden a shock and are greatly comforted in the Belief that all that could be done to save her *was* done—

Yours evermore
D Wordsworth

If you leave London in the Ludlow Mail any evening, you will arrive at Ludlow the following Evening at the same hour. (Sara believes at 8 oclock). You are then 19 miles from Hindwell by the Wigmore Lingen and Presteyn Road. If you hire a horse at Ludlow it can go back from Hindwell the next day. If you take a Chaise you will go by Knighton, which is some miles further. This Sara says is the most expeditious way. There is a coach to Kington but it is very slow. Sara knows nothing about the Kington Coach, but Tom Monkhouse or R^d Addison perhaps can tell you.

We propose burying the beloved Girl on Monday. This we do for the best, and we hope you will both be satisfied. If we had

---

[1] This letter follows *MY* pt. ii, L. 246. It arrived after W. W. had left for Bocking on the 8th, and did not reach him there until the 10th.

attempted to keep her till you and her Mother could come, you would not have been able to look upon her face, she would then be so changed, and it will be a calmer sorrow to visit her Grave. Mr Scambler has been all that we could desire in such a melancholy case, and we both felt the most perfect reliance on his judgement.

Sara will write to Tom[1] to reach him about the time that she will reckon upon your arrival in Wales, to inform you how we go on. Farewell, we shall bear up under it all.—Pray write to tell us how you are, and what you determine upon doing.—

W. W. to M. W.[2]

Address: Mrs Wordsworth, Mr Hutchinson's, Radnor.
Franked: London June sixth 1812 Byron.
Postmark: 6 June 1812.
MS. WL.
LL, p. 234.

Saturday morning. June 6th [1812]

My sweetest Mary,

This will be a very short Letter.—I ought to have provided myself with a couple of quires of very thin and light paper, when I first came to London; for I have found several times that I have overloaded my franks, and if sent in that state we should have lost as much by one of those, as we have saved by three or 4. Yesterday, on this account I was obliged to send a Letter to Grasmere in a very garbled state.—To day you are returned or probably will return from your, I trust, fortunate and pleasant excursion.[3]—I have a frank for Monday, the day I go to Bocking you may therefore expect another short Letter from me by your Wednesdays post.—but to continue my Journal.

On Wednesday afternoon T. Monkhouse took me up with his Gig and carried me to Hampstead. Where I sate three hours with Mr and Mrs and Miss Robson[4] and T. M– and then by previous engagement drank tea with Miss Baillie; returned about 11 and supped with the Robsons where I slept. Next morning returned to the City with T. M– Called in passing on one of the

---

[1] Thomas Hutchinson.
[2] This letter, and the next, follow *MY* pt. ii, L. 247.   [3] To the Wye.
[4] The Robisons were London friends of Thomas Monkhouse. M. W. referred to Miss Robison as 'my oldest acquaintance' (*MW*, p. 29).

Mackereths,[1] T. M— stated to me that he was under great obligation in his business to Robson which he had no present means or prospect of future means of discharging. He added that Robson was of the Fish-Mongers' Company the wealthiest and most respectable of London; that the Court which governs this company consisted of about 30 Members, who had very considerable patronage etc etc, and that he was sure it would be very gratifying[2] to Robson to be in the way of becoming a Member. Now your Friend, Richard Sharp said T. M. is Warden or chief officer of this company, and if he would at your request take Robson by the hand, it would probably bring about in course of time his appointment; and I should then in some degree repay the great obligation I am under to him. I replied that I would take up the business immediately; accordingly I called on Sharp yesterday, stated the Case, he allowed me to bring T. M— to him, and told him what he could and would do to promote the object; and Robson is to call upon Sharp in the course of the week: This business took me up the whole of yester morning At 3 I attended Coleridges lecture,[3] hurried home and he Chris[r] Sergeant Rough and myself dined with the Beaumonts. This morning I am going to have an interview with Mont:[4] and Woodriff about Luffs Money; which has been a heavy restraint and plague to me.[5]—T. M. advises me also to make a Copy of the Letter to be sent to France,[6] and send the Duplicate by another conveyance. This will be an hours work; and I assure you in writing such long Letters to Grasmere as well as to you I have employed many a long and let me say happy hour, farewell my darling, it grieves me to send so short a Letter—

---

[1] Probably William Mackereth, one of the Grasmere family of that name, who lived in Finsbury Square.

[2] *Written* gratified.　　　　　　　　　　　　　[3] See *HCR* i. 102.

[4] Montagu.

[5] In her letter of 6 June, M. W. was uneasy about refusing the money to Luff: '. . . I think the loss (should it prove a loss) would be *even to us* so small that I would risk it rather than have the pain of thinking that you had wounded the feelings of a *poor Man who* has the highest respect for you.' (*WL MSS.*).

[6] Annette *deleted*. M. W. had referred to Annette's recent letter to D. W.: 'Dear Caroline and Annette I cannot help recurring to them again the account they give of themselves is very affecting—and creditable to the Mother—She must be a nice Girl—but I should hope that her time is not so completely shut out from all exercise and pleasure in life, except what they find in each other . . .'

W. W. to M. W.[1]

Address: Mʳˢ Wordsworth, Mʳ Hutchinson's, Radnor.
Franked: London June eight 1812. Rᵈ Sharp.
Postmark: 8 June 1812.
MS. WL.
LL, p. 240.

[7–8 June 1812]
Sunday 2 o clock

My dearest Love,

I have been occupied nearly three hours this Morning in making a Duplicate of a Long letter of Dorothy to France[2] and of my own. T. Monkhouse who will forward these Letters by the means of Merchants of his acquaintance who have licenses advised me so to do as not one Letter in three reaches its destination; I have also called on the Davies,[3] and Sir H— is to send me a fishing Rod to Grosvenor Square, which I shall bring down with me to Hindwell. I called also on the Ladies Fleming[4] but did not find them at home; I called there also yester day morning; so that I have done my duty here.—To morrow I depart for Bocking at 3 o clock in the afternoon—so that the morning is all which remains for me to settle the business with Montagu and Woodriff.—I called yesterday on Mrs M— who affects and *perhaps* feels great kindness towards you but says nothing of Dorothy and Sara—I should have written you a Long Letter this morning; but you have been told how my time has been occupied, nothing can be conceived more tedious than copying french, especially when like mine and poor D.'s also it is not good—

Now let me tell you my Sweet Love, that on returning home last night I was gree[te]d by your fondly expected Letter with Abergavenny Post Mark.[5] How happy am I that you have been

---

[1] This letter was written the day before, and on the morning of, W. W's departure for Bocking with C. W. He was still ignorant of Catharine W.'s death, and so was M. W.

[2] To Annette.   [3] Sir Humphry and Lady Davy.

[4] Lady le Fleming of Rydal Hall and her daughter.

[5] M. W.'s letter of 2–3 June from Chepstow and Abergavenny containing her account of the Wye tour: 'O William what enchanting scenes have we passed through—but you know it all—only I must say longings to have you by my side have this day been painful to me beyond expression. We coursed the back of the Wye all the way from Monmouth to Tintern Abbey—the River on our left hand—now *close* to us now at the distance of a stones throw—and now and then we were separated by a part of the wood which hangs over the Margin—I hope

delighted and that you stand the fatigues so well. I knew that if
the weather favored you would be charmed with the Country;
but I was very apprehensive that the fatigue would injure you;
and your health is above every thing precious to me.—The
Olives[1] are worthless creatures without any heart. These last
words explain why they did not trouble themselves to see you,
you measured their enthusiasm by your own sweet nature; further as you mentioned your B[r] and Sister they were probably
afraid that you should accept the Beds which they must have felt
themselves bound to make you an offer of. Next; they probably
thought it very hard to pay their money for the play, and not
have their penn'orths. I am sorry very sorry that the stupid
Roscius[2] led you back to Hereford; and could earnestly have
wished that instead you had gone up the Usk as far as Brecon,
and then returned by the Hay. I have twice been up the Usk and
a charming country it is; this really mortifies me; I paced this
tract once alone on foot, and great part of it in the same way
with Dorothy and C.[3] You cannot think how much dearer the
Wye is to me since you have seen it; I loved it deeply before on
most tender remembrances and considerations but now that you
have seen it also and know it, and we [?now] can talk of it
together what a sanctity will it attain in my mind, and of all my
Poems The one [in] which I speak of it will be the most beloved
by me.—

Here I was interrupted; it is now eight Monday Morning. I
have been up an hour, washing, dressing, putting my things in
order for my journey to day etc etc—I shall leave my trunk till
my return, and take as few things as possible.—I am quite
puzzled how to act on my return to London; the Beaumonts will
be going or gone;—I do not like to quarrel with Mrs Mont:[4] nor
can I bring my mind to give her such a public testimony of
regard as would be implied by putting myself under her roof—

you have paced this blind track—for never did path lead amongst so much love-
liness—' (*WL MSS.*).

   [1] John Oliff and his wife were former Grasmere residents, who had moved to
the Usk valley. They had declined to meet D. W. and the Hutchinsons.

   [2] William Henry West Betty (1791–1874), actor, called the 'Young Roscius'.
See *EY*, L. 236.

   [3] Coleridge. W. W.'s first visit was in 1793: the second, five years later, in
1798.

   [4] Mrs. Montagu.

therefore I am as yet quite undecided where I shall be during the week I purpose to spend in town on my return.—You cannot conceive also what a trouble I have had and time I have lost in this affair of Luffs too, I have at least made ten calls about it; nor have I yet brought it to an issue. This morning I shall have to betake myself to it again. It was a most unwarrantable application on Luffs part; and on every account I do exceedingly regret that it was ever made.—

Yesterday (it is now Monday morning observe) Coleridge was to have called on me by appointment at eleven to walk in the Park.—Soon after came that good Creature Morgan with an apology that he was ill in bed—in fact he had been (2nd slip of paper) quacking,[1] and brought on the pain in his bowels.—I employed the morning in writing, and between two and three called on the Addisons[2] whom I found at dinner, Mrs A– Miss Hindson and Mr and Mrs Rich^d A– and a young Lady I suppose Miss A– I sate, I think an hour with them, and then called on C– I found Mrs Morg: at home, and C– appeared shortly. Mrs M– I think, I once described as a handsome woman, but she is not so—She has a round face, dark eyes, an upturned or a pug nose, nevertheless as her complection is good, her eyes bright, and her countenance animated and goodnatured and she has the appearance of being in redundant health, she is, what would be called, a desireable woman; neither too fat nor too lean; but just what, in that I respect, I and your other friends would wish you dearest Mary to be. The other Sister[3] has a smaller round face, an upturned nose also, and is thinner and more delicate in appearance and of more still and gentle manners; not that there is any thing unpleasan[t] in Mrs M– on this score; but Mrs M.'s carriage [   ] person is more uneasy luxuriant and joyous.—I fear [   ] with all these words I give you no distinct Idea of [   ][4] I sate there about an hour. Coleridge upon the whole is much better in health, and appears to live far more rationally than he did with us, so that he has changed for the better assuredly; and I think his present situation and employments upon the whole quite eligible for him.

Tell me frankly, can you decypher the scrawls I send you. I am never so happy as when writing to you, what a pity that my penmanship is not better.—Lady Davy has engaged to give me 4.4

---

[1] i.e. playing the quack, dabbling in medicine.
[2] Richard Addison's mother and aunt.
[3] Miss Brent.   [4] MS. torn.

for three subscriptions of the Friend;[1] so that, by little and little, some are picked up.—Coleridge proposed to come down for a couple of days to Bocking, and if we can manage it, we are to cross the Country to Chatham to see Capt[n] Pasley for a day and a half, I know not how far this will be practicable. He seemed to enjoy himself so much, and the Country air and objects appeared to do him so much good, the day he walked with me to Hampstead, that on this account I shall be happy as far as depends on myself to give effect to his proposal.—So that upon the whole there appears small likelihood of my leaving Town till comes a month dating from last friday afternoon, for on a Friday afternoon I certainly take my departure with T. M.[2]—

Examine upon the Maps if you are able how Oxford lies in respect to Hindwell as to distance etc—Thomas[3] and I settled that he was to meet me at Worcester, but if by leaving out Worcester he, by the addition of thirty miles or so, could meet T. M.– at Oxford it would be a high treat to us both, and T. might see Oxford and Blenheim two of the finest things in their several ways in the world. Do mention this. How much my darling, do I regret that when we returned to Coleorton we did not make a deviation to include these. Observe what I mean it is forty miles, if I mistake not, from Hindwell to Worcester, now if by the nearest road, Oxford should prove to be no more than 70, would it not be worth T.'s while to make a push for the sake of seeing it.—I ask this with diffidence, but it would be a pleasant thing if practicable.—

You will risk no extravagance but this very moment I have parted with no less than 20 shillings thus: a 5 and sixpence piece to the person who has made my bed while here, another to him who has cleaned my shoes etc and three 3 shilling pieces to Sir Georges' Servant, for his personal attendance upon me. Is this too much? or would less have sufficed? I purchased on Saturday the Tatler,[4] unbound a neat Copy for 4.6 This is surely very reasonable, and we do not possess the Book. I could buy many works which we want reasonably[5] had I the money.—Coleridge says that he shall soon be clear of all his embarrassments, and that he

---

[1] Coleridge was talking of resuming publication of *The Friend*.

[2] Thomas Monkhouse.   [3] Thomas Hutchinson.

[4] The periodical begun in Apr. 1709 by Sir Richard Steele (1672–1729), and continued with Joseph Addison's help till Jan. 1711.

[5] *Written* reasonable.

finds fagging pleasant to him.—Certainly he is quite punctual as to his Lectures—How gladly could I scribble away[1]

[*cetera desunt*]

W. W. to THOMAS HUTCHINSON[2]

Address: Mr Hutchinson, Hindwell, Radnor.
Postmark: 11 June 1812.
MS. WL. Hitherto unpublished.

Grosvenor Square Thursday
[11 June 1812]

My dear Thomas,

It was Dorothys and Saras wish that I should myself communicate to our dear Mary the melancholy intelligence of the death of her daughter Catharine. I came from Bocking to Town this morning with that intention, but on consulting with my friends they are unanimously of opinion, that it is better that she should receive this intelligence from you the particulars of which I have reason to believe have already reached you from Grasmere. I request then that you would impart the fact to Mary, telling her as soon as may be afterwards that I shall be at Hindwell on Sunday.—It is my intention to set off by the Hereford Coach at one oclock and on Saturday evening or night I shall be at Hereford, where Mr Monkhouse or George[3] will be so kind as to

---

[1] M. W.'s letter to W. W. of 8–10 June followed him from Bocking to Hindwell, and was later endorsed: 'Our Child had been 4 days dead!' In it she had referred to the unsettled political situation and her forthcoming reunion with W. W.: 'No parliament formed yet! it is quite painful to me to think of this suspension—it is plain there is no one competent to be placed at the head of affairs or this could not be—all here wish *you* were the chosen one and then they are sure things would go right—for my part worlds should not tempt me to consent to your being in a situation of so much danger or of your being subject to so much anxiety—No my darling let us have our own dear retirement—with a little more money for the sake of more ease, and ability to enjoy the pleasures we derive from a little travelling the short time that it remains to be a pleasure to us—but if this cannot be, if we are only to be blessed with life and each others society and—health and power to make our Children what we would wish to be—we shall be happy—But how miserable should I be to see thee subject to irritation envy and ever in danger from thy situation to tempt the hand of the Murderer.' (*WL MSS.*).

[2] This letter, and the next two, follow *MY* pt. ii, L. 248.

[3] George Hutchinson.

meet me in the Gig, to set off for Hindwell on Sunday. If the Gig should not be at liberty a Horse would do, but I shall prefer the Gig both for myself and my trunks.—

If the particulars should not have reached you, which is not likely as I know they purposed to write, it may be proper to say, that Catharine was seized with convulsions last Wednesday night and died after seven hours illness during which time she was insensible to all bodily suffering. These convulsions were not the consequence of any negligence or improper food as was proved, and every thing was done for her which could be done. I have a most satisfactory letter from Mr Scambler[1] on this point. Your love and that of all about you will suggest to Mary every consolation that you are able.

I have thought that Mary having to look forward to my arrival will be of far more use to her than my actual presence in the first instance. Your most affectionate

Brother and friend
Wm Wordsworth

I shall be at the Greyhound Hereford and should like the Gig to be there on the Saturday night, if Mr Monkhouse or George can come with it.

D. W. to W. W. and M. W.

Address: Mr Wordsworth, at Mr Hutchinson's, Hindwell, near Radnor, Radnorshire.
Stamp: Kendal Penny Post,
MS. WL. Hitherto unpublished.

Grasmere, Saturday morning
13th June [1812]

My dearest William and Mary,

By last night's post we received a letter from Lady Beaumont telling us that you had left Grosvenor Square about an hour before my letter arrived with the sad tidings of our sweet Catharine's Death. We had been very anxious for Friday night, yet not without strong hopes that a letter from yourself or Lady B would come to inform us that you had not left London so soon as the time of delivery of letters—and yet we are doubtful about it, as your Frank is dated Monday, Woodruff's rooms.[2] It is possi-

---

[1] This letter is among the *WL MSS*.

[2] See the latter part of W. W.'s letter to M. W. of 7-8 June.

ble you might do your business after you had parted from the Beaumonts yet if they knew by what coach you were to go they surely would have sent a Servant after you to the Coach house to stop your departure.

We have been inexpressibly anxious for your arrival at Hindwell before Sara's letter to Tom, and in that hope we are disappointed—our only remaining hope is, that Mary did not see the letter before it was put into her Brother's hands. If she did not we think he would conceal its contents in the expectation of your arrival, which we trust would be on Friday morning at the latest.[1] We are most anxious to be certified in this respect, as we dread the effects of a sudden communication of the event to Mary. Oh! let her think what a blessing it was to see the child stretched out in peace after her hard struggle, which must have left her deprived of the use of her limbs, if not of her senses, if it had pleased God to spare her life—but he took her to himself a blessed and innocent spirit and she is happy—and if we knew that her Mother and you were calm and resigned we would think of her with tender comfort. We cannot be at rest till Sunday night, when surely we shall have a letter from you if not from Hindwell, from London or Worcester—but surely you would be in London on Tuesday night, and why had not we a letter by last night's post to tell us so? We are very much perplexed and cannot help fearing some miscarriage of my letter and Mr Scambler's[2] which were enclosed by Lady Beaumont under cover to Christopher.

We expect dearest Dorothy[3] on Thursday morning. Poor thing she wept bitterly for above an hour when she heard of her Sister's death; but the rest of the day she was tolerably cheerful, and the day after played with her Companions as usual.

John went to Mr Dawes[4] on Tuesday morning, came home very happy at night, and continues to be pleased with his School. He has sunk deeper into our hearts than ever since Catharine's death he has shewn so much thoughtful and tender sensibility. He has a generous innocent soul and I trust that if he lives he will be a good Man, William's spots are mended and he is beginning to look like himself again. He is very lively and perfectly well.

[1] See previous letter, which makes clear that W. W. did not expect to reach Hindwell till Sunday, 14th.

[2] W. W. had received the physician's letter and D. W.'s accompanying letter at Bocking.

[3] Dora W.   [4] John W.'s new school at Ambleside, run by Mr. Dawes.

If you determine to stay a short time in Wales we shall consider it as a proof that Mary has not sunk under her affliction and is willing to receive consolation—but we are very anxious to know your determination. Perhaps there may be some lonely publick house in some of the retired and beautiful parts of Wales where you may pass some days together.—Whatever you determine upon you may be assured that we shall be resigned and comfortable if we hear that Mary bears her loss with fortitude.

The child was buried near the Thorn[1] on Monday afternoon at 5 o'clock. All who attended her Remains I believe were sincere mourners. Fanny and Sarah followed us three, and the Body was borne by Sarah's Mother, Fanny's, Mary Williamson's and Mary Dawson's.[2] Hartley and Derwent were here. We sent for them to follow her to the grave.

God bless you, my dearest Friends. Be comforted in thinking how she is blessed compared with what she would have been if she had been with us, lingering in weakness.

> Evermore yours
> D Wordsworth

With respect to the 100£ to be advanced to Woodruff for Luff I can only say I am sorry you did not do it yourself; but I think if you resolved against that, knowing Sarah's determination, you ought to have done it for her. She is now placed in a very unpleasant situation. She cannot act for herself in connection with Woodruff because after your refusal it would appear to him as if she acted in opposition to you. Her determination remains unshaken: and she wishes you still to procure the money for her. I hope you will do it, it is the kindest thing you can do for her in respect to this affair, for it will be a hard thing for her, to have to act herself after your refusal. You may do it and there will be nothing strange in your altering your mind. My dear Brother pray do not give her pain by further opposition. I am sure you ought not.

We are all well.

---

[1] In Grasmere churchyard.
[2] The mothers of the Wordsworths' four servants.

D. W. to W. W.

Address: Mr Wordsworth, Hindwell, Radnor, Single.
Stamp: Kendal Penny Post.
MS. WL. Hitherto unpublished.

Wed. Night 17 June—[1812]

I went up to Mr Scambler's as soon as I had read dear Mary's
questions and put the first to him concerning the sickness. He
explained to me many causes of convulsions which are not necessary in the present case to state. I remember then Catharine's case
he said was decidedly from the Brain the symptoms were all
unequivocal—when this is the case sickness always follows. If a
man falls from a horse and his body is injured he becomes insensible and vomits instantly. He has no doubt but that the brain was
injured with the first convulsions[1] and the tendency to a sickness
remained. 'In short, Miss H' said he most earnestly and solemnly,
'had we been forewarned it is my firm belief that nothing could
have been done to prevent this. We might have tried but they are
never foreseen, come on without warning, instantly, therefore no
preventative is known', nor can Mr Scambler form any conjec-
ture as to what might be a preventative.[2] Sara did not ask M^r
Scambler about the child's ear; for she could not recollect it at
the time, nor even if she *had* recollected it she would have considered him as answering that question in the other, namely by
his opinion, nay his faith and confidence that the previous seizure
lay in the brain; not that this would have prevented her asking
the question if she had recollected it. For myself I must say that
the ear healed gradually, as a common sore ear does heal; but was
not entirely well when she died—I washed her that very day and
she cried when I washed that ear. Mr Scambler thinks from our
representation of the appearance of the child that she had only
just been seized, when we went to her, however Sara must have
been 20 minutes (at least while her porridge was making and she
had finished eating it and mixed some porridge and milk for the
cat who was eating in the Room with us) at the time when John
called out. The sitting-room had been open all this while till I
came in to my supper, and in the mean time I had been in my
own Room or backwards and forwards from one Room to the
other, therefore if she had made any noise we *must* have heard it.
Mary Williamson came after the clock had struck nine—Fanny

---

[1] i.e. in Apr. 1810 (see *MY* pt. i, L. 188).

[2] Up to this point the letter is written by S. H.

went with her to turn the beds down, and carried Mary into the Room to see Catharine—she drew the Blind back that M might look at her, and Catharine sate up in bed, being awake, and Fanny said to Mary 'it is very odd she should not be asleep—lie still Honey—here's Mary Williamson come,' which, she thought would please her as Catharine was very fond of her. C. laid down as she bade her which proves that she was sensible, and if she had been in pain she would have given some token of it—Therefore it is probable she had no *species of illness* upon her then; and the disease of which she died is marked by *immediate insensibility.*— The cat was not in the Room, as you will have perceived. As to Fanny's having frightened her I should not have even suspected that if she had not told her story in the presence of Mary Williamson; for the dear, mild innocent Child has been so very tractable that even Fanny has never had need to speak a harsh word to her. She was perfectly quiet with her eyes wide open and fixed when I called to Sara. *So* she was lying when she came in, and she was not visibly convulsed till a few minutes after we had brought her into the sitting room. Fanny's mother was in the house, and immediately after Fanny and M left Catharine they went as quickly as possible back again—We were entering the gate before they came upon the Bridge—we talked a little to them, and then came up stairs. There was no noise then—and if there had been any before the old woman must have heard it, the house being so very quiet. You will observe the clock had struck 9 when Mary W. came into the house. It was about ¼ before 10 when we found her lying as I have described, after having got our suppers in the next room to her.—I do not believe they have even been left a moment in the house[1] [ ] asleep or awake since you left home—[ ] of hearing and listening have been better [ ] besides one is naturally [ ] when they are left by you. Sara omitted [ ] part of the matter that when Mr Scambler [?] tried [ ] by evacuating the [?bowels] and it was proved that these were in a proper [?order]. I can say no more. She has been a blessing [?and] she is taken away, and if we had known [ ] over her we should never have had an easy [ ] her innocent smiles, her loving ways and [ ] pain of anguish along with these. It was [ ] sight to see her lying an image of peace and [ ] compared with what we had so lately looked [ ] have been for long years to come. No [ ] do not grieve that she is removed from [ ]

---

[1] *Side of sheet torn away.*

dearest dearest Friend. Mrs King[1] tells [ ] had no return of the
disorder for several [ ] would have been the greatest reason [ ]
at a certain age—and these have [ ] when every year would
have [?strengthened] [ ]. Mr Scambler was never confident,
never [ ] her and happy it was we did not know it [ ] he had
seen her wonderful amendment he has too [ ] and Sara noticed
it when he came to [ ] eagerly he looked at her when [ ] as if
he could hardly believe that he saw her so well.—We have had
the greatest comfort (except that you were absent and it was a
misery to us to think of that) but it has been the greatest comfort
to us that every thing else fell out the most fortunately that could
have been. Sara was at home, a blessing this for me! It was a
blessing that she slept with John; for if Fanny had been her Bed-
fellow She would have gone much later to bed, and we should
not have gone to look at her til just before *our* bed-time—M^r
Scambler came as soon as possible—Fanny's mother was in the
house with us, and nothing was mismanaged, nothing forgotten
in our distress and confusion—indeed when I look back on it I
wonder that we were so much masters of ourselves. It was the
excess of the calamity that supported us.—

William! you say that you should have been better satisfied if
Mr S. had stayed with us to the last [ ] Mr Scambler you would
have thought that what [ ] right—he stayed two hours but Sara
[ ] saw, and I *might* have seen if I had [ ] the child who was on
my knee, that she had [ ] went away he *told us as much*, and that
no [ ] had been done, therefore he could only [ ] and we did
not wait therefore. Why keep [ ] when he might be of use to
others? Mr [?Scambler said] that in all cases of disease from the
Brain [ ] vomiting was a symptom, and it appears [ ] what he
said that the convulsions also were [ ] symptom of her disease in
the Brain, and not [ ] though the tendency had before been
produced by the [ ] convulsions which first proceeded from the
Stomach.

I suppose when you say 'write to the Montagues' that you
have not seen them or told them of Catharine's death. Indeed
William I cannot do it. I cannot repeat the news late to them—if
Mary continues to be bent on coming.

Give our kindest love to all—Her grief will be removed at
coming home and perhaps the sooner it is over the better.—That
useless letter to Tom,[2] what a pity we sent it, but we did all for

---

[1] Of The Hollens, Grasmere.   [2] Tom *written twice.*

the best—but her anguish has been prolonged by your absence. I wish you had told her yourself.—

We had a most affecting letter from Mr de Quincey last night.[1] He says he intends to leave London on Saturday, hopes that nothing will delay him longer—shall be at Liverpool on Monday. He should leave it on Tuesday or Wednesday. He says if we want to write to him we must direct to him at Mr Merrit's[2] N° 60 Castle Street, Liverpool. If you should come home so soon you might perhaps meet him there—or you might come in a chaise together, which would be the best way of travelling for Mary.

Dorothy[3] is arrived and is very well and looks very well. I feel very grateful to Miss Weir.

W. W. and M. W. to D. W. and S. H.[4]

Address: Miss Wordsworth, Grasmere, Kendal.
Stamp: Radnor.
MS. WL. Hitherto unpublished.

[Hindwell]
Friday Evening [19 June 1812]

My dear Friends,

I sit down to write to you, but of matter of fact I have nothing new to say; and as to the feelings of my mind I do not think that any good could come for giving way to them. Mary is very sorrowful, and heavy; and as she is considerably reduced in strength I do not think it adviseable that we should begin our journey to Grasmere immediately; even if there were not some ground for hope that a little interposition of time and of new objects in this part of the country might be of service to her. In this respect I am quite at a loss; only I feel that she ought not to move on account of the state of her health, for some little time. She kept her room while the Wheelrights[5] were here, they left us this morning at nine.—

I have written short letters to most of my friends, reporting how I found Mary, and have received one from Mrs C–[6] in answer to mine from Bocking. Her distress of course was great.—

Little Thomas is very well, cheerful, and happy; seeing that his mother is melancholy he naturally avoids her. He is rather worsened in his reading; and in particular articulates much worse.

---

[1] See Jordan, p. 264.   [2] De Quincey's bookseller friend.   [3] Dora W.
[4] This letter, and the next, follow *MY* pt. ii, L.250.
[5] Thomas Monkhouse's business partner and his wife.   [6] Mrs. Clarkson.

Your account of John gives me much pleasure.—Yesterday we received your letter—giving account of the funeral of the Darling. I am pleased with the place you have [?picked] upon for her grave. We have broken ground in that Churchyard through God's blessing, as gently as well could have been. I hope that we shall all be sensible of this, and shew our dear remembrance and feeling of it by additional tenderness and kindness to each other. Catharine is gone before to prepare the way for us and make it somewhat less forbidding; sweet Innocent—I have yet not felt my own sorrow, only I know well that it is to come.—But as I said before, I do not mean to yield to the emotions of my heart on this sad and unexpected privation.—I long to hear how little Dorothy is and how she is looking—take care of the water, and of fire, and of all dangers; especially for William. I appear to have said all that I mean to say; for our life here is wholly unvaried— Mary walks out a little but cannot go far without resting, nor does she seem to relish any thing but Sadness,—Sara will expect some thing to be said about the money; I can have no control over [her] in this and she must act as she thinks proper; only I do not see what connection she has with the affair at all. Luff tells me he would rather he than that I should run any risk of losing the principal; upon the supposition that no risk is to be incurred. I promise to advance the money; as soon as I have an opportunity of examining the security. I find it not worth a Button; and therefore withhold the money, as Luff I am compelled to think were he Master of the funds would ask me to do. And here the matter ends.—

Yours most affectionately
W. W.

[*M. W adds*]

Saturday morn^g

My dearest Sisters,

William left this letter for me to close, he is gone with his Son Thomas before him this morning along with John to Kington in search of old Books—I find he has given you a worse account of me than he ought to have done—My health is not bad. I have had no one thing in this respect to complain of except some-times, which it was impossible should have been otherwise, a head-ache—My bowels have been quite regular and I have slept a great deal—It is true that I am weakened and cannot walk far without resting and my flesh is gone from me of course, but this is all that is complained of in respect to my health. Believe me my darlings that I am completely resigned to my loss and have a firm faith that this deprivation will in the end be salutary to us all. That it is a great gain to an innocent child we can none of us question. But sorrow will have its time—to fight or argue against it only aggravates the evil—that I should regain my spirits before I have *at home* become familiar with this change seems to argue an expectation that my nature should be changed—Some allowance must be made in consideration of the suddenness of the blow—I *such a distance* from you and having up to the very time had such formidable, such flattering accounts!—But forgive me I did not mean to write this. Depend upon me I will do my best to be chearful—this is all I want for I am quite comforted—I trust dearest Dorothy your expression 'hard struggle' in your [letter][1] did not imply any thing in contradiction to the former comfortable assurances that we had that the Blessing was from the first [ ] insensible to all bodily pain—I trust it did not.

Dear Mrs Clarkson's was a sweet letter and has done me more good than any thing by her pure and perfect sympathy. When you write to her tell her so, tell her that I would myself have thanked her but from the fear of agitating her—I am grieved that W. did not go to her tho' certainly he has been a great blessing to me for I believe I owe my good nights' rest to his being by my side. You will be happy to hear that he is and looks uncommonly well—on thursday evening he told me that he had had a most excellent appetite since he came here and that his digestion was *perfectly good*—last night I was not surprized to hear him say that he had felt some uneasiness in this respect for I had observed the quick manner in which he eat a large dinner with great pain. I could not but think at the time that if he digested a dinner so eaten he was the strongest of all men. What do you think of his going to the pool at ¼ before 10 last night to fish, when, to use his own words it was raining pell mell. He said afterwards that he went on account of his stomach but I am persuaded that it was the boyish spirit that was working in him—a continuance of which may God prolong—W. now puts our remaining here a while longer upon the footing of his own desires—says it may be long before he sees the place again—so I cannot press the matter further—but as to my consenting to travel for the sake of *my see-*

[1] *Seal.*

132

ing the country it would be idle to spend so much money at a time when I know and feel that I could not enjoy it.—

I am very sorry about the business of Luff's. W. has talked very *angrily* to me when I opposed his determination—he means to write to Luff stating his sentiments,—pray dearest Sara do not distress yourself about it. W. has mentioned the affair to Tom, who thinks W. has acted right. W. read a letter slightly over before he went out from Annette—the substance of which seemed to be a statement of Caroline's great expectations from her uncles—but the letter on acc^t of the publicity of the correspondence was written so ambiguously that it is scarcely possible to understand it—but the main drift of it seems to be that she wishes in order to secure advantages to C. to pass for William's wife. She speaks of an old uncle who died some time ago and who left all his property to her, but that for the sake of his child's expectations and other considerations she relinquished the whole to his Brother or *her* Brother the husband's heir. She says that C. has begun to learn English. Requires money to Mons. Devaux,[1] for this is the sum of what I can recollect.—I think W. will see the young man and he means to advance him more money— £20 he has sent by Tom Monkhouse's means, £10 of which he, T., advanced—so we shall have this to pay, and when we get home £13 which W. received from Mr Tuffin for the Greens[2]— so I think it behoves us to get home as frugally as we can—but W. tells me that if we take a tour it is to cost us nothing for he has money for that purpose and for no other—this consideration however cannot at this time act as an inducement to me. If I felt in my own heart that I was doing W. good for his own sake of course I would not hesitate to make the sacrifice of being so much longer from you all but nothing short of this could induce me to it.—

Sarah I shall never forget thee for exerting thyself so far as to send me that [ ][3] account of my darling's departure—I wish another letter much to enter into particulars how you are now going on—from which I may better gather that you are so than by express facts written for the purpose of saying you are well etc. I have a thousand anxieties about you all when I think of what you have gone through. Tom is sadly gone back lately at his book—he has been too busy riding horses to learn his book—he

---

[1] Or Deveraux, an intermediary with Annette.

[2] i.e. the fund for the Green orphans.   [3] *Two illegible words.*

is a great man today, he has patiently waited for this journey to Kington ever since Mrs Donaldson gave him a sixpence—he means to buy something here for his 'dear Willy'—God in heaven bless that child and you all. O that I had him in my arms—and my sweet Dorothy I long to see her and beloved John. God bless you all!—Joanna has been a kind friend to me— and every one of them. God bless them. Thomas is a good sort— but they are all so.—Geo will put this into the Post at Ludlow—he goes this afternoon and expects to return with Miss W.[1] tomorrow night. I am thankful for dear Joanna's sake that Miss W. is coming for she would have felt herself solitary after we leave here with nobody but my aunt being at home.

farewell M. W.

Give my love to the good fr[iends] at Hacket.[2]

W. W. to JOHN HUTCHINSON[3]

MS. WL. Hitherto unpublished

[Hindwell]

[*c.* 20 June 1812]

My dear John,

It gives me great concern that I was hurried out of London by the account of the death of my Child Catharine, without having seen your Daughter Elizabeth. The Cause which prevented my seeing her long before was this; I was to have breakfasted and dined also with Mr Stuart[4] at Brompton by appointment, and as Sloane street lies on the way to his House, I purposed to call on Bessy in my way thither or on my return; Mr Stuart was obliged from time to time to defer these engagements with me, till at last I was hurried away unexpectedly by the news of Catharine's death. I am very sorry for this disappointment, as I should have much liked to have seen her and to have let you know how she looked.—

Your Brother Thomas has shewed me a Letter in which my name is mentioned with reference to your late Uncles[5] disposal of his property by Will.—I have no hesitation in saying that *as far as I am competent to judge*, the partiality of your Uncle is less to be

---

[1] Miss Weir.

[2] Betty and Jonathan Youdell.

[3] M. W.'s eldest brother.

[4] Daniel Stuart of the *Courier*.

[5] Henry Hutchinson of Stockton (see letter of 19 Aug. 1810 above).

complained of in your case than in any other; I meant to say that your claim upon his notice appears stronger than that of any other person.

My wife has invited me to give an opinion upon your arrangement with respect to Henry:[1] I am not sure that I am justified in so doing. As a friend however and so nearly allied with the family, I may say that as to the *amount* of your intended provision for Henry it appears such as every one ought to be satisfied with, and does honour to your paternal feelings, while it expresses your determination to rectify an act of gross injustice on the part of your deceased Uncle. At the same time, you will not blame me I hope if I add, that the *manner* of this provision, though it may satisfy Henry's mind, is not such as ought, I think, if naturally considered, to satisfy completely your own. It is not enough that Henry should have no doubts concerning the payment of his annuity in both cases of your life and death (though by the bye in the latter case I do not see how he can have such assurance with a legal provision by will or otherwise) but it appears to me that for your own sake you should put this affair by a legal instrument completely out of the possibility of being affected by any change of circumstances of disposition in your self.—You remember the lines of Pope

> Manners with fortunes, humours turn with climes,
> Tenets with books and principles with times.—[2]

You might continue punctually to Henry his allowance, if no revision of fortune prevented it; but age chills the generous disposition of us all; and not suspecting you of any worse falling off than we all as human beings are subject to in this respect, I cannot but press upon you for your own sake the reasonableness and the duty of obviating this evil. Observe that I do not speak this in contemplation of a change in your disposition to the extent of the possibility of your withholding from Henry at some future period any part of the full amount of what you had promised to grant, while you had it in your power to keep your engagement; but who could guarantee to himself the unabated continuance of the same liberal disposition, through all changes of life and

---

[1] M. W.'s sailor brother. John Hutchinson was attempting to rectify the injustice of his uncle's will by paying an annuity to Henry, his younger brother, but John already had two daughters by his first wife, and four sons and two daughters by his second, all of whom might be thought to have prior claims on him.

[2] *Moral Essays*, I, 166–7.

circumstance; so that what was not withheld might yet be granted much less freely and willingly. Besides is it not desirable that whatever is done for Henry should be relieved from all weight of obligation as much as possible; it should be placed upon its true footing, viz, an act of justice; but, can this be done so effectually or even done at all, without removing the intended benefit at once from all dependence upon your Will, power, or pleasure, and locking it fast in the abstract security of a legal form.—Excuse what I have said, and attribute it to the request of your Sister, my beloved wife, that I would state my opinion, and to the interest which I take in all that relates to the family of Hutchinson.

I shall do all in my power to point out for George[1] another Agency; whose conduct appears wholly unexceptionable, and with whom every body here is much pleased. Your Sister Mary is of course in great dejection, which nothing but time can be expected to alleviate much.

Believe me your affectionate friend and Brother
W. Wordsworth

D. W. to W. W.[2]

Address: Mr Wordsworth, Hindwell, Radnor, *Single*.
Stamp: Keswick.
MS. *WL. Hitherto unpublished.*

Monday night—[22nd] June—[1812]

My dearest William,

We walked to the top of the hill this evening to meet Algernon Montagu[3] whom we had desired to bring our letters. He brought us Mary's, and upon the whole it has given us great comfort; for your and Mary Monkhouse's last had made us very uneasy about Mary; we had hoped that the letter received tonight would have fixed the time of your return; for the more we thought about it the more we were convinced, from the state in which she was, that the best thing that could be done was to come home immediately; thus getting over that fresh access of

---

[1] George Hutchinson.

[2] This letter follows *MY* pt. ii, L. 252. It is dated 21st June, but Monday was the 22nd.

[3] Basil Montagu's son.

sorrow which home will bring; and at the same time satisfying her mind respecting those particulars which disturbed her. I am afraid that our letter which you would receive on Thursday would *not* satisfy her; as she seems to have considered the action of a blister as a drain, analogous to what sore ears may in some cases be supposed to be;—whereas it was only applied in Catharine's case as an external stimulant, which *might* tend to divert the action from the Brain—but it was applied without hope. Of this I will speak after, when I have uttered what is more upon our minds, namely our earnest desire that you would come home without delay. If every thing had been managed as we had intended—if you had yourself communicated the sad tidings, or even if she had not had so long to wait in expectation of you it might we thought have been of use to her to stay a short time with her kind dear Friends, and she might have received consolation from visiting some beautiful spots in Wales with you: but it is now plain from the tenor of her letter, and the evident state of her mind, that nothing can restore her to tranquillity and chearfulness till she has got over the last sorrow of returning home;—and where all her doubts may be satisfied, which we cannot I am sure satisfy by letter. She has only consented to stay because she perceives that you *wish* it, therefore from the moment you receive this I pray you give up all thoughts of staying longer; if she appears willing to stay it is only because she cannot endure to oppose her will to yours it being always in the habit of her mind to submit, and depend upon it that she will receive no benefit; but only be rendered less capable of receiving it speedily when she returns to us. We are very anxious about her; and our anxiety must continue till we see her, knowing that she only *submits* to stay and *desires* the contrary; and our anxiety must continue till we see her.

Now my beloved Mary I will try to satisfy your doubts respecting Mr Scambler; but I almost dread to enter upon the subject being so liable to fall into inaccuracy of expression, and to misinterpretations on your part—not on your part *as* yours, but because all letters are subject to misinterpretation. Mr Scambler never said to us that he had apprehended that this would be the end—he had taken no merit himself as having foreseen it. What he said to Mrs King[1] was said long ago. With respect to the dear child's final recovery; you know my dearest Mary, that all our

---

[1] Of The Hollens, Grasmere.

questions to him were respecting her *lameness* and he spoke of her recovery from that as a thing to be *hoped* for—he never said it could not be—but it was always as if, when he spoke to me, he was yielding his judgment rather to our wishes when he said he *hoped*; for he never said he *expected*. It was from these recollections that I formed the belief, that he had had in his inner mind a fear of something much worse than the lameness—of which at the time I never had any misgivings. I do not believe that he could conceive to himself any preventative; therefore it was the wisest and the most benevolent part which he acted in keeping those fears to himself. Certainly he had no notion of a *drain* acting as a preventative. The Blister was applied as an external stimulant; and we have no reason to suppose that a perpetual Blister, or perpetual external stimulant would have prevented the disease. Perhaps it might have produced partial or general mobility. With respect to the Electricity, when we mentioned that we had the machine in the house and that we were thankful we had not used it; he said *he* was also; for he might have been apt to attribute the present seizure to the application of that stimulus; and he never had any idea that it could do her good; but this he said in the most humble, unboastful manner, as if feeling the powerlessness of all medical efforts in this case, and as if glad to seize upon any thing that could afford us consolation; and it is certain that he never had any apprehension that it would do her any harm— only he seemed to have comfort in rejoicing with us that it had not been tried; and as if he could not be so presumptuous as not to have had misgivings if it *had been tried*. To return again to the Blister. Blisters are never used as[1] drains; but to divert any evil action that there may be in the Body to another part, as in the case of inflammation in the side, in the lungs etc etc—[?][2] and issues are used as drains but I should think that all these things would have a debilitating tendency, and it has been the object of all the medical efforts and advice to strengthen Catharine. We know that many children are very subject to convulsions and may often have no bad effects; but the disease in Catharine was the paralysis—and the injury alone to the Brain was the cause of the second and last attack.—

My dearest Friends, I hope I have satisfied you. I wish I could write as plainly as I feel the truth—but I *cannot* write more, and if you are not satisfied by what I say do trust that all has been well.

[1] as *written twice.*   [2] *MS. obscure.*

If you had seen Mr Scambler—if you had seen the humility, the tenderness, the watchfulness with which he administered the medicines—if you had heard him speak with the calm confidence and satisfaction that *we* did you would have been satisfied. You could not have wished for any thing to have been different. You would have seen that it was the Will of God to take this blessing from us and that we could not prevent it by any human foresight.

—Dorothy is very well and very happy—and John is the sweetest creature in the world. John should never be alone—he appears ten thousand degrees more amiable when D is with him—takes pains with his Book, is interested in every thing—and his thoughtfulness is wonderful. He makes up, and more than makes up, in thoughtfulness what she gains in superior quickness. God bless her she is [? willed][1] as ever; but a tender spirit—reads very prettily sews well, and is industrious at her work—very good to Willy and John and they are inseparable. They work in the garden together—and get off tasks together. John goes over the old Road[2] therefore he is out of the way of the Quarry—he goes to, and returns from school equally happy with his tin Bottle over his shoulder, and his Basket in hand. Willy is very happy with Dorothy and she is very good to him—he is a sweet lively creature.—

Pray give my love to Miss Weir and tell her we are very grateful for her care of Dorothy. I can never sufficiently express my sense of the kindness she has done us. With respect to Mary Monkhouse we think it would be better for her to come with Miss Weir; both because Miss Weir will be most desirous of her presence at Hindwell, and of her company on the journey, and because it will be better for Mary to come when our dear Mary has composed her mind after her first sorrow on returning; unless Mary wishes for the consolation of Mary Monkhouse's society in the journey, in which case Miss Weir, we are sure, will chearfully give her up.

If a letter can reach us before your arrival pray write that our minds may be prepared to expect you—we always get a letter on the 4th day after it is put into the post office. Sara joins with me in kindest love to all—God bless you both my dearest Friend. God strengthen thee, my Mary—and preserve to us the blessings we yet possess! Farewell and may peace follow our meeting.

Yours evermore

D W

[1] *MS. obscure.*   [2] The road over White Moss to Ambleside.

Mrs Cookson's[1] mother is dead. She was prepared to set off to see her. Fanny's mother is still with us. We have been loath to part with her. Fanny has been very good and is an excellent servant in her present place—much better than Sarah, and far better than herself in her former place.—We like Molly very much— she appears to be an exceedingly good Girl, and of a most sweet temper, with good sense.

W. W. to ELIZABETH MONKHOUSE[2]

Address: Mrs Monkhouse, Hindwell, Radnor.
Stamp: Kendal Penny Post.
MS. WL. Hitherto unpublished.

Grasmere Sunday Dec^br 6th [1812]

My dear Madam,

I write this to you, I mean I address it to you, in consequence of having been very uneasy at having omitted your name when I wrote my last most unhappy Letter:[3] in fact, when I begged Mr Monkhouse to communicate the sad tidings to the family at Hindwell, it escaped my recollection that you were resident there. But I have already said too much of this; you cannot for a moment suppose that I could be insensible to the degree in which you would be afflicted by our loss; often have I thought of it and suffered for you much and heavily; as indeed I have suffered in some degree for every body who knew him; as no loving creature ever did without loving him.—Sweet Lamb he was laid by the side of his sister[4] yesterday, and we all support ourselves by the blessing of God better than before he died, far better than we could have ventured to hope But it is not to be concealed that our loss is dreadful, and would be insupportable but that we acknowledge in it the will of God and feel that it is our duty to submit.—None of the other three children have yet sickened and though John and Dorothy have at times after the manner of children been grievously distressed, they have also thrown off their sorrow as lightly, and are at this moment quite chearful. God grant that they pass safely through, we are not alarmed, and we repose upon God's mercy.—

---

[1] Mrs. Elizabeth Cookson, of Kendal.
[2] This letter to 'Aunt' Monkhouse follows MY pt. ii, L. 267.
[3] Announcing the death of his son Thomas on 1 Dec.
[4] Catharine, buried in Grasmere churchyard.

Sara's health has somewhat suffered; the pain in her side returned upon her last night, but it is gone to day, and I do not fear that by riding exercise, for which the weather is at present quite favorable, she will be able to keep it down.—Never child was more deeply or generally deplored than our sweet Thomas; he was the darling of old and young; his little Schoolfellows weep for him, and his new Master was stricken with heart felt sorrow when he heard that his Favorite was no more. This is a melanchdy consolation but a consolation in some degree it is; nothing however can sustain us under our affliction but reliance in God's Goodness, and a firm belief that it is for *our* Good, as we cannot doubt it was for his, that he should be removed from this sinful and troublesome world.[1] He was too good for us; we did not deserve such a blessing—and we must endeavour to correct and amend every thing that is wrong in us and our bitter sorrow will in time become sweet and kindly, and never such, at no moment such, as we should wish to part with—Farewell, best love to all—

Yours very affectionately
W. W.

W. W. to WILLIAM WHITE[2]

Address: Mr White.
MS. Cornell. Hitherto unpublished.

Rydal Mount Tues: June 22nd 1813

. . . answer well for us Both.—

Please to return my kindest regards to Mr Blakeney[3] and say that Mrs W. and I will not fail to let him know beforehand of our visit.

I am dear Sir
yours truly
Wm Wordsworth

[1] W. W.'s aunt Dorothy Cookson wrote to D. W. on 4 Jan 1813: 'Gladly would I offer consolation were it in my power to suggest any thing which the well-regulated and religious minds of your brother and sister have not had recourse to for comfort.' (WL MSS.).

[2] W. W.'s Sub-distributor of Stamps at Whitehaven. This letter follows *MY* pt. ii, L. 295.

[3] Secretary to the Whitehaven Harbour Trustees.

W. W. to UNKNOWN CORRESPONDENT[1]

MS. Cornell. Hitherto unpublished.

Rydale Mount near Ambleside
July 13th 1813.

. . . they may be returned to me at some future opportunity.—I
thought it adviseable, in order to avoid troubling the Board on
small occasions, to defer the mention of the Returned Stamp and
the mistake relative to it, till the settling of the first Quarterly
account, also [ ]² on my part to supply you punctually with
every thing that you may have occasion for—

with great regard
your humble Ser^{vnt}
Wm Wordsworth

D. W. to THOMAS DE QUINCEY[3]

MS. Brown University Library.
Mark Reed, '*Wordsworth Letters, New Items*', NQ *ccxvii* (1972), 93–6.

Sunday Eveng
[?Autumn 1813]

My dear Friend,

We are very sorry to hear that you have been so poorly. Pray if
you are well enough to come tomorrow bring yourself a pair of
slippers and stockings that you may not have to sit with wet feet.
Dorothy⁴ is quite well, and Willy has no apparent ailment but ill-
humour. John has been very languid all day; but he is better
tonight. God bless you.

believe me ever your affec^{te}
D Wordsworth

---

¹ This letter on Stamp Office business, which follows *MY* pt. ii, L. 298, is
addressed to one of W. W.'s Sub-distributors.

² *Several sentences cut away.*

³ This letter is impossible to date with any certainty, but it was written appar-
ently from Rydal Mount sometime after the deaths of W. W.'s children
Catharine and Thomas, and before De Quincey's estrangement from the
Wordsworths.

⁴ i.e. Dora W.

W. W. to WILLIAM WHITE[1]

Address: Mr White *[delivered by hand]*
MS. J. Robert Barth, S. J. Hitherto unpublished.

[1813–14]

. . . Will you also take the trouble for me to desire Mr
Sawyers[2] of the Custom House to let me know how many
parcels of Stamps he has had from me, and to give an acknowledgement for the whole amount.

> With much regard
> I am Sir
> Your obedient Ser^vnt
> Wm Wordsworth

Turn over
[ ]Find them in the list of Stock transferred from Mrs
Bulfield.[3] —W. W.

W. W. to SIR GEORGE BEAUMONT[4]

Address: To Sir George Beaumont Bart., Grosvenor Square, London.
Postmark: 27 June 1814. *Stamp*: Kendal Penny Post.
MS. Cornell. Hitherto unpublished.

Rydal Mount June 23^d [1814]

My dear Sir George,
It was very good in you to sit down and write to me at this
festive time,[5] when every head almost in London is turned topsy-
turvy by the presence of so many illustrious and distinguished

---

[1] Sub-distributor of Stamps at Whitehaven. This fragment is impossible to
date exactly, but it probably belongs to the first or second year of W. W.'s
Distributorship, which, from the date of his appointment in Apr. 1813, included
Whitehaven (see *MY* pt. ii, L.289).

[2] William Sawyers, Comptroller and Surveyor of Warehouses for the Port of
Whitehaven.

[3] Apparently Mr. White's predecessor as Sub-distributor (see L. 295).

[4] This letter follows *MY* pt. ii, L.322.

[5] Sir George Beaumont had written on 2 June about 'the morbid irritability of
my nerves which inhibits all effort.' 'Your conversation would certainly have
been a cordial to me—As it is I have the consolation to perceive that the film
which has so long blinded the public and prevented their being sensible of your
excellence is gradually dissolving—and I have no doubt will soon have 'created
the taste by which you are to be relished.' (*WL MSS*).

personages. This kindness was more than I had a right to expect; particularly as I was a Letter in your debt.—If I had not thought it right, on Mrs Wordsworth's account, to persist in my intentions of conducting her and her Sister through the most striking scenes of Scotland during this summer I should have certainly been in London at the present time. But I feel so strong a persuasion that our intended Tour will be beneficial to Mrs W's health and spirits, that I am quite reconciled to the sacrifice which I have made—Your account of Keene the actor[1] interests me much and I should have found in him not the least considerable of the attractions which London at present holds out.—I should have been very glad to fix my eyes on the veteran Blucher,[2] who has excited in me the same admiration as the body of the people seem to feel towards him. I cannot help fancying also that the King of Prussia[3] must have an impressive countenance, and with his two Sons must make an interesting spectacle.

You will be pleased to hear that Lord Lonsdale had permitted me at my request to dedicate my intended publication to him;[4] and I need not say to you that his assent was conveyed in a manner that enhanced the obligation.—Mr Lee Hunt whose 'amende honorable' you mention had not read a word of my Poems, at the time he wrote his sarcasms.[5] This I know from an

---

[1] Beaumont considered Kean 'likely to restore once more nature to the stage,' though 'I must tell you he is deficient in many qualities generally esteemed requisite to an accomplished actor—person—deportment—voice, and declamatory powers—but then he has true feeling for the quick and animating touches of nature; he makes you feel—he electrifies you.' Edmund Kean (1787–1833) had made a comeback to the stage of Drury Lane the previous January in the part of Shylock, and was now playing Richard III, one of his favourite roles.

[2] Gebhard Leberecht von Blücher (1742–1819), Prussian field marshall, had decisively defeated the French at Leipzig, and in May 1814 entered Paris with the other victorious allied commanders. He was created Prince of Wahlstadt by Frederick William III, and following the allied sovereigns to England, received the freedom of the City of London and an honorary degree at Oxford. After Napoleon's return in 1815, Blücher assumed command of the Prussian forces in Belgium and helped secure the victory at Waterloo.

[3] Frederick William III (1770–1840) reigned from 1797. His sons were Frederick William, later Frederick William IV (1795–1861), who reigned from 1840 to 1858, and William, later William I (1797–1888), who ruled as regent from 1858 and succeeded his brother as king in 1861.

[4] The Dedication to *The Excursion* took the form of a sonnet (*PW* v. 1).

[5] In *The Feast of the Poets*, first published in *The Reflector* in 1811, Leigh Hunt (1784–1859) criticised W. W. and S. T. C. for 'gath'ring the refuse that others

acquaintance of his; so that neither the censure nor the praise of such people is in *itself* of any value. It however affects the immediate sale of works, and authors who are tender of their own reputation would be glad to secure Mr Hunt's commendations. For my own part, my *dignity* absolutely requires an indifference upon this point. The Editor of the Champion (Mr De Quincey, a friend of mine informs me) is a Lawyer, and though once a desperate Enemy of mine, may become in time what the Quakers call, a convinced Friend.[1]

I agree with you, my dear Sir George, in thinking that these facts are indications that in the end I shall get the better of my foes. In what I am now going to publish I make more than one desparate assault on their prejudices; and though I doubt not that the portion of my Poem[2] now almost ready for the light will attach to me some enthusiastic admirers I am equally sure that the herd of minute critics will be astounded and thrown upon their backs, from which shock they will recover only to vent their

reject', and had Apollo drive them from the feast. Hunt's hostile remarks were largely retained in the 1814 edition, but in the Preface and Notes to the 1815 edition he made some amends, paying tribute to W. W. as 'a great living poet', and writing to him on 28 May 1815: 'Whatever may be the objections, which I have ventured to make to some parts of your poetic theory, and which perhaps would not exist with persons who felt your poetry less than myself, I am known for one of the most ardent of your general admirers, and even hope that I have not been altogether uninstrumental in procuring you some, who knew as little of you at first as I did. My objections, such as they are, still exist; but my admiration has been increased since the publication of the Excursion, and I have been delaying from day to day in hopes of sending you the second edition of a little work which [appeared] last year, and which contains a suitable increase in its mention of you.' As Haydon remarked in a letter to W. W. of 15 Apr. 1817, 'he never holds one opinion one month he does not sophisticate himself out of before the next is over' (*WL MSS.*). According to Leigh Hunt's *Autobiography* (ed. J. E. Morpurgo, 1949, pp. 253–5), W. W. called on him on 11 June 1815 'to thank me for the zeal I had shown in advocating the cause of his genius', but he continued to criticise W. W. from time to time for his poetic theories and growing conformism.

[1] W. W. began to correspond with John Scott the following year. He had been a schoolfellow of Byron's and went on to Marischal College, Aberdeen, before moving to London and employment in the War Office (and not, apparently, in the legal profession). Scott started a weekly paper *The Censor* and *Drakard's Newspaper*, the name of which was changed to *The Champion* on 2 Jan. 1814.

[2] *The Excursion* was described on the title-page as 'A Portion of *The Recluse*'.

malice more bitterly. I have dedicated to Lord Lonsdale; and I wish my very dear and honored friend, to give you some public testimony of my respect.—If you are stout enough to bear a part with me in the indignities which may yet perhaps for some time be heaped upon my miscellaneous Poems which I am going to republish, arranged in a manner that will greatly illustrate them I should be happy to inscribe the Volume with [your][1] name. They will include my share of the Lyrical Ballads and my small Pieces already published, with additions.—I have just finished the White Doe,[2] and pretty well to my satisfaction; I shall publish it shortly, and if you prefer that offering to the other, I should be happy to make it: or Peter Bell,[3] which you have condescended to illustrate by your pencil. Take your choice; but do not deny me the satisfaction I solicit—I long to see the late works of your pencil; I have very frequently before my memory the two last delightful pictures which I have seen of your execution. I live in some degree of hope that we may meet at Coleorton this Autumn; I will do my utmost to accomplish it.—I have not left myself room to say more than to thank Lady Beaumont for her account of Haydon;[4] and to mention that the title of what I am now publishing is, The Excursion, a portion of the *Recluse*. Mrs Wordsworth and my Sister unite in kindest remembrances. You do not mention your mother in your last; we therefore hope she is comfortable in her slow decline. Adieu.

Yours most faithfuly friend
W. Wordsworth

[1] *MS. torn.* For the Dedication to *Poems*, 1815, see L. 192. As the Preface (*Prose Works*, iii. 26 ff.) explained, the poems were for the first time arranged in sequences, according to a system of classification which W. W. continued to refine in subsequent editions.

[2] *The White Doe of Rylstone.* It was eventually dedicated to M. W. (see *PW* iii. 281).

[3] *Peter Bell*, eventually published in 1819, was dedicated to Southey (see *PW* ii. 331). The frontispiece was engraved by J. C. Bromley after a painting by Sir George Beaumont.

[4] Lady Beaumont had considered Haydon's 'Judgment of Solomon', exhibited this spring, to be 'a magnificent work', according to Sir George's letter of 2 June. The painting had been produced under great personal stress, and Haydon had quoted lines from 'The Happy Warrior', 'as if they had cheered him through all his stormy path.'

W. W. to D. W.[1]

Address: Miss Wordsworth, Rydal Mount, Kendal, Westmorland.
Postmark: 24 Aug. 1814.
Stamp: Alloa.
MS. WL.
Letters of William Wordsworth, ed. Alan G. Hill, *1984, p. 165 (—).*

> Perth, Sunday Morn. 10 oclock
> August 19 or 20 [1814]

My dearest Dorothy,

As our Letter from Dunkeld would inform you our Tour has advanced much more slowly than we expected. Yesterday we walked on both sides [of] the Tay; but only ascended the high ground on the side approach[ing] the Town. You have a beautiful view of the Abbey from the bridge, and see it also very pleasingly, as you walk up the river side, when you have crossed. We were unusually pleased, I should say delighted with the view from the high ground, up and down the Tay; it is magnificent and lovely at the same time.—I was much more struck with this than I recalled to have been when we saw it together.[2] Our Car met us near Rumbling Bridge, and we slept at Amelrig.[3] Passed the narrow Glen, about 8 yesterday morning—an hour too late; a very fine morning, but the Scene not so interesting as when we saw it. When we had ascended to the top of the hill we turned with the Course of the Almond towards Perth. Unfortunately we were misdirected by a Man upon the spot and went a mile and a half about, two miles and past up a steep hill instead of half a mile. Came to the Bridge of Buckarty, a beautiful little spot with a mill, Rocks and a Waterfall upon the Almond, thence 4 or five miles over a moor, an[d] rejoined the Almond, at Lyne-dock—

---

[1] This letter follows *MY* pt. ii, L. 325, and is apparently the only one of W. W.'s to have survived from the Scottish tour of 1814. Hitherto, the only sources available for this tour have been two letters of S. H. (see *SH*, pp. 71–80), and two MS. journals, the first in S. H.'s hand, the second and longer one, a reworking and expansion of the first, in M. W.'s hand (*WL MSS.*). For full details of the itinerary, which was more extensive than the tour of 1803 but less productive of poetry, see Reed, pp. 556–71. W. W., M. W. and S. H. set out on 18 July, journeying through the Borders to Glasgow and on through the western Highlands to Fort William and Inverness, returning by way of Perthshire and Edinburgh. See W. W.'s *Memorials of a Tour in Scotland, 1814 (PW* iii. 97–108).

[2] In 1803. See *DWJ* i. 358–60.

[3] i.e. Amulree.

General Graham,[1] the place from which he takes his title; visited here the burial place of Bessy Bell and Mary Gray[2], which I shall describe to you when we see you. Arrived at Perth about six, dined[3] and walked about the Town. Rose this morning at six; Mary and I walked to the summit of Kinnoul-Hill—not quite a mile and a half; and had an extensive and fine view of the course of the Tay seawards. This is a fine prospect in all directions, almost, but the sky was disturbed and threatening, and a sullen haze concealed two thirds of the prospect. We mean to stay at Perth to day; and tomorrow, weather permitting, shall go to Kinross, near Lock Leven, thence to Stirling by Clackmannon and Alloa. I do not exactly know the distance. Yesterday was much the finest day for weather we have had, the narrow Glen was less solemn than when we saw it; but very attractive, Cattle grazing peacefully along its bottom, with a [?] and sweet image of the Ideal of pastoral Life.

The Course of the Almond is naturally very interest[ing] if the Road had kept near the River, but unfortunately it shews little or nothing of it, going over a moorish Country now under a course of interesting improvement; and the River ungraciously conceal-ing itself in its own rough Bed.—Perth disappointed me, not the county which is fine, but the town, it has only two Churches, not large, with beggarly steeples, and no kind of public Buildings to crown the Body of the Town, which with the exception of these two sorry steeples, presents to view nothing but Roofs and Chimneys. There is a bridge very respectable but much inferior to the new one at Dunkeld. Dunkeld is indeed vastly improved since we saw it together and the Duke[4] is going to build a splen-did mansion. The weather was delightful from Blair to Dunkeld and the Garry, Tay and Tummel delighted us. The Tay is

---

[1] General Thomas Graham, Baron Lynedoch (1748–1843), agriculturalist and Whig M.P. for Perthshire, 1794–1807, served under Moore at Corunna, and with Wellington in the Peninsula.

[2] Figures from a popular Scottish ballad, reputedly buried in Methven church-yard. See Arthur Quiller Couch, *Oxford Book of Ballads*, 1910, p. 865.

[3] 'Perth. 6 oclock very hungry. Dinner promised in 10 minutes—and to our surprize the promise fulfilled—excellent pie delightful Salmon and capital Scotch soup etc—but as usual the bones by some former party were thrown upon the floor—in other respects a handsome and comfortable place.' (*M. W.'s MS. journal*).

[4] John Murray, 4th Duke of Atholl (1755–1830), of Blair Atholl Castle and St. Adamnan's Cottage, Dunkeld.

unquestionably the noblest river in Britain for its own dignity and the beauty and variety of the scenes it flows through.—We are sadly disheartened about the state of the weather to day, quite mortifying, as yesterday we confidently calculated upon a course of fine days, which would have carried us sure enough into Harbor at Edinburgh.—I forgot to say, that I stepped yesterday evening into a Bookseller's shop with a sneaking hope that I might hear something about the Excursion,[1] but not a word; on the contrary, inquiry of the Bookseller what a poetical parcel which he was then opening consisted of, he said, that it was a new Poem, called Lara, a most exquisite thing, supposed to be written by Lord Byron, and that all the world were running wild after it: this parcel they had down by the Coach—they had received one the day before which was carried off immediately. Now dont you think I am quite a hero not to be envious. You I assume yet bring philosophy as proof against all this. I took the book in my hand, and saw 'Jacqueline' in the same column with Lara;[2] what's this, oh said the bookseller, Jacqueline is a sweet Thing supposed to be by Rogers the author of The Pleasures of Memory. Here was another rap for poor me if I had been of the commonly supposed poetic constitution. You remember that when I wrote to Rogers last, I said that it was impossible for any honest Poet to thrive while his friend Lord B. was flourishing daily at such a rate—Here I must stop, as we are going to Church to hear the *grunting* Priest of the old Kirk. This elegant portrait is supplied by Miss H. I am better of my complaint.—

[*M. W. writes*]

Alloa Tuesday Morn 12 oClock—

Here we are my dearest D. worse beset with our old Enemy than ever—for it seems to be fairly *set in* for wet weather and we can neither stir one way or other and as we get nearer to the end of our journey we are become more impatient—Wm left off when we wanted him to go to church—but instead of the 'grunting' Scotch Priest we heard a most eloquent American travelling

[1] Publ. *c.* 17 Aug. W. W. bought from this bookseller 'a small Ed. of Ossian and the Perth Guide' (*M. W.'s MS. journal*), and probably the inscribed copy of the *Poetical Works of Burns*, 1813, now at the *WL*.

[2] Byron's *Lara* and Rogers's *Jacqueline* were published together anon. in 1814, and went through three editions in that form. H. C. R. called the one 'rather an imitation than a work by himself', and the other, 'very flat and insipid' (*HCR* i. 147).

minister with whom we were all so much impressed and delighted that we attended him again in the afternoon, when he preached in a different division of the same old Church, which has formerly been a fine old edifice but being divided and subdivided is now a sad confined place to sit in for 2 hours amid a greasy looking crowded assembly; but we were well repaid for our confinement.[1] We were sorry we could not learn any thing about this man [? who had] pleased us so much—he was more like one [of] the [ ][2] than any thing else. In the evening we walked [? to the] castle, the rain favoring us for a little while, it be[ing] sunset, but before we reached the inn it came on ag[ain as] bad as ever.[3] The morning (Monday) being fair, we de[parted] at 6 oClock and breakfasted at the Brig of Earn about 4 miles from Perth, having by the way ascended Moncrief hill (a climb of a long mile) to see an extensive prospect—in this our aim was defeated for smoking fogs veiled the distance—but we had a pleasing view of the entrance of the Earn into the Tay and the immediate country round, which is peculiarly interesting, seeing at the same time what W. says is the best part of Strathearn and parts of the vale of the Tay—a rich and fertile scene. Reached Kinross about 1 oClock—a sweet pensive place. Loch Leven is more like one of our own Lakes and the Loch of Moncrief than any of the Scotch Lochs—The island with the Castle is very beautiful[4]—a square Tower—we had a perfect view of this from the shore, so did not take a Boat—For the sake of poor Bruce the Poet[5] we felt much interested in this Vale and should have wished to have lingered longer. A Latin Epitaph in the Burying Ground occupied too much of our time which W. and S. transcribed and we did not get off on our journey to this Place, to

[1] 'West end of the old church—heard an American Minister Dr Romaine, most eloquent discourse—best Preacher we had ever heard.—Afternoon heard him again in the middle Kirk did not like him so well he ranted a little. Church full close and hot—curious rushing noise when the congregation rose and sate down . . .' (*M. W.'s MS. journal*). The minister was Dr. Jeremiah Romayne, the Calvinist divine (see also *MY* pt. ii. L. 330).

[2] *MS. tom.*

[3] According to *M. W.'s MS. journal*, their evening walk was to Scone Palace, seat of the Earls of Mansfield, and the site of the ancient Abbey.

[4] Mary Queen of Scots was imprisoned there, 1567–8.

[5] Michael Bruce (see *MY* pt. ii, L. 541), was born at Kinesswood on the eastern shore of Loch Leven, and later taught in the school at Cleish on the western shore.

which we were recommended at Glasgow in order to see fine prospects from Clackmannan Tower (a mile distant hence) Alloa Tower etc, until we were driven too late to see in our road the rumbling Brig and Cauldron Linn—at least W. only saw in a hurried way the rumbling Brig and none of us the Cauldron Linn (about these places see Currie's life of Burns and Correspondence[1]), being afraid of being benighted. Here therefore we arrived, without rain at 8 oClock, but had the mortification of passing thro' a beautiful high tract without enjoying the pleasure which a clear day would have given us.—This morning we should have walked to Clackmannan Tower to have overlooked the firth of Forth and an expanse of country, but we have no chance of seeing any thing, nor no hope of being any better when we reach Sterling (8 miles off), should we be enabled to go even that short distance in the course of the day.—We see the Forth from one of the windows of a handsome room where we are. W. is dozing over the fire, and S. reading Ossian. The Coal waggons pass under the windows from the Pits so we have the comfort of a glorious fire, and it is a very pretty place if we could but see it surrounded with roomy Gardens—nothing Scotch in its appearance, except the Church which stands opposite with its window shutters.—I should have told you before that on our return from our walk on Sunday night at Perth, W. put into my hands Wednesday's *Courier* announcing Mr Wordsworth's Poem with the Dedication[2]—We hailed it with great pleasure. It almost seems as if that Dedication had been written for the purpose of the Poem being advantageously advertized—for it answers so nicely that it will surely appear in all the Papers. We shall in all liklihood meet with the Poem at Edinburgh—if we have any luck we hope to be there the day after tomorrow at the latest. We shall be most cruelly disappointed if there is not a letter for us

[1] James Currie, M.D. (1756–1805) edited *The Works of Robert Burns*, with a Life, in 1800 (see *R.M. Cat.*, no. 480). Burns had visited Rumbling Brig and the Cauldron Linn, a cataract on the Devon river, during his tour (1787) of Clackmannan and Perthshire with Dr. James Adair, who sent Dr. Currie an account of their excursions from Clackmannan, 'to visit parts of the surrounding scenery, inferior to none in Scotland, in beauty, sublimity, and romantic interest.' (i. 170–1)

[2] The sonnet to the Earl of Lonsdale dated Rydal Mount, 29 July, 1814, can scarcely have been written during the Scottish tour: either 'July' is a mistake for 'June', or W. W. instructed Longman's to date it as nearly as possible to the proposed date of publication.

at Sterling[1]—we hoped for one at Perth.—With respect to rain we have been most unlucky, for while we were in the Western Highlands they had nothing but westerly winds here, which are always accompanied with fair weather. Now the wind is in the east and rain must follow—

Sarah says it is going to brighten, but I do not see any such prospect—God bless you! S. says J. Carter is to mind to hoe all about the Brocoli well—Kiss the darlings—I hope to have a letter from John[2] at Edinburgh—Yours M.W.

We hope to be able to depart from E.[3] on the third day. Shall probably go by Peebles and Melross to Kelso[4] and return by Jedbro' and Hawick to Langholm.[5] So write either to Melross or Kelso.

[1] They reached Stirling on 24 Aug. and went on to Falkirk and Linlithgow. 'The view of Sterling Castle looking back from Falkirk road very fine. Passed through the pleasure grounds of Callender house. No mud huts, yet still the women without hats and the children bare-foot. Falkirk a dirty old Town with a new Spire in the midst built by the Inhabitants for ornament. Some interesting monuments in the churchyard—Linlithgow—The Castle—Church—Fountain— A very neat comfortable new Inn—but all the town dirty and old—remains of former splendor . . .' (*M. W.'s MS. journal*).

[2] John W. had accompanied them on their outward journey as far as Burnfoot on the Esk, where he was left with the Miss Malcolms (see *MY* pt. ii, Ls. 304 and 354), to attend the local school (see *SH*, pp. 73–4), until their return *c*. 4 Sept.

[3] They arrived in Edinburgh on 25 Aug. and left on the 30th, having met 'all the *wits* who were in town' at Mrs. Wilson's, the mother of John Wilson of Elleray. These included his youngest brother James Wilson, the naturalist (see *LY* pt. iv. L. 1671), R. P. Gillies (see *MY* pt. ii, L. 333), James Hogg, the 'Ettrick Shepherd', Charles Kirkpatrick Sharpe (1781?–1851), the antiquarian and friend of Scott, J. M. Lappenberg, the German historian (see *LY* pt. iii, L. 1060), and Lord Buchan (see *MW*, p. 19). Excursions included Holyrood House, a walk up Corstophine Hill, and a visit to Roslin Chapel and Castle. See Robert Pearce Gillies, *Memoirs of a Literary Veteran*, 3 vols., 1851, ii. 142–4.

[4] At Traquhair they fell in with Dr. Robert Anderson (see *MY* pt. ii, L. 326) and James Hogg, who undertook to conduct them to the Yarrow which W. W. and D. W. had left 'unvisited' in 1803. See *PW* iii. 450–1; *The Works of the Ettrick Shepherd*, ed. T. Thomson, 2 vols., 1865–6, ii. 463; and James Russell, *Reminiscences of Yarrow*, 2nd edn. 1894, pp. 198–9. W. W.'s poem 'Yarrow Visited' (*PW* iii. 106) was probably begun the same day (1 Sept.). On 2 Sept. W. W., M. W. and S. H. breakfasted with Mrs. Scott at Abbotsford (Scott himself being away in the Shetlands), visited Melrose Abbey, and went on to have lunch with Lord Buchan at Dryburgh Abbey, before journeying along the Tweed to Kelso, where they passed the night.

[5] W. W., M. W. and S. H. arrived home on 9 Sept., having collected John W. from the Malcolms', to find that James Hogg had already arrived at Rydal

½ past 4 oclock—we have seen a sort of half view from the Towers—the rain continues and we despair of getting to Sterling tonight.

Britain[1] continues to perform very well and is a great favorite, but in spite of all our care and good feeding he is grown thin—he has never failed to eat his corn chearfully and never once been in a sweat but the hot day we went to Glasgow.

W. W. to ABIGAIL HODGSON[2]

Address: To Abigail Hodgson, 21 Great George Street, Liverpool. [*In M. W.'s hand*]

MS. Ray Collection, Pierpont Morgan Library. Hitherto unpublished.

Rydal Mount near Ambleside
September 26th 1814.

Madam,

I have ever been indifferent to the opinions of professed Critics concerning my writings; and as much as I have slighted these, even so much have I been accustomed to value the judgements of persons speaking or writing from their hearts and inner spirit. From these sources have flowed the language which you have addressed to me; it could not therefore but be acceptable; and I sincerely thank you, for the assurances which (through means of your Letter) I have received from one who is a stranger to me, that in my Poem of the 'Excursion', I have moved the affections and excited the Imagination to salutary purposes. Assurances of this kind given by Friends, however judicious, are liable to a suspicion of personal particularity, but when they proceed from Strangers an Author is convinced that it is the book and the book

Mount. Two days later was the dinner party at which Hogg supposed himself to have been slighted by W. W. (see *LY* pt. ii, L. 693).

[1] The horse, which was drawing their jaunting-car.

[2] This letter follows *MY* pt. ii, L. 327. The addressee is unidentified and may not have been a permanent resident in Liverpool, and her letter to W. W. has not survived. W. W. was to receive a similar letter in praise of *The Excursion* from the minor novelist Letitia Matilda Hawkins, who as a young woman had known Dr. Johnson. She wrote from Twickenham on 27 June 1815: '. . . in all the sincerity of a Christian and with the gratitude of a traveller directed on his way, I from my heart join the many who, whatever be the worldly success of your labour, must have cause, and I hope the will, to acknowledge the benefit you have offered to the world.' (*WL MSS.*).

alone to which he is indebted for the tribute of gratitude and praise which he receives. Great, then, must be the pleasure, when, as in the present case, there is accompanying evidence that fervent admiration is the result of comprehensive thought, and feelings at once deep and delicately discriminative.—

I have only to add that if you should ever be led to revisit the scenes which have proved delightful[1] to you, I hope you will not pass my door without favoring me with a call. With deep esteem and regard I remain

Madam
Your sincere friend
Wm Wordsworth

W. W. to ROBERT PEARCE GILLIES[2]

Address: R. P. Gillies Esqre, 3 King Street, Edinburgh. [*In M. W.'s hand*]
Postmark: 23 Nov. 1814.
MS. Miss Lisa Jean Duncan.[3]
Gillies(—). *K(*—).

Rydal Mount Nov^{br} 23^d 1814

My dear Sir,

You must have feared that notwithstanding your care the parcel has not reached its destination; I have however the gratification of saying that it arrived punctually at Kendal. That we did not receive it in due time was owing entirely to the neglect of our worthy friends, in that place, to whom it was consigned.—On my return from Whitehaven, yesterday, I found it here, and beg you to accept my sincere thanks for the pleasure it has already afforded me. Had I not imagined, so much delay having already taken place, that you would be under some anxiety to hear of its arrival, I should have deferred writing, till I had perused the whole of its contents; at present I have only glanced over the several Volumes, here and there. I have to thank you also for Egbert,[4] which is pleasingly and vigorously written, and

---

[1] *Written* delighted.

[2] Part of this letter was published as *MY* pt. ii, L. 334. For Gillies, see also the I. F. note, *PW* iii. 425. [3] Since sold.

[4] *Egbert, or, The Suicide*, publ. in *Illustrations of the Poetical Character in six Tales*, 2nd edn. enlarged, 1816.

proves that with a due sacrifice of exertion you will be capable of performing things that will have a strong claim upon the regards of posterity.—But keep I pray you to the great models; there is in some parts of this tale particularly page 4th too much of a bad writer, Lord Byron; and I will observe that towards the conclusion, the intervention of the Peasant is not only unnecessary, but injurious to the tale, inasmuch as it takes away from that species of credibility on which it rests. The Peasant does nothing; and by making him a hearer of the intercourse between the Demon and the Suicide, he becomes responsible for an account which the reader would readily receive upon the Poet's authority, but which he feels inclined to reject when thus superfluously vouched for, or attested. Besides, there are no incidents in the previous part of the story nor is there any thing in the character of the distress of the Sufferers, which fits him or his fate for being introduced with rustic or popular superstitions. I have peeped into the Ruminator,[1] and turned to your first Letter, which is well executed, and seizes the attention very agreeably. Your Poem[2] I have barely looked into, but I promise myself no inconsiderable pleasure in the perusal of this.

I thank you for the Queen's Wake;[3] since I saw you in Edinburgh I have read it. It does Mr Hogg great credit. Of the tales, I liked best, much the best, the Witch of Fife, the former part of Kilmenie, and the Abbot Mackinnon. Mr H– himself I remember, seemed most partial to Mary Scott: though he thought it too long. For my own part, though I always deem the opinion of an able Writer upon his own works entitled to consideration, I cannot agree with Mr H– in this preference. The story of Mary Scott appears to me extremely improbable, and not

---

[1] *The Ruminator: containing a series of moral, critical, and sentimental essays* by R. P. Gillies and Sir Egerton Brydges (see *MY* pt. ii, L. 334; *LY* pt. i, L. 145, pt. ii, Ls. 474, 754, 792, and pt. iii, Ls. 888, 963). Gillies's essay on the delights of solitude, which W. W. commends here, was criticised by Byron for dwelling too much on 'sensibility'. 'This young man can know nothing of life; and, if he cherishes the disposition which runs through his papers, will become useless, and, perhaps, not ever a poet, after all, which he seems determined to be.' (*Byron's Letters and Journals*, ed. Leslie A. Marchand, 12 vols., 1973–82, iii. 217).

[2] *Childe Alarique, a poet's reverie, with other poems*, 1814.

[3] *The Queen's Wake: a legendary poem* by James Hogg, author of *The Private Memoirs and Confessions of a Justified Sinner*, anon. 1824. Byron had recommended it for publication to John Murray the previous year.

skillfully conducted—besides, the style of the piece is often vicious.—The intermediate parts of the Queen's Wake are done with much spirit; but the style here also is often disfigured by false finery, and in too many places it recalls Mr Scott to one's mind. Mr Hogg has too much genius to require that support however respectable in itself. As to Style, if I had an opportunity I should like to converse with you thereupon. Such is your sensibility and your power of mind, that I am sure I could induce you to abandon many favorite modes of speech—for example, why should you write, Where the lake gleams beneath the *autumn Sun*, instead of 'the autumnal', surely much more natural and harmonious. We say '*summer* Sun', because we have no adjective termination for that season; but vernal and autumnal are both unexceptionable words. Miss Seward[1] uses 'hybernal', and I think it is to be regretted that the word is not familiar. But these discussions render a letter extremely dull. I sent the alterations of Yarrow Visited[2] to Miss Hutchinson and my Sister, in Wales, who think them great improvements, and are delighted with the Poem as it now stands. Second parts if much inferior to the first, are always disgusting, and as I had succeeded in Yarrow Unvisited,[3] I was anxious that there should be no more falling off; but that was unavoidable perhaps, from the subject: as Imagination almost always transcends reality.—I remain, hoping that you will excuse this most hasty scrawl, with great regard and respect yours most truly

Wm Wordsworth

Pray say to Mr Hogg that the printing of my two volumes, of which both the Yarrows are a part, advances so [?rapidly][4] that there is no probability of its answering his purpose. If I write any thing else in time for his publication I shall [?send] it.[5]

---

[1] The 'Swan of Lichfield' (see *MY* pt. ii, L. 334).

[2] Begun 1 or 2 Sept. (see *SH*, p. 79) and publ. in *Poems*, 2 vols., 1815. W. W. had now revised the poem (see *MY* pt. ii, L. 333), having sent an earlier version to Hogg for inclusion in a projected miscellany, which never appeared.

[3] *PW* iii. 83, written during the Scottish tour of 1803.

[4] *Word blotted.*

[5] Hogg abandoned the project, but later produced a volume of parodies of modern poets, including W. W. (see letter to Charles Lamb below, 21 Nov. 1816).

W. W. to JOHN EDWARDS[1]

MS. *Arizona State University Library*.
Mark Reed, 'Wordsworth Letters, New Items', *NQ ccxvii* (1972), 93–6.

[*c.* 20 Mar. 1815]

My dear Sir

I take up the pen (meaning merely to scrawl a few words) in order that you may be put in the way of receiving my Poems,[2] about to be published, without expense. On the other side, you will find an order to that effect; which I hope you will be able to make use of in such a manner, as that the books may be received by you without costing you a penny, if possible. I cannot bear that after laying out so large a sum as two guineas [upon] the Excursion,[3] you should have to pay any thing [ ] I thank you for your most [ ] domestic [ ][4] Mr Montgomery's praise was highly grateful to me—pray tell him so when you write; and add that I am happy to have repayed in kind the great pleasure which his writings have afforded me.—Excuse extreme haste. The White Doe[5] is mine. Let me hear from you at your leisure.

And believe me with great respect
And sincere regard
Your friend
W Wordsworth

W. W. to MESSRS. LONGMAN AND CO.

MS. *Cornell. Hitherto unpublished.*

Rydal March 29th [1815]

[*In M.W.'s hand*]

Mr Wordsworth requests Messrs Longman and Co to give to the Bearer Mr Monkhouse[6] a Copy of his Poems.

---

[1] Of Derby (see *MY* pt. i, L.219). This letter, and the next one, follow *MY* pt. ii, L. 357.   [2] *Poems*, 2 vols., 1815.

[3] Edwards's recent letter to W.W., received at Rydal Mount on 15 Mar., had been full of praise for *The Excursion*, and had cited Montgomery's equally high estimate of the poem. D.W. had quoted both views in letters to C.C. and S.H. (see Ls. 353 and 357).   [4] *Several lines torn away.*

[5] *The White Doe of Rystone* was finally published this year.

[6] See M.W.'s letter to Thomas Monkhouse, *MW*, p. 29. This slip was presumably enclosed with the letter.

W. W. to WILLIAM WILBERFORCE[1]

Address: William Wilberforce Esqr, Kensington Gore [*readdressed to*] Mr Hatchard, Bookseller, Piccadilly.
Postmark: 20 May 1815.
Endorsed: Mr Wordsworth asks vote for his friend Mr Southey Candidate for office of Phys^n to Mdx Hospital.
MS. Bodleian Library. Hitherto unpublished.

May 20th [1815]
24 Edward Street
Cavendish Sq^{re}

Mr W. Wordsworth presents his Comp^{ts} to Mr Wilberforce and takes the liberty of soliciting his vote for the vacant place of Physician to the Middlesex Hospital[2] (if not preengaged) for Mr Wordsworth's Friend Dr Southey,[3] Brother of the Poet. Mr Wordsworth cannot help taking this opportunity to express his regret that there is little chance of finding a day on which Mr Wilberforce may be disengaged, to give him the pleasure of meeting him at Sir George and Lady Beaumont's, as his stay in Town will not be more than a fortnight.

---

[1] This letter follows *MY* pt. ii, L. 366. W. W. met Wilberforce for the first time during this visit to London, though Wilberforce was a College friend of his uncle William Cookson's and D. W. had known him at Forncett in 1790 (see *EY*, L. 8). It was perhaps with that contact in mind that W. W. had included Wilberforce among the 'persons of eminence' to whom he sent complimentary copies of the 2nd edn. of *Lyrical Ballads* (see *EY*, Appendix vi). Wilberforce wrote to W. W. on 23 May, accepting Lady Beaumont's invitation to meet him at Grosvenor Square ('I have resolved to claim what I hope you will admit as the right, grounded in our many common friends, to become acquainted with you by the earliest practicable means'), and inviting him to breakfast. (*WL MSS.*).

[2] One of the 'new' 18th century hospitals in London, built 1755–75 by James Paine (1716–89), the Palladian country-house architect.

[3] Dr. Henry Herbert Southey, now in practice in Queen Anne Street. He had probably called on the Wordsworths since their return from escorting Hartley Coleridge to Oxford (see Curry, ii. 122). Wilberforce agreed to support his candidature 'if I could thereby gratify the Poet Southey.'

W. W. to WILLIAM WILBERFORCE[1]

Address: William Wilberforce Esq[re], Kensington Gore.
Postmark: 25 May 1815.
Endorsed: M[r] Wordsworth.
MS. Bodleian Library. Hitherto unpublished.

24th May 1815
24 Edward Street
Cavendish Sq[re]

My dear Sir,

I am very sorry that I am engaged for breakfast every day this week, although on Friday only conditionally. If on that day Mr Heber[2] and Mr Walter Scott[3] should be at liberty, I am under promise to meet them at Sir George Beaumont's to breakfast, thence to proceed to the City with Sir George and Lady Beaumont to view an original Portrait of Milton[4] (a very fine one) recently rescued from the dust of a Broker's Shop.—

If this arrangement cannot be effected, it will give me great pleasure to wait upon you on Friday, otherwise I must defer that gratification till Monday Morning[5]—In the mean while permit me to thank you for your most kind note, and to express my regret on account of your illness, and earnest wishes for your speedy and perfect recovery.

I have the honor to be
my dear Sir
With great respect
Your obedient Ser[vt]
W[m] Wordsworth

---

[1] This letter follows *MY* pt. ii, L. 368.

[2] Richard Heber, the book collector.

[3] According to Lockhart, Scott returned to Edinburgh on the 22nd, but L. 368 to Scott, which Scott sent on to Heber with a covering note on the 25th, shows that Scott was staying on in London for several days more.

[4] See *LY* pt. i, L. 47.

[5] According to Wilberforce's Diary, W. W. breakfasted with him on the 29th, 'and it being the first time, staid long'; and on 9 June Wilberforce dined at Sir George Beaumont's to meet W. W., who was 'very manly, sensible, and full of knowledge, but independent almost to *rudeness*.' (R. I. Wilberforce and Samuel Wilberforce, *The Life of William Wilberforce*, 5 vols., 1838, iv. 260.)

W. W. to MESSRS. LONGMAN AND CO.[1]

MS. Bodleian Library. Hitherto unpublished.

[late Apr. 1816]

This Letter is very correctly printed, and the Author begs that what remains to be done of the Poetry,[2] may be as carefully executed; as he does not wish the Publication to be delayed by being sent down a 2nd time. The Parcel was 6 days on the road instead of two.

W. W. to J. COLIN SATTERTHWAITE[3]

Endorsed: Copy of Agreement between Mr Wordsworth and Mr Satterthwaite concerning St. Leonard's.
MS. Transcript in private collection. Hitherto unpublished.
Copy

To J.C. Satterthwaite Esqr   Cockermouth 3^d Octr 1816

D Sir

I agree to let you the small Field late the Property of my deceased Brother Wordsworth for the Term of Seven Years from Candlemas next, at the annual Rent of Seventeen Pounds, reserv-

---

[1] A note on p. 37 of the corrected proof sheets of *A Letter to a Friend of Robert Burns* (*Prose Works*, iii. 111 ff.), which follows *MY* pt. ii, L. 399. W. W.'s *Letter* seems to have been published on 1 May (hence the dating of this letter), and formed a considered response to James Gray's invitation on 28 Nov. 1815 (*WL MSS.*) to set out his views: 'In a conversation that passed at your house respecting Burns I was delighted, tho not surprised to discover that you were one of the few individuals I had met who had taken a true view of the character of that extraordinary man. I am happy now to be able to inform you that his brother Gilbert, a man of sound head and some skill in composition is about to undertake a vindication of the Poets name from the calumnies of Reviewers and pamphleteers. . . . I repeated to him some of the remarks you had made, which struck him so much that he is exceedingly desirous of obtaining your opinion as to the best mode of conducting the defence.' James Gray (d.1830), a schoolmaster at the Edinburgh High School (1801–22) and subsequently at the Belfast Academy, wrote on 19 Jan. 1823 (*WL MSS.*) recalling their friendship and his abiding love of W. W.'s poems: 'The Excursion has long been familiar to me and over its sublime and moral page I have often found a solace amid the evils that are inseparable from life.'

[2] *Thanksgiving Ode, January 18, 1816. With Other Short Pieces*, which also appeared this May.

[3] This letter about the administration of the late R.W.'s estate, follows *MY* pt. ii, L. 419. See also Ls. 421 and 429.

ing to myself the Power to sell it, at any time I please on condition of my granting you a Lease for the said Term of Seven Years which I promise to do.

Wm Wordsworth

W. W. to CHARLES LAMB[1]

MS. WL.
Letters of William Wordsworth, ed. Alan G. Hill, 1984, p. 195.

Rydal Mount 21st Nov^r [1816]

Dear Lamb,

Miss H. writes that you may *read*.[2]—W. H.[3] is much such a drawer of characters, as, judging from the specimens of art which he has left in this country, he is a portrait painter. He tried his hand upon me. My brother Richard happened to come into the room where his work was suspended, saw, stopt, I believe recoiled, and exclaimed *God Zounds*! a criticism as emphatic as it was concise. He was literally *struck* with the strength of the sign-board likeness; but never, till that moment, had he conceived that so much of the diabolical lurked under the innocent features of his quondam playmate, and respected Friend and dear Brother. Devils may be divided into two large classes, first, the malignant and mischievous,—those who are bent upon all of evil-doing that is prayed against in the Litany; and secondly those which have so thorough a sense of their own damnation, and the misery consequent upon it, as to be incapable of labouring a thought injurious to the tranquility of others. The pencil of W. H. is potent in delineating both kinds of physiognomy. My Portrait was an example of the one; and a Picture of Coleridge, now in existence at Keswick (mine has been burnt) is of the other. This piece of art is not producable for fear of fatal consequences to married

---

[1] This letter follows *MY* pt. ii, L. 426. See also Winifred Courtney, 'Lamb and Hazlitt, 1816–1826; Some Notes to a Relationship', *Charles Lamb Bulletin*, July 1988.

[2] Lamb had recently complained about W. W.'s handwriting: 'Your manual graphy is terrible, dark as Lycophron . . . Well, God bless you and continue to give you power to write with a finger of power upon our hearts what you fail to impress in corresponding lucidness upon our outward eyesight.' (*Lamb*, ii. 187–8).

[3] William Hazlitt, who had painted portraits of W. W. and S. T. C. for Sir George Beaumont in 1803. See *LY* pt. ii, L. 612a, and Griggs, ii. 957–8, 960.

Ladies, but is kept in a private room, as a special treat to those who may wish to sup upon horrors. As H. served the person of Coleridge, fifteen[1] years ago, now has he served his mind;[2] a likeness, it must be acknowledged there is, but one takes refuge from the spectacle in detestation (in this latter instance) of the malevolence by which the montrous caricature was elaborated.

By the bye, an event has lately occured in our neighbourhood which would raise the character of its population in the estimation of that roving God Pan, who some years ago made his appearance among us.[3] You will recollect, and Mr Henry Robinson will more easily recollect, that a little Friend of our's was profuse in praises of the 'more than beauty'—'the angelic sweetness'—that pervaded the features of a fair young Cottager dwelling upon the banks of Rydal mere.[4] To be brief, Love and opportunity have wrought so much upon the tender frame of this terrestrial angel, that, to the surprize of Gods, Men, and Matrons, she has lately brought forth a Man child to be known, and honored, by the name of *William*, and so called for a deceased Brother[5] of its acknowledging Father Thomas de Q–. Such, in these later times, are the fruits of philosophy ripening under the shelter of our Arcadian mountains. A marriage is expected by some; but, from the known procrastination of one of the parties, it is not looked for by others till the commencement of the millenium. In the meanwhile he has a proud employment in nursing the new-born.

Let me hear that the Shoemaker has not bullied you out of your intention of completing the meditated Essays.[6] Southey, of

[1] In fact, thirteen.

[2] In the *Examiner* of 8 Sept. 1816, Hazlitt had anticipated the forthcoming publication of the *Statesman's Manual* by launching an abusive personal attack on S. T. C. as 'the Dog in the Manger of literature'. Earlier, in the *Examiner* of 2 June, 1816, he had denigrated the *Christabel* volume. See Griggs, iv. 669, 685, 700; *Lamb*, ii. 195–6.

[3] A jocular reference, apparently, to Hazlitt's escapades at Grasmere in autumn 1803, for which see *HCR* i. 169.

[4] Margaret Simpson of the Nab, whom De Quincey married the following Feb. H. C. R., who had paid his first visit to Rydal the previous Sept., noted that 'though Wordsworth was reserved on the subject,' De Quincey 'has entangled himself in an unfortunate *acquaintance* with a woman.' See *HCR* i. 187, 195–6.

[5] William, De Quincey's domineering eldest brother, who died at the age of 15, is recalled in his *Autobiography* (*Works*, ed. Masson, 1. 58 ff.).

[6] Lamb had written on 23 Sept.: 'Gifford (whom God curse) has persuaded squinting Murray (whom may God not bless) not to accede to an offer Field

whom H. affects to talk contemptuously, beats us all hollow in interesting and productive power.[1] If he reads, if he talks, if he is talked to, he turns it all to account: behold! it is upon paper, it is in print; and the whole world reads, or many read it, sure of being always entertained, and often instructed. If the attainment of just notions be an evidence of ability, Southey will be cherished by posterity when the reputation of those, who now so insolently decry him, will be rotted away and dispersed upon the winds. I wish to hear from you, and not unfrequently. You are better off than we—inasmuch as London contains one person whose conversation is worth listening to—whereas here we are in an utter desert, notwithstanding we have a very amiable and edifying Parson; an intelligent Doctor; an honest Attorney (for he is without practice), a Lady of the Manor, who has a Spice of the romantic; Landscape Painters who are fraught with admiration, at least of their own walls; Irish Refugees, and Liverpool Bankrupts, without number.—Have you seen a thing advertized called the *Poetic Mirror*?[2] a parody which selects, as a Subject for my Muse, 'The flying Taylor'. You will call to mind that I told you there was a person, in this neighbourhood, who from his agility, had acquired this name—hence a thought crossed my mind that the Author of this *Skit*[3] might be of your acquaintance; but as he has

made for me to print 2 vols. of essays, to include the one on Hogarth, and 1 or 2 more, but most of the matter to be new, but I dare say I should never have found time to make them . . .' (*Lamb*, ii. 197). The essays were published, with poems, as *The Works of Charles Lamb* in 2 vols. by Charles and James Ollier in 1818.

[1] 'How is Southey?—' Lamb had asked, 'I hope his pen will continue to move many years smoothly and continuously for all the rubs of the rogue Examiner. A pertinacious foul-mouthed villain it is!' Southey had recently published *The Poet's Pilgrimage to Waterloo*, and was about to bring out the 2nd vol. of his *History of Brazil*, as well as his regular contributions to the *Quarterly*. See also *MY* pt. ii, L. 447.

[2] By James Hogg (see L. 333), a series of parodies of Byron, Scott, Wordsworth, Southey, Coleridge, John Wilson, and Hogg himself. W. W. was represented by three blank verse pieces, *The Stranger*, *The Flying Tailor*, and *James Rigg*, each described as 'a further portion of *The Recluse*'. Hogg thought he had been slighted by W. W. during his visit to Rydal Mount in Sept. 1814 (see *LY* pt. ii, L. 693), but he later came to believe that De Quincey's account of the alleged affront was less than trustworthy, and W. W. himself later dismissed it as 'silly'. His lasting admiration for Hogg was recorded in his *Extempore Effusion upon the Death of James Hogg* (see *LY* pt. iii, Ls. 947–8).

[3] A new colloquialism (the first recorded instance in this sense in the *O.E.D.* is 1820).

selected *three* Scotish Poets—Hogg, Scott, and Wilson—to the exclusion of English ones of near equal eminence and more merit, I conclude that he is some Sawney ayont the Tweed, who has been resident in this Country and probably about the time when the annual sports[1] bring the flying Taylor into notice. To conclude—I remain, in good health, and not bad spirits notwithstanding the bad weather and hard times,

Your friend to command,
[*signed*] Wm Wordsworth

W. W. to JOHN MAY[2]

Endorsed: 1817 Rydale Mount 1st June Wm Wordsworth rec^d 4th d^o. ans^d 30th d^o
    as by copy annexed and letter of 24th do^o, C. B. f° 249.
MS Cornell. Hitherto unpublished.

Rydal Mount
near Ambleside.
June 1st 1817

Dear Sir

It gives me pleasure to say that I have a £1000 which will be at the service of Mr Southey, on unexceptionable Mortgage security being furnished.

I do not know exactly how the Property which Mr S. wishes to purchase at Keswick is circumstanced, but I apprehend that difficulties may be found in procuring a satisfactory Title.

Mrs Wordsworth returns her thanks for your obliging recollections. She begs her kind regards. Hoping that our mutual Friend may not be disappointed in his views upon the Property at Keswick, I remain dear Sir

With much respect
very truly yours
Wm Wordsworth

[1] The Grasmere sports in September.

[2] This letter, and the next one, follow *MY* pt. ii, L. 451. John May (1775–1856), Southey's early benefactor and lifelong friend, whom he first met at Lisbon in 1796, came of a prosperous family of wine merchants which suffered losses as a result of the French occupation of Portugal. He lived at first in affluent circumstances at Richmond, but later on his fortunes declined, and in 1827 he went to manage a bank in Bristol. In May 1817, Southey was planning to buy Greta Hall, which he held on a lease, and during his absence on the Continent he had entrusted the negotiations to W. W. and John May. See also L. 455.

W. W. to THOMAS HUTTON[1]

Address: Thomas Hutton Esq., Sol[r], Penrith.
MS. Private Collection. Hitherto unpublished.

> Rydal Mount
> 1817 June 2nd

My dear Sir,

Mr Lightfoot[2] has called upon me here: he submits the following Proposal to my consideration.

'I propose to pay Mr Hutton the Expenses already incurred down and to give a cognovit with stay of Execution untill the first of August.'

> John Lightfoot
> 2nd June 1817

In answer I have to say; that supposing, as was my Brother's wish, you were acting as joint Executor with me, and you yourself, under the circumstances would then have acceded to this proposal, I hereby accede to it, but not otherwise, leaving the conduct of the business to your superior judgement.—

> I am my dear Sir
> with great respect
> very truly yours
> W[m] Wordsworth

W. W. to JOHN TAYLOR[3]

Address: To John Taylor Esq[re], Sun Newspaper, Office, Strand, London.
Postmark: 14 Mar. 1818. *Stamp*: Kendal.
MS. Massachusetts Historical Society.
David Bonnell Green, 'Wordsworth in the Westmorland Election of 1818: A New Letter to John Taylor', *MLR lxii(1967), 606–7.*

> Rydal Mount near Kendall
> March 10th 1818

My dear Sir,

Do you happen to know, or can you find out, any person competent to undertake the management of a weekly News

---

[1] A letter about the administration of the late R. W.'s estate.
[2] The Keswick attorney who later married R. W.'s widow.
[3] Editor of *The Sun*. This letter follows *MY* pt. ii, L. 481.

paper?[1] Certain Gentlemen Inhabitants of Kendal and its neighbourhood are desirous of setting up a Paper in that Town upon
constitutional Principles, to counteract a Journal which has done
much harm by pervading public opinion in this County—If you
know of a Person who would suit them be so good as to write to
Mr Harrison[2] Surgeon Kendal, and I should esteem it as a favor
done to myself—They propose a Salary of 150 per ann.

Their expectations will be stated below.—

I remain my dear Sir
very faithfully yours
Wm Wordsworth

W. W. to BENJAMIN ROBERT HAYDON[3]

MS. Kenneth Spencer Research Library, University of Kansas.
Hitherto unpublished.

Rydal Mount
Sept^{br} 2 1818

My dear Sir,

Having an opportunity of procuring a Frank, I write to inquire
after your health and pursuits, and to remind you of the beautiful
drawing[4] of which my head was at least the 'motive' and which
you so kindly presented to Mrs Wordsworth. We long to have it
in our possession, and it will be most welcome when you can
spare it—I wrote *conveniently* spare it, but struck the word out,
least you should interpret it too liberally.

—I have to thank you for an interesting pamphlet, on the new
churches,[5] received some time ago. I fear the Age is not

---

[1] The proposed *Westmorland Gazette*, launched in May in opposition to the
Kendal Chronicle (see Ls. 494 and 503).

[2] See L. 476. Harrison wrote to Taylor the next day with details of the post.
The editor was expected 'to arrange the matter:—write the Summary of Politics
and such observations as may be necessary and to revise the Press. If he would
engage in any other part of the management so much the better.' (*Massachusetts
Historical Society MSS.*).

[3] This letter follows *MY* pt. ii, L. 504.   [4] See L. 571.

[5] *New churches considered with respect to the opportunities they afford for the encouragement of Painting*, 1818, in which Haydon had argued that the provision of altar
pieces should be an integral part of the building programme of the Church
Commission. 'It is not mere decoration, senseless ornament we want', he wrote
in his *Diary*, 'no, but we wish to combine painting, music, and prayer, that when

sufficiently liberal to act upon your proposal.—Sir George and Lady Beaumont are at Keswick—the former uncommonly well—Lady B. I am sorry to say yet something of an invalid. Collins[1] is there.—Do let me hear from you soon, and tell me how you are, and how the Crest comes on. We have been immersed in politics in West^nd—

ever my dear Sir
faithfully yours
W. Wordsworth

W. W. to UNKNOWN CORRESPONDENT[2]

MS. untraced.
Bookseller's Catalogue.

[*In M. W.'s hand*]

Rydal Mount
15 Sep. 1818

I thank you for your prompt reply to my enquiries concerning the Publications in your hands, the results of which do not differ from what I expected. I will avail myself of your kind offer for them to remain some time longer with you;—but as I have not for a considerable space of time had any communication with the Person to whom you allude, I must beg that you will not in future consider him as being connected with this arrangement.

[cetera desunt]

the soul is turned to a holy musing by the solemn roar of the organ, its pious feelings may receive additional warmth by contemplating the actions of the Divine founder. Is such a consequence to be classed as a mere decoration, with the efforts of the house-painter, the white-washer, and the carpenter?' (*Diary*, ed. Pope, ii. 189). Though favourably noticed by Southey in the *Quarterly* for July 1820, however, Haydon's proposals made little headway with the Government.

[1] William Collins, R. A.

[2] This letter, which follows *MY* pt.ii, L. 505, seems to be addressed to a bookseller, and perhaps concerns the remaining stock of W. W.'s *Two Addresses to the Freeholders of Westmorland*.

W. W. to [? THOMAS HUTTON]¹

MS. WL. Hitherto unpublished.

[*c.* 1 Oct. 1818]

My dear Sir,
    I have not replied to this Letter from Mr Rudd, but supposing that the demand is proper, I shall write to him to day, apprizing him that the admittance may be forwarded to you, and that you will pay the money—

[*unsigned*]

W. W. to GEORGE TICKNOR²

MS. Baker Library, Dartmouth College.
Judson Stanley Lyon, 'Wordsworth and Ticknor', PMLA lxvi(1951), 432–40.

[late Apr. 1819]

Dear Sir,
    I am afraid you will have thought me more ready at promise than performance; in fact I have been absent from home, and very much engaged, so you must excuse me.—
    I cannot make out every particular respecting my profits. But I am confident not reckoning £100, from the White Doe, a very

---

¹ This note, which probably follows *MY* pt. ii, L. 509, is written on a letter of William Rudd, the Cockermouth attorney, to W. W., dated 29 Sept. 1818, about the sale of a portion of the late R. W.'s lands to Southey's friend, Major Humphrey Senhouse of Netherhall.

² The American author (see *MY* pt. ii, L. 520), who had visited W. W. on 21 Mar., noted his 'grave and tranquil manner, a Roman caste of appearance, and Roman dignity and simplicity', and D. W.'s 'spirit' and 'more than common talent and knowledge'. W. W. showed him the manuscript of *The Prelude*, and read out *Peter Bell*, 'a long tale, with many beauties but much greater defects; and another similar story "The Waggoner" . . . The whole amused me a good deal; it was a specimen of the lake life, doctrines, and manners, more perfect than I had found at Southey's, and, as such, very curious.' Later, they discussed Scott, Campbell and Byron: 'For Campbell he did not seem to have so much regard; and for Lord Byron none at all, since,—though he admired his talent, he seemed to have a deep-rooted abhorrence of his character, and besides, I thought, felt a little bitterness against him for having taken something of his own *lakish* manner lately, and, what is worse, borrowed some of his thoughts. On the whole, however, he seemd fairly disposed to do justice to his contemporaries and rivals.' (*Life, Letters, and Journals of George Ticknor*, Boston, 1876, i. 287–8). This letter follows *MY* pt. ii, L. 542.

bad bargain for the Bookseller, that the nett amount, little, if at all, exceeds 250.—

Peter Bell is gone to the Press.[1]

What a pity your stay with us was so short.[2] The weather is charming, and the fields now as green as Emerald. Not venturing to hope that we shall ever meet again in this world, whatever be my wishes, and praying that you may find all your friends well and arrive happily in your Country

I remain dear Sir
Very truly yours
Wm Wordsworth

Mrs Wordsworth and my sister I see, both send their best wishes.—

Your House of Representatives, and your *good* City of York, have, both taken up the Ruffian Jackson.[3] America would be a

---

[1] Ticknor had written on 11 Apr. (*WL MSS.*) to enquire about the publication of *Peter Bell*, now finally to appear in its revised form (see *SH*, p. 46).

[2] In his letter Ticknor recalled his recent visit to Rydal Mount: 'When I was so hospitably entertained under your roof, we talked a good deal of American literature and the progress the knowledge and letters of the old world are making in the new; and you seemed curious to see the style in which we reprint European Books.' And he sent with his letter (or separately) a copy of Obelin's Tacitus, 'as a very honest specimen of the style of our Press,' i.e. *Caius Cornelius Tacitus qualem omni parte illustratum postremo publicavit J. J. Obelin, cui postremas ejusdem annotationes et selecta variorum additamenta subjunxit* J. Naudet, 1819. This was perhaps the American book referred to in *LY* pt. iii, L. 1089, but it is not recorded in any of the lists of W. W.'s library, and was possibly given to John W. in the poet's lifetime. Jérémie Jacques Obelin (1735–1806), Professor of Latin at Strasburg from 1770, published philological works and editions of Ovid, Horace, Tacitus (Leipzig, 1801), and Caesar.

[3] Andrew Jackson (1767–1845), President of the United States from 1828, made his mark in frontier politics in Tennessee, and later defended New Orleans against the British (1815), thereby becoming a national hero. In 1818 he was accused of exceeding his authority in the Seminole war against the Indians in Florida by occupying Spanish territory, hanging two British subjects, and making one of his subordinates military governor of the area. His expansionist aims thereafter made him a controversial figure in Democratic politics. W. W. had voiced his fears of Jackson's ambitions to another American visitor, the Quaker scientist John Griscom (1774–1852), on 21 Apr.: 'The proceedings of a certain general in the Seminole war, appear to have left a strong impression upon his mind, of danger from this quarter; and there are certainly many persons, taking into view the conduct of this individual in relation to the Indians, that will not wonder at those impressions.' (John Griscom, *A Year in Europe, Comprising a Journal of Observations ... in 1818 and 1819*, 2 vols., New York, 1824, ii. 332).

charming region were it peopled with such men as your Self and Alston.

Do not, I pray you, read the poem[1] which I send to Mr Als [ton] (at least in England) to any of your Friends who may be writers of Verse.

W. W. to VISCOUNT LOWTHER[2]

Address: To The Lord Viscount Lowther, London.
Stamp: Kendal Penny Post.
MS. Lonsdale MSS. Hitherto unpublished.

[mid–Oct. 1819]

My dear Lord Lowther,

The Beauties of Cobbet, announced in your Note have just arrived. Neither Cobbett nor Paine are, I think, much known in this neighbourhood through the medium, at least, of their own writings—but I will take care to disperse the books where they are most likely to be of use.—[3]

George Mackereth[4] (you probably recollect him) Parish Clerk of Grasmere, and a respectable Yeoman is anxious to have a Granddaughter of his admitted into the West[nd] School.[5] There are six fatherless children two of whom he has taken to his own

---

[1] 'Composed upon an Evening of extraordinary Splendour and Beauty' (*PW* iv. 10).

[2] This undated letter probably follows *MY* pt. ii, L. 560.

[3] *The Beauties of Cobbett*, 1819, consisted of extracts from the earlier writings of William Cobbett, designed to discredit him. The second part provided 'instructive observations' on Tom Paine's *Age of Reason*, 1793, which had recently been reissued as part of his *Theological Works* in 1818. The following year, Richard Carlile (1790–1843), the radical freethinker, brought out Paine's *Political and Miscellaneous Works*, with a Life, and he was subsequently prosecuted and imprisoned at Dorchester for six years (1819–25), issuing his paper *The Republican* from prison. Earlier, he had attracted the attention of government by distributing Jonathan Wooler's *Black Dwarf* (1817) and by printing and selling Southey's early republican drama *Wat Tyler*.

[4] See L. 304. He voted for the Lowther candidates in the 1820 and 1826 elections.

[5] The Free Grammar School in Appleby, of medieval origins, was refounded in 1574 by Queen Elizabeth, and had a special connection with Queen's College, Oxford.

house; and some of the others will probably prove burthernsome to him, so that his claim is strong. He is a Freeholder, and a staunch Yellow, being one of those in Grasmere who wishes also to turn over a Freehold to his Son (a business in which I am sorry to say no progress has yet been made, though it has been mentioned several times to Johnson[1]).—This worthy man being informed that there are several Votes in the Lowther family begged me to mention this case to your Lordship or to Lord Lonsdale, which I promised to do.—

I am sorry for Mrs Luff's disappointment;[2] she is truly sensible of your kind exertions, as indeed are we all.—

The legislative measures likely to be adopted by Parliament,[3] promise to be effectual.—That which relates to exacting previous security from Publishers to meet possible penalties, I think is called for by the times; but I exceedingly regret that it was not proposed for a *limited* period. I cannot reconcile myself to the notion of this being made permanently part of the Law of this Country. Every body rejects with horror the idea of a government licence for the circulation of thought; and surely this regulation is of the same character; it *prejudges*, it presumes that the circulation of the opinions or reasonings of *poor* men must upon the whole be *unavoidably mischievous*. This is surely an unpalatable doctrine; I like it neither as a man nor an Englishman, and wish earnestly that when an enactment grounded on this principle was proposed, a hope had been held out by making its operation limited as to duration, that we may hereafter get rid of it.—A Report has just reached me that the Radicals have attempted to seize the arms in the Castle at Carlisle!—the sooner these deluded men take such courses the better. Your reference to the Poll-Book

---

[1] The Kendal attorney (see L. 471).

[2] She had applied for a pension. See L. 565.

[3] To curb the freedom of the press. See L. 564. 'The abuses of the press are so various', Lord Lowther wrote in answer to W. W.'s misgivings in this letter, 'the means of evading the laws so ingenious, that most vigorous enactments are necessary. Indeed no Gov^t could exist, with the present licence and latitude of the press. The publishers are either beggars or prefer going to Gaol instead of paying. So to check the inundation of Blasphemy Treason and Sedition, some such permanent law is necessary.—Cobbett—Wooler's Black Dwarf—The Republican—The Cap of Liberty—The Medusa—Black Book—and a list as long as the daily papers sell weekly for 20, to 30,000 copies. This cannot be endured.' (*WL MSS.*).

completely destroys every plea for a County meeting being held at Kendal—I was not aware of the fact it establishes.—

> I remain my dear Lord Lowther
> very faithfully your friend
> Wm Wordsworth

Mr. Johnson has this morning called; he has prepared the writings[1] for the Grasmere Freeholders above mentioned.—

The Form put into my hands is,

Westmorland School

The favor of your vote and interest is solicited for the ensuing Vacancy in the Institution for Lucy Mackereth aged 7 years daughter of Mary Mackereth, a Widow, having a family of six Children totally unprovided for.

recommended by
Stephen Cleasby.[2]

W. W. to WILLIAM WESTALL[3]

Address: William Westall Esqre, No 11 Seymour Crescent, Somers Town. [*In M. W.'s hand*]

Postmark: 25 Nov. 1819. *Stamp*: Holborn.
MS. Wesleyan University Library, Middletown, Connecticut. Hitherto unpublished.

Rydal Mount 22nd November [1819]

My dear Sir,

I cannot see that Mr Stephens' family[4] will be benefited in the way you propose. In the first place nothing can be done publickly without the sanction of the nearest Relations on both sides, and specially of those of them who undertake to act for the children.—A *public* subscription, I cannot but think, would tend if it had any success to slacken efforts which would be much more permanently serviceable. Mr Stephens had the rank of a Gentleman, and a thing of that sort would lower the family very much, so that people would be less likely to exert themselves to

---

[1] i.e. the applications for enrolment as freeholders.

[2] Stephen Cleasby (d. 1844), of Warcop, nr. Appleby: a prosperous Russia broker in Broad Street, London, and father of Richard Cleasby (1797–1847), the Icelandic scholar.   [3] The artist. This letter follows *MY* pt. ii, L. 562.

[4] See Ls. 562 and 565, and *SH*, pp. 160, 166.

place the children in respectable situations. The most effectual way of serving the family, in my humble opinion would be through the medium of public establishments; not but that something might be done without discredit by subscription in a private way. I shall write this day to Mr Crackanthorp[1] and to my Brother; and I will take care to mention the case to Lord Lonsdale, as soon as I am fully acquainted with it. The merits of Mr Stephens, especially in the earlier part of his life were great; but, I assure you, the belief is general that he was intemperate in the use of liquor; and that principally from this cause the School latterly became under his management, a sinecure. This unfavorable impression is another objection to a public subscription.—

You may depend upon it that I will do every thing in my slender power to serve his poor family, for whose condition I assure you I feel much. If you are in correspondence with those of his Relations who act on behalf of the deceased, pray say as much to them; and if they can point out any way in which I can serve the orphans, beg them to do so.

In the mean while my dear Westall, with best regards from all here I remain

sincerely yours
W Wordsworth

P. S.—I enclose Mr Harrison's[2] Letter to me.—

On reconsidering the subject I have determined to write to Mr Bland,[3] to learn what is doing, so that you need not address the Relations of the orphans on my account.

[*D. W. writes*]

My Brother has set me to correct his illegible letter. I fear you will have had hard work to read it after all.

With best wishes believe me truly
yours
D Wordsworth

---

[1] William Crackanthorpe of Newbiggin Hall, W. W.'s cousin, had been a pupil at Sedbergh.

[2] Probably Thomas Harrison, the Kendal surgeon.

[3] The Revd. Miles Bland, D.D., F.R.S. (1786–1868), mathematician, and a former pupil of the school: Fellow and tutor of St. John's College, Cambridge, from 1808, rector of Lilley, Herts., from 1823, and Prebendary of Wells from 1826.

W. W. to FRANCIS WRANGHAM[1]

MS. untraced.
Bookseller's Catalogue.

Rydal Mount
Dec 17th 1819

My dear Wrangham,

Do exert yourself in behalf of poor Stephens's family,[2] of which you have an account on the opposite side.—In about 3 weeks time there will be a sale of his Books at Kendal; Catalogues are to be had of Miss Stephens,[3] Dress Maker, 39 St James's place, if you wish for any thing I could procure for you.—

I am afraid my last Scrawl perplexed you; be assured I am always happy to hear from you; and you should hear often from me and at greater length if I was an endurable Penman. As you are a Reader of and contributor to Blackwood's Mag. you probably have read Peter's Letters,[4] which is undoubtedly from some of the Conductors of that Journal—A friend of mine wrote this motto in a copy I happened to see.

> Here's a braw Scots what say you to that?
> And here's another as good as that,
> And here the best of a' the three,
> And there's my Lord Provost of Auld Reekie!![5]

With best wishes for yourself and yours I remain my dear Wrangham

Your faithful friend
W. Wordsworth

---

[1] This letter follows *MY* pt. ii, L. 564.

[2] The orphans of the late headmaster of Sedbergh.

[3] William Stevens's sister, a dressmaker in London, who was to care for two of her orphaned nieces (see *MW*, p. 54).

[4] *Peter's Letters to His Kinsfolk*, 1819, by Peter Morris the Odontist, the pseudonym of John Gibson Lockhart (1794–1854), Sir Walter Scott's future son-in-law and biographer, and editor of the *Quarterly Review* from 1825. Lockhart had begun to write for *Blackwood's* in 1817, and some of the material in this volume was probably supplied by John Wilson, 'Christopher North'. According to S. H., it was 'a most audacious and unprincipled performance—full of gossip and personality—and contradictions' (*SH*, p. 166), but it contained a notable appreciation of W. W.'s poetry in the eleventh 'letter'.

[5] S. H. also quotes this epigram, without indicating the author.

W. W. TO THE COMMISSIONERS OF STAMPS[1]

Address: To The Hon'ble Commissioners, Stamp Office, London.
Postmark: 8 Jan. 1820.
Stamp: Kendal Penny Post.
Endorsed: Wm Wordsworth Rydal Mount Ambleside 4 Jan[ry] 1820 rec[d] from the
    Board 8 Jan/20. Ansd—10th Jany 1820—
MS. Public Record Office. Hitherto unpublished.

[*In John Carter's hand*]

Rydal Mount, Ambleside
4 Jany 1820—

Hon'ble Sirs,

That I may be enabled to give the intended effect to the
Directions Contained in your Circular Letter respecting the Legacy
Duties, I must beg to be informed, whether, in cases of Receipts
being returned from *my* Office, for correction, without having
been forwarded to the Head Office, it will be proper to insert such
Rec[ts] if not duly returned, in my Quarterly Account of Rec[ts] (not
received back from the Parties) returned from the *Head* Office.

I beg leave to state that my monthly Parcel of Receipts was
forwarded Today.

> I have the Honor to be,
> Honorable Sirs,
> Your obedient Servant,
> [signed] Wm Wordsworth

W. W. to MESSRS. LONGMAN AND CO.[2]

Address: To Mess[rs] Longman and Co, Peternoster Row, London.
Postmark: 15 Apr. 1820.
Stamp: Kendal Penny Post.
Endorsed: W. Wordsworth 11 Ap[l] 1820.
MS. Archives of the Longman Group Ltd. Hitherto unpublished.

Apr 11th [1820]

Dear Sirs,

Will you please to transmit the following additional corrections
and Errata[3] to the Printer without delay. My Brother, and Sister

---

[1] This letter follows *MY* pt. ii, L.567. Like other letters to the Commissioners,
it may possibly have been drafted by John Carter, and only signed by W. W.

[2] This letter follows *MY* pt. ii, L. 580.

[3] For *The River Duddon* volume, 1820 (see L. 583).

(who is now in London) will speak to you about reprinting my miscellaneous Poems. I had agreed with them that they should be printed in 3 vol. the same size as the last Edition—but I prefer a smaller size in 4 vols.[1] and likewise a Paper more of a cream colour than has recently been used. Shew my Sister a copy of Southey's Madoc,[2] one of those pages contains as many lines, without being crowded, as my two volumes, which are so much larger size.

> I am Sirs yours etc
> W Wordsworth

Announce in the Ad: the Topographical description of the lakes.

Page 61 two lines from the bottom dele 'and'
62 for 'Birkett's' read Burkitt's,[3]
79 to be yet again, Disparted dele comma after again
127 first line dele comma after 'claw,'
158 'woods and crags;' for the semicolon substitute a comma
200 'beams of light;' substitute a comma for the semicolon
208 2ᵈ line for 'and Power' read, with power

W. W. to UNKNOWN CORRESPONDENT[4]

MS. Mr. W. Hugh Peal. Hitherto unpublished.

> Rydal Mount
> 1ˢᵗ May 1820

Sir,

It is several weeks since I was honored by the Receipt of a small Volume of Poems from your hand: but happening to be called from home immediately after, I was prevented reading them with such care as they appeared to require previous to my returning thanks for this agreeable mark of your attention.—I have since perused them more than once with much pleasure; the tendency is more than good—it is excellent, the Spirit they

---

[1] The *Miscellaneous Poems* in 4 vols. appeared in the autumn.

[2] Publ. 1805.

[3] From W. W.'s *Memoir of the Rev. Robert Walker*, appended to *The River Duddon* sonnets (see *PW* iii. 518). William Burkitt (1650–1703), the Biblical commentator, was vicar of Dedham, Essex, from 1692. His *Expository Notes* appeared posthumously in 1724 and was frequently reissued up to W. W.'s own time. But the spelling of his name here was not corrected.

[4] This letter follows *MY* pt. ii, L. 584.

breathe pure and amiable, and the execution is pleasing. I should be insensible, were it not gratifying to me to learn, both from the Elegant Sonnet you have addressed to the Author of the Excursion, and from other pages of your little Volume, that my Labours had won your approbation, and been to you a source of profitable pleasure.—

You will excuse me, if having been ever of opinion, that, in order to be a good Poet it is necessary to be a good Man, I differ from you in respect to the Genius of the Author of Don Juan. With Lord B's private life I have nothing to do—I know nothing of it—but confining our notice to his *Works*, it cannot be questioned that they afford abundant proofs of sensual, corrupt, and malignant propensities. The Soul, and with the Soul, the Genius, suffers as these prevail. This is the ordinance of Providence. The fabrics which Lord B. has raised are unsound in their foundations and perishable in their materials; can he be, then, a *discerning* Spirit that will work under such conditions, and to such ends— and in what is blindness but incapacity? This misguided power, is want of Power.—Bring *his* pathos and *his* sublimity to the test by placing them side by side with what successive ages have pronounced to be genuine, and this spurious character will appear at once.

I do not expect immediate acquiescence with this censure; but I am confident that such will be the decision of Posterity.

I am Sir respectfully
your obliged h^{ble} Ser^{vnt}
[*signature cut away*]

D. W. to CHARLES LLOYD SNR.[1]

Address: To Charles Lloyd Esqre, Birmingham.
Postmark: 26 May 1820.
Endorsed: Dorothy Wordsworth 26/5 1820.
MS. Mr. W. N. Tolfree. Hitherto unpublished.

Lambeth Friday 26th May 1820.

My dear Sir,
I am happy to have it in my power to tell you that your Son-in-law is we trust recovering, though slowly. I should have

---

[1] This letter follows *MY* pt. ii, L. 592. D. W. had been staying with C. W. at the rectory, Lambeth, since early Apr. For his father-in-law, Charles Lloyd, snr., the Quaker banker and Classical scholar, see also L. 379.

written to you before, but that, in the beginning of his illness, I was unwilling to communicate painful tidings without the consolation, at the same time, of assuring you that he was getting better: and afterwards, (judging that you must have heard of us through your Son and Daughter)[1] I thought it unnecessary to write till I could say something comfortable, which, thank God! I can now do. The fever is abated; his head is much more easy; and he has had three better nights, with some sleep in the course of them, a blessing which did not visit him for five nights at the commencement of his illness. The medical attendants do not expect a speedy restoration to perfect health, and strength, slow fevers being such *hanging lingering* disorders; but they consider my Brother is *convalescent*. The most perfect quiet, and abstinence from all thoughts connected with business have been strictly injoined; and, indeed, he has suffered too much pain in the head, and has felt too much of oppression and weakness to have any desire to depart from the rules of the Physician.

Most likely you have seen my Brother William and his Wife ere this: they talked of setting off from Rydal last Monday; but I have not yet heard whether they fulfilled their intention. I addressed a letter to them a few days ago at your house,[2] to tell them that it was desireable that they should go into lodgings on their first coming to London, and not come hither, as they had designed. You may be sure it has hurt my Brother C^r not a little that he cannot receive them at Lambeth.—

—This very moment I have been reading a note from your Daughter-in-law Sophia, which tells me that you are coming to the Yearly Meeting: but that Charles had informed you that my Brother was not in a state to receive you as a constant guest here. How grievous this is! When we were at Birmingham you thought you should not come to the Yearly Meeting: but on hearing, a while ago, that there was some prospect of your coming, you can hardly imagine how much I was pleased—and this is the end of it! but I have little doubt of [my][3] Brother's being able to see you, and converse with you without injury in your quiet way, and I trust, though you will not be resident at the Rectory, nothing will prevent you attending the Meeting. It will be a great pleasure to me to see you. I shall not communicate Mrs C. Lloyd's note to my Brother till tomorrow morning, the time

---

[1] Charles and Sophia Lloyd.   [2] At Bingley, Birmingham.
[3] *MS. torn.*

when we give him his letters, because I know it will worry him to think that you cannot come at once to Lambeth.

I was very grateful to my kind Friend, your wife, for her letter; but sorry that she should have troubled herself with writing to me: for I recollect, when I was at Birmingham, she spoke of it as one of the infirmities of her years that letter-writing had become troublesome to her. Tell her, if she will promise not to answer my letter I will write to her again when I have seen my Nephews, her Grand-children.[1]

With best regards to every member of your good Family whom I have the pleasure of knowing, believe me, my dear Sir,

your grateful and affectionate Friend
Dorothy Wordsworth

The Boys *were* to have come home last Saturday for the Whitsuntide holidays: but we wrote to prevent their coming, on account of their Father's illness.

D. W. to CHARLES LLOYD SNR.[2]

Address: To Charles Lloyd Esqre, Birmingham.
Postmark: 31 May [18]20.
Endorsed: D. Wordsworth 30/5 1820.
MS. Mr. W. N. Tolfree. Hitherto unpublished.

May 30th, 1820
Lambeth, Rectory House.

My dear Sir,

Since I wrote to you my Brother[3] had had no serious relapse; therefore I may say that he has been in the way of amendment, but the progress is so very slow as to be scarcely perceptible. He is now, however, allowed to take a little light animal food, and a small portion of wine; and the Physician hopes soon to be able to administer the Bark, and if this agrees with him, I hope we may see him advance with better speed then hitherto.

My Brother is very sorry (and I heartily join with him in this regret) that you have been prevented by want of strength from undertaking to attend at the Yearly meeting; yet it is matter of congratulation that you are not suffering under bodily disease at

---

[1] i.e. C. W.'s sons, John, Charles, and Christopher.
[2] This letter follows *MY* pt. ii, L. 594.   [3] C. W.

present; and I trust the little loss of strength which you speak of may be owing to the bad cold and cough you had, not long ago.

Be so good as to keep my letter addressed to Mrs Wm Wordsworth till her arrival at Birmingham. It was her intention and my Brother's to leave Rydal a fortnight ago and to spend one day at Birmingham in their way to London: and I wrote to apprize them that my Brother Chris^r on account of his illness, could not, at their first coming, receive them as inmates in his house. I do not know whether they are still at Rydal or not; for I received a letter from my Sister written last Wednesday, in which she said she *hoped* they might be able to set off the next day; but were quite uncertain, as they had been detained by a return of the inflammation in my Brother's eyes, and, till this was abated, they could not venture upon the journey. You may be sure I am not a little anxious to hear that the eyes are better.

Pray make my kind regards to Mrs Lloyd. I have no news for her respecting her Grand-children, excepting that they were well when we last heard. I shall not see them till the holidays, when I hope their dear Father will be well enough to enjoy their company.

My Brother has not yet seen any one; and he wholly abstains from all business.

He begs to be most kindly remembered to you, to Mrs Lloyd, and all your Family; and I can assure you for him, (which I know will be a great satisfaction to you) that he is disposed to take great care of himself.

I remain, dear Sir,
your obliged and faithful Friend
Dorothy Wordsworth

D. W. to HENRY HANDLEY NORRIS[1]

MS. untraced.
Bookseller's Catalogue.

[Lambeth]
[early June 1820]

. . . anxieties, and I shall rejoice with you all in Mrs Norris's perfect recovery, and your Brother's.[2]

My Brother William and Mrs Wordsworth are now in this house; but as there was a little access of fever the day before yesterday, and as my B^r (D^r W) was a little worried yesterday he will not see them today. I think he has never been quite so comfortable as this morning since the commencement of his illness.

With earnest wishes for the Return of health and spirits to all the members of your Families, believe me, dear Sir

faithfully yours
Dorothy Wordsworth

If you do not hear from me again for two or three days, conclude that we go on well.

W. W. to SIR FRANCIS LEGATT CHANTREY[3]

Address:—Chantry Esqre, Belgrave Place, Pimlico.
Postmark: 10 Nov. 1820. *Stamp:* Holborn.
MS. Lilly Library, Indiana University. Hitherto unpublished.

76 Oxford Street
Thursday Novr 8th [1820]

[*In M. W.'s hand*]

My dear Sir,

This morn^g I have arrived from the Continent—be so kind as let me know when it would suit you that I should call; with a

---

[1] This letter follows *MY* pt. ii, L. 595. For Henry Handley Norris, the Hackney high-churchman, see *LY* pt. i, L. 135. He was prominent in the S. P. C. K. and the *British Critic*, published pamphlets on church issues, and was commonly called 'the Bishop-maker' on account of the influence he reputedly exerted on Lord Liverpool's appointments to vacant sees.

[2] The reference is probably to his brother-in-law Archdeacon Watson (see *LY* pt. iii, L. 1048).

[3] This letter follows *MY* pt. ii, L. 609. For Sir Francis Chantrey and his bust of W. W., see L. 598.

181

view to your completing the Bust. Mrs W. and my Sister join me in best regards to yourself and Mrs Chantry.

> Believe me d^r Sir
> very respectfully yours
> [*signed*] W. Wordsworth

M. W. to LADY BEAUMONT[1]

Address: To Lady Beaumont, Coleorton Hall, Ashby de la Zouch. Lecestershire. Single Sheet.
Stamp: Kendal Penny Post.
MS. Pierpont Morgan Library.
K(—).

Feb^ry 5th 1823

My dear Lady Beaumont,

I have delayed sending you the Poem, and also to reply to your last kind letter, in the hope of being able to speak decisively about the intended visit to Coleorton, but your letter to my Sister rec^d this morning causes me to reproach myself for having done so—as I cannot even now give the answer I could wish—and I might, time since have prevented your imagining that our Silence was occasioned by anxiety on William's[2] account.— Thank God he is now going on well and with reasonable attention, we are full of trust that he may continue to do so—Notwithstanding which, there are other reasons, that I need not trouble you with, which make W. unwilling to leave home just now—therefore my dear Lady B. as the time of your going to London draws so near I fear our expected pleasure must be deferred—altho' I have the utmost confidence that the delight it would be to W. to see Sir George and yourself at Coleorton would be of *infinite service to him*—he wants a little relaxation, and not being able, from the state of his eyes, to read himself, stands more in need of a change of society. This being my own deep feeling as well as my Sister's, we cannot but ardently even yet hope that after the receipt of a letter which he is daily expecting, upon business, he may determine to fulfil his first intention.

We rejoice to find that Sir George and you have passed the winter hitherto so comfortably—long may good health permit

---

[1] Part of this letter was printed as *LY* pt. i, L.93.   [2] Willy W.

you to do so! We too have been much interested and gratified by Southey's book[1]—we shall lose no time to communicate your report and desires to him—He did speak of going Southwards in Feb[ry] but I have heard nothing of it lately.

M[rs] C. and Sara have been some time at Highgate. She wrote soon after their arrival there, and gave a chearful account of C. She spoke of going into Devonshire about the middle of March—We seldom see Hartley, but as we hear little of him, and that little in his favour, we hope he is spending his time to some good purpose—but as to the discipline of Mr Dawes' School, that cannot much restrain him, as I believe there are not more than four Boys.

You have before now heard that there was no truth in the paragraph stating Ld Lonsdale's second accident—we saw it contradicted, after W. had written, as you had done, to Lady L. It must be a bad feeling that can invent these things—we were all made very uneasy by it.

I hope the verses will afford you pleasure. Her Ladyship wrote a very proper reply when they were sent to her—but how far they may have power to act as a 'peace-offering' we much doubt, but heartily wish they may.—The severe weather has put a stop to all progress with the work—if you or Sir George could send us any hints, or sketch for a chapel that would look well in this situation, it is possible that we could have it made useful—through her agents.[2] We are very anxious that nothing should be done to disfigure the Village—they might, good taste directing them, add much to its beauty. The site chosen is the orchard opposite the door leading to the lower waterfall.—

My Sister will write to you shortly. She is very well, my Sister Sarah not quite so—tho' she is only waiting for a companion to induce her to set out at this Season for London. She is going to visit M[r] and M[rs] Monkhouse[3]—M[rs] M. is confined to her couch by a spinal weakness. We have been much delighted by many of Charles Lamb's essays lately published from the London Mag: under the title of 'Elia'[4]—altho there is much to object to [in] many of his statements.—Adieu d[r] Lady Beaumont with best

---

[1] The first volume of his *History of the Peninsular War* (see L. 61).

[2] The architect finally chosen was George Webster of Kendal (see letter of 18 Feb. 1826, below), but his building failed to satisfy W. W. It was eventually enlarged in 1884.

[3] M. W.'s cousins, in Gloucester Place, off Portman Square.

[4] See also L. 87.

wishes from all around me believe me very sincerely and affly your obliged M. Wordsworth.

P.S. It is long since we have heard of good Mrs Fermor,[1]—I trust she is well?

[Enclosed is a copy in M. W.'s hand of the second version of To the Lady le Fleming *composed upon seeing the Foundation preparing for the erection of a Chapel in the Village of Rydal Jan*ry *1823, as in PW iii. 165, with the omission of the fifth stanza, added later, and with the MS. variants noted in app.crit.]*

W. W. to THE COMMISSIONERS OF STAMPS[2]

MS. Public Record Office. Hitherto unpublished.

2 Jan. 1824

[In John Carter's hand]

I have to express my regret that I did not when the Receipts were sent up, require a *written* statement from the Party setting forth the cause of the mutilation, which I am sorry for as the late Subdistributor might have erased the Receipt for the duty without injuring the Form.

Wm Wordsworth[3]

W. W. to HENRY TESHMAKER THOMPSON[4]

Address: H. T. Thompson Esqr, Castle, Cockermouth.
MS. Record Office, Carlisle. Hitherto unpublished.
[In M. W.'s hand]

Rydal Mount Tuesday
Jany 12th [1824]

Sir,

Your obliging letter was not delivered to me till the Coach had passed for Cockermouth this morng, so that I could not reply to

---

[1] Lady Beaumont's sister.

[2] This letter, which follows *LY* pt. i, L. 121, refers to a case of mutilation to a form of legacy discharges.

[3] Signed by John Carter on W. W.'s behalf.

[4] Lord Egremont's agent at Cockermouth Castle (see *LY* pt. i, L. 124). This letter follows L. 122.

it earlier. I shall be glad to see you on Friday, or any other day that may suit you.

My Clerk is a ready and correct Arithmetician and will be happy to do every thing necessary in drawing out the accounts, and other parts of the business which he perfectly understands.

We have a bed at your service which I shall be much disappointed if you do not make use of, and should you have a day to spare I shall be happy to shew you any thing in our beautiful neighbourhood if the weather continues as favourable as at present.

With many thanks for your invitation to the Castle,[1] which I shall with pleasure profit by on some future occasion.

I am Sir very sincerely your obliged S^t
[*signed*] Wm Wordsworth

[*W. W. writes*]

I have been obliged to employ an Amanuensis on account of an inflammation in my eyes.—I have directed my clerk to write you also by Post, in fear this might not be punctually delivered.

W. W. and D. W. to THOMAS and CATHERINE CLARKSON[2]

Address: Thomas Clarkson Esqre, Playford Hall, Ipswich.
Postmark: 20 Mar. 1824.
Endorsed: W. W. 20 March 1824.
MS. Cornell.
Ronald Tetreault, 'Wordsworth on Enthusiasm: A New Letter to Thomas Clarkson on the Slavery Question', MP, lxxv (1977), 53–8.

67 Gloucester Place
20th March [1824]

My dear Friend

Your letter was forwarded to me from Rydal. Sincerely do I congratulate you on having health strength and spirits to go through so much in so good a cause, and also upon the favorable dispositions which you found every where existing.—

---

[1] Cockermouth Castle was besieged and dismantled by the parliamentary forces during the Civil War, but the gate-house and a set of adjoining rooms had been restored as an occasional residence for Lord Egremont.

[2] This letter, written from Thomas Monkhouse's London residence, follows *LY* pt. i, L. 129.

As probably you have learned from Mrs Clarkson, I could make little use of the Papers your Society[1] sent me. We have no Quakers at Ambleside, nor any Species of Dissenters, and no coffee house where People meet and talk on Politics and public measures; the Papers were therefore sent partly to Kendal and partly to Hawkshead, except a Copy of Each which I gave to the Man who keeps the circulating library to send to any persons whom he thought they might interest.—

I shall not return to West^nd in time to be of use in the matter of the petition; which I do not regret because nobody at Ambleside appeared in the least interested in the question; and really, anxiously as I desire to see the condition of the Negroes improved, and slavery abolished,[2] I feel the Question involved in so many difficulties, that I am inclined to leave it to the discretion of the Government. The Petitions you are so desirous of obtaining may be of use in giving Ministers courage to act up to their own wishes; but is it not possible that those very petitions may make the Negroes impatient under their present condition; and excite them to disturbance. I should like much to have the benefit of your knowledge on this subject.

Be so good as mention to Mrs Clarkson that I called at the Post off. Oxford;[3] but found no letter from her. I could not have been of any use; knowing nobody in that Place.

Ever my dear Friend
most faithfully yours
Wm Wordsworth

[*D. W. writes*]
  To Mrs Clarkson

My dear Friend,

As my Brother has told you, he knows no influential persons at Oxford—his sole acquaintances are in New College and with a few other young men, but we should have called on your Friend had we known where to find him. We left Coleorton on Tuesday after a very pleasant residence and had a delightful jour-

---

[1] The Anti-slavery Society had been formed the previous year, with Clarkson and Wilberforce as vice-presidents.

[2] In 1823 Clarkson had published *Thoughts on the Necessity for improving the Condition of the Slaves in the British Colonies, with a view to their ultimate emancipation*. For W. W.'s view on the issue, see *LY* pt. ii, L. 755.

[3] W. W. and D. W. had been visiting John W. at New College.

ney hither—saw Mrs Lloyd[1] at [? Bingley]—she all at sixes and sevens—removing—no beds for us—hardly one for herself and Daughter—going to Versailles—Charles somewhat better—very happy under his present delusions and this is an alleviation of his affliction. We arrived here last night—and now (12 o'clock) are going to see Mrs Luff. Poor Mrs M[2] is confined to the Sofa, but is, and *looks* very well. Not so her Husband. I never saw him look so ill. He has been harassed with Partnership business. I think W^m and he will go to Lea Priory[3] for a few days next week in hopes that country air may mend him. Your account of y^r eyes distressed me much. I know not exactly when Easter holidays end; but I think I shall be ready to come to you about the 3rd week in April—certainly not sooner. I fear William will not be able to accompany me I wish he could though but for a few days, but he will be anxious to get home. When I have seen Mrs Luff I shall know more of your plans but I do not like the notion of your *giving up* your London journey for my sake. Perhaps you will go a little *later?*—On second thoughts perhaps it will be the last week of April before I am ready—but all our plans are uncertain except that we take Doro with us to Cambridge, that I must stay with her till she leaves and that the approaching Musical festival would certainly drive us away, but of this festival I knew nothing till Mrs Lloyd told us—nor do I know when it is to be—Perhaps (nay probably) not till some time after our visit would of itself be ended—God bless you dearest friend—Ever your affec^{te}—D. Wordsworth. In greatest possible haste. John well and happy at Oxford. We go to Hendon tomorrow to see Doro—and she must stay there till her father comes back from Lee.

W. W. to LORD LONSDALE[4]

MS. Lonsdale MSS. Hitherto unpublished.

[*In M. W.'s hand*]

Rydal Mount Decr 6th 1824

My Lord,

As I shall have to trouble you at some length, to spare your eyes, and indeed my own are not in their best state, I am induced to employ Mrs W. as my Amanuensis.

---

[1] Mrs. Charles Lloyd and her family were about to move to Versailles.

[2] Monkhouse.   [3] To stay with E. Q.

[4] This letter follows *LY* pt. i, L. 147.

The Townships of Grasmere and Loughrig have lately been thrown into much agitation by a public notice, that an application was to be made to Parliament during next Session for leave to bring in a Bill to enclose their Wastes and Commons. This Advertisement excited much astonishment and indeed no little indignation, for it appeared in the Kendal Papers and was posted at the Church door, without any previous meeting being called, or the least suspicion on the part of any, but the 3 or 4 Persons with whom it originated, that such a Measure was designed. Immediately upon the knowledge of this step coming to me, which was shortly after my return to Rydal,[1] I sought an interview with Mr Jackson[2] who I had learnt was the principle mover—he informed me that they had been driven to this by the encroachments and abuses committed by many who had an interest in these Commons; and I also gathered from him, tho' he did not positively assert it, that if these abuses could be prevented the Measure should not be proceeded in. If he had been explicit upon this point, and his assertion had been confirmed by others, I should not have had occasion to trouble your Lordship, but would have applied my exertions exclusively to consider of the best means of putting a stop to all trespasses, and to opening the eyes of the offenders to their misconduct, and its possible consequences.

While I am persuaded that there is but too much ground for the alledged complaint, and that it is not a pretext to cover the odium of the proceeding, I see that there is much resentment in the minds of those who have suffered from the encroachments, and that attempts to stop these abuses (inveterate as they are) will be impossible; I see also that a few who have money to spare, are flattered by a hope of gaining by the Enclosure; and I therefore apprehend that the measure *may* be proceeded in.

It is now time that I should declare to your Lordship that the Enclosures long ago having been carried very high up these mountains, there is not the least probability that the remaining part of this vast tract, from its steepness, boggy and stony surface would defray the first expence of enclosure—not to speak of the cost of keeping up fences upon ground that runs for miles, in some places, 3000 ft above the level of the Sea—and there are but a very few acres of the whole tract capable of cultivation.

[1] W. W., M. W. and Dora W. had toured North Wales this autumn, spending some time at The Stow and at Hindwell.

[2] Thomas Jackson of Waterhead, Lady le Fleming's agent at Rydal Hall.

This consideration alone ought to prevent the Enclosure—but what has troubled me most in it, is, that the Proprietors being, much the greater part of them, Persons of small estate and who find, in no few instances, the expence of keeping up the already existing mountain enclosures burthensome, would be deterred from fencing their allotments, or if they attempted it, might thereby be entangled in ruinous engagements. In fact the benefit (if any) of the new, must be squeezed out of the old land.

A meeting took place in the vestry last Saturday—when two resolutions were passed—1st that the proposed En: would not pay the expence, and next that another meeting should be held Sat: fortnight to lay down the best plan for preventing the admitted abuses.

Thus the matter now stands, and I have only to beg of your Lordship, that if the intention of bringing this into Parliament should be persisted in, that you as Lord of the Manor of Grasmere would permit its opposers to lay before you all the peculiarities of the case before the measure secures your approbation and Consent. My own conviction is, that if carried, it would displace, and that very speedily, the greatest part of the present valuable race of inhabitants, who are already too much supplanted by other causes—and this probably will be done without advantage to any; for the Ground, if enclosed, would be of little use but for planting, and situations much more favourable, might be had for that purpose elsewhere.

Looking at this question so seriously I have not adverted to the irreparable injury which Enclosure would be to the beauty and dignity of the Vales of Grasmere or Rydal. Lady Fleming knows nothing about matters of this kind and is guided entirely by Mr Jackson her Agent. *She* has already not less I think than 2000 acres of the best of this sort of land of which the fences have been suffered to fall into decay, or where that is not the case, the ground is neglected and turned to little account—this is of course entre nous.

You will be be much concerned to hear that my excellent Friend Mr Tho⁵ Monkhouse[1] is gone into Devonshire, with little hope among his friends of his recovering from the Pulmonary Consumption with which he is afflicted. I was with him several weeks during my late absence, which was prolonged on his account. I may say that he was zealously attached to your

---

[1] M. W.'s cousin, whom they had met 'on the banks of the Wye' (see L. 142).

Lordship's political Interests, and I have often heard him regret that the state of his health left him little prospect of his being *personally* of any further use. I returned to West^d when the Family were about moving from Lowther. Had we arrived a few days earlier, I should have hurried over.

I have the honour to be, etc. [*signed*] Wm Wordsworth

W. W. to LUPTON RELFE[1]

Address: To Mr Relfe, 13 Cornhill, London.
Postmark: 1 Mar. 1825. *Stamp*: Kendal Penny Post.
MS. WL. Hitherto unpublished.

[*In M. W.'s hand*]

Rydal Mount Feb^ry 26th 1825

Dear Sir,

You are more attentive to me than I deserve—the hope of procuring a frank, in which I have been disappointed, induced me to defer my acknowledgements for the 2 copies of your beautiful annual Offering—which I received punctually thro' the hands of Miss Dowling.[2] You have much improved upon the last in elegance of appearance, and also in the value of the matter;[3]

---

[1] Publisher of *Friendship's Offering* (see *LY* pt. i, Ls. 211 and 243). This letter follows L. 162.

[2] Eliza Dowling.

[3] A copy of *Friendship's Offering* for 1824–25 cannot be traced. The Preface to the following volume, dated 10 Nov. 1825, announced a change in the character and plan of the annual, 'and in the dismissal of its more toy-like attributes, for the purpose of combining, with the increased beauty of its embellishments, a high literary character.' Along with predictable contributions from Bernard Barton, W. L. Bowles, L. E. L., Miss Mitford, James Montgomery, and many other regular contributors to the annuals, the volume for 1826 included (pp. 388 ff.) four unpublished poems by James Thomson, author of *The Seasons*, from the collection of the Earl of Buchan, including 'Hymn to God's Power', and Southey's 'Inscription for a Tablet at Banarvie, on the Caledonian Canal' (p. 167). But W. W.'s decision not to contribute would probably have been strengthened had he known that Byron was to feature so largely in the volume. It included two poems of his: 'Stanzas to her who can best understand them' (p. 102), 'from the Album of Captain Medwin', and 'Lines addressed to Lady Caroline Lamb, sixteen years ago', (p. 230), 'taken from the note-book of her Ladyship'. There was also an Ode on the death of Lord Byron by the Revd C. C. Colton (?1780–1832), eccentric author of *Lacon*, and of an earlier satire,

and you have my best wishes for your success in this and your other undertakings:—this sentiment is far from being uttered as a matter of form, for I have understood from Miss D. that you are just entering upon business and I have reason to believe you are likely to conduct it in a mode that will deserve its reward.

Since your first application to me I have had a request from an old friend the Conductor of a London Journal,[1] so strongly urged that I could not have refused to comply with it, however averse, except upon the ground of my having invariably declined entering upon this field of literature. I mention this to you because it reconciled me still more to the necessity of abiding by my first resolution. Of course circumstances may occur requiring a change in this resolution.[2]

I remain dear Sir,
faithfully your ob^d St.
[*signed*] Wm Wordsworth

W. W. to GEORGE WEBSTER[3]

MS. Rare Book Room, Smith College Library. Hitherto unpublished.

Rydal Mount
Saturday 18th Feb^{ry} 1826

Dear Sir,
I wish you to come over to Rydal for the benefit of your Plans and judgement in respect to the House I design building there—I have particular reasons for wishing to see you as early in the ensuing week as possible—I shall not go from home; but pray let

Hypocrisy (1812), modelled on *The Dunciad*, in which the poets of the new age, including 'wild' Wordsworth (p. 18), were held up to scorn by comparison with their predecessors. The illustrators of the new annual included R. Westall, Vernet, Bonington, and W. W.'s friend Sir Robert Ker Porter.

[1] Probably Alaric Watts, proprietor of the *Literary Souvenir* (see Ls. 144 and 189).

[2] For W. W.'s contributions to *The Keepsake* in 1829, see Ls. 322 and 327.

[3] This letter follows *LY* pt. i, L.216, and refers to W. W.'s plans to build on 'the Rash', if he was forced to vacate Rydal Mount (see L.206). George Webster (1797–1864), the Kendal architect and monumental sculptor, had become a partner in his father's firm some four years before he built Rydal Chapel in 1824 (see L.153). He subsequently designed many churches, public buildings, and mansions in the north-west, including Underley Hall nr. Kirkby Lonsdale (see *LY* pt. iv, L.1826), and was mayor of Kendal in 1829.

me know when I [can]¹ expect you; and bring as many plans as you think may be of use to me.—if it suits you to stay all night I have a bed at your service.

> I remain dear Sir
> your humble Ser^vt
> Wm Wordsworth

W. W. to JOHN WORDSWORTH²

Address: John Wordsworth Esq., Trinity College, Cambridge. [*In S. H.'s hand*]
Postmark: 15 Apr. 1826.
Stamp: Kendal.
Endorsed: My Uncle to dear John. Testimonial for Birmingham.³
MS. Mitchell Library, Glasgow. Hitherto unpublished.

15 Apr. 1826

. . . We shall be glad to see Owen⁴—If Chris: be with you remember me to him affectionately, and believe me my dear nephew most faithfully yours

Wm Wordsworth

Dora is returned from Keswick⁵ and sends her love, as does her mother.—

William⁶ had a severe attack of the nettle rash a few days ago, with fever—these liabilities to disease prevent us from sending him to School, by which his progress in books is much retarded—

---

¹ *Word dropped out.*

² C. W.'s eldest son. This letter follows *LY* pt. i, L. 223.

³ The endorsement is puzzling. John Wordsworth was not quite 21 at this date, and in the middle of a brilliant career at Trinity College, Cambridge. This year he won the University Porson prize for Greek verse, the Second Latin Declamation prize at Trinity, and a College scholarship; but he was not elected to a Fellowship till 1830. It is inconceivable that he could have contemplated leaving the University at this juncture for a post in Birmingham for which he was not yet fully equipped. On the other hand, he was an unsuccessful candidate for the Headmastership of King Edward's School in Apr. 1838, and W. W. wrote him a testimonial (*LY* pt. iii, L. 1227). It seems very likely therefore that the endorsement was added to the wrong letter by mistake after John Wordsworth's death (1839), when his papers were being put in order.

⁴ Charles Lloyd's son, educated at Trinity, and later curate of Langdale.

⁵ She had been visiting the Southeys.   ⁶ Willy W.

W. W. to WILLIAM WILLIAMSON[1]

Address: D[r] Williamson, Park Square, Leeds [*In Dora W.'s hand*]
Stamp: Harrowgate.
MS. Washington University Library, St. Louis, Missouri.
Hitherto unpublished.

Harrowgate
Monday Evening [?4 June 1827][2]

Dear Sir,

My Daughter joins me in thanks to yourself and Sister for your hospitable invitation of which we shall gladly avail ourselves—As she cannot travel in the heat of the day I fear we shall not be able to reach Leeds much before 9 in the evening—

The weather being so settled I need scarcely add that should it unfortunately change to rain, you will not expect us—

I remain dear Sir
your obliged Ser[nt]
W[m] Wordsworth

W. W. to MARY FRANCES HOWLEY[3]

MS. Lambeth Palace Library. Hitherto unpublished.

Vicarage
July 25 [? *c.* 9 Aug. 1828]

My dear M[rs] Howley,

After meeting the Bishop I wrote a note to my wife from Walham Green[4] which will fill her with sorrow. But we know

[1] Of Sidney Sussex College, Cambridge, and later perpetual curate of Headingley (see *LY* pt. iii, L. 893). His wife was a relation of M. W.

[2] This letter seems to refer to W. W.'s and Dora W.'s visit to Harrogate to take the waters in June 1827 (see *LY* pt. i, L. 290). It follows L. 289.

[3] Wife of Dr. William Howley, Bishop of London (see *MY* pt. ii, L. 554). The exact circumstances in which this letter was written are not entirely clear. It seems to refer to Dr. Howley's translation from the diocese of London to the Archbishopric of Canterbury (and therefore to Lambeth Palace as his official residence) in late July 1828 (see *LY* pt. i, L.353); but if so, it must have been misdated, as W. W. was away on the Continent with Dora W. and S. T. C. throughout July, while M. W. was keeping house for John W. at Whitwick Rectory. A date soon after his return to London on 6 Aug. is indicated, and the letter perhaps follows L. 353. The 'Vicarage' from which W. W. writes is unidentified.

[4] Walham Green is close to Fulham Palace. W. W. had evidently visited Dr. Howley at his London residence.

very well that the Bishop must go to Lambeth, nobody else being half so fit. I say nothing more about it now, lest my note should be too late.

Ever y^{rs},

etc etc—

W. W.

W. W. to WILLIAM GODWIN[1]

MS. Private Collection. Hitherto unpublished.

Sat Morn—[?mid-Aug. 1828]

Mr Wordsworth will thank Mr Godwin when he has read Dr W^s Pamphlet[2] to forward it under Cover to Mr Aders[3] No 11 Euston Square.

W. W. to ROBERT COTTON MONEY[4]

Address: R. Money Esqre, W.S. Bombay. To the care of
Messrs Forbes and Co, Bombay. [*In Dora W.'s hand*] [*readdressed to*] Bhovj.
Stamp: (1) [?Bombay] (2) Forwarded by Forbes and Co, Bombay.
MS. Private Collection. Hitherto unpublished.

Rydal Mount near Ambleside

Tenth October, 1828

My dear Sir,

Your letter of the 13th March, I received a couple of days ago—as I owe the pleasure it gave me to your verses I will begin with them: These specimens are so creditable to your sensibility, that I should have no scruple in encouraging you to write, were I convinced that Poetry co[u]ld be followed by you, without encroaching too much upon your time, and a risk of dispositions being generated by the practice of the art which might make business distasteful to you. I fear this;—my own experience com-

---

[1] For W. W.'s later relations with Godwin, see above, letter of 21 Apr. 1807. This letter was written from London just before, or more likely, just after, W. W.'s Continental tour of 1828, and perhaps follows *LY* pt. i, L. 355.

[2] C. W.'s second pamphlet on the authorship of the *Icon Basilike* (see L. 362).

[3] Charles Aders, H. C. R.'s friend (see Ls. 342 and 350).

[4] An Edinburgh lawyer living in India: author of *Journal of a Tour in Persia during the years 1824 and 1825*, 1828, and of pamphlets on Indian education and currency. This letter follows *LY* pt. i, L. 361.

pels me to do so; for I do not think I could have reconciled any laborious employment of mere dry business with the excitement indispensible to successful poetic composition.—But this is perhaps a good deal an affair of constitution—one man may find it easy to pass from a state of emotion to drudgery, or mechanic employment when duty calls, and another may be too weak and irresolute for such a conquest over enclination. It follows therefore that I cannot advise; all I can say is that I have been much pleased with the spirit of your verses and should auger very favourabl[y][1] of them as effusions of a writer too young to be practised in the structure of composition. You have much to learn, in the art of management of Words; and nothing but practise can teach this. Your verses upon the Nautilus interested me most, but elegant and striking as the piece is—the composition is in some places very objectionable—e.g. I can scarcely guess what is meant by, 'as curtained in the eye of Beauty', and the word '*so*' at the beginning of the next stanza ought to be 'then' or I cannot make any sense of it. But it is a long way to send these minutiae, which you must excuse as necessary to explain my meaning when I say that you have much to learn; nor would it be well were it not so, young as you are.

What you say of my old Friend Mr Gray[2] and his labours gives me great pleasure. Pray, if you fall in his way, present my kind remembrances to him, and my best wishes for the continuance of so useful [a][3] life.

Accept my thanks for the account you give me of yourself, and of the manners of the people among whom you and your Acquaintance reside. The Opium-eater of this neighbourhood to whom you seem to allude has been, for many months residence in Edinburgh; his Family however continues to occupy a Cottage in the Vale of Grasmere, in which I dwelt many years. Professor Wilson also has in a great measure ceased to frequent the Country.—The 1st account I have read of India, is in Bp Hebers journal,[4] which is written with simplicity, and apparently with

---

[1] *Written over edge of sheet.*

[2] James Gray, to whom the *Letter to a Friend of Robert Burns* had been addressed.   [3] *Word dropped out.*

[4] Bishop Reginald Heber's widow (see also *LY* pt. ii, L. 561) had this year published his *Narrative of a journey through the Upper Provinces of India from Calcutta to Bombay, 1824–25 (with notes upon Ceylon); An account of a journey to Madras and the Southern Provinces, 1826, and letters written in India*, in 2 vols. It went through three editions in one year.

accuracy and truth. From some passages in that work one cannot but apprehend that the governing Powers in India, I mean the British, are not sincere in their endeavours to promote Christianity. Should this be so, nothing can be less desirable than the situation of a Christian Bp in that Country, or indeed of any Christian minister.

I cannot conclude without a few words upon writing verse. I have already spoken of the necessity of feeling, if not of something like inspiration, to produce it; and of the difficulty of passing from such a state of excitement to dull and ordinary business—I wish to add that thought and labour are equally necessary for the production of correct verse—such as likely to please extensively and permanently.—This observation is made from a conviction of its importance. The Poetry of our day is not wanting in spirit—but it is deplorably deficient in workmanship—and a great deal of it must unavoidably perish on that account. The severest logic is required for good verse—and few Authors of our day take the trouble to bestow it upon their effusions. This remark is made not to intimidate you, but to direct your attention to a truth which must be impressed upon all who would turn their poetic sensibilities to account for the benefit and permanent pleasure of others—I must now conclude a letter which seems scarcely worth sending so far—but should it be so you must take part of the blame to yourself.

I remain my dear Sir, with much respect
very sincerely yours
Wm Wordsworth

D. W. to S. T. C.[1]

Address: S. T. Coleridge Esqre, Highgate.
Postmark: (1) 17 Nov. 18 [ ] (2) 17 Nov. 1829.
MS. Berg Collection, New York Public Library. Hitherto unpublished.

Rydal Mount—14th November [1829]

My dear Friend,

It is so long since I have written to you that you will hardly recognise the hand-writing, without a turn to the Signature; Sara and Henry[2] will have told you about all of us at Rydal Mount,

---

[1] This letter follows *LY* pt. ii, L. 478.

[2] Sara Coleridge had married her cousin Henry Nelson Coleridge at Keswick on 3 Sept.

and I hope the latter has delivered the messages of affectionate remembrance with which I charged him—therefore to the points at once concerning which I have set myself to write to you.

We enclose the catalogue of your Books[1] which are ready to be sent off; but my Sister and Mr Carter, who have been the active agents, wait to know *how* you wish to have them sent—whether by Canal or Sea carriage. The Catalogue contains the whole of the Books which, as yet, we have found among my Brother's: but Hartley wishes to keep for his own use, if you have no objection, Milton's and Bacon's Works[2] (in folio) together with Carmina Italiana and some others (amounting altogether to about 40 volumes) of which he will himself, send you a list, along with a list of those which he has had in his possession for some time, and my Brother will take the Liberty to obtain Pausanias's History of Greece[3] with your permission. Be so good as to inform Mrs Wordsworth without delay *how* the Books are to be sent.

Mrs Coleridge, who spent a few days with us previous to her departure from the North, told us that among letters which she had forwarded to you from Keswick, there was a bundle of our letters—i.e. of my Brother's and other members of this Family. Now at this day such abominable use is made of every scrap of

---

[1] In his will, dated 17 Sept. 1829 (see Griggs, vi. 998–1002), S. T. C. had left instructions for the sale of his library for the benefit of his widow and children. Many of his books had remained behind with the Wordsworths when he moved to London many years before, and these had been designated as his in the manuscript catalogue of W. W.'s library drawn up around this time by John Carter (*Harvard University Library MSS.*). A separate list of S. T. C.'s books had also been made, and D. W. was now forwarding this to him. As no reply to this letter has survived, it is unclear whether the books were sent down to Coleridge straightaway, or whether they remained for some time longer at Rydal Mount. See Chester L. Shaver and Alice C. Shaver, *Wordsworth's Library, A Catalogue*, 1979, pp. xx–xxiii.

[2] *A complete collection of the historical, political, and miscellaneous works of John Milton . . . With an historical and critical account of the life and writings of the author . . .*, 2 vols., 1738 (Shaver, p. 343), compiled by Thomas Birch (1705–66), historian and Secretary of the Royal Society; and *The Works of Francis Bacon . . . To which is prefixed a life of the author by Mr Mallet* (Shaver, p. 315). David Mallet (?1705–65), the poet, was a friend of James Thomson and author of *The Excursion*, 1728. 'Carmina Italiana' is untraced, and was probably published in Italy.

[3] *The description of Greece . . . translated with notes*, 3 vols., 1794. The translator was Thomas Taylor (1758–1835), the Platonist. See *R. M. Cat.*, no. 147 and Shaver, p. 347.

private anecdote, or transient or permanent sentiment, of every one whose name has ever been at all known by the publick that we are very desirous these letters should be destroyed; and therefore, my dear Coleridge, I must beg of you either to *send the letters to us immediately*, or that you will yourself destroy them, *and give us an assurance, by writing*, that this has been done.

You have, no doubt, heard of my Brother's pleasant tour in Ireland; and of his great activity in climbing mountains etc etc—I hope *my* day is not quite over, though at present I confine myself to garden-walks; and drives in the poney chaise, to guard against returns of serious derangements of the Bowels which have troubled me since last March. You will, I know, be glad to hear that I am now quite well.—Mary is almost as strong, and quite as active as ever—and Sarah H. is, in constitution, stronger than she used to be.—Dora is certainly very far from strong; but she is always chearful and gay—She begs her very kind Love to the Family God-father.—

Will it not be possible for Henry or Sara to persuade you to accompany them when they pay their first visit to the North? We had them twice at Rydal; and their first visit was perfectly happy; but during the second poor Sara had little even of comfort, being constantly tormented by the tooth-ache. We are anxious to hear that she has got rid of this sad annoyance, and is comfortably settled in a home of [her] own. We were very much pleased with Henry.

I have nothing new to say, except that since they left us we have heard the sad tidings of our poor Racedown and Allfoxden Peggy having been burnt to death by her own fire-side. She has left a family of nine children, having borne sixteen. Dr Rudge,[1] the Rector of Hawkechurch wrote to me to inform us of this melancholy event. He gives the highest possible character of the Deceased, and of her two eldest Daughters, who alas! are *unhappily* married. You will remember poor Peggy's blooming cheeks, her sweet voice, and her active habits.

William and Mary, Sarah H. and Dora all unite with me in affectionate remembrances, and also give our kind regards to M^r and Mrs Gillman, and believe me, dear Coleridge,

ever your faithful and affectionate Friend
D Wordsworth

---

[1] The Revd. James Horace Rudge, D.D., F.R.S. (1785–*c*. 1853), chaplain to the Duke of Sussex (1821), and to the Duke of York (1825), and rector of Hawkchurch, nr. Axminster, Devon, 1828–52.

I should be glad to hear of an improvement in Mrs Gillman's health.

If you can spare them my Brother will keep besides Pausanias, Taylor's Cratylus,[1] and [?Kircher Polit.][2]

W. W. to GEORGE HUNTLY GORDON[3]

MS. untraced.
Bookseller's Catalogue.

Rydal 18th [Mar.1830]

. . . We had the flourish of a Storm just when it told most, in the heart of one of our finest mountain passes.—through the rest of the rapid tour we had the happiest bursts and gleams of sunshine, exactly in the right places, with black shadows and sweeping lights over the lakes and mountains . . .

W. W. to JULIUS CHARLES HARE[4]

Address: The Revd Julius Hare, Trin: Coll: Cambridge.
Stamp: Kendal Penny Post.
MS. Mr. R. L. Bayne-Powell. Hitherto unpublished.

Mar: 20th [1830]

My dear Sir,

I thank you heartily for your Sermon[5] and Vindication[6]—the former is very eloquent and all the objections I might have been

---

[1] *The Cratylus, Phaedo, Parmenides and Timaeus of Plato, translated from the Greek by Thomas Taylor*, 1793 (see *R. M. Cat.*, no. 408 and Shaver, p. 202).

[2] *MS. obscure.* The reference seems to be to the *Principis christiani archetypon politicum, sive Sapientia Regnatrix . . .* 1672, of Athanasius Kircher, the Jesuit scholar and scientist (see also *LY* pt. i, L. 382). See *R. M. Cat.*, no. 262 and Shaver, p. 145.

[3] This letter, and the next one, follow *LY* pt. ii, L. 510. It describes W.W.'s recent journey on Stamp Office business to Ulverston. He returned by way of the Duddon Valley and over the Wrynose Pass.

[4] See *LY* pt. i, L. 123, and pt. iii, L. 1239.

[5] *The Children of Light. A Sermon Preached Before the University of Cambridge . . . on Advent Sunday*, 1828.

[6] *A Vindication of Niebuhr's History of Rome from the Charges of the Quarterly Review*, 1829. In the *Quarterly* for Jan. 1829 (xxxix. 1–41), in the course of a discussion of Augustus Granville's travels in Russia, Sir John Barrow (1764–1848),

disposed to make to it are anticipated in the very judicious preface. Take the trouble to compare what you say page 18 upon Reason in connection with personal immortality,[1] with what I have written in the former part of an Essay on Epitaphs,[2] appended to the Excursion, and you will see that upon this part of your subject I must have stood in especial need of the explanation of terms which your Preface supplies.[3] As to a demonstrative assurance of a blessed personal Immortality being given by Reason even in the highest sense of the word, no Man worth listening to will contend for it—on the other hand, I cannot perceive for my own part, that without a mediator or an atonement such a *hope* is in *Repugnance* to reason; I say *hope* to make a distinction between something far short of absolute Belief, and the mere *wish* which the instincts of nature give birth to.—

Your *Vindication* is triumphant—the obnoxious passage would

geographer and Secretary to the Admiralty, had made disparaging remarks about Niebuhr and Hare's role as his translator.

[1] Discussing the shadowy idea of a future state among pre-Christian peoples, Hare had concluded: 'The unquenchable hope of immortality, implanted within the human breast, was fain to seek something external that might justify and uphold it; for bare naked Reason could not do so: indeed so far is Reason from conveying or possessing any assurance of a blessed immortality, that a blessed immortality, without a mediator, without an atonement, is in direct repugnance to Reason.'

[2] See *Prose Works*, ii. 50–1, where W. W. concludes: 'We may, then, be justified in asserting, that the sense of immortality, if not a co-existent and twin birth with Reason, is among the earliest of her offspring: and we may further assert, that from these conjoined, and under their countenance, the human affections are gradually formed and opened out.'

[3] Hare's closely-argued Preface to the sermon, which reflects W. W.'s and Coleridge's influence, sets out to distinguish between the various uses of the word 'Reason', contrasting Reason 'as the whole complex of the reflective faculties', which needs to be refreshed 'by influxes of the imagination and the heart', with Reason 'as the logical faculty or the power of drawing inferences', which had been 'since the middle of the last century, so fruitful a parent of error and mischief . . . It costs so much less trouble to construct a system out of one's own brain, than to labour in the quarries of Nature to obtain the materials for rearing it.' For it to function properly, Reason needs 'the lordly splendour and living energy of the Imagination': it is 'so far from being all sufficient in itself, that, without the ministerial offices of the other faculties, it has no hold and is utterly unable to act upon anything external: and if, instead of acknowledging their rights, it attempts to trample upon them, it is sure in the end to become the creature and slave of its slaves . . .'

never have been worthy a moment's notice but for the vehicle that conveys it to the world. The consciousness of the advantage that each of these continuous and multifarious publications possesses in facility of circulation over detached works, is the main cause of the recklessness with which they scatter their Calumnies, and their carelessness as to facts.—The notice of Niebuhr and his translator is an instance of restless slander,[1] that of myself, of unreflecting disregard to truth[2]—in the one there is malignity, in the other not.—Some of the Remarks which you make upon good and able Men lending their support to such Publications and their giving wings to their mischief, I have repeatedly made to my Friend Southey—A more upright and highminded man is not easily to be found—What then is his answer.—I am ready says he to unite with men of another temper, but where are they to be found?—Had Coleridge, and others, yourself (said he) included been here whose habits and turn of mind would have allowed you perseveringly to cooperate with me, then something might have been done—I advert to this merely to shew you that [?][3] is more easily talked upon than effected.—Notwithstanding your able defence, I should have been better pleased if any evidence could have been adduced that Niebuhr was a Believer—I mean on account of the *Profession* of his Translator. Had the Book contained nothing impugning the credibility of the Scriptures, this would have been of no importance—as it is, there is cause for regret—and it is not sufficient for the doing away of this regret to bring forth animated expression in belief of a superintending Providence.[4]—Such possibly may be found in the writings of Voltaire—at all events Voltaire thought himself a Deist.—

I must not omit thanking you for correcting the mistake in

[1] Barrow had written of Niebuhr's 'absurd and shallow doctrines', embodied in 'some of the most offensive paragraphs which have appeared since the days of the Philosophical Directory, though unnoticed by his latest translators ... who have exercised the right of adding notes to Niebuhr's text wherever they fancied they had anything worth hearing to offer.'

[2] Barrow had added: 'But Niebuhr *is*, what Mr. Wordsworth should not have called Voltaire, 'a pert *dull* scoffer.'

[3] *MS. obscure.*

[4] Hare defended Niebuhr's political writings as applications of the principles outlined in his *History*, and more redolent of Burke than Rousseau in their admiration for English institutions. In his faith in an overruling Providence, Niebuhr had more in common with Milton than with Voltaire.

regard to myself. It is done with your usual sagacity and Spirit.[1]
One material circumstance however is overlooked. The words
are not in my own person, but in the mouth of one of my
Dramatis personae; one the fundamental position of whose faith
he himself thus expresses,

> one adequate support
> For the calamities of mortal life,
> Exists, one *only*—an assured belief
> That the procession of our fate, however
> Sad or disturbed, is ordered by a Being
> Of infinite benevolence and power;
> Whose everlasting purposes embrace
> All accidents, converting them to *good*
>
> See Ex.[2] p. 31 Last Edition

Again, he is one who while his mind is filled with uneasy
thoughts, says

> That what we feel of sorrow and despair
> From ruin and from change, and all the grief
> The passing shows of being leave behind
> appeared an idle dream that could not live
> where meditation was.[3] ibid p. 42

To such a one how could the Candide, met with under such circumstances, appear otherwise than stupid. But he selects the
word 'dull' as in opposition to the vulgar opinion and with an
especial allusion to the tastes of [a] Friend[4]—a man of shewy talents, but of feelings that ought to have raised him to, and kept
him among, higher things.—

Pray let me ask whether the favourers of Concession in your
University have not been dazzled by principles somewhat too
abstract for the present state of human knowledge, equality of
civil rights without regard to religious creeds, and the belief that
the Church of England, if a true Church, is competent to defend
herself, and therefore should be left to do so.—As to her
Doctrines, that is perfectly reasonable—but as to her property

---

[1] Hare corrected Barrow's misquotation of the Wanderer's words at *Excursion*,
ii. 484. 'Many a sneer has been put forth against our great moral poet in our
magazines and other literary smallcraft.' (*Vindication*, pp.40–1).

[2] *Exc.*, iv. 10–17.

[3] Ibid. i. 949–53 (1814 text, altered in 1845).

[4] The Solitary.

and [? endowments], which are creatures of Law, I demur. This distinction I fear has not been sufficiently meditated.

    farewell—with genuine regard I remain faithfully yours

                    Wm Wordsworth

Your parcel reached me with the seal broken—no letter in it—Through Mr Whewell.[1] I have thanked Digby[2] for his Orlandus—it has since afforded me a subject for a poem[3] of 138 lines which I should be proud to read to him.

W. W. and D. W. to MARIA JANE JEWSBURY[4]

Address: To Miss Jewsbury, Grosvenor [Street], Oxf[ord Road], Man[chester].
Stamp: Kendal Penny Post.
MS. Private Collection. Hitherto unpublished.

                    Rydal Mount
                    23rd March 1830

This our life exempt from public haunt
Finds tongues in trees books in the running brooks
Sermons in stones and good in every thing[5]

                    Wm Wordsworth

---

[1] William Whewell (see *LY* pt. i, L. 382).

[2] Kenelm Henry Digby (see *LY* pt. i, L. 376), had expanded *The Broad Stone of Honour* into 4 volumes, the fourth of which, *Orlandus* (1829), dealt with the spirit of Christian chivalry.

[3] 'The Armenian Lady's Love' (*PW* ii. 96), published 1835 with a dedication to Digby. The published version has 156 lines.

[4] For Miss Jewsbury see *LY* pt. i, L. 171. This year she published her last and most successful book, *The Three Histories: being the History of an Enthusiast, the History of a Nonchalant, the History of a Realist*. This fragment, presumably preserved for the autographed quotation, is all that has survived of a longer letter from D. W. to Miss Jewsbury, of which only the corner and her signature remain. It follows *LY* pt. ii, L. 511.

[5] See *As You Like It*, II. ii. 15–17.

W. W. to MR. MATTHEWS[1]

MS. WL. Hitherto unpublished.

[*c.* 19 Apr. 1830]

Dear Mr Matthews—

Miss Jewsbury[2] is in Town—you will find her till next Friday at 9 upper Charlotte Street Fitzroy Square—on that day she goes into the Country. Your name sent in will be a sufficient Introduction, as she [is] apprized of your wish to know her.

You were so kind as to offer to procure me Books at the best market—Could you get me the Oxford Edit. of South's Sermons,[3] 7 volumes—1823—and let it be sent to Whitaker's,[4] I suppose there is only one Bookseller of that name, to be forwarded in Mr Troughton's[5] first parcel to Ambleside.

—My Sister begs me to apologize for giving you so much trouble with her load of foreign letters.[6] We have a dismally wet seed-time—I never remember so much rain in April.

Excuse this miserable Scrawl—I have tired myself with a desperate long folio sheet to Mr Dyce, who has been so kind as to send me his Edition of Webster just published—[7]

ever faithfully
Your much obliged Friend
Wm Wordsworth

[1] Unidentified, but probably a bookseller or publisher, and perhaps a connection of W. W.'s early friend William Mathews and the comic actor Charles Mathews (see *EY*, L. 13).

[2] Maria Jane Jewsbury (see above, letter of 23 Mar. 1830) was on a visit to London, where she went to live the following year.

[3] Robert South (see also *LY* pt. ii, L. 561), the distinguished court preacher, noted for his homely and witty pulpit manner. W. W. owned an 18th century edition of his *Sermons Preached upon Several Occasions* (6 vols., 1727), *R. M. Cat.*, no. 295, but there is no evidence that he actually acquired the collected edition referred to here.

[4] The London booksellers.

[5] The Ambleside bookseller.

[6] D. W.'s correspondents abroad included Miss Barker (see *LY* pt. ii, L. 486, and *MW*, p. 181); but the letter may also refer to a renewed correspondence with Annette Vallon and the Baudouins (see also *LY* pt. ii, L.526).

[7] See *LY* pt. ii, L.519. W. W.'s long letter of thanks to Alexander Dyce (L.521), establishes the date and placing of this letter.

W. W. to [?JOHN WILSON CROKER][1]

MS. *New York Public Library. Hitherto unpublished.*

Rydal Mount
Kendal
June 6th [1830]

My Dear Sir,

Mr Quillinan a friend of mine and a Countryman of yours wishes to be among the first 100 of the Athenaeum to be selected by a Committee of which you are a member. Mr Q–'s name was put down by Mr Lodge,[2] he has the support of Mr Rogers, and his lively talents and agreeable manners would make him an acquisition to any Society.

Let me beg of you to favour him with your support, but should this application be too[3] late, pray be so kind as to assist it upon the second selection which I understand will be made by the Votes of the whole Society.—

Believe me faithfully yours
Wm Wordsworth

W. W. to FELICIA DOROTHEA HEMANS[4]

Address: Mrs Hemans, Dove's Nest [*delivered by hand*]
MS. *The Robert H. Taylor Collection, Princeton, N.J. Hitherto unpublished.*

[11 July 1830]

Dear Mrs Hemmans,

I cannot but be persuaded that it will be agreeable to you to be broken in upon in your Solitude by the Rev. Professor

---

[1] This letter follows *LY* pt. ii, L. 538, and was addressed either to John Wilson Croker (see L. 506) or to Thomas Moore (see *MY* pt. ii, L. 606), the two Committee members of Irish extraction to whom W. W. wrote about E. Q.'s candidature for the Athenaeum (see *LY* pt. ii, L. 541). The club was founded in 1823, largely on Croker's initiative, and was now moving into Decimus Burton's new building in Pall Mall. Croker was shortly to resign from the Admiralty, but was to remain in the House of Commons as M.P. for Aldborough till 1832.

[2] Probably Edmund Lodge (1756–1839), the biographer and genealogist: author of the memoirs attached to *Portraits of Illustrious Personages of Great Britain, engraved from authentic pictures* . . ., 4 vols., 1821–34, and several works on the peerage.

[3] *Written to.*   [4] See *LY* pt. i, L. 246. This letter follows *LY* pt. ii, L. 553.

MacVickar and his family from New York.[1] They had proceeded this far on their way to Keswick, but learning from us that you were at Low Wood, they have not been able to resist the temptation of returning for the sake of visiting you.—The party will by their conversation sufficiently recommend themselves—and I shall merely add that they are introduced to me by Bp Hobart.

ever faithfully
Yours in great [?haste][2]
Wm Wordsworth

D. W. to C. W.[3]

Address: To The Revd Dr Wordsworth, Trinity Lodge, Cambridge.
Stamp: Kendal Penny Post.
MS. WL. Hitherto unpublished.

Wednesday—6th October [1830]

My dear Brother,

We were grateful to you for writing to us previous to the public decision; for our anxiety was great in dear John's account[4]—*so* great indeed was mine that I hardly sent a wish after poor Chris, being well able to encounter a disappointment for *him*, in the assurance of his after success. May God bless them both and grant them many long years of happy and useful life!—Our small remaining household—William, Miss Hutchinson[5] and myself join in sincerest congratulations to you and them and especially to you my dear Brother on this completion of your satisfaction in your Sons' progress through the University.

Dora left us for Moresby yesterday morning side by side with Isabella[6] in her little carriage, driven by Mr Curwen's Servant. It was an affecting sight to me when I saw them drive away—very sisterly and very pretty they looked. Both left their congratulations for you and the Cousins—for your *letter* had arrived the day before—and yester morn the Cambridge paper, which they took

---

[1] See L. 554. [2] *MS. torn.* [3] This letter follows *LY* pt. ii, L.569.

[4] C.W.'s sons John and Christopher were elected Fellows of Trinity College, Cambridge, this autumn.

[5] i.e. S.H.

[6] Isabella Curwen, whom John W. was to marry later this month (see Ls. 571 and 574). M.W. was making ready their house at Moresby, John W.'s living near Whitehaven.

on for John and his mother. She went to Moresby last Monday to begin to prepare the house—and our Brother will follow on Saturday. The wedding is to be on Monday, and the young couple will proceed to Edinburgh; but will only be absent two Sundays.

Mary's business in the house will hardly be finished before the end of another week. William will stay with her, and Dora at Moresby. This arrangement leaves but little time for preparations for their long journey and we think they cannot set off before from the 22nd to the 25th. William has written to Sir G Beaumont to say that if convenient they will stay three or four days at Coleorton in their way—and if so they cannot be with you till the end of the month. But should not the Beaumonts receive them they *may* be sooner with you if it should make much difference in regard to your convenience.—But if it be equal, or nearly so to you, they will have ample employment for that time intended to be given to Coleorton, having other Friends who wish to detain them on their road.—Perhaps Mrs Watson's[1] unfortunate illness may make their early arrival at Cambridge of less consequence, as, at all events, the visit of that Family will probably be at least *delayed*. I was much shocked and concerned at hearing of her severe and dangerous illness; and the more so as happening at this time when your plans had been as we thought so happily arranged for a family meeting.

I have at length finally given up the idea of accompanying the Three[2] to Cambridge—reluctantly, as you may believe—for such an opportunity of meeting you and your three Sons together under the Roof of Trinity Lodge may never again occur. My Resolve has been made chiefly in consideration of the win[?ter][3] being a bad one for excursions and travelling—and of my being now well, and that therefore it may be wiser to run no risques till I have had longer experience of re-established health. Add to this—that if I should suffer by my hardihood, it would be such a distress to me to disturb the comfort and happiness of others.—If we do not hear again from you *immediately* we shall conclude that it will not put you to much inconvenience if they do not arrive till the end of the month, but if you have particular reasons for wishing it otherwise, pray write.

---

[1] Wife of Joshua Watson, the prominent Anglican layman (see *MY* pt. ii, L. 590).

[2] W.W., M.W. and Dora W.   [3] *Seal.*

Give my kind love to all my nephews, and believe me, my
dear Brother

ever yours D. Wordsworth

The Eichbaum property[1] is held under Lord Lonsdale, and not
[?burdensome][2]—but no difficulty in enfranchising—Mr E. willing to sell—demands £800, which is one hundred more than
specified by Mr Harrison[3] on account of the Stable lately built,
and other improvements. The sole objection[4] is Mr Greaves's
lease—*certain* for 3 years—and at his option for three years more.
But on the other hand, he and his Wife are likely to tire of his
Bargain—and even if they do not, it would be no bad investment
for idle money. Rent is £50 annually furnished, which[5] for the
time probably might be bought with the house for £100, or less.
Further: if inclined to come before Mr Greaves goes you might
certainly rent Mrs Barlow's.[6]

I have spent ten days very pleasantly at Hallsteads[7]—you much
inquired after there and at Paterdale.[8]

W^m on his walk to day met Owen Lloyd,[9] who sent his congratulations.

Of course when you write you will tell us what you hear of
Mrs Watson, as we are anxious for her recovery.

---

[1] Ferney Green, near Bowness, at present leased to Capt. Robert Greaves. The
reference is to C.W.'s unfulfilled plan to acquire or rent a property in the Lake
District.

[2] *Illegible word.*

[3] Benson Harrison of Green Bank, Ambleside.

[4] Objection *written twice.*

[5] i.e. the furniture.

[6] Owner of another house near Bowness, and a friend of the Wordsworths
(see *LY* pt. ii, Ls. 484 and 527).

[7] Home of the Marshalls on Ullswater.

[8] i.e. Patterdale Hall, home of the Marshalls' son William and his family.

[9] Curate of Langdale (see *LY* pt. i, L. 152).

W. W. to JOHN WALKER ORD[1]

Address: J.W. Ord Esq. 39 Montague Street, Edinburgh.
MS. Private Collection. Hitherto unpublished.

12 Bryanstone Street
London Jan^ry 1st 1831

Sir,

I regret that you should have had the trouble of writing twice upon such an occasion.

I have been absent from home—the contents of your former Letter were transmitted to me but they slipped my memory—

I now send you the autograph requested and remain

sincerely yours
Wm Wordsworth

They hand in hand with wandering steps and slow
Through Eden took their solitary way.
The world was all before them where to chuse
Their place of rest and Providence their guide.[2]

W.W.

W. W. to MESSRS. A. G. MORYER AND CO.[3]

MS. Mr. Sherman R. Emery. Hitherto unpublished.

[*In M. W.'s hand*]

London 2 April 1831.

Messrs A. G. Moryer and C°.

Gentlemen,

Mr Henderson[4] H. M.'s Consul General recently from Bogota, has recommended your establishment to me, for the purpose of

[1] John Walker Ord (1811–53), topographer, minor poet and journalist: friend of Professor Wilson and Hogg while a medical student in Edinburgh. He abandoned medicine and came to London to start the *Metropolitan Literary Journal*, and was the author of *England, A Historical Poem*, 2 vols., 1834–5, and *The History and Antiquities of Cleveland*, 1846. This letter follows *LY* pt. ii, L. 586.

[2] *Paradise Lost*, xii. 646–9.

[3] This letter follows *LY* pt. ii, L. 598, and was written from E. Q.'s lodgings at 12 Bryanston Street. Messrs. Moryer have not been further identified, and perhaps W. W. misspelt the name.

[4] James Henderson, F.R.S. (?1783–1848), a native of Cumberland or Westmorland, travelled in South America and became Consul-General for Colom-

effecting a purchase for me to the extent of Fifty Pounds in the Colombian 5 p^r Cent domestic Stock;[1] provided that can be done at the rate of from 1½ to 2 per Cent—and I should not wish you under any circumstances to exceed 2½ or 3 per cent.

Should you be able to make this purchase you will draw on Messrs Masterman and Co Bankers London for the Sum mentioned, giving me through Mr Henderson timely notice of your so doing.

[*W. W. writes*]

I remain Sirs
your obedient Servant
Wm Wordsworth

W. W. to SIR ROBERT KER PORTER[2]

Address: Sir Robert Ker Porter, Caracas.
MS. untraced.
Bookseller's Catalogue (——).

[*In M. W.'s hand*]

Rydal Mount,
10 September 1831

. . . I am obliged to employ my Wife's pen, in consequence of an inflammation in my eye-lids . . .

. . . It was the great instability, in my judgment, of all European securities which tempted me to try in a small way this expedient . . .[3]

[*cetera desunt*]

bia. He wrote a history of Brazil (1822) and works on Spain and on commercial questions.

[1] This investment is odd, in view of Joanna Hutchinson's 'sad' experience of Columbian Bonds (see Ls. 494 and 757).

[2] A letter which also discusses William Green and his *Guide to the Lakes* ('voluminous . . . tho' with much merit . . . unsuccessful . . . his end was hastened . . . by the labors'), and looks forward to seeing Ker Porter either at Moxon's or at Rydal Mount ('if the beauties of the scenery should ever tempt you to renew your acquaintance with this neighbourhood'). This fragment follows *LY* pt. ii, L. 639. For Sir Robert Ker Porter and his previous visit to the Lakes, see L. 679.

[3] W. W.'s investment in Columbian bonds.

W. W. to ROBERT JONES[1]

MS. WL Transcript. Hitherto unpublished.

Rydal Mount Decr 18th 1831.

[*In M. W.'s hand*]

My dear Jones

Your letter was duly received, and we were all glad to hear that you arrived at home[2] safe, and that your Sisters were well; it would have been answered sooner, but I waited to be able to tell you that I had received your Dictionary,[3] which arrived yesterday, and I am happy to possess it as a memorial of our long Friendship, tho' it would certainly have been more useful to me if one of the volumes had been Welsh and English. I also wished you to know that I had given orders for my Poems being sent to you—not precisely according to the address you left (it had been mislaid) but I requested Mr Longman to enclose the volumes in his first Parcel to the Bookseller either at Denbigh or Ruthen—so if you have not already received them—let the parcel be enquired for occasionally.

My nephew John[4] is still with us—I wish you and he had paid your long expected visit at a less anxious and melancholy time—for what with the Reform Bill, and now with the Cholera, which in all probability will now be at Carlisle (where our son Wm is) and at Kendal, we have more than enough to cloud our fireside, however otherwise disposed we might have been to cheerfulness. My Son John has just left us after a stay of a few days—he is looking very well, brought good accounts of his Wife's health; and but for matters in which all the Nation is concerned would be as happy, I think, as any man need be. Dora has been much plagued with the tooth ache which makes her look thin and ill. The rest of us are quite well. Let me tell you however that three of us—Sister, Dora, and myself—had in our little carriage the other day, a very narrow escape—the Horse (one that John had lent to us) having been fed above any work he had to do—and not having been well broken in—suddenly took to kicking up his heels, in play, got one leg over the shaft and became desperately

---

[1] This letter follows *LY* pt. ii, L.658.

[2] Robert Jones had stayed at Rydal Mount the previous October.

[3] *An Abridgement of the Welsh and English Dictionary*, 1826 (first publ. 1803), by William Owen Pughe (1759–1835). See *R.M.Cat.*, no. 412.

[4] John Wordsworth was spending the winter at Rydal Mount.

frightened: Broke both Shafts and but for several happy interventions—and especially the courage and presence of mind of our neighbour Mr Harrison,[1] who happened to be passing, some grievous or fatal mischief would probably have befallen us. God be thanked nobody was any worse.

Poor Mr Fleming's[2] eyes are now in a very bad state, and his general health not good—and this day after *evening service*, I met him riding as fast as his horse could carry him to do some duty for Sir Rd[3] at Grasmere—who seems to be disabled about every other Sunday in all probability by his bad habits—before Mr F. could well get there a very heavy storm of fierce and sleaty rain came on—only think of this, and feel for the poor man, who was obliged, from the state of his eyes and health, to decline coming up the other day to dine here with my Son and Nephew—and who, for the same reason, cannot have the gratification of visiting us in an evening for conversation, or to hear the Newspapers read. Henry Curwen[4] who is here, on his way to Workington, from Trinity Coll., tells us that the young Man who lately made the attempt to blow up the letter box at Cambridge is undoubtedly insane. H. C. says that he was himself upon the Hustings during the Election for Cambridgeshire,[5] and that Dr Lamb's[6] speech was much more violent than as reported in the Newspapers. Indeed that it was too shocking to be given faithfully by a Paper of any side.

I am not aware that anything has occurred worth mentioning since your departure. Our course of life, at this season, as you must know has little variety. I have heard nothing from or of Sir Walter Scott[7]—but a letter from Rogers tells me that he himself was very ill in the summer.

All unite with me in the kindest remembrances to yourself, and those about you; and thanking you for having come so far to see us, and hoping that, till we may by God's blessing, meet,

---

[1] Benson Harrison.

[2] The Revd. Fletcher Fleming, curate of Rydal.

[3] Sir Richard le Fleming, the 'inhibited' rector of Grasmere.

[4] Younger brother of John W.'s wife Isabella (see *LY* pt. ii, L.482).

[5] The previous May.

[6] The Revd. John Lamb, D.D. (1789–1850), Master of Corpus Christi College, Cambridge, from 1822, and Dean of Bristol from 1837. A convinced Whig, he wrote *A Historical Account of the 39 Articles*, 1829, and works on the history of Cambridge.

[7] Scott was now at Naples for the winter.

again, you will let us hear from you from time to time—believe me ever to remain

Your faithful friend,
Wm Wordsworth

I have had another slight attack of inflammation in my eyes, they are better but I am afraid to use them.

W. W. to JULIUS CHARLES HARE[1]

Address: The Revd Julius Hare, Trinity Coll., Cambridge.
Stamp: Kendal Penny Post.
MS. Mr. R. L. Bayne-Powell. Hitherto unpublished.

Rydal Mount
August 28th or 9th [1832]

My dear Sir,

Your letter followed me to Lowther where, welcome as it was, the state of my eyes barely allowed me to read it; and since my return home I have been engaged in a perpetual round of summer dissipation, part of which it would not have been disagreeable to you to share.[2] We all wish much that you could join us to day;—our intention is, if the weather will permit, to dine under the Hill in the Centre of Grasmere Vale. One of our Company a London Lady sings most delightfully; her low notes and her high being managed with equal feeling and judgement, and her articulation exquisitely distinct. It gives us all great pleasure to learn from your Letter[3] that your Residence here was so agreeable and

---

[1] This letter follows *LY* pt. ii, L. 716.

[2] Julius Hare, who had been in the Lakes for more than a month earlier this summer, was one of a number of notable visitors from Trinity College, Cambridge, whose names are recorded in *RMVB*. He had called in July, accompanied by J. W. Blakesley and James Heywood (1810–97), later M.P. for N. Lancs., editor of the Cambridge University and College Statutes (1840), and author of *Academic Reform and University Representation*, 1860. The 'London Lady' whom W. W. goes on to describe, was probably Maria Kinnaird, Richard Sharp's ward (see *LY* pt. i, L. 79), referred to as 'the Nightingale' in *SH*, p. 390. W. W. and Dora W. had stayed with the two of them at Storrs recently.

[3] Hare had written from Wales on 4 Aug.: 'The obligations my mind has been under to your writings, almost from the earliest dawn of my understanding, I cannot easily estimate: but I think you yourself must have recognised, since you have always been good enough to take some notice of what I have attempted in literature, that, if there was anything good therein, the main part of it sprang

your Friends, of whom I have seen several, confirm the belief we
ourselves had, that your health was much improved by mountain
air and exercise. Your intended journey to Italy[1] will, I trust, set
you to rights completely. I am gratified by your wish that I
should join you in that Tour—but I feel it to be quite impossible.
My poor Sister is still in a languid state. While I was at Lowther
she rallied wonderfully, we were full of hope, but change of
weather brought back her weakness, and she is now again pretty
much as when you left us. She has been reading Scherer's tour in
Germany,[2] where I stumbled upon a passage that brought to my
mind the fine Incident you reported from Anastasius[3] of the
power supposed to exist in the Innocence of children. Scherer
says 'that the King of Prussia when at Darmstadt breakfasted *alone*
in a certain cabinet, and sate there opposite a Portrait of himself
taken when he was a little child. An anecdote like this (continues
the author) I love, it shows a King confessing his alliance with
our common kind, wishing himself again perhaps the little

originally from you. And now to the advantage and instruction I have received
from your poems, I may add the still greater of your conversation for so many
days. If the former has borne any fruit, the latter ought to do so more plenteously.' (*WL MSS.*).

[1] With Landor. See *LY* pt. ii, L. 711.

[2] Joseph Moyle Sherer (1789–1869), *Notes and Reflections during a Ramble in
Germany. By the author of 'Recollections in the Peninsula etc.'*, 1826. Sherer served in
the Peninsula and in the Indian army, publishing the popular *Military Memoirs of
Field Marshall the Duke of Wellington*, 2 vols., 1830, in Lardner's Cabinet Library,
as well as travel books and novels.

[3] *Anastasius, or Memoirs of a Greek written at the close of the Eighteenth Century*,
published anon. 1819 and at first attributed to Byron, was the work of Thomas
Hope (?1770–1831), of Deepdene, Surrey, the connoisseur and patron of
Canova, Thorwaldsen and Flaxman. According to Hare, W. W. had mentioned
this romance as 'the only novel you wished to read', but 'It is one of the most
monstrous works I ever met with, containing several passages of great power,
along with many that are quite revolting, in which Byron's extravagant misan-
thropical sentimentality is mixt up with the levity and persiflage of Voltaire. But
the account of Egypt is exceedingly interesting. One of the scenes described is
among the sublimest I ever heard of.' During the famine of 1786 the priests had
no longer ventured to offer up prayers except through the voices of young children who were taken by the imams to the tops of the minarets while the population listened in silence below. But they only begged that a pestilence might
deliver them from lingering suffering. 'What sort of person Mr Hope was, you
may judge from his subjoining to this description, "This humble request God in
his mercy granted." So blind was his heart to the grandeur of what he himself
had been telling of.'

uncrowned king that played free in a nursery. Childhood is the season of true royalty; they command us all, they bid us do this and do that, come here and go there, shew this picture or tell the story, or sing the song, and we do it all with delighted obedience. It is innocence we serve, nay, we feel them in so much beings of a higher order, we forget not that of such is the Kingdom of heaven, etc.'—

You will have inferred from my continuing to scrawl in this way with my own hand that my eyes are better, indeed they are much improved within these few days, and I have the prospect, agreeable about measure, of being again able to read, without a likelihood of my eyes being sacrificed to newspapers as they were during the debates on the Catholic Relief Bill and upon the pestilent Reform Bill. We shall have something like a respite for at least a couple of months. You will not be sorry to learn that the registering of both now complete has shewn that the spirit of the people in our two counties, is far from being as bad as many feared. Two Conservatives *might* be returned in connection with the Lowther interest, for Westmorland, and that I cannot doubt, easily.[1] Whether the Friends of moderate measures will act up to their powers is uncertain; but whatever may be done in this part of the Country, one cannot but fear that the cause will be lost by the timidity and love of present ease, which has always proved in difficult times the besetting sin of humane and good men, and men of property and influence.—

Dr Arnold has determined to purchase the little estate we looked at together.[2] I am rather sorry for this, as I think it will involve him in more expense and trouble, should he build, this he is aware of. Mr Hamilton[3] is of the same opinion. He has purchased Mr Tillbrook's, for 1700, very dear I think; but he is likely to have his enjoyment of it, and promises to make a pleasant neighbour for us, only I fear that he will draw around him some persons whom this quiet village would rather be without.

Yesterday Peacock and Thorpe[4] called here on their way to

[1] At the General Election in December, Lord Lowther and Col. H. C. Lowther were again returned for Westmorland.

[2] Dr. Thomas Arnold, who lodged with his family at Brathay this summer, arranged to buy Fox How the following month.

[3] Capt. Thomas Hamilton (see *LY* pt. ii, L. 673) had bought the Ivy Cottage, below Rydal Mount, from Samuel Tillbrooke (see *MY* pt. i, L. 174).

[4] George Peacock and Thomas Thorp (see *LY* pt. ii, Ls. 593 and 619), Fellows of Trinity. See *RMVB*.

Keswick. We thought Thorp was looking ill—Unluckily for us we had a party of Strangers breakfasting with us at that time, of whom Sir James Grant[1] proved to be a Relation of Thorpe's, so that we had little conversation with them. In a day or two I am expecting Mr Pickersgill,[2] who is so kind as to come all the way from London to paint my portrait for St John's Coll.—the last of my sittings.—

I fear that with so much to see you will be sadly hurried in your projected Tour. Dresden, Prague and Vienna, you ought to include if possible, and snatch a sight of Saltzburg and its romantic neighbourhood. Then there is Munich also, which one would like to have a peep at.

I wish you could have told me that Mrs Dashwood[3] was in better health. Mr Barber's[4] Sister is come to occupy his Cottage permanently. Say every thing that is kind to Landor[5] and add that I still hope to shake him by the hand in Italy.—Should your Route lead you going or returning to the Lake of Lucerne, take what I have not done a look at Weggs[6] between Husnach and Gerisane, and walk along that shore of the lake, as far as Brunen. Mr Thorp tells me that the seclusion is most delightful, and he is a good judge of scenery. There is also an Inn at Bellagio upon the Lake of Como, which he speaks of as a charming abode.

My wife, Sister and Daugher and Miss H– all unite with me in Kindest remembrances. Pray let us hear from you at your convenience, and be indulgent if I shall not reply as soon as I ought and shall be sure of wishing to do.

Believe me your
affectionate friend W. Wordsworth

[1] Sir James Grant, C.B. (1773–1864), Inspector General of Army hospitals, 1814, and chief medical officer at Waterloo.

[2] Henry William Pickersgill, R. A. (see *LY* pt. ii, Ls. 621 and 694).

[3] Hare's cousin Anna Maria (see also *LY* pt. iii, L. 1219), to whom he had been for a time engaged. She was second daughter of William Davies Shipley (1745–1826), Dean of St Asaph, and elder sister of Reginald Heber's widow, and had married Col. Charles Armand Dashwood (d. 1812), a descendant of the Dashwoods of Kirtlington Park, Oxon.

[4] For Samuel Barber, the local eccentric, see *MY* pt. ii, L. 523; *SH*, p. 383, and *LY* pt. ii, L. 686.

[5] Walter Savage Landor had visited W. W. at Rydal Mount in June (see *RMVB*), and was now about to return to Florence by way of Germany, in the company of Julius Hare and Thomas Worsley (see *LY* pt. iii, L. 877).

[6] i.e. Weggis.

In your copy of the Excursion page 82 line 11, read 'earthy' and 149 for 'infinite', 'finite'.[1]

D. W. to KATE SOUTHEY[2]

Address. To Miss [? Southey] By Jane.
MS. WL (Moorsom Papers).

Monday mor^{ning}
[Oct.—Nov. 1833][3]

My dear Friend, little Kate,

I have just destroyed a note which I wrote on Friday for Jane to inquire about the Mitts; when she was gone, the explanation arrived, and I was glad the coach could [?not][4] receive her. She will pay 4/- with thanks.

This morning is bright and I hope she will get off. We have a nice little Maiden in her place: would that some of you were now on the road to us!

My dear Brother is much better and my Sister tells me he hopes you will come—Company begins now to be of great use to him. I am in good plight,[5] and shall enjoy chatting with Edith, and I hope become acquainted with her intended companion for life.

My dear Kate, if you can send me any Books that you think will interest and amuse an invalid I know you will set them aside to be brought by Jane at her return. My taste lies in the *Biography*, *Missionary* and *Travels* line.

I write in bed—so excuse me for adding no more—and with love to Father, Mother, Aunt, Sister etc—and shall I add Brothers?

Your affectionate Friend
D. Wordsworth

[1] See *Exc.*, iii. 31, and iv. 993.

[2] This letter perhaps follows *LY* pt. ii, L. 790.

[3] Dated by reference to W. W.'s eye-trouble in autumn 1833, and the forthcoming marriage of Edith Southey to John Wood Warter in Jan. 1834.

[4] *Written* no.

[5] D. W. had now partially recovered from her devastating illness earlier in the year, but was to remain an invalid for the rest of her life. Samuel Crosthwaite's portrait of her, now hanging again at Rydal Mount, belongs to this autumn. See L. 796.

W. W. to FELICIA DOROTHEA HEMANS[1]

Address: Mrs Hemans, 20 Dawson Street, Dublin.
Franked: Stamford December Twenty Seven 1833 H. C. Lowther
Postmark: (1) 27 Dec. 1833 (2) 30 Dec.
Stamp: (1) Stamford (2) Dublin.
MS. WL. Hitherto unpublished.

[*In M. W.'s hand*]

[27 Dec. 1833]

. . . my Sonnet on Saragossa[2]—I am glad you have seen Mr Archer,[3] why does not he write either to Mr Hamilton, or myself—he is often thought of and talked about at Rydal. I have not rec^d any letter or parcel from him—so of course have not seen, which I must regret, the translation from Filicaia.[4] I delivered your message to Mr Hamilton, who is about to be married to Lady Townshend Farquhar,[5] an amiable friend of ours.

My eyes you will be glad to hear are all but well, tho' I do not venture to use them yet in writing, which must be my excuse for so dull a letter which is merely intended as one of business—My dear Sister is in her better way. Pray remember me kindly to Charles[6] and to both the Mr Gs[7]—Mrs W. my Sister and Dora unite with me in kind regards and the good wishes of the season to you and yours, and believe me d^r Mrs H. to be your faithful friend

[*signed*]
Wm Wordsworth

---

[1] Part of the missing portion of *LY* pt. ii, L. 797. For Mrs Hemans, see *LY* pt. i, L. 246.

[2] See *PW* iii. 132, 458.

[3] Edward Archer of Dublin, a recent visitor to Grasmere (see *LY* pt. ii, L. 580a).

[4] Vincenzio Filicaia, the Florentine poet (1642–1707), noted for his sonnets mourning the degradation of Italy: 'the greatest lyric poet of modern times', according to Macaulay. For W. W.'s estimate of him, see *PW* iii. 461. See also Morley i. 262; *R. M. Cat.*, no. 531, and Alan G. Hill, 'Wordsworth and Italy', *Journal of Anglo-Italian Studies*, i (1991), 111–25.

[5] See *LY* pt. ii, L. 673.

[6] Her son, the antiquary, author of works on Roman history and archaeology.

[7] The Revd. R. P. Graves and his brother Charles (see *LY* pt. ii, L. 776, and letter of early Aug. 1836, below).

W. W. to EDWIN HILL HANDLEY[1]

Address: Edwin Hill Handley Esqre, Lower Wick, near Worcester.
Stamp: Kendal Penny Post.
MS. Stanford University Library. Hitherto unpublished.

[*In M. W.'s hand*]

Rydal Mount Octr 29th [1835]

My dear Sir,

A few words may suffice to congratulate you, which I do most heartily, upon your restoration to health and strength; with corresponding and still higher blessings vouchsafed to the mind and spirits. Be assured also, it was not with indifference that I heard of the improvement you mention in your outward circumstances; and above all of your being married to a Lady of congenial sensibility, accomplished in vocal and instrumental harmony, and I doubt not in the music of daily and hourly life, as it makes itself felt in good actions and kind looks; and emotions encouraged only as far as they are under a regulation rational, and, without presumption, it may be said, divine.

As to the mode in which you propose to express the gratitude you feel for the benefit you have derived from my writings, if you have happened to see 2 Sonnets, to be found in p. 183 in the 3^d vol: of the last Ed: of my Poems, printed in 1832, you will be aware of the view I take of the rite of baptism, and the obligations of Sponsorship.[2]—I wish to refer you also, to one of the miscellaneous Sonnets beginning 'Rotha my spiritual child'[3] from there you will learn, that, advanced in life as I am, I feel myself unfit to incur the responsibilities ordinarily attached to the connection, and with a declaration to this effect I have replied, even for nearly the last 20 years, to requests of the same kind as that you have just honored me with. But the objection has been overruled by considerations which have induced you to desire me to stand in that relation to your child—and therefore, tho' not without some reluctance I gave way, as I cannot help doing on the present occasion: hoping that the influence of my writings, upon the young Persons with whom I am so connected, may be thereby so far aided, as to compensate in some degree for those substantial and palpable Services living Godfathers and

---

[1] This letter, and the next, follow *LY* pt. iii, L. 936. For Edwin Hill Handley, C. W. jnr.'s college friend, see *LY* pt. ii, L. 569; pt. iii, L. 976.

[2] See *PW* iii. 394.   [3] ibid. 47.

Godmothers ought to keep in view, and have not unfrequently an opportunity of rendering.

If I had wanted any inducements beyond the wish to see you and Mrs Handley for visiting your abode, they would be supplied by the charming country you live in—not above two days ago, I had occasion to say, as I have said over and over, that if I were forced to quit the district in which I was born and much the greatest part of my life has been spent, and had a choice, it would settle upon the neighbourhood of Malvern.—

Domestic circumstances, and to you I may say, afflictions, have put and continue to put it out of my power to leave home—I do however cherish the hope of seeing you and your life's Partner in this country—and of personally bestowing a Blessing upon my new Godson.

Believe me to be, with sincere thanks for your long and confiding letter, and with my best wishes for yourself and Mrs H,

faithfully yours

[unsigned]

In consequence of a severe sprain in my [?right][1] arm, I am obliged to employ Mrs W's pen which you will excuse.

W. W. to EDWIN HILL HANDLEY

Address: E. H. Handley Esqre, Lower Wick, Worcester.
Franked: Whitehaven November one 1835—Lonsdale.
Stamp: 1 Nov. 1835.
MS. Stanford University Library. Hitherto unpublished.

[In Isabella Wordsworth's hand]

Rectory Workington[2]
Octr 30th 1835

My dear Sir,

You would indeed be surprised to find my yesterday's letter to you was without a signature: as my best apology and I trust you will think it a sufficient one, let me tell you how that happened. As soon as I had dictated the letter to Mrs W. I went out, to take a walk, meaning to read the letter on my return, when I thought I might have to add a few words from my own pen; and I

---

[1] *MS. torn.*

[2] W. W. had gone to stay with John W., and to dine with Lord Lonsdale at Whitehaven Castle.

intended to sign the letter at the same time. Mʳˢ W. folded it up, and left it on my desk, with the address upon it, and soon after my daughter finding it there, sealed it as she is accustomed to do on like occasions, and sent it to the Post: my surprise was mixed with some vexation, and now upon inquiring for the letter on my return from my walk, I found that it was nearly half way on its road to Kendal. I left home this morning and am now in the house of my Son, whose Lady (the same to whom the poem is addressed, which you mention in your letter)¹ is now kindly acting as my amanuensis, but I will take care that the letter shall be signed, and by myself, before my pen is laid down. This morning I received from America a letter written by a female disciple of mine² as she calls herself, full as ardent and devoted as yourself, it is occasioned by my last volume and at some future time I may have the pleasure of reading it to you. I remain my dear Sir

faithfully yours
[*signed*] Wᵐ Wordsworth

W. W. to ROBERT FLETCHER HOUSMAN³

Endorsed: The date is a mistake; it should be Janʸ 15. R. F. Housman
MS. untraced.
Bookseller's Catalogue (—).

[*In M. W.'s hand*]

Rydal Mount
Dec 15ᵗʰ [15 Jan. 1836]

Dear Sir,

    I am sorry that you should have had any anxiety on the subject of your letter recᵈ this morning. Messʳˢ Longman have not been

---

¹ 'To— upon the Birth of her First-born Child, March, 1833' (see *PW* iv. 107, 426).

² Elizabeth Peabody (see *LY* pt. iii, L. 937). Her letter from Boston on 7 Sept. referred to W. W. as 'the Columbus of Poetry' and 'the Messiah of the reign of the Saints—a true Christian prophet', praising what he had done for women in his poems, and describing the use to which she put *Peter Bell* in the moral education of her pupils (*WL MSS.*).

³ The Revd. Robert Fletcher Housman, of Lune Bank, Lancaster, son of the Revd. Robert Housman (1759–1836), a close associate of Simeon and Venn, and builder and incumbent of St. Anne's, Lancaster, 1796–1836. R. F. Housman published a monumental *Life and Remains* of his father in 1841: earlier, in 1835, he

221

in communication with me upon it. They must however be supposed to know their business better than I can do; and as they have an interest in the work they no doubt felt themselves justified in threatening an injunction. But it could only be their zeal in promoting my interest that induced them to say, that they were satisfied I should take such proceedings, without communication with me.

Private considerations of regard to yourself will have entirely prevented me, as far as I am concerned, from taking such a step. Besides I have no reason to think that extracts even as copious as those you have done me the honor to make from my Sonnets would tend to obstruct the circulation of my Works. I have, it is true, often stated to Messrs L. the injury I felt as being done to me by the Paris editions[1] and the remembrance of that fact probably caused them to pre-conclude that I should act as they stated to Messrs Whitaker. You will then d^r Sir understand that I on my own part make no complaint and do not think it probable that my publishers will proceed on the business. As a friendly caution however allow me to say that should you be disposed to make any Collections in future, it would be better to ask permission of the respective Authors and Proprietors before you proceed to print . . .

> I remain my d^r Sir
> faithfully yours
> [*signed*] Wm Wordsworth

W. W. to FRANCIS MEREWETHER[2]

MS. untraced.
Bookseller's Catalogue (—).

> Rydal Mount
> 7th March 1836

. . . I do not wonder at your shrinking from the thought of your little boys leaving home—after a bustling family—how silent the fireside must feel . . . with *one daughter*, and yet you will look to

had edited *A Collection of English Sonnets* from Surrey to Tennyson, containing no less than 56 sonnets by Wordsworth (*R. M. Cat.*, no. 565). The volume included a lengthy essay on the art of the sonnet, discussing the views of Dr. Johnson, Capel Lofft, and Sir Egerton Brydges. This letter follows *LY* pt. iii, L. 967.

[1] By Galignani (see *LY* pt. i, Ls. 370–1, 387).
[2] This is part of the missing portion of *LY* pt. iii, L. 984.

the holidays . . . for the boys' return to you—We have outlived
that regular expectation—and our hearth was and is a more bereft
one than even yours, while our poor sister . . . is confined to her
room and our only daughter to her couch—*Her* progress to
amendment is very slow and often interrupted—but we are
grateful that she is no worse . . . We are blessed by our two sons
being . . . affectionate and dutiful, that they lose no opportunity
. . . [*half a sheet missing*] When you have occasion to write either
to John[1] or us, pray never omit speaking of Sir George
Beaumont[2] or his dear little orphans. Pray tell him that I long . . .
to see my Godson.[3] We hope Mrs Merewether and yourself and
family are well . . .

Wm Wordsworth

W. W. to LORD LONSDALE[4]

Endorsed: 29 March 1836. Copy f^m Mr Wordsworth to Ld L.—
MS. Lonsdale MSS. Hitherto unpublished.

[*In unidentified hand*] Copy

29 March 1836

My Lord,
    I am going to write upon a point of business which you will be
surprised that I should meddle with.—

    Henry Lancaster a shoemaker of Troutbeck came to me the
other day to tell me, he had discovered a Vein of Black Lead in
your Lordship's Royalty[5] in that neighbourhood. The object of
his calling upon me was to entreat that I would endeavour to
procure for him liberty to work the same. He then told me that
he had made two several applications to Mr Benn[6] without any
result, and put into my Hands a copy of a Letter which had been
addressed to Mr Benn together with an Agreement between
himself and certain persons purposing to work the Mine and
share the profits.

    I then put such questions to him as I thought proper, and tho
the man has a manner singularly shy and odd, his account seemed

---

[1] John W. had been Merewether's curate at Whitwick in 1828.
[2] i. e. the 8th Baronet, whose wife had died in 1834.
[3] Sir George's younger son William.
[4] This letter follows *LY* pt. iii, L. 988.   [5] Lord Lonsdale's mineral rights.
[6] Agent at Lowther.

to be deserving of attention. I have since inquired about him and learn nothing to his prejudice. He says when he saw Mr Benn he told him not to meddle with the Ore. He said further, that when he first discovered the Vein he brought away a specimen, parts of which I believe were seen by several persons—but the piece he kept for himself was either thrown into the Fire by accident, or otherwise destroyed by his children. I told him, as he might be mistaken as to the quality of the Mineral, I should like to see a specimen, before I troubled your Lordship, but he will not meddle with it, even for this purpose without authority.—

I know nothing of the circumstances under which Black Lead is usually found, but as the Man says, it here lies only a spade's depth from the surface, it could not cost much to ascertain whether there is any thing in this supposed discovery.

If your Lordship would grant me permission I would myself venture, in conjunction with this poor man to make a trial; upon such terms and under such arrangements as are usual in Royalties where Mines lie—though this, if there should be anything in it, is a thing of rare occurrence. My neighbour Mr Benson Harrison[1] has had a good deal to do with Mining, and I should have the benefit of his advice as to the manner of proceeding, and of his cooperation if expedient.—

One result, at all events there would be—the poor man, who has had this weighing upon his mind, I think he told me for 4 years, would probably soon be set at ease, one way or other.—I take the liberty to enclose the Agreement between the man and his Friends, *if such they be*, which as to one of them especially, I have good reason to doubt, and therefore wishing him out of that individuals hands, I have had little scruple in making the above proposal. The paper upon the face of it does not appear entitled to much respect.—My proposal could not be acceded to by your Lordship without setting it aside altogether: if it should be thought there is any unfairness in this, I should at once drop the idea of personally mixing with the affair, further than to assist in securing to Lancaster any recompence that might be due to him for his discovery, should it prove of any Value.—Such was my first and principal object in attending to his story, and such it now is in troubling your Lordship.—

Ever faithfully yours
Wm Wordsworth

[1] The ironmaster, of Green Bank (see *MY* pt. ii, L. 304).

W. W. to LORD NORTHAMPTON[1]

MS. The Marquess of Northampton. Hitherto unpublished.

[?late May 1836]

My dear Lord,

Be assured that I was duly sensible of the honor done me by your Present of a Copy of the unpublished Poem of Irene with the miscellaneous Pieces annexed, and that thanks would have been immediately returned had I not persuaded myself they would be more acceptable if I were enabled to say that I had perused the Volume. Much do I regret that innumerable and harrassing engagements[2] have deprived me hitherto of that pleasure, but the smaller pieces to which you kindly pointed my attention I have several times read, and I can sincerely say with very great delight. They are written with simplicity pathos and energy. I have also read part of Irene, but not yet the passages which you mentioned. I reserve them and the whole in its order for a time when I shall be more capable of enjoying things that are good. But I can no longer defer my acknowledgements nor deny myself the gratification of declaring that in my opinion (whatever may be its value), these pieces give proof of a poetical feeling, and talent, which by culture might have been carried to a high degree of excellence.

Believe me my Lord
With thanks for your Letter
faithfully
your obliged
Wm Wordsworth

---

[1] This letter perhaps follows *LY* pt. iii, L. 1023. Spencer Compton, 2nd Marquess of Northampton, a liberal-minded Tory, had succeeded Spencer Perceval as M. P. for Northampton, and supported Wilberforce on emancipation and Sir James Macintosh on criminal law reform. In 1815 he married Margaret, eldest daughter of Maj. Gen. Douglas Maclean Clephane of Kirkness, Kinross, and a close friend of Scott (see J. G. Lockhart, *Memoirs of the Life of Sir Walter Scott, Bart.*, 7 vols., 1837–8, iii. 299–300, 347). He lived in Italy, 1820–30, interesting himself in artistic matters and liberal politics, and meeting H. C. R. there (see Sadler, ii. 257–8); but he returned to England on his wife's death in childbirth in Rome. In 1833 he printed her poem *Irene* for private circulation (see *R. M. Cat.*, no. 548), and several of her other poems were later published in *The Tribute* (see below, letter of *c.* 1 Mar. 1837). W. W. does not appear to have made Lord Northampton's acquaintance until his London visit in summer, 1836 (see *LY* pt. iii, L. 1017): hence the suggested dating for this letter.

[2] Particularly, perhaps, his discussions with Longman and Moxon over a new edition of his poems.

M. W. and W. W. to UNKNOWN CORRESPONDENT[1]

MS. untraced.
Bookseller's Catalogue.

[London]
Saturday Morn^g
[?May–June 1836]

My dear Sir,

Mr Wordsworth has desired me to inform you that you will find us at ½ past eleven oClock at Mr Rogers' when we shall be happy to be conducted by you to see your Picture etc.

I am dear Sir
respectfully yours
M. Wordsworth

[*W. W. adds*]

I was very sorry I did not see you last night and more for the dinner, but I entirely approve of your prudence and firmness. Take care of yourself.

W. W. to CHARLES GRAVES[2]

Address: Charles Graves Esqre, Bowness.
Stamp: Kendal Penny Post.
MS. Private Collection. Hitherto unpublished.

Wednesday [early Aug.1836]

My dear Sir,

This note is written to beg you not to trouble yourself with coming to Rydal sooner than is quite convenient. I have been so much interrupted as to have had little time with corrections[3] since I had the pleasure of seeing you. Besides I have now a Gentleman staying with me, Mr Quillinan, who is likely to prove

---

[1] This letter was written during one of W. W.'s visits to London, most likely in the 1830s, but it cannot be dated with any certainty; nor can the addressee be identified, though it may possibly have been B. R. Haydon.

[2] The Revd. Charles Graves, D.D., F.R.S. (1812–99), R. P. Graves's brother, Fellow of Trinity College, Dublin, from 1836 and Professor of Mathematics from 1843. He became Dean of Clonfert in 1864, and Bishop of Limerick two years later. This letter follows *LY* pt. ii, L.1061.

[3] W. W. was revising his poems, with E. Q.'s help.

very useful in this irksome labour. Now take care that you understand this rightly. I shall be truly glad to see you at any time—I only wish to prevent your putting yourself to inconvenience.

Pray make our kind remembrances to your Brother and Sisters.

Y^{rs} faithfully,
Wm Wordsworth

W. W. to UNKNOWN CORRESPONDENT[1]

MS. Private Collection. Hitherto unpublished.

[*In M. W.'s hand*]

Rydal Mount
Sepr 20th [1836]

Dear Sir,

On returning home this evening, I have found your obliging letter, and cannot deny myself the pleasure of thanking you for the zealous exertions you have made in my Son's favour. Whatever may be the result of his offering himself as a Candidate for the employment in question,[2] it will always be a pleasure to me to reflect upon the active endeavours of the friends who have been applied to, as a testimony of respect either for himself or his nearest connections.

I have the honor to be
dear Sir
Your much ob^l St.[3]
[*signed*] Wm Wordsworth

---

[1] This letter follows *LY* pt. iii, L. 1069, and may possibly be addressed to the same correspondent.

[2] W. W. jnr. had applied for the Secretaryship to the Birmingham and Derby Railway. See also L. 1090.

[3] i.e. obliged Servant.

W. W. to ISAAC GREEN[1]

Address: The Revd I. Green, Sedbergh,
Stamp: Kendal Penny Post.
MS. Private Collection. Hitherto unpublished.

[*In M. W.'s hand*]

Rydal Mount Novr 12th [1836]

. . . I shall value as a memorial of the Place for which I have long felt a lively interest.

I was sorry not to have seen you when you were last in the neighbourhood—or I should have given you my Subscription of £2—which I shall not forget when I have the pleasure to see you, which I imagine may be in a few weeks—else I should have sent it to you.

Mrs W. joins me in kind regards to yourself, and believe me to be dear Sir,

very sincerely yours,
[signed] Wm Wordsworth

W. W. to JAMES STANGER[2]

Address: James Stanger Esqre, Keswick.
Stamp: Kendal Penny Post.
MS. WL (Moorsom Papers). Hitherto unpublished.

[*In M. W.'s hand*]

Rydal Mount
Novr 14th [1836]

My dear Sir,
You must have been disappointed in not hearing from me, I assure you it has not been my fault. From some cause or other

---

[1] See *LY* pt. i, L. 365, and pt. iii, L. 1088. This letter, which is incomplete, concerns the restoration (1838) of Howgill Church, on the Lune, near Sedbergh, and follows L. 1088.

[2] The Keswick churchman and philanthropist (see *LY* pt. i, L. 42), whose portrait hangs in Crosthwaite Church. This letter, which precedes *LY* pt. iii, L. 1089, is the first of several additional letters concerned with the protracted negotiations about the provision of a new church in W. W.'s native town of Cockermouth (see *LY* pt. iii, L. 978).

my letter was long in reaching Mr Watson,[1] and when his answer came, I found him unable to reply to my enquiries as to what assistance could be derived from the Societies on account of the absence of the Official Returns from Mr Fawcett.[2] It is some time since the Bp:[3] wrote to the Secretary, upon the matter of a Ch: at Cockermouth, and in compliance with his Lordship's request the Sec^ry applied to Mr F. by letter, to make the requisite Returns, which to my great mortification upon passing thro' Cockermouth 12 days ago, I learned he had not done. Having since that time been exceedingly engaged, and from home, I have been at a loss how to proceed with due delicacy to Mr Fawcett. I have been inclined to write to the Bp: myself, but it would be more agreeable to me to apply to him thro' Mr Watson, and still more so; that the Official Returns should be made by Mr F without my being put to the necessity of addressing our Diocesan either directly or indirectly.

If you are likely to be in Cockermouth shortly perhaps you might not be unwilling to introduce the Subject to Mr Fawcett and might perhaps prevail upon him to send the returns without delay as officially requested. At all events, having now taken time to consider this matter, I shall write again to Mr Watson in a few days.

Believe me in the mean while, dear Sir faithfully yours,

[*signed*] Wm Wordsworth

D. W. to UNKNOWN CORRESPONDENT[4]

MS. *Cornell. Hitherto unpublished.*

January 5th 1837

Christmas Day

This is the day when kindred meet
Round one accustomed social fire:

[1] Joshua Watson (see *MY* pt. ii, L. 590), the leading Anglican layman, who at W. W.'s request was approaching the Church Building Societies for financial support.

[2] The Revd. Edward Fawcett, perpetual curate of Cockermouth (see *LY* pt. iii, L. 933).

[3] The Bishop of Carlisle, Dr. Hugh Percy (see *LY* pt. ii, L. 477).

[4] This poem, copied out in an unidentified hand, was probably included in a letter addressed to some local friend, and follows *LY* pt. iii, L. 1101. D.W. enjoyed some remission of her illness around Christmas 1836, as is clear from her

If still survive the hoary Sire
In patriarchal age, beside his honour'd feet
His Children's Children claim the appropriate seat;
And if the Partner of his youthful days,
His dear supporter through the uncertain ways
Of busy life—if *she* be spared,
She who all joy, all grief has shared
Now is their happiness complete:
Their Children, and their Children's Children meet:
Beneath the Grandsire's reverenced roof,
Where faithful love through trying years has stood all proof.

Dorothy Wordsworth

W. W. to JAMES STANGER[1]

Address: James Stanger Esqr, 17 Cheapside.
Postmark: 17 Jan. 1837.
Stamp: Fleet St.
MS. WL (Moonsom Papers). Hitherto unpublished.

[*In M. W.'s hand*]

Rydal Mount
Jan^{ry} 14th—37

My dear Sir,

I was about to write to you at Keswick, when I received your
letter dated St Anne's Hill[2] having the day before received a
Letter from Lord Londsdale and some days previous, a communication from Mr Watson. The purpose of both I wished you to be
made acquainted with. Mr W. transmitted to me a Copy of a
Return, at length, made by Mr Fawcett and this he sent Mr W.
(not to the board) who found it so imperfect that he was doubt-

letter to Jane Marshall (L.1095), and she remembered old friends to the end. As
late as May 1851, M.W. was writing to Mrs. Sarah Greenwood (*née* Staniforth),
niece of Mrs. Bolton of Storrs: 'My poor Sister was much gratified by your
remembrance of her—She begs me to say she forgets none of her old friends—
and your dear Mother was an especial favourite with her, as was the case with us
all. My Sister's bodily health enables her to go out in almost all weathers—but
she suffers much from nervous restlessness.' (*MS. Mrs. Greenwood, Swarcliffe Hall,
Harrogate*).

[1] This letter follows *LY* pt. iii, L. 1106.
[2] Stanger's London residence in Wandsworth.

ful whether to lay it before the Commissioners[1] or not, and he wrote to me for advice. The letter from Lord Lonsdale permits me to mention, where I think it may be useful so to do, that his Lordship is 'prepared to provide an Endowment for a new Church at Cockermouth to the amount of £150 per ann', and in all such cases he presumes the clergyman derives some Benefit from Pews. This munificent proposal from Lord Lonsdale, if I have any thing (beyond my own Subscription) to do with the business, decides for me where the Patronage must rest.

I am far from certain that any Committee which may be formed in support of a measure based upon this principle, may not lose certain intended Subscriptions, nor can I be sure that the requisite Sum for building the Church can be raised, I will therefore frankly own that I am not a little anxious about the issue—but I am resolved to do my utmost out of affection for the Place—and must be permitted to express to you the exceeding regret that I feel, from the declaration you made to me, that we are not likely to have your support beyond that of a small Subscription.

I have mentioned to Mr Watson that you have obligingly proposed to call upon him—and knowing that his important engagements might cause you a useless journey, if you waited upon him with merely my introduction, I have requested him to send you a note appointing a time when you might be sure to find him at home. Therefore, if you do not hear from him you may conclude that he cannot command leisure within the time of your remaining in Town.

We should have been glad if your letter had mentioned your Brother and Sister.[2] I hope their health may have withstood the attacks of this unusually changeable Season.

Pray give our united affectionate regards to them, and accept the like yourself, from d^r Sir,

faithfully yours
[*signed*] Wm Wordsworth

P.S. I hope you will contrive to give us a call at least, on your way to Keswick.

If a very small packet should be sent to your address for me, may I request the favor that you will bring it down for me.

---

[1] The Church Building Commissioners (see L. 1102).

[2] Joshua Stanger (see *LY* pt. i, L. 166, where he is incorrectly described as the son of James Stanger), and his wife, *née* Mary Calvert.

W.W. to JAMES STANGER[1]

Address: James Stanger Esqre, Keswick.
Stamp: Kendal Penny Post.
MS. WL(Moorsom Papers). Hitherto unpublished.

Rydal Mount Feb 9th [1837]

[*In M.W.'s hand*]

My dear Sir,

I have to thank you for your letter reporting your interview with Mr Watson. It was to me a matter of much regret that you were obliged to pass thro' by the coach without my seeing you. But this disappointment I felt less, as I had not received Lord Lonsdale's answer to Mr Wood's final communication[2]—This post has brought it; and I must now, however reluctantly, declare that I feel myself obliged to withdraw from present connection with the project of a new Church at C—. Nor, considering my advanced years, is it likely I shall ever have it in my power to benefit however humbly my native Place in that way. Whatever may have been my views at first, I feel so hurt at the manner in which Lord Lonsdale's munificent offer has been received—knowing also, as I do, further dispositions of his regarding the point—that I cannot bring myself to cooperate with Persons who entertain such decisive opinions in opposition to a proceeding which would I am convinced have been beneficial in an eminent degree to the Place.

You will of course have concluded that Lord Lonsdale's letter expressed an opinion—that, in consequence of the indisposition of the Inhabitants, as far as he was concerned, the project should be suspended, and further discussion on the Subject at an end. And such was my own opinion after the receipt of the Lord's letter.

Mrs W. and my daughter unite with me in kind regards, and believe me my dear Sir

to be sincerely yours
[*signed*] Wm Wordsworth

---

[1] This letter follows *LY* pt. iii, L.1114.
[2] See L. 1113. William Wood was Lord Lonsdale's law agent.

W. W. to JAMES STANGER[1]

Address: James Stanger Esqre, Keswick.
Stamp: Kendal Penny Post.
MS. WL (Moorsom Papers). Hitherto unpublished.

[*In M. W.'s hand*]

Feb. 15th [1837]

My dear Sir,

I am very anxious to see you before I leave the country—especially as I feel myself (upon a communication this morn^g from Ld L–)[2] at liberty to speak in *confidence* to you, more explicitly than when I last wrote to you, upon the Subject which has interested us both so much. I therefore write to say that if Friday is not a stormy day I intend calling upon you at Keswick—and hope that I may find you at home.

I am dear Sir
Sincerely yours
[*signed*] Wm Wordsworth

W. W. to LORD NORTHAMPTON[3]

MS. The Marquess of Northampton. Hitherto unpublished.

[*c.* 1 Mar. 1837]

My dear Lord,

It cannot but be a subject of thankfulness to poor Mr Smedley's[4] Friends that his sufferings are closed.—I rejoice to

---

[1] This letter follows *LY* pt. iii, L.1116.   [2] Lord Lonsdale.

[3] This letter probably follows *LY* pt. iii, L. 1121.

[4] The Revd. Edward Smedley (1788–1836), educated at Westminster School and Trinity College, Cambridge, and Fellow of Sidney Sussex College, 1812–16, won the Seatonian Prize for English verse in 1813, 1814, 1827 and 1828. On leaving Cambridge, he held several curacies before devoting himself entirely to literary work from 1822, editing the *Encyclopaedia Metropolitana* and contributing to the *British Critic* and the *Penny Cyclopaedia*. He published numerous volumes of verse and works on French history; his *Poems*, with a memoir, were published posthumously by his wife in 1837. *The Tribute*, edited by Lord Northampton, 1837, was projected as a benefit for him in his last illness, and then as a memorial to him. W. W.'s stanzas 'The Moon that sails along the sky' (see *PW* iv. 77 and I. F. note, p. 417), were given pride of place in the volume (p.3), following Bernard Barton's introductory verses, and many of his acquaintances also contributed, including Rogers, Landor, and Moore. Tennyson's offering (p.244), was

hear that Mrs Smedley[1] has been so fortunate, and should be well pleased to think that your benevolent exertion in her behalf, may add some little to her Comforts. As to the trifle from my own pen I have only to regret that it is not worthier of the Volume in which it will appear, and of the place which your partiality has assigned to it.—

Mr Southey has just returned to Keswick after an absence of four months. You will not be displeased, I am sure, if I mention the project to him, which I shall do with a hope that he may have a few verses to spare.[2]

> I have the honor to be
> My dear Lord,
> faithfully yours
> Wm Wordsworth

Towards the end of next week I purpose to start for London, and perhaps for the Continent. My Tour last summer was put off.

W. W. to BENJAMIN ROBERT HAYDON

Address: B. R. Haydon Esqre [*delivered by hand*]
MS. Rare Book Room, Smith College Library. Hitherto unpublished.

> [London]
> [?17 Aug. 1837][3]

My dear Haydon,

I go out of Town at 2 oclock this day, and I shall not return for a week or ten days; and much fear that I shall only remain a couple of days on my return—But I will contrive to see you if possi-

---

an early version of 'Oh! that 'twere possible', which was eventually used as the germ for *Maud* (see R. B. Martin, *Tennyson, The Unquiet Heart*, 1980, pp.226–8).

[1] She was Mary, youngest daughter of James Hume, of Wandsworth Common, Secretary of the Customs, and had married Smedley in 1816.

[2] In his letter of 6 Mar. (*MS. Marquess of Northampton*), Southey suggested that a private subscription 'among old Westminsters' would yield more for Smedley's family than the proposed volume. His contribution to *The Tribute* (p.280) was 'Brough Bells', written 1828 (*Poems of Robert Southey*, ed. Maurice H. Fitzgerald, 1909, p.376).

[3] This letter cannot be dated with any certainty, but it probably belongs to the 1830s, and was perhaps written soon after W. W.'s return to London from his Continental tour of 1837, and before he set out on a visit to Chatham and Broadstairs (see *LY* pt. iii, L. 1157). If so, it perhaps follows L. 1154.

ble, though I see little prospect of being able to dine with you and Mrs Haydon.

ever faithfully yours
W. Wordsworth

W. W. to CATHERINE CLARKSON[1]

Address: Mrs. Clarkson, Playford Hall, near Ipswich. [*In H. C. R.'s hand*]
Postmark: 2 Sept. 1837.
MS. untraced.
Bookseller's Catalogue (—).

44 Dover Street
Sept^br 2nd [1837]

My dear Mrs Clarkson,

Mr Robinson is going to write to you, and I cannot omit the occasion of letting you know that we have had a most agreeable tour together as far as Rome (the cholera would not allow of our going to Naples), and have both returned in good health. About the time when you receive this you will have also a letter forwarded, from my dear Sister, which will at least show you that wreck as she is both in mind and body, she still remembers and thinks of her dear old Friends.[2]

Let me hope my dear Friend that you and your excellent husband, have through God's goodness, been by this time enabled to bear with Christian resignation your afflicting loss. With a world of good wishes for you both

I remain faithfully and affectionately yours
Wm Wordsworth

[1] This letter follows *LY* pt. iii, L. 1160. W. W. had returned to London on 1 Sept., having spent a week and a half at Broadstairs with the Moxons on his return from his Continental tour.

[2] C. C. wrote to H. C. R. on 5 Sept.: 'I hope you will send me dear Miss Wordsworths note—I would gladly pay postage for it. I cannot tell you how much it touched me to hear that she thought and talked of me in the hour of my sorrow. I felt a strong desire at the moment to write to her thinking that perhaps it might rouse her but my poor head would not let me write at that time. Give my very best love and my very best thanks to dear Mr Wordsworth for both his Letters.—Tell him I remembered how I felt when the Abergavenny was lost and knew how he would feel for me.' (Morley, i. 347). C. C. had recently lost her only son Tom (see *LY* pt. iii, L. 1124).

My daughter is writing by my side. Her health is much improved. Friday next we shall start for Hereford.—[1]

[*There follows a letter from H. C. R. to Mrs. Clarkson*]

W. W. to HIS FAMILY[2]

Address: Mrs Wordsworth, Rydal, Kendal.
Franked: Penrith November twelve 1837 Lonsdale.
Postmark: 12 Nov. 1837. *Stamp*: Penrith.
MS. Armit Library, Ambleside. Hitherto unpublished.

[Lowther]
[12 Nov. 1837]

Dearest Friends,

It is settled that I do not go till Wednesday morning,[3] so dearest Mary by all means meet me by the coach on that day at Keswick. I shall be off early, to give the horse time to rest at Keswick and probably may bait also before we reach that place.—My eyes are not bad, but certainly weaker than I could wish, the lids reddening and the balls watering when exposed to strong light or sharp air, but very little bloodshot.

Most affectionately yours
W W

I have not yet had private talk with Lord L—he was much amused with Dora's Letter,[4] as were the rest of the party.—You may write again on Monday if any thing occurs, but not later as I shall be off on Wednesday before post time. Pray be so kind as to send a note to the Wood, telling, for Mr Luther Watson's[5] information, how long we shall be absent that he need not call till our return.

---

[1] To visit the Hutchinsons at Brinsop, on their way back to Rydal Mount.
[2] This letter follows *LY* pt. iii, L. 1180.
[3] W. W. was bound for Brigham to stay with John W. (see *MW*, p. 193).
[4] Dora W. was at Dover with I. F.
[5] For Richard Luther Watson of The Wood, Windermere, see *LY* pt. ii, L. 667.

W. W. to LORD NORTHAMPTON[1]

MS. The Marquess of Northampton. Hitherto unpublished.

[*In M. W.'s hand*]

Rydal Mount
Dec[r] 21st 1837

My dear Lord,

The autumnal quarter ends today—so that I fear the hope your letter holds out of my seeing you here *this* Autumn, is not likely to be realized. If your journey be deferred, and you could give me 3 hours, or even less, and the day proved tolerable, I could lead you a walk or ride out of the common Way, with which, acquainted as you are with foreign landscape you would be not a little pleased. I feel flattered by your preference of the English to the Scotch Lakes, because I was born and have lived the greatest part of my time near or among them. Nor is my love or admiration of this district the least abated, by having at different times in my life, seen the lakes of Scotland, Ireland, Switzerland, Italy, Austria and Bavaria: tho' not the whole in the last named country, being driven from them last summer by bad weather into Munich.

My Italian tour[2] fully answered my expectations in every thing—but that it was cut short by the fear of Cholera, or rather the Quarantine, so that we went Southward no farther than Albano and its neighbourhood, where we had unluckily 3 days of bad weather out of four.

The Tribute[3] was duly forwarded to me, and I only deferred thanking your Lordship for it, till the inflammation from which my eyes have suffered several months, should abate, and I might be enabled to report to you the pleasure which I trust is in store for me. A few pieces have been read with which I was much pleased—and particularly struck by one entitled Julia's dream.[4]

---

[1] This letter follows *LY* pt.iii, L. 1192.   [2] The previous summer.

[3] *The Tribute: A Collection of Miscellaneous Unpublished Poems, by Various Authors*, edited by Lord Northampton, had appeared recently. See above, letter of *c.*1 Mar. 1837. The Subscription List was headed by the Queen, and many of W. W.'s own acquaintances were included.

[4] 'Julia's Dream', by Miss A. Bradstreet (p.129), who also wrote 'Julia in her Garden' (p.29), and 'A Father to his Daughter' (p.153). Miss Bradstreet is unidentified, but she was probably related to Robert Bradstreet (1766–1836), of Higham Hall, Raydon, Suffolk, author of *The Sabine Farm, a Poem*, 1810, and of a prologue for the reopening of Drury Lane Theatre in 1812. A Mrs. Bradstreet is listed among the subscribers to *The Tribute*.

The conceptions are vivid, and are expressed in correspondent language. If this Lady be young, she is surely a person of great promise. The Miscellany will, I think sell—so as to benefit Mrs Smedley still more—nothwithstanding the market for Poetry even when, as in the case of The Tribute superior quality, has been a good deal spoiled by over-production.

The death of Mrs Southey[1] was a deliverance for her afflicted husband and family—and a merciful removal to herself—her sufferings having been very great. Southey is well, tho' his daughter told us by letter some little time ago, that he was looking worn and thin. I saw him at Keswick the day before his poor wife expired.

If you come northward you must enquire for us, at Ambleside—as Rydal Mount, my residence is nearly 3 miles south of Grasmere, where you suppose it to be. If you could manage to let me know *when* you would be at Ambleside I would meet your Lordship there with great pleasure.

I have the honor to be My Lord,

faithfully yours
[*signed*] Wm Wordsworth

W. W. to DORA W.[2]

MS. Wordsworth Centre, Lancaster University. Hitherto unpublished.

Thursday afternoon,
4 oclock Feb^{ry} 8th [1838]

At Dover[3]

From the Pier's head, long time and with encrease
Of wonder had I watched this seaside Town,
Under the white Cliff's battlemented crown,
Hushed to a depth of more than sabbath peace.
What love of order guards this strange release

---

[1] On 16 Nov.

[2] This item, perhaps included in a letter of M. W. to Dora W., follows *LY* pt. iii, L.1203. Dora W. was staying with I. F. at Dover.

[3] This sonnet (see *PW* iii. 198 and *app. crit.*, and I. F. note, p.488), composed this month, was published in revised form in *The Sonnets of William Wordsworth*, 1838, and found its final place, after further revisions, in the *Memorials of a Tour on the Continent, 1820* in 1845.

From noise and bustle? or are both but flown
Soon to return? Then Ocean cried, '*I* drown
Each petty turmoil; let thy wonder cease:
My overpowering murmurs have set free
Thy sense from pressure of life's hourly din,
As the dread voice that speaks from out the sea
Of God's eternal word, the voice of Time
Deadens,—the shocks of faction, shrieks of crime,
The Shouts of folly, and the groans of sin.

Suggested by a passage in your journal, and sent as a peace-offering,[1] at your dear Mother's request.

[*unsigned*]

W. W. to LORD NORTHAMPTON[2]

MS. The Marquess of Northampton. Hitherto unpublished.

Rydal Mount
Sept.ʳ 14 [1838]

My dear Lord,
    Immediately after we had the pleasure of seeing you, and the Professor[3] at Rydal my old autumnal enemy inflammation of the eyes attacked me, so that I could neither read nor write; you will therefore I know excuse my not forwarding earlier Sir Wˢ verses, according to my promise. I have now read them carefully, and cannot refrain from saying that I think your good nature prompted you to speak somewhat too favorably of them. The thoughts do not appear to me happily connected; and neither the diction nor versification please me as much as I would wish in the performance of One whom I think so very highly of, and admire and love so much.[4]

[1] Possibly an oblique reference to Dora W.'s wish to marry E. Q., to which her family was increasingly opposed (see *LY* pt. iv, Ls. 1189 and 1225.

[2] This letter follows *LY* pt. iii, L. 1275.

[3] Sir William Rowan Hamilton (see *LY* pt. i, L. 297), had called at Rydal Mount on 30 Aug. on the way back from the meeting of the British Association at Newcastle. Lord Northampton, a keen student of the sciences and one of the earliest Presidents of the Geological Society, had presided over the meeting of the British Association at Bristol in 1836, and was to preside again at Swansea in 1848.

[4] Hamilton's 'Lines Addressed to the Poet Wordsworth' had been included in *The Tribute* (p. 34).

Many years ago I took the liberty of saying to Sir W^m, when he showed me some of his verses, that his genius pointed to another course, and that to write verses worthy of his extraordinary powers, *skill* which could not be acquired without more pains than *he* ought to bestow, was absolutely necessary. Notwithstanding the many praiseworthy pieces of Poetry that Sir W— has thrown off I am still of the same opinion, and though I do not like to touch so delicate a subject by Letter, when we meet again, I shall not fail to tell him so.

And now my dear Lord, let me thank you for your very friendly Letter, and express my satisfaction in learning from it that you and Lady Mary-Anne[1] passed your time agreeably during the few hours we had the pleasure of seeing you under our roof. I was glad also to learn, that you and Sir W^m fell in with each other again at Warrington. He is a great favorite with us. Most delightful it is to find so eminent a Genius and such profound knowledge united with such warmth of feeling, and a confiding simplicity that is almost unique.—

Mrs Wordsworth and my Daughter join with me in offering respectful remembrances to yourself and Lady Mary-Anne, and believe my dear Lord

faithfully yours
Wm Wordsworth

My health is quite restored.

W. W. to WILLIAM HARNESS[2]

Address: The Revd Wm Harness, 19 Heathcote St, Mecklenburg Sq.
Postmark: 2 Jan. 1839.
MS. WL. Hitherto unpublished.

[c. 1 Jan. 1839]

My dear Sir,

You are not aware perhaps that Penrith is 27 miles from this place with a mountain between of more than a thousand feet high and a very bad road over it, so that there is little chance of my

---

[1] Lord Northampton's eldest daughter, Marianne Spencer Compton (1817–88), who married (1841) John Hume, Viscount Alford (d. 1851), eldest son of John, 1st Earl Brownlow, of Belton House, Grantham, and Ashridge Park, Berkhampsted.

[2] See *LY* pt. iii, L. 1013. This letter follows L. 1288.

being able to call upon your Friends residing in that neighbourhood. All that I can do is to request you would say to them that I
should be pleased if they would look in upon me, should they
happen to visit, which it is most likely they will, this beautiful spot
where I live.—I need scarcely add that it would give me much
pleasure to pay any attention in my power to Friends of yours.

Mr Kenyon kindly took upon him to present my farewell
respects to you, with the expression of my hope you would
excuse the formality of a call.[1] With good wishes for yourself and
your Sister, in which Mrs W. unites

I remain faithfully yours
W. Wordsworth

W. W. to CHARLES HENRY PARRY[2]

MS. untraced.
Saleroom Catalogue.

[Bath]
Wednesday 5th noon [Apr. 1839]

My dear Sir,

Having procured Mr Wade's[3] address, I no longer defer thanking you for the elegant and valuable present you have just made
me of the Memoir of Peregrine Bertie,[4] which I have no doubt
will afford me much pleasure in the Perusal.

. . . Mr Robinson has seen the Portrait, since he called upon
you along with me; and he concurs with us in thinking it an
admirable likeness.

. . . My spare time and strength find a good deal of employment in walks and drives about Bath. Last evening we were at
Charlcomb[5] which with its seclusion and its rural church and
churchyard interested us much.

---

[1] Presumably when W. W. was last in London, in Aug. or Sept. 1837.

[2] See *LY* pt. iii, L. 1307. This letter probably follows L. 1302.

[3] For Josiah Wade, the then owner of Washington Allston's portrait of S. T.
C., see L. 1341.

[4] See L. 1314. Peregrine Bertie, 11th Lord Willoughby de Eresby
(1555–1601), was commander of the English Protestant forces in the Low
Countries, 1587.

[5] A village a few miles north of Bath. The church has been extensively
restored since W. W.'s time, but retains the striking monument to Lady Barbara
Montagu (d. 1765).

Believe me with kind regards to Mrs Parry and your amiable Daughters to be

faithfully my dear Sir
Your much obliged
Wm Wordsworth

W. W. to LAURA CARR[1]

MS. Private Collection. Hitherto unpublished.

Rydal Mount
4th May 1840

My dear Miss Carr,

Upon the opposite leaf I have ventured to transcribe a Sonnet which I wrote a few weeks ago upon the subject of John the Baptist,[2] and I send it as the most appropriate return I can make for the delicate mark of attention you have paid me by your Present just received of the beautiful Engraving of the Prophet of the Wilderness by Morgan[3] from Raphael. I feel myself rich in the possession of it for its own sake and, as with sincerity I may say, still more for yours.

How much I regret that Miss Fenwick saw but little of you during her short residence in Town, and my Daughter scarcely anything. She, as you know probably was a Prisoner, during the greatest part of her sojourn, by two successive colds both severe, the former even formidably so. I grieve to say that the latter she has brought with her, and when it is to be shaken off we know not. Miss Fenwick is quite well. She leaves us to day, having been kindly under our roof since she came into Westmorland about ten days ago.—Perhaps you know she has been able to take

---

[1] Later Lady Cranworth (see *LY* pt. i, L. 279; pt. iv, L.1381). This letter follows *LY* pt. iv, L.1406. The original is tipped into a copy of the one-volume *Poems of William Wordsworth*, 1845, sent as a present to her on the occasion of her marriage to W. W.'s friend Robert Monsey Rolfe, Lord Cranworth (see *LY* pt. iv, Ls. 1930 and 1935), and inscribed 'To Laura Rolfe from her affectionate Friend William Wordsworth Rydal Mount 15th Novr 1845.'

[2] 'Before the Picture of the Baptist, by Raphael, in the Gallery at Florence'. See *PW* iii. 225 and the I. F. note, p.500. The sonnet was composed in Apr. 1840 (see *MW*, pp.242–3), and published in the *Memorials of a Tour in Italy, 1837* in 1842.

[3] Rafaello Morghen (1758–1833), Professor at the Academy of Florence from 1793, noted for his engravings of the masterpieces of the Italian Renaissance.

for 4 months a pretty large House[1] very near the one she lived in
when you were her Guest, which I hope you will be again
before I grow too old or infirm to renew those plans and rambles
which we enjoyed so much together. [?Spring][2] has been a glorious opening; twelve weeks all but two or three days of uninter-
rupted fair weather; and never were the wild flowers more
profuse and beautiful, Rydal Mount has been in beauty a perfect
paradise.—

Dora has just come in; she begs me to say how deeply she
regrets that she only saw you once. She had not heard till she met
Miss Fenwick at Birmingham of the anxiety you were suffering
on account of your Brother's severe indisposition. We all hope
that the illness has by this time abated. Miss Fenwick is anxious
to hear from you again, and I mean to write in a few days.—I
must now conclude with the united best remembrances of this
Household, and believe [me] my dear Miss Carr

> very faithfully your much obliged Friend
> Wm Wordsworth

[*There follows* The Baptist *as in PW iii. 225*, 'transcribed for Laura
Carr by W.W.']

M. W. and W. W. to EMMELINE FISHER[3]

MS. Cornell. Hitherto unpublished.

[? Feb. 1841]

. . . We have the pleasure of having good tidings of the health of
all your cousins Crackanthorpe.[4]

As you do not, dear Emmie, say aught to the contrary, we trust
your home circle are all well, and that you have no anxieties in
connection with those of your family who are absent.

You shall hear from me again before it is very long—
Meanwhile hoping that we *may* meet in Summer and with the
dear love of all your Cousins, and with thanks to your Papa and

---

[1] See *LY* pt. iv, L.1393.   [2] *MS. obscure.*

[3] This extensively damaged fragment perhaps follows *LY* pt. iv, L. 1493. It
seems to belong to early 1841, when Emmie Fisher's visit to Rydal Mount the
following summer was first mooted. For W. W.'s cousin, Emmie, her mother
and father, and her aunt, all mentioned below, see *LY* pt. iii, Ls. 1185 and 1323.

[4] The family at Newbiggin.

Mamma for allowing us the prospect of seeing you, believe me
dear Emmie to be ever

Your affectionate Cousin
M. Wordsworth

[*W. W. writes*]

My dear Emmie,

I have read Mrs Wordsworth's [   ] it states the case [   ] only
to add from [   ] not young [   ] we should [   ] as well as your
mother.

ever your
affectionate friend and cousin,
Wm Wordsworth

Give my love to your mother and to your aunt Mary, when
you have an opportunity, and kind remembrances to your Father
and the rest of your family. Also to my old Friend Mr Bowles[1]
whom I never forget.—

W. W. to [? THOMAS HARTREE CORNISH][2]

MS. Private Collection. Hitherto unpublished.

20th May [1841]
Bagborough
near Taunton.

My dear Sir,

Your Letter gave me much pleasure as a proof of your kind
remembrance of me; and be assured it causes me no little regret
that I am unable to profit by your obliging invitation.

Our travels westward are limited to Plymouth, by engagements
which make it impossible for us to extend them further.

You will be pleased however to know, that my short residence
in this neighbourhood has allowed me to visit here the old
haunts of Mr Coleridge and myself more than 40 years ago, when
I lived at Alfoxden under the Quantock Hills on that northern
side; I am at present as you know on the southern. On Saturday
we proceed to Exeter, with our friend Miss Fenwick, then to

---

[1] William Lisle Bowles.

[2] Or possibly his elder brother. For Cornish, see *LY* pt. iv, L. 1598. The family came from Barnstaple. This letter follows L. 1512.

Plymouth, and mean to return along the coast to Lyme and by Salisbury and Winchester to London for a short stay there.

I have only to repeat my regret that my allowance of time is so nearly expired, and to add that it would give great pleasure to renew our acquaintance in any part of England, which I say not without a hope that our beautiful district in the north may tempt you to visit it.

Believe me my dear Sir with Compts to Mrs Cornish and your brother if with you

very faithfully yours,
Wm Wordsworth

W. W. to JOSEPH COTTLE[1]

MS. Stanford University Library. Hitherto unpublished.

Rydal Mount
Ambleside
April 22nd—43.

My dear Mr Cottle,
    The Ex^{rs} [2] of our lamented Friend R. Southey are endeavouring to collect his Letters from all the Persons with whom he is *known* or supposed to have corresponded. In the former class I have confidently placed you, and undertaken to request that you would furnish them with such as may be in your possession, and that you may think would prove interesting if published in the whole or in part. Any communication of this kind made to Henry Taylor Esqre 16 Blandford Square London (who is one of the Ex^{rs}, Southey's Brother D^r S— being the other would be thankfully received.

I don't enter into particulars concerning the Laureatship,[3] for these you must have read reported with sufficient accuracy in the newspapers.

Pray accept the accompanying Copy of verses of which I had some impressions struck off a few weeks ago.[4] They got surreptitiously into a provincial newspaper, and perhaps you may have seen them. This Copy may however prove more correct.

I hope that both you and your Sister have enjoyed good health

---

[1] This letter follows *LY* pt. iv, L. 1698.   [2] Executors.
[3] See Ls. 1687–9.   [4] 'Grace Darling' (see L. 1672).

during the past winter, as I and my little Household have done, for so I may say as my poor dear Sister has been no worse.

Believe me to remain, with many most interesting remembrances, and with best good wishes

my dear Mr Cottle
faithfully yours
Wm Wordsworth

Be so kind as to enclose this Letter to Mr Peace[1] who will understand that through it the same request is made to himself.

W. W. to C. W. JNR.[2]

MS. WL. Hitherto unpublished.

Brinsop Court
near Hereford
Sept^{br} 25 1843

My dear Chris,

Your letter to Dora announcing the birth of a Son,[3] has been forwarded to us at this place; we heartily congratulate you and dear Susan upon the event and offer our best wishes for the health, welldoing and happiness of the newborn, and of your other children—

I have to thank you for your Sermon accompanying the Translation from St. Chrysostom[4] which I received some time ago; and both of which gave me much pleasure.

We left our Sister Joanna[5] in improved health but still weak, and likely we fear to remain so. This improvement was gratifying, but our visit upon the whole was the most distressing I ever paid in my life. Mr Sutton[6] every day became more and more

---

[1] John Peace, City Librarian at Bristol (see *LY* pt. iii, L. 1313).

[2] This letter follows *LY* pt. iv, L. 1736.

[3] John Wordsworth (1843–1911), later Fellow of Brasenose College, Oxford, Oriel Professor of the Interpretation of Holy Scripture (1883), and Bishop of Salisbury from 1885: author of *The Episcopate of Charles Wordsworth*, 1899, *The Ministry of Grace*, 1901, and numerous other works.

[4] Unidentified, and perhaps never published.

[5] W. W. and M. W. had visited Joanna Hutchinson at Elton, near Stockton-on-Tees (see L. 1730), before travelling down to Brinsop to stay with Thomas and Mary Hutchinson.

[6] M. W.'s nephew (see *MY* pt. ii, L. 466), the details of whose illness are given in *LY* pt. iv, L. 1735).

excited in mind; and by the advice of his Stockton medical attendant, I procured from a Physician, Dr Belcombe at York, a person accustomed to the care of insane persons, and under him Mr S– is now placed, in his own House.

We have also had great anxiety since we came here. On the night of the second day after our arrival, our excellent Maidservant,[1] who has lived with us thirteen years, was seized with pleurisy. Blistering, bleeding, and all other usual remedies have been resorted to; and She continues very ill though better today than yesterday.

One of Mrs Hutchinson's Daughters is also so unwell, that she must leave us in a day or two, to take the Invalid to the Sea side, as advised by her Doctor. So that anxiety which we left at home, has attended us all the way.—The accounts from Isabella[2] are far from good, and your cousin John of Keswick[3] though something better I cannot but consider in a precarious state.

Why did not you mention your own health. With Love to Susan in which Mary unites, I remain your affectionate Uncle

W. Wordsworth

W. W. to HENRY TAYLOR[4]

MS. WL. Hitherto unpublished.

[? late 1843]

My dear Mr Taylor,

Having often talked to my intelligent neighbour (a medical Man, Mr Carr),[5] upon precautions for [? preserving][6] Health abroad, I send you the notes he was so obliging as to furnish me with, assuming you will pay to them the attention which they

---

[1] Jane, who died soon afterwards. [2] John W.'s wife.

[3] R. W.'s son.

[4] Of the Colonial Office: author of *Philip van Artevelde*, etc. (see *LY* pt. i, L. 120). This letter seems to refer to his trip to Italy in search of health in the winter of 1843–4 (see *Autobiography of Henry Taylor*, i. 343), and possibly follows *LY* pt. iv, L. 1744.

[5] Thomas Carr, the Ambleside surgeon (see *LY* pt i, L. 66), who had written to W. W.: 'I enclose you the notes such as they are, in truth little worth, but you will take the word for the deed. I am ignorant of the road Mr Taylor intends to travel and therefore all is guess work.' (*WL MSS.*)

[6] *MS. torn.*

deserve. God grant that you and Mrs Taylor may benefit by the change, as you have good reason to hope!

ever affectionately yours
Wm Wordsworth

W. W. to EDWARD MOXON[1]

MS. New York Public Library. Hitherto unpublished.

Rydal
2nd Augst 1844

Dear Mr Moxon,
   Will you be so kind as to get these spectacles mended at the Shop near you in Bond Street and bring them down with you in a new case.

ever faithfully yours
W. W.

W. W. to BASIL MONTAGU[2]

MS. Mugar Memorial Library, Boston University. Hitherto unpublished.

[?Sept. 1844]

My dear Montagu,
   Thanks for your ready compliance with my request. I see no objection to Mrs Montagu keeping two or three Letters for the considerations she mentions in her Postscript to Mrs Wordsworth for which she thanks her; and also for her kind intention of forwarding them to Rydal.
   You have not given me a definite answer as to what I am to do with yours. If you have no objection to my destroying them I will do so; for it seems to me that in this gossiping age it is not desireable, to leave to others the discretion of making any kind of public use of documents if evidently private.—
   The least objection to publishing private Letters or parts of them is that they are a burthen to the Press, and their perusal a waste of time.

---

[1] This letter follows *LY* pt. iv, L. 1818. Moxon was to visit Rydal Mount later in the month (see L. 1826).

[2] This letter perhaps follows *LY* pt. iv, L.1826. The approximate date is indicated by L. 1836.

With kind remembrances to Mrs Montagu in which Mrs W joins, I remain

> my dear Montagu
> your faithful friend
> Wm Wordsworth

W. W. to UNKNOWN CORRESPONDENT[1]

MS. Ella Strong Denison Library, Scripps College, Claremont, California. Hitherto unpublished.

> Rydal Mount
> Novr 17th—44

Dear Sir,

Your obliging Letter ought to have been much earlier acknowledged, but I was from home when it came and I have been a Wanderer almost ever since I received it. You will, therefore be so kind as to excuse the apparent neglect.

We are still threatened with the nuisance of a Railway to the Vale of Windermere—but the Terminus is now not intended to come so near Ambleside but to stop a little below Orrest Head, about a mile from Bowness; by this arrangement the opposition will in some quarters be diminished, in others not at all; for what we most dread is that after they have come so far, they will not rest there, but a new attempt will be made to carry the mischief through the whole of our beautiful district, in order to join it with a like nuisance now set on foot on the Banks of the river Derwent at Workington with the intention of pushing it on to Keswick.[2]

Your hints about making the embankment of the line less offensive are very good; but I fear would not meet with the slightest attention from the managers of such undertakings.

The tree, an oak,[3] reverenced so much, is still standing; a fine tree it is, and its owner, whose name is William Birkett,[4] is still

---

[1] This letter on the proposed Kendal and Windermere Railway follows *LY* pt. iv, L. 1848.

[2] The projected Workington and Cockermouth Railway (see L. 1856) was threatening to disturb the privacy of John W.'s rectory at Brigham.

[3] See W. W.'s prefatory remarks to his pamphlet *Kendal and Windermere Railway. Two Letters Re-printed from the Morning Post* (see *Prose Works*, iii. 339).

[4] A farmer whose land lay between Waterhead and Troutbeck Bridge.

living and, is furious at the thought of the Railway going through his little Property. He has declared that he would give a thousand pound to prevent it.

Believe me dear Sir, in haste truly your obliged
Wm Wordsworth

W. W. to LORD NORTHAMPTON[1]

Address: The Marquis of Northampton [*delivered by hand*]
MS. The Marquess of Northampton. Hitherto unpublished.

[*In unidentified hand*]

44 Dover Street
[5 May 1845]

My dear Lord,

Having heard through Mr Rogers that you will be so kind as to take me under Your Wing to the Levee tomorrow, may I request that either I may be allowed to call upon you or that you would take me up here at the usual hour. I have the honour to be your lordship's

Much obliged
[*signed*] Wm Wordsworth

W. W. to CHARLES BONER[2]

MS. Ella Strong Denison Library, Scripps College, Claremont, California. Hitherto unpublished.

Brinsop Court
Hereford
20th Octr 45

My dear Mr Boner,

I have this moment received your Letter. I cannot advise printing at your own expense, because I fear you would have still more to pay than 30£, and because your Publisher would take no pains to make your work known.

---

[1] This letter follows *LY* pt. iv, L. 1887. For W. W.'s presentation at Court, see L. 1886. See also *HCR* ii. 653.

[2] This letter follows *LY* pt. iv, L. 1921. For Charles Boner of Ratisbon, see Ls. 1882, 1915 and 1918. His complete poems were eventually published in 1858.

As to the other method proposed it is far from attractive, but it seems to me the less objectionable of the two. But the fact is, the Magazines have so much Trash sent to them, and[1] judging from what I occasionally see of Blackwood,[2] they appear to print so much that your chance of having your work acknowledged would not be very good. I should therefore recommend to you to hold back, and make your Poems as good as you possibly can, and then you would feel that you have done your duty to yourself and to that Art of which you hold so just a notion.

I have little hope that the Edition of my own Poems which I am preparing[3] will bring me satisfaction by its Sale. The world is in general little disposed to Poetry; and at this time in particular nothing but Railways engages public attention; which is another strong reason why you should defer Publication.

Mrs Wordsworth thanks you for your kind enquiries, She is well in health, and presents you her Compts and best wishes. We shall not return to Rydal before the middle of the first week in next month.—I hope you will have a pleasant journey, and that you may find your German Friends well.

Believe me ever faithfully and with the kindest good wishes,

Yours Wm Wordsworth

It was very good in you coming so far that we might be personally acquainted.

W. W. to MARY STANGER[4]

MS. WL (Moorsom Papers). Hitherto unpublished.

2^d: March 1846—

[*M. W. writes*]

I hold the pen for my husband whose eyes do not allow him to use his own—M. W.

My dear Mrs Stanger,

I was sorry to learn thro' a letter written by Kate Southey to Miss Fenwick, that you had been distressed by a report, the truth of which you had no doubt of, that our dear Isabella[5] was dead.

---

[1] and *written twice.* [2] *Blackwood's Magazine.*

[3] *Poetical Works,* 1845.

[4] *Née* Calvert. This letter follows *LY* pt. iv, L. 1974. [5] John W.'s wife.

The same report had come to Miss Dowling from West Cumb. With the addition that John having taken her away from Rome with her children, she had died of fatigue at Florence. Now I need not say to you that the Persons who set on foot such reports act worse than silly—My excellent cousin Mrs H[1] of Green Bank who is not in strong health, passed a sleepless night in consequence of this statement, and was made very ill by it. In the whole Story there was not a word of truth, except that John, at my most earnest request, in conjunction with his own strong desire, had taken the children from Rome—not doubting but that Isabella, if she was not able herself to accompany them, which we hoped might have been the case, would have sanctioned the step. I had urged this from my own knowledge how dangerous the climate of Rome is in the Spring Season, and especially from having witnessed, during my residence there in March and April,[2] how liable they, who like our Children, had suffered from the fever were to a recurrence of it. I had also seen, at the time when John went for the purpose of removing his family, a letter from a Sister of D[r] Babington[3] then residing with her B[r] in Rome, in which was given a deplorable character of the state of the disease and the danger attending it—often requiring of him 3 visits to the same patient in one day. I am aware that D[r] Deacon[4] has written in very different terms of the disease, to Workington—But I have little respect for *his* judgement—and his conduct in taking Isa: and her Children, *to suit his own convenience*, to Rome in the month of Dec[r] was highly reprehensible—it was at least 8 weeks, say 10, too soon. In fact except during the latter part of Dec[r], Jan, and Feb. a residence in Rome, for English Children especially, is attended with great hazards.—So pray do not let John be blamed, as he has been most unjustly, for '*taking his Children from* his wife'[5]—for my own part I shall never be tolerably at ease till they are all back in their own country. And as Mrs Curwen says, She found her daughter better than when She parted with her. We trust *she* will be able to return with her mother. English Children who have their bread to gain in their own Country ought above all others to be brought up in it,— and no Parent who is not improperly biassed, or in utter igno-

---

[1] Dorothy Benson Harrison.   [2] In 1837.

[3] Of Guy's Hospital (see L. 1960).

[4] An English physician resident in Rome.

[5] For John W.'s deteriorating relationship with his wife, see Ls. 1964 and 1974.

rance *can* remain free from dread of Italian religion, morals and manners and the corruption that is in them all.

I have written thus to you, trusting that it may contribute to your tranquillity of mind, and guard you against giving too easy credit to reports or one-sided Statements from any quarter prejudicial to others.

I remain with kind regards to your husband, in which Mrs W joins,

affectionately dear Mary
Yours
[*signed*] Wm Wordsworth

W. W. to EDWARD MOXON[1]

Address: Edward Moxon Esq, 44 Dover St [*In M. W.'s hand*]
MS. WL. Hitherto unpublished.

Rydal Mount
19th april 1846

The Bearer is Captain Alexander Robertson,[2] going to India: be so kind as to let him have any Books published by you at Trade price and you will oblige

Yours Sincerely
W Wordsworth

---

[1] This letter follows *LY* pt. iv, L. 1981.
[2] Perhaps Alexander Robertson of Struan, Perth (1805–84), sometime resident in Jamaica.

W. W. to ANNE MARSH[1]

Address: Mrs Marsh, Eastbury, Watford, Herts.
Postmark: (1) 3 May 1846 (2) 5 May 1846.
Stamp: (1) Ambleside (2) Watford.
MS. Rare Book Room, Smith College Library. Hitherto unpublished.

Rydal Mount
3^d May—1846

Dear Madam,

Pray accept my acknowledgements for your Emilia Wyndham and for the honor you have done me by the Dedication,[2] and by the manner in which your sentiments in respect to my writings is expressed. The Book just received by me will I have no doubt be read both by myself, and the members of my family, with much interest.

Wishing that these volumes may in all respects answer the purpose for which you have written and published them, I have the honor to be

dear Madam
respectfully
your obliged
Wm Wordsworth

---

[1] This letter follows *LY* pt. iv, L. 1982. Anne Marsh, later Marsh-Caldwell, was the author of *Two Old Men's Tales, Emilia Wyndham,* 1846, and numerous other novels, many of which were published in 'The Parlour Library'. She also wrote *The Protestant Reformation in France, or the History of the Huguenots,* 1847, and translated *The Song of Roland,* 1854. Harriet Martineau had forwarded to W. W. her request for permission to dedicate *Emilia Wyndham* to him, and in her accompanying letter had described Mrs. Marsh as a London friend of hers, 'though we differ as widely as possible in our opinions on very important subjects, and are neither of us the most cold blooded of womankind.' She added: 'I am afraid my writing tonight is *almost* as illegible as hers,—from my having been out foraging in the woods today,—digging out some pretty tough roots.' (*WL MSS.*)

[2] The Dedication of *Emilia Wyndham* ran: 'To William Wordsworth, Esq., one from the countless numbers of those deeply indebted for the advancement of their moral life to the fine influences of his poetry, offers this imperfect tribute of admiration and gratitude.' The last six lines of 'She was a phantom of delight' (*PW* ii. 214) formed the epigraph on the title-page. The presentation copy is now in the *WL*.

W. W. to C. W. JNR.[1]

MS. WL. Hitherto unpublished.

Rydal Mount
May 17th—1846

My dear Nephew,

Your Aunt and I were glad to hear of the addition to your Family[2] and that Mother and the new born were both doing well; so we infer as to the latter, as you do not say any thing to the contrary—

I have ventured to propose a slight addition to your dear Father's Epitaph.[3] His Portrait[4] will I hope be left in Trin. Coll—

John left us yesterday after a weeks stay. He had a prosperous journey from Italy with his five children,[5] two of whom have been placed at the new Church of England School near Fleetwood, Lancashire—[6] The Eldest, his Daughter, is at Mrs Gee's School,[7] Hendon, and is kindly noticed by our excellent Friend, Mrs Hoare.[8] The two younger Boys have been with us since their return, and will remain till their mother arrives, who is on her way from Italy accompanied by her own mother.— Your poor Aunt Dorothy continues struggling on in her old way; your Aunt W. is very well and as active in mind and body as is possible for any one at her age—She is at the moment hearing her eldest (3[d]) Grandson's lesson[9] in the Bible. He is a slow Boy, his Sister very quick, as is W[m]—and Charles the youngest promises to be; I mention this as of some consequence for they will have their fortunes to make, themselves. Your cousin W[m] [10] is I am told looking unusually well—

Archbishop Whately[11] is on a visit to Mrs Arnold and preached this day at Ambleside.—

---

[1] This letter follows *LY* pt. iv, L. 1985. [2] His fifth child Susanna.

[3] C. W. had died at Buxted on 2 Feb. (see L. 1967), and was buried in Buxted churchyard.

[4] The portrait by George Robson, reproduced as the *Frontispiece* to *LY* pt. i.

[5] John W. had five surviving children, Jane, Henry, William, John and Charles.

[6] Rossall School (see *LY* pt. iv, L. 1980).

[7] Widow of Capt. George Gee and formerly resident in Grasmere and Rydal. After her husband's death, she opened a school at Hendon (see *LY* pt. i, L. 327).

[8] Hannah Hoare, the Wordsworths' Hampstead friend.

[9] *Written* Grandson a lesson.

[10] Willy W., who had succeeded his father as Distributor of Stamps at Carlisle.

[11] See *LY* pt. iv, L. 1986.

I am utterly disgusted with the present Ministers[1] and abominate that speech of Sir James Graham[2] spoken the other day—his talk of Protectionists, who shall soon I fear have nothing left worth protecting—but good God will take care of us in spite of our present baseness—

Heartily do I wish you success in your endeavours to procure the means of building the Churches you mention—[3] But pray take care you do not wear yourself away by your intense and various labours: People say you look very thin.—Kindest love to yourself and Susan with best wishes from your Aunts and myself and believe [me] my dear Chris your affectionate Uncle

W. Wordsworth

W. W. to HARRIET MARTINEAU[4]

MS. Harold B. Lee Library, Brigham Young University. Hitherto unpublished.

Rydal Mount
24th July 1846

Dear Miss Martineau,

Pray present my thanks to your Friend[5] for her beautiful drawing of Rydal Lake, which I shall value as it deserves.

faithfully yours
Wm Wordsworth

---

[1] Peel was now committed to the repeal of the Corn Laws (see L. 1974), in the face of continued opposition from protectionists in his own party. See Sir Llewellyn Woodward, *The Age of Reform*, 2nd edn. 1961, pp. 122–4.

[2] The Home Secretary (see *MY* pt. ii, L. 542), a powerful advocate for repeal. After the fall of Peel's ministry later in 1846, Graham declined to serve under Lord John Russell but supported him against the protectionists; and he was eventually returned for his old constituency of Carlisle in 1852, serving as First Lord of the Admiralty in Lord Aberdeen's coalition ministry and under Palmerston.

[3] Soon after his appointment as Canon of Westminster, C. W. jnr. had become secretary of the Westminster Spiritual Aid Fund, which aimed to provide new churches, schools, parsonages, and clergy for the neglected and overcrowded streets surrounding the Abbey, which was itself still unrestored.

[4] See *LY* pt. iii, L. 1190. This letter follows pt. iv, L. 1998.

[5] Miss Carpenter, to whom Harriet Martineau sent this letter with a covering note. Mary Carpenter (1807–77), eldest child of Dr. Lant Carpenter (1780–1840), the Unitarian divine, hymnologist, and writer on education, founded 'ragged schools' in Bristol for poor children (1846), and later, with the support of her

W. W to UNKNOWN CORRESPONDENT[1]

MS. Private Collection. Hitherto unpublished.

Rydal Mount
13th Jan^{ry} 1848

Dear Madam,

Pray accept my cordial thanks for your interesting Present of the Box made from the wreck of the Royal George.[2] It may be worth while to mention to you that I owe to the kindness of a Friend a Box made from the wreck of the Royal William built in 1719; which Ship remained in the service 90 years—the oldest ship on record. The small centre piece of the same box is from the Royal George, and the lath on the lid is a piece from the Standard[3] of the Victory, against which Lord Nelson reclined in Death.[4] I also have had the pleasure of receiving from General Pasley a Walking-stick made from the Royal George headed by a piece of the Copper from the same Vessel, and pointed at the bottom by part of one of her Bullets.—

The Poet Cowper would have had a better claim to these Reliques than I feel that I possess.[5] They are valued however not only by myself but by my family—I have the honor to remain

dear Madam
Your obliged Ser^{vnt}
Wm Wordsworth

---

friend Lady Byron, opened a reformatory at Kingswood (1852). Her *Morning and Evening Meditations* (in prose and verse), 1845, passed through several editions, and she wrote extensively on the problems of juvenile delinquency, advising on education and prison policy in India, the United States, and Canada. Her brother was Philip Pearsall Carpenter (1819–77), presbyterian minister at Warrington Chapel (1846–61) and an eminent conchologist. See *Harriet Martineau's Autobiography*, 3 vols., 1877, i. 95–6; *Harriet Martineau, Selected Letters*, ed. Valerie Sanders, 1990, pp. 135–6; and J. Estlin Carpenter, *The Life and Work of Mary Carpenter*, 1879.

[1] This letter follows *LY* pt. iv, L. 2069.

[2] The ship sank at her moorings in Portsmouth Harbour on 29 Aug. 1782, with the loss of over 500 lives.

[3] An inverted knee timber for connecting the stern posts of a vessel to the deck beams.

[4] Nelson (see also *MY* pt. i, Ls. 5 and 79) died at Trafalgar on 21 Oct. 1805 at 4.30 p.m., at the moment of victory.

[5] See Cowper's poem in Latin and English versions, 'On the Loss of the Royal George', to be sung as a dirge to the march in Handel's *Scipio*. See his letter to

W. W. to UNKNOWN CORRESPONDENT[1]

MS. untraced. (Photocopy supplied by Mr. Ulrick Funk).

Rydal Mount
near Ambleside
9th June 1848—

Dear Sir,

Be assured that I am sensible of your kindness in communicating the intelligence of the decease of Mr Watt,[2] my Friend, for so I may call him though we had not personally much intercourse. Of one day passed in his company, I have a most lively remembrance.[3] We clomb Helvellyn together nearly to its summit,

the Revd. William Unwin, 4 Aug. 1783 (*Letters and Prose Writings*, ed. James King and Charles Ryskamp, 5 vols., 1979–86, ii. 154–5).

[1] This letter follows *LY* pt. iv, L.2078. It was probably addressed to James Patrick Muirhead (1813–98), an Edinburgh advocate and collateral descendant of James Watt's mother: author of *The Life of James Watt*, 1858, and other works relating to his inventions. Muirhead had visited W. W. in Aug. 1841 (see *RMVB*), with an introduction from his friend James Watt, jnr. His recollections of the visit, and of the poet's opinions on political, literary, and historical matters, as recorded in his letters to his mother from Keswick, 1–2 Sept., are set out in 'A Day with Wordsworth', *Blackwood's Magazine*, ccxxi (1927), 728–43.

[2] James Watt, jnr. (1769–1848), of Aston Hall, Warwickshire, son of the great engineer, had died unmarried on 2 June. He had gone to Paris as a young man in 1789 to pursue his scientific studies, and became actively involved with the Girondins and Jacobins during the Revolution. As he later told Southey, he had on one occasion intervened to prevent a duel between Danton and Robespierre (see Southey, vi. 209). Along with Dr. Thomas Cooper (1759–1840), the scientist and radical friend of Priestley, he was denounced by Burke in the House of Commons on 4 Mar. 1793 for seditious practices, and Cooper published a violent pamphlet in reply. Like W. W., Watt was horrified by the September Massacres, voicing his disgust publicly and vigorously rebutting Robespierre's accusations at the Jacobin Club that he was an emissary of Pitt. As a result of this public altercation, he was forced to flee from Paris, and eventually from France, making his way back to England by way of Italy. See *Life of James Watt*, pp. 491–4, and Moorman, i. 205–6. Soon after his return he became a partner in his father's Soho works, Birmingham (1794), and after his father's death in 1819, he took over management of his concerns in partnership with Matthew Boulton's son, developing the application of steam power to marine engines. His voyage in the refitted Caledonia as far as Coblentz on the Rhine (1817) was the first occasion on which a steamboat put out from an English port onto the high seas. He wrote the memoir of his father in the *Encyclopaedia Britannica*, 6th edn., 1823.

[3] In his conversations with Muirhead, W. W. recalled his rambles in the Lake country with Watt, but the date of Watt's visit, or visits, is uncertain. Whether

when a cloud overspread the mountain top, and barred our further progress. We descended almost to the Valley, when observing that the veil had disappeared we mounted again, and came again as near to the summit, when as dense a cloud disappointed us again, so that after waiting some time we returned with our wish ungratified as before. Mr Watt was at Paris during the earlier part of the French Revolution, I was in that Country for nearly a year and a half of the same period;[1] but I was only a Spectator, while Mr Watt took an active part in that great event,[2] and had a conflict with Robespierre of which no doubt you must have heard. But I must conclude begging you to believe me, dear Sir,

your much obliged
William Wordsworth

they had known each other much earlier, in Paris, is also unclear from Muirhead's recollections of W. W.'s words in 1841, and from the slightly different version he included in his *Life of James Watt*, and his statements in this letter do little to settle the issue. See also Mark L. Reed, *Wordsworth, The Chronology of the Early Years, 1770–1799*, Cambridge, Mass., 1967, p. 125.

[1] W. W. was in France from 27 Nov. 1791 till late Nov. or early Dec. 1792, and he probably returned in late summer 1793, witnessing the execution of Gorsas in Paris on 7 Oct., as he later told Thomas Carlyle (see Reed, *Chronology of the Early Years*, pp. 124, 138–9, 147). These two visits, if taken together, could be thought to amount roughly to a period of 'nearly a year and a half', as W. W. says. Elsewhere, however, in *MY* pt. ii, L.366, in the 'Autobiographical Memoir' in *Mem.*, and in *The Prelude*, Bk.x, his memories of the length of his stay in revolutionary France vary between a year and a period of 15 or 16 months, and while the evidence for his second visit remains inconclusive, it is difficult to see how these various statements can be reconciled.

[2] In the *Life of James Watt*, p. 494, W. W. is quoted as saying, 'I went over to Paris at the time of the revolution in 1792 or 1793 ['1792 and 1793' in the *Blackwood's* version], and so was *pretty hot in it*; But I found Mr. Watt there before me, and *quite* as warm in the same cause. We thus both began life as ardent and thoughtless radicals . . .'

W. W. to THE DUCHESS OF ARGYLL[1]

MS. Private Collection. Hitherto unpublished.

Rydal Mount
2nd Sept[r] 1848

M[r] Wordsworth will be happy to see the Duchess of Argyle whenever it may be agreeable to her Grace to honor him with a call at Rydal Mount.

W. W. to UNKNOWN CORRESPONDENT[2]

MS. Special Collections Department, Robert W. Woodruff Library, Emory University. Hitherto unpublished.

Rydal Mount
18 Sept[r]—1848

My dear Sir,

Your Letter of acknowledgement was duly received; and I am much annoyed at the trouble which the non-appearance of the other ½ Note[3] has occasioned, particularly as Mrs Wordsworth, who kindly undertakes these matters for me, has no distinct recollection of having forwarded it; but as it is not found in the place where She usually makes such deposits, She thinks She must have sent it to the Post-office. As you hold the half-note, perhaps it might not be inconvenient to you to get it replaced by a whole one, upon proper application to the Bank. I understand this may be done; otherwise please to return it, and I shall, through some other Friend endeavour to do so.

Believe me
dear Sir
with much respect
faithfully yours
W[m] Wordsworth

[1] This letter follows *LY* pt. iv, L. 2081. For the visit of the Duke and Duchess of Argyll to Rydal Mount, see L. 2101; and for the wider significance of their meeting with W. W., see Alan G. Hill, 'Poetry and Ecumenism: the Legacy of the Wordsworths', in the *Annual Review of Lambeth Palace Library*, 1992.

[2] This letter follows *LY* pt. iv, L. 2082. [3] i.e. banknote.

After the above was written Mrs W. has found the Note, and she begs you would excuse the trouble given through the fault of her recollection.—

W. W. to UNKNOWN CORRESPONDENT[1]

MS. Rare Book Room, Smith College Library. Hitherto unpublished.

Rydal Mount
near Ambleside
Decr 8th—1848

Dear Madam,

It will give me pleasure that my name should be added to the list of subscribers to your forth-coming little volume, along with those of Mrs W's Relatives—

Mrs Wordsworth joins me in kind remembrances.

Believe me dear Madam
ever faithfully yours
W Wordsworth

Would not 'Poems upon sacred Subjects' be a better title for your Vol: than 'Sacred Poems'?[2]

W. W. to ROBERT FERGUSON[3]

MS. Mr. J. F. Chance.[4] Hitherto unpublished.

Rydal Mount
12 Decr 1848

My dear Sir,

Upon my return from a visit to my Son at Brigham I found your little vol: of Travels in Palestine etc.,[5] which has been read

---

[1] This letter follows *LY* pt. iv, L. 2089.

[2] This volume, if published, is untraced, but it was possibly renamed *Sacred Hours* (*R. M. Cat.*, no. 249).

[3] This letter follows *LY* pt. iv, L.2091. Robert Ferguson, traveller, dialectologist, and head of the family textile business in Carlisle, published sonnets (1847) and travel books. During his visit to America (1864), he got to know Longfellow, with whom he corresponded about his translation of Dante, and who visited him at Carlisle in 1868. He was later mayor of Carlisle, and active in many branches of local affairs. His son Joseph Ferguson (1785–1863), of Morton, was proprietor of a mill at Holme Head, and Whig M.P. for Carlisle, 1852–7.

[4] Since sold (1988).

[5] *The Pipe of Repose: or, Recollections of Eastern Travel*, 1849.

to me by Mrs Wordsworth—We were both *much* pleased with the account which you give of what you saw and felt in that most interesting region. All I have to say on the opposite side is, that you have treated Mademoiselle Martineau with much more respect than She deserves.[1] She is above measure conceited and self-opinionated. Have you seen a notice of your book which appeared lately in the Guardian? I have not read it myself, but am told that it speaks very favourably of your performance in comparison with most of the other travellers who have preceded you.

> I remain
> My dear Sir
> faithfully your
> much obliged
> Wm Wordsworth

[1] Soon after her return from Palestine earlier this year, Harriet Martineau had published *Eastern Life* (see L.2078). In his book, Ferguson crossed swords with her on several matters, particularly her entry in the visitors' book at Mount Carmel: 'The Religion of Nature, and the Religion of Christ being found here, all minor distinctions may be forgotten, and all who meet may feel as brethren.' (p. 135).

APPENDIX I

DECEPTION EXPOSED;[1]

OR,

An Antidote for the Poison of the Westmorland Yeoman's Address,

Lately re-published in 'The Kendal Chronicle'

No. 1.

This pretended Yeoman[2] affirms, that 'the comforts and privileges of those to whom he addresses himself are sacrificed to the present state of their Representation in Parliament; and that the Constitution has received a bias which, if it be not resisted, will gradually circumscribe their privileges, and leave their liberties and property at the mercy of the Aristocracy.'—How does he attempt to prove these bold assertions? First, by referring to the Militia Laws, which are 'so constituted,' he says, 'as to amount to a Conscription among the lower classes of society, while, to the higher, they are nothing but an insignificant poll-tax.'—*A Conscription*!!! Why were not the exceptions stated, or alluded to? namely, 'That no poor man who has more than one child born in wedlock shall be liable to serve personally, or to provide a substitute: nor any Constable, nor Peace-Officer, Seamen, or Seafaring man, nor any Person employed in his Majesty's Docks, or Yards, etc, etc. nor any Clerk or Apprentice, nor any Licenced Teacher of any separate Congregation,' though it is well known that numbers of these belong to the humblest classes of society: and

---

[1] These two articles were for the first time attributed to W. W. in *The Middle Years*, Part 2, and listed among his contributions to the Westmorland Election of 1818 (see Ls. 497–8 for a full discussion), and they are now reprinted in full from the *Westmorland Gazette* for 23 May and 6 June 1818. More recently, a copy of the handbill *Deception Exposed*, which corresponds to the first of these items (with some few variations, the most important of which are noted below), has come to light in the Paul Betz Collection, thereby somewhat strengthening the original argument for W. W.'s authorship of the two pieces. The handbill is endorsed: 'circulated at Kendal May 2 1818.'

[2] The Yeoman was widely supposed to be Henry Brougham himself.

lastly, no person under the age of eighteen, or above forty-five. Such and so numerous were the exceptions in favour of those classes. Among the persons actually liable to serve, the calculation was that the lot fell upon one in eighteen, and the drawn man, if he served in person, was entitled to his discharge at the end of five years, and was exonerated from future ballot. Every one knows that the service of the militia was confined to the united kingdoms. In almost every parish may be found some individual who, from his own experience, can report the manifold comforts, privileges and indulgences the militia soldier enjoyed; what care was taken of his health and general conduct; what provisions were made for his lodging, clothing, and nourishment; and what favourable opportunities were afforded him to acquire money, if so disposed, by the exercise of his craft, or by any sort of labour in demand where he might be quartered. During the period of service, an allowance of two shillings a week was made from the parish for the wife and each child of a married man. Yet these considerate laws accompanied with such humane regulations are termed a *Conscription!*—a most reprehensible abuse of words, intended to convey the notion and feeling that the laws of England are, in this particular, as tyrannical as those of France were during the despotism of Bonaparte. For the word *Conscription* is not known to the English law, and would have been scarcely known to the English language, but for the tremendous process which in France was designated by that term.[1]

In the proportion of one to eighteen among those liable to be enrolled, a man of the lower classes was subject to this easy and pleasant service; but, if he had better prospects, or preferred another kind of life, by only taking the precaution of entering into a society or club, as was usually done, he might ensure himself against the contingency, at a very trifling rate, probably at less than three shillings and sixpence per annum, for any five years during the war, or if towards the close of the war the high price

---

[1] The word was first used in this sense in connection with a law of the French Republic, 5 Sept. 1798, which provided that recruits required for service in the army should be compulsorily enrolled from young men between the ages of 20 and 25, whom it declared to be legally liable for military service. The distinction urged here is between compulsory conscription of this kind and the tradition of voluntary enlistment advocated, for example, in Machiavelli's *Art of War*, which lasted on in 'citizen armies' and, in modified form, in the militia system of the Napoleonic era.

of the substitute caused an exception, this was owing to the increased price of labour, so that the parties liable were better able to meet the demand. It is indeed true, as the pretended Yeoman affirms, 'that the Freeholder of forty shillings a year, or the Labourer without property,' (with the exception of the cases above stated, and some others where the parish made up the deficiency,) 'did, where service was commuted for money, contribute *as largely*, for the defence of the country, while subject to the militia ballot, as a Nobleman, (he ought to have said Gentleman, Peers being excepted) with an annual income of £40,000 per annum.' We have already stated the amount of this *large* contribution, upon an average three shillings and sixpence per annum at the utmost. Is there an Englishman, however low his rank, with a spark of English feeling in his breast, who would deem an equality of contribution to such a small amount, and for such a purpose, partial and oppressive? Would he not rather esteem it an honour that the legislator has called upon him to take a part in the defence of his native land,[1] in common with the wealthiest subject in the kingdom? Yet this self-styled Yeoman, without respect either to the feelings, understandings, or knowledge of his readers, has dared to apply[2] the odious term *Conscription* to the English Militia Laws; falsifying their character in order to excite discontent.

The next instance brought forward to make out the Yeoman's case is the 'Tax on riding horses, which is charged at the same rate on a yeoman of £20 a year, as upon a nobleman or an esquire of £20,000.' So much is here insidiously suppressed, that the statement amounts to a gross falsehood. A yeoman with one horse, if subject to riding horse-duty, is, we allow, charged £2.17.6d.; but the rate is progressive, and does in fact fall the heaviest upon the class immediately above the yeoman: for, a gentleman keeping two saddle horses pays four guineas and a half for each; if he keeps *three*, he pays five pounds four shillings for each: should he keep ten, the duty upon his horses would amount to £63.10s. per annum; and if twenty, to £132 per annum: so that what the nobleman or gentleman would pay for each of his twenty saddle or pleasure horses exceeds what the yeoman pays, who keeps only one, in the sum of £3.14s.6d. for each horse, which is considerably more than double the sum paid

---

[1] to stand upon the same footing in this mode of defending his native land *handbill*.

[2] Blush then, blush self-styled Yeoman, at having applied *handbill*.

by the yeoman. This is dwelt upon because it is the aim of the writer, whom we are unmasking, to persuade, at any cost of truth and fair dealing, that worthy class of men, whom he feigns himself to belong to, that they are treated by the laws with peculiar hardship. As a further proof of disingenuous suppression of facts, the reader of the Yeoman's Address must be reminded that if a person rents land, in value under £70 per annum, or occupies his own under £35, he is at liberty to use a horse for all the ordinary purposes of his business, such as attending markets, fairs, etc., or for the purpose of procuring medical assistance, and is also entitled to ride to places of public worship, to assizes, quarter sessions, meetings of commissioners, and to elections, without being subject to any other duty than 3s. the rate on husbandry horses, occasionally used for riding by small farmers; and, if he belongs to a yeomanry corps, whatever may be the rent of his farm, he is then exempted. The Act expressly exempts horses used '*for the purpose of procuring medical assistance*,' and yet this writer, by implication, charges the legislature with inhumanity upon this score![1] Take his own words. 'Nor is it the worst feature of this tax, that it amounts to an absolute prohibition to the Yeoman from the use of his own horse, however pressing the emergency. For the Surveyor, concluding that every man, on some necessity or other (*especially if he, or any individual of his family, be afflicted with sickness*) will use his horse at least once in the year, sends him a surcharge at a venture, and puts him upon his oath, etc.' So that the very instance by which the laws most pointedly shew their consideration for that class of Yeomen who are much the most numerous, is, by disguising the truth, made an occasion of vilifying the Legislature. Let it be borne in mind also, that by an act past in 1816, exemptions from duties upon one horse used occasionally for the purpose of riding, were carried much farther.

The next instance cited as a specimen of oppressive taxation is treated still more unfairly. 'If', says the writer, 'the yeoman occupied his own freehold, he was made liable, in addition to his ten per cent as proprietor, to a duty of 7½ per cent as occupier; and thus the small proprietors were paying 3s.6d. while their legislators were so modest as to be satisfied with contributing from their own pockets 2s. in the pound.' Now the fact is, that the occupier of his own land did not, in respect of his occupancy, pay a farthing, if, upon a fair valuation, it was not worth more

---

[1] *Rest of paragraph omitted by handbill.*

than £46 per annum; nor did he become subject to the tax of seven and a half per cent as occupier of his own land, if its value fell below £86 per annum. The scale, was, as given in the note*.

Why, but for the purpose of deception, was the actual state of the case kept out of sight? And when it is said that 'the legislators were *so modest* as to be satisfied with contributing from their own pockets only two shillings in the pound,' how justly does the irony apply to a writer who omits to mention that if the legislator or rich landholder occupies his own land, (a case *universal* to a considerable extent, and *general* to a very great one, during the late and still existing passion for agricultural pursuits among the gentry,) he was subject to the full rate of duty of 3s 6d in the pound, while the smaller proprietor and occupier was relieved in the manner above detailed. Let this hypocritical writer refer to the accounts presented to Parliament in 1813: he will there find, that out of £15,000 charged on the farmers in Westmorland, at the rate of 1s.6d in the pound, little more than £7,000 was required by government, which sum was paid by the *large* and *wealthy* occupiers. The small occupiers, amounting to 3,000 in number, were entirely relieved from the remainder of the tenant's duty, amounting to more than £3,000 annually!!

The 'Yeoman's address' has been re-published[1] in the Kendal Chronicle, from a hope that this tissue of falsehoods and misrepresentations will dispose the freeholders to vote for Mr Brougham. Mr James Brougham[2] has been a most active canvasser in his brother's behalf, and is said to be at this time so engaged.—Let the Yeomanry, to whom he applies for their votes, and who may think that they have cause of complaint, ask that gentleman if the statements of the present writer be not accurate. Mr James Brougham must know: for in the year 1808 he accepted a commission from the tax-office, and actually went into Scotland to enquire into the complaints of his countrymen, the small Scotch farmers. What benefit they derived from his exertions, is not known. What benefit Mr James Brougham derived, he seems either to have forgotten, or will forget to tell

---

[1] Announced for republication *handbill*.

[2] Henry Brougham's brother (see *MY* pt. ii, L. 472) and his supporter in the election campaign. Little is known about him before he was returned for Kendal in 1832, except that he had successively represented the closed boroughs of Tregony, Downton, and Winchelsea for short periods. When Henry Brougham became Lord Chancellor, he appointed him to the posts of Registrar of Affidavits and Clerk of Letters Patent, which he performed through a deputy.

his Westmorland friends; and, as the party to which he belongs have spared no pains to fix a stigma of unprincipled selfishness upon the motives of every man connected with government, who takes any part in the present contest in opposition to their own, it may not be amiss if the Westmorland Freeholders should ask of Mr James Brougham whether, on his return from the above named excursion into his native country, he did not apply for permanent employment under the tax-office.—We shall return to the pseudo Yeoman and his Friends.[1]

* It appears from a most careful examination of the Act, that a person occupying his own land is granted an allowance equal to the whole duty in respect of the occupation, till their annual value amounts to £47; and that the duty of 1s.6d. does not take its full effect till the annual value amounts to £86. From £47 to £86 the duty increases as the allowance decreases.

Annual Value   £46 pays nothing
47 pays nearly 0 ¾d in the Pound
50 .... 0 3
60 .... 0 9
70 .... 1 1¼
80 .... 1 4½
85 .... 1 5¾
86 and upwards 1 6

ANTI-JANUS

DECEPTION EXPOSED;

OR,

An Antidote for the Poison of the Westmorland Yeoman's Address,

No.2.

'The *excess* of taxation, however,' continues the Yeoman, 'is still more demonstrative of the subserviency of the House of Commons to the executive Government than the *apportionment* of it, oppressive as it is.' 'During the reign of his present Majesty,

---

[1] Enough for the present:—we shall probably return . . . at our leisure *handbill*. Evidently a second handbill was projected, but the second part of *Deception Exposed* was not apparently first published in that form.

the annual taxes have been increased by fifty millions, nor has that been sufficient to meet the wasteful expenditure of Ministers; for there has been added to the national debt, during the same space of time, the enormous sum of seven hundred millions!'—'a burthen under which they (the people) are not able to stand.'

True it is that the pressure, towards the close of the late war and after that period, was felt in many quarters very severely. But the several interests that suffered have been rapidly recovering. The Chancellor of the Exchequer,[1] in his speech on Mr. Tierney's motion,[2] May 1st, assure us that there has been an increase of six millions in the aggregate of our exports and imports; and that in our internal trade the increase has been in a much greater proportion; which could not have happened without a correspondent revival of agricultural prosperity. Let my neighbours who would see the subject of the national debt comprehensively treated, refer to those extracts lately given in the 'Carlisle Patriot,' from Mr. Fellows' pamphlet,[3] which demonstrate, that not only is the country able to stand under this burthen, 'but its productive powers, for the last hundred years, have increased in a greater proportion than the debt.' Making due allowance for the depreciation of money, the debt that existed about a hundred years ago may fairly be computed at *one-eighth* part of the present debt; but whoever will examine the records of the Custom-house, Excise, and Post-Office duties (which falling chiefly upon articles of luxury and indulgence, or indicating increased industry, may therefore be regarded as no unfair criterion of public wealth at different periods) will find, that the produce of those duties in the times of Geo. I. fell considerably *below* one-*eighth* part of their present amount. With these documents, others concur to prove, that the national debt, whatever may be its operation, and however vast its accumulation, bears a less proportion to the actual resources of the country than the public

[1] Nicholas Vansittart, 1st Lord Bexley (1766–1851), M.P., latterly for Harwich (1796–1823), and Chancellor of the Exchequer, 1812–23, during one of the most difficult periods of the nineteenth century.

[2] The Motion of George Tierney (see *MY* pt. ii, L. 538) on the state of the circulating medium and resumption of cash payments.

[3] *The Rights of Property Vindicated Against the Claims of Universal Suffrage*, 1818, extracts from which appeared in the *Carlisle Patriot* between 11 Apr. and 6 June 1818. Robert Fellowes (1771–1847), editor of the *Critical Review*, 1804–11, and a benefactor of London University, published *Morality United with Policy* (1800), and *The Religion of the Universe* (1836).

debt a century ago did to the resources of that period. A comparison between the state of things at the commencement of the late war, and at the present time, when it has been victoriously terminated, leads to a conclusion as satisfactory. 'That taxation,' continues Mr. Fellows, who gives the details from which these inferences are made, 'cannot be oppressive, under which, in proportion as it has increased, the wealth of the country has increased in a triple or quadruple proportion; nor can that debt, whatever may be the number of millions to which it amounts, be regarded as an overwhelming weight, and of terrifying magnitude, which does not equal twice the amount of the property created by the varied industry of the people of Great Britain and Ireland in a single year.'[1]

So loud is the outcry against taxation and the national debt that it requires some courage to ask what benefit has been derived from these sources;—yet they who are not so perverse as to prefer error along with sullen dissatisfaction, to truth with contentment, will not find it difficult to perceive that these benefits are great and numerous. Taxation quickens industry, by transferring superabundance in one quarter to supply deficiency in another. It is the means of making the luxurious propensities of the wealthy and indolent minister to the wants of the industrious labourer; and it extorts from the miser what charity would not be strong enough to induce him to part with. By pressing upon those who are thriving, it urges them to fresh exertions; and if, as must unavoidably happen, taxation sometimes presses too hard, and exhausts, where in a less degree it might only have stimulated, this evil is invariably remedied, as far as circumstances will allow, as soon as it is perceived. In the mean while, let those who complain, not without reason, consider what would have been the rate of the interest of money, if there had been no such establishment as the public funds. In how small a degree would superfluous capital have been productive of permanent income compared to what we now see, not to say that the principal itself in a thousand instances could never have come into existence! Who would wish to be driven to the melancholy expedient of living upon the principal of his money, for want of opportunity to place it where it might be turned to better account, as being more needed than in his own hands? And, after all, comes the apprehension of housebreakers, who, laying their hands upon a

---

[1] This is the last sentence of the extract published on 16 May.

strong box, could in one night sweep away the whole of the amplest treasure. As for those who have little more than they work for, from day to day, it is obvious that the wages of labour, were it not for the funds and public expenditure, must be as low as they were in former times; so that the artisan and tiller of the soil would find themselves in a worse instead of a better condition, if the national debt was annihilated. This subject, for want of room, is very slightly touched, and may be well, though somewhat abruptly concluded, with a *political* consideration relating to it, *viz.* the stability which the government derives from the immense numbers of proprietors of all ranks, through their possessions in the funds, interested in its support.[1]

To the above, and other important points the 'Westmorland Yeoman,' from ignorance, or from still more discreditable causes, pays no attention. So that he appears before us representing that to be an intolerable grievance which, notwithstanding the partial hardships unavoidably accompanying it, is upon the whole, a very great benefit; and this he does for the express purpose of slandering the Legislature of his country; which he describes as consisting of 'men, who, *allured each by his individual interest,* voted millions after millions out of the pockets of the people.' This sweeping condemnation includes both sides of the House of Commons— every member who may have supported the Government, whether under Mr. Pitt, Mr. Fox, or any succeeding Minister. In expressing this defamatory opinion the 'Westmorland Yeoman' may possibly be sincere; but if they also hold it who have republished his address, with a view to promote the election of Mr. B. for the County of Westmorland, what absurdity have they fallen into! for Mr. B. anxiously endeavoured to recommend himself to the Foxite Administration,[2] who converted the Income Tax of six into the Property Tax of ten, per cent.; and the same

[1] In the extract on 2 May, Fellowes had argued that 'It is for the interest of the labouring classes that the number of proprietors should be increased as much as possible; for the industry of a country is stimulated in proportion as its proprietors are multiplied . . . The funds tend to give a more rapid circulation to the wealth of the country; and by creating an order of proprietors, different from the landed gentry, and often of more active and more enlightened minds, they open new avenues to civilisation, and increase the diffusion of urbanity and affluence. I say nothing of the safe place of deposit which the funds furnish for the savings of industry . . .' The National Debt, he maintained, had had a salutary effect: 'It rather invigorates exertion than depresses industry.'

[2] See *MY* pt. ii, L.467.

Mr. B. upon whom the hopes of these Independants, who ascribe all existing political evils to a rapacious Aristocracy, are founded, owes the seat in the House of Commons which he now fills, to the nomination of a Peer![1]

But were it actually true, that a national debt to the amount of that of Great Britain is ruinous, or even injurious, instead of being, as it is, the contrary, the Government would not be censurable for any part of that debt, which the aggressions of foreign powers had forced it to incur. Now that a great majority of the people, and especially those most competent to judge, deemed the late war both just and necessary,[2] and sanctioned the resistance against Bonaparte to the utmost, cannot be questioned by any unprejudiced mind. Yet, the 'Westmorland Yeoman,' without hinting at any concurring cause from without, imputes the annual taxation and the addition to the national debt to the intrinsic depravity of Parliament. Doubtless in one point of view taxation has been carried to what, adopting his own term, we may justly call *excess*; expenditure having often gone beyond the amount necessary to maintain the security and support the honour of the State. Allowing this, what do we more than admit that the British Government, consisting of human instruments, and having to deal with men, is not exempt from the errors and infirmities of our common nature. It is not enough to establish the conclusions of this pretended Yeoman and other intermeddlers, that the resources of the country have been misapplied, and that economy has not prevailed as it ought to have done.—It is incumbent upon them to shew, by the testimony of experience, that a Government more popularly constituted than ours, and subject, in a greater degree, to the changeable influences of public opinion, would be more judicious in respect to measures adopted, and more economical in carrying them into effect. Unless this can be shewn, nothing is accomplished, and all history discountenances such expectations. A single instance shall suffice from that of our own country: Milton,[3] strenuous friend of lib-

---

[1] Brougham sat for Lord Darlington's pocket borough of Winchelsea.

[2] A phrase in frequent use: for example in W. W.'s *Convention of Cintra* (*Prose Works*, i. 226, 373) and in the second of his *Two Addresses to the Freeholders of Westmorland* (*Prose Works*, ii. 164–5).

[3] See *The Digression to Milton's History of Britain*, reissued, anon. 1681, under the title of *Mr. John Milton's Character of the Long Parliament and Assembly of Divines in MDCXLI* (*Complete Prose Works*, v (1971), 443–4). The same work is cited three times in the *Convention of Cintra* (see *Prose Works*, i. 302, 314, 343).

erty, thus delineates the proceedings of a body of reformers of his own time, whom he had zealously favoured till their misconduct extinguished his hopes. 'A Parliament,' he says, 'being called, to redress many things, as 'twas thought, the people, with great courage and expectation, to be eased of what discontented them, chose to their behoof in Parliament such as they thought best affected to the public good, and some indeed men of wisdom and integrity; the rest (to be sure the greater part) whom wealth or ample possessions, or bold and active ambition (rather than merit) has commended to the same place.

But when once the superficial zeal and popular fumes that acted their new magistracy, were cooled, and spent in them, straight every one betook himself (setting the common-wealth behind, his private ends before) to do as his own profit or ambition led him. Then was justice delayed, and soon after decryed: spite and favour determined all. Hence faction, thence treachery, both at home and in the field: every where wrong and oppression; foul and horrid deeds committed daily, or maintained in secret, or in open. Some who had been called from shops and warehouses, without other merit, to sit in supreme Councils and Committees (as their breeding was) fell to huckster the common-wealth. Others did thereafter as men could sooth and humour them best; so he who would give most, or, under covert of hypocritical zeal, insinuate basest, enjoyed unworthily, the rewards of learning and fidelity; or escaped the punishment of his crimes and misdeeds. Their votes and ordinances, which men looked should have contained *the repealing of bad laws*, and *the immediate constitution of better*, resounded with nothing else but NEW IMPOSITION, TAXES, EXCISES; YEARLY, MONTHLY, WEEKLY.'[1]

Recommending a serious reflection upon the above, to those Electors of Westmorland who may be disposed to favour Mr. Brougham, not long since the abettor of Lord Cochrane's principles;[2] and also to the Electors of Carlisle, who may have

[1] Milton's sentence runs on: 'not to reck'n the offices, gifts and other preferments bestow'd and shar'd among themselves.'

[2] Thomas Cochrane, 10th Earl of Dundonald (1775–1860), admiral and M. P. for Westminster (1807), whose controversial and colourful career brought him much notoriety. See *MY* pt. i, L.142. In 1814 he was implicated in a stock exchange scandal, fined, imprisoned, and expelled from the navy, but was at once re-elected by his constituents, and his fines were paid by subscriptions from the public. Later, he commanded the Chilean navy in their war of independence against Spain (1819–22), helped to secure the independence of Brazil (1823–5),

encouraged an individual,[1] whose credentials on his first public introduction to that city are given in a panegryrical letter from his lordship, as factious and inflammatory as any thing that has proceeded from the press for some years. I take my leave of the 'Westmorland Yeoman,' for the present.

ANTI-JANUS.

and served as an admiral in the Greek navy (1827–8). He was finally reinstated in the British navy in 1832, and urged the introduction of steam-power and screw-propellers in warships. In the second of his *Two Addresses to the Freeholders of Westmorland*, W. W. had linked Lord Cochrane with Henry Brougham as advocates of annual parliaments and universal suffrage. See *Prose Works*, iii. 177–9, 217–19.

[1] In the turbulent Carlisle election of 1818, a local candidate named Perkins had come forward as a Whig with testimonials from Lord Cochrane, in opposition to the sitting Tory and Whig members, Sir James Graham and J. C. Curwen respectively. They both repudiated him, and so did Henry Brougham, and he came out at the bottom of the poll with 49 votes.

APPENDIX II

Letter from Annette Vallon to Dorothy Wordsworth, April 1835[1]

Address: Mademoiselle Dorothée Wordsworth, Grasner Ridelmonde,[2] Kendal, Westermorland, angleterre.
Postmark: (1) FPO 4 Apr. 1835 (2) 4 Apr. 1835.
MS. WL.
Robert Gittings and Jo Manton, *Dorothy Wordsworth*, 1985, p. 280.

2 avril 1835
Boulevard des Filles du Calvaire au 15

C'est avec plaisir et chagrin que je vous ecris ma Bien chere Dorothée ses sentimens opposés n'en sont pas moins ces que j'eprouve j'attendois une reponse á la lettre que jai ecrit á votre frere j'esperois une pronte Satisfaction a mes justes reclamations il

---

[1] For the occasion of this letter, which has only recently come to light among the *WL MSS.*, see *LY* pt. iii, L.879. Since the marriage of his 'French' daughter Caroline Baudouin in 1816 (see *MY* pt. ii, L.395), W. W. had paid her an annuity of £30; but owing to his own precarious financial position early in 1835, he sought through the good offices of H. C. R. to substitute for the annuity a lump sum of £400 to be invested in French bonds by Caroline and her husband. Unfortunately, as the Baudouins were quick to point out, this sum was not expected to yield more than half the original annuity, which they regarded as their right under French law, the father being under a legal obligation to contribute to his child's marriage settlement. Annette had already appealed to W. W., in a letter which has not survived, for a prompt settlement of her 'just claims', and in this further letter she now repeated her anguished plea that the original arrangements should be upheld. In the event, H. C. R. seems to have convinced the Baudouins that W. W. could not afford more than was on offer and the matter seems to have been settled on that basis, as W. W. went to see them when he was in Paris in 1837 (see *LY* pt. iii, L.1132), and subsequently sent them presents (see Ls. 1212 and 1270). When W. W. was granted his state pension in 1842, Jean Baptiste Baudouin seems to have applied to him for more money (see *HCR* ii. 623 and Morley i. 467), and he applied again to the Wordsworth family after the poet's death (see below, Appendix III), apparently in the belief that under French law W. W.'s illegitimate daughter was entitled to some provision from her father's will. Baudouin, chef de bureau au Mont de Piété, died in 1854, his wife Caroline in 1862.

[2] i.e. Grasmere, Rydal Mount. Annette's spelling is idiosyncratic and sometimes old-fashioned.

prolonge mes Souffrances, et le chagrin qui me tue, cette pensée
doit le tourmenté parce je le supose toujours avec cette noblesse
de coeur que je lui ai naguere connu et constament admiré. Sa
position de famille peu l'embarassé mais la mienne doit le toucher
et Sa fille doit le déterminé á acquitté une promesse faite; ce qu'il
envoye ne represente point á Son mari la Somme donnée par Son
contra de marriage; je ne rescenderai Sur des détails deja donné
dans ma precedent lettre. Le passé avec tous les Souvenirs qu'il
me laisse n'a rien que d'affligent, le present m'occupe par amour
pour ma fille et Son avenir me tourmente Si vous ne determiné
pas votre frere á remplir noblement ce que je crois qu'il doit tant
de motifs D'honneur et délicatesse lui en sont la loi que je presume que vous n'aurai pas de peine a le décidée a faire cesser cet
etat painible, les fonds sont sans interet ils reposent entre les
mains du Banquer sans nulle benifite pour M Beaudoin il est Bon
mari Bon pere mais cest en raison de ces qualités qu'il est plus
Strique á demander pour eux.

je vous le demande au nom de l'amitié que je vous ai voue et
au nom de mes malheurs qui doivent parlé haut dans Son coeur
de terminer ces reclamations si painible pour moi. Ma chere fille
si admirable dans les qualités que possede Son père merite toute
Sa tendresse par la ressemblance morale qu'elle a avec lui, elle me
charge de lui offrire toute l'etendue de Son respect de sa tendresse elle lembrasse avec toute la chaleur de son coeur et vous
Bonne Dorothée qu'elle aime tant en qui elle á la plus Grande
confiance justifié ce sentiment en prenant les interets de votre
niece et laissé mourire sa mere en paix je ne tiens guere á la vie
dieu peut en abregé la cour quant il lui plaira.[1]

Vos nieces sont[2] charmantes elles Sont parfaitement élevées la
jeune vas faire Sa première communion ma derniere invocation
sadresse Bien vivement a votre frere Cest entre ces mains que
reposent les derniers jours de ma carriere.

Je vous embrasse avec de sentiments qui ne peuvent changer.

---

[1] Annette Vallon died in straitened circumstances on 10 Jan. 1841 at the age of
75, at the address in the 8th *arrondissement* of Paris from which this letter is written. See Émile Legouis, *William Wordsworth and Annette Vallon*, rev. edn. 1967,
pp. 110–11.

[2] Caroline had two surviving daughters at this time: Louise Marie Caroline
Dorothée (1816–69), who was twice married, the second time to Théophile
Vauchelet (1802–73), the artist, and Marie Marguerite Caroline (1823–64), who
married M. Marquet, a prison official at Melun. W. W. would have seen the
elder of the two during his visit to the family in 1820 (see *MY* pt. ii, L.608).

Appendix II

Mes respects á Madame Words qu'elle sois mon avocat je serai
sure du Sucès
adieu votre Malheureuse Annette W.[1]

---

[1] Annette was known as 'Madame William' or 'Williams'.

APPENDIX III

Additional Letters of Mary Wordsworth
Concerning the Publication of C. W. jnr.'s
Memoirs of William Wordsworth (1851)

M. W. to I. F.

Address: Miss Fenwick, Kelston Knoll, near Bath.
Postmark: (1) 27 Dec. (2) 28 Dec. 1847. *Stamp*: (1) Ambleside (2) Bath.
MS. WL.
MW, p. 289(—).

27th Dec^r. [1847]

My dearly beloved friend,

Thro' Mr Taylor's kindness we had heard of your having performed your journey to Kelston prosperously—but it was a great
comfort to us to receive this satisfactory account from yourself,
and God bless you for writing to us—but pray dear friend spare
yourself, so long as you find the effort irksome. We shall be contented with a line now and then from dear Louisa,[1] who I know
will be ready to prevent us anxiety. Give my dear love to her and
tell her so. And of her Father, whom you do not mention we
shall be glad to hear.

I have received, and distributed according to your direction,
the £30. No doubt you will receive the thanks of the Parties—all
of whom were grateful to have the power to dispence so much
comfort as your charity gives them.—And as you suggest, I trust
you have afforded an object of interest to the 2 Quillinans[2] that
may be of use to them.

We have this morning parted with our Grandaughter—who,
together with Clara Broadwood[3] arrived along with Mr
Robinson on the 18th. Clara went forward to Workington Hall
on the 21st but we kept Jane with us over Xmas day. And a great
comfort she is to us—a more intelligent, lively Child cannot
be—and tho' I do not think her situation at Present equal to

---

[1] I. F.'s niece.   [2] E. Q.'s daughters.
[3] A Curwen relative, whose father was in India.

Hendon, she will make a fine Woman. She goes on today to Workington Hall—to see an Aunt (Clara's Grandmother) who leaves in a few days, before she joins her Father and Brothers at Brigham—the School boys[1] spent 10 days with us on their way, but they were gone before their Sister arrived. Upon the whole we were pleased with the Boys but hitherto the School does not seem to give general satisfaction—but as changes are contemplated, their Father means to give it another ½ year's trial. *This is* your Godson's 12th birthday.

Mr Robinson has written to you and reported of us—so that I have not much to say of ourselves. My husband and I still *bark* a little one against the other—his cough has been of much longer standing than mine, but for a time I was more oppressed by the cold than he has been;—indeed I am most thankful to say that his *bodily* health has been marvellously supported. Our poor Sister too, continues in her usual way—she comes down every Evening—but I cannot say that (except *any* change may be useful), she derives much good from the visit. She is more restless than ever, and it is a perpetual move from her own chair to that of her Brother the whole time she is down stairs.

Of dear Mrs Arnold's sorrow I know you are acquainted—but not perhaps that poor Mary[2] is now at Fox how, and so changed—so thin and pale! It was deemed quite necessary on every account that, however unwillingly, she should come home—and a hard trial it must be for her. They do not speak openly of the afflicted *state* of her Husband, only that it is quite improper that he should see her, or his family—Paralysis of the Brain—and extreme weakness is the state in which he is, as far as we can gather. Yet we understand that he has muscular strength that enables him to walk in a considerable way. This, as it appears there is not the slightest hope of recovery, is to be lamented—as causing fear of a long continuance in so very distressing a state.

Sorrows, my beloved friend, as at our age we must expect, are gathering upon us. Our invaluable friend Mrs Hoare is at this time in that state of weakness as to make us fearful that the next post may tell us she is no more. On the 4th of the month she wrote me a long and tender letter—speaking of *her* she loved so dearly[3]—and wishing to know what winterly comfort she could send me, that might have been thought of *by* her whom *I* had

---

[1] John W.'s sons Henry and William, now at Sedbergh.

[2] Mary Arnold, now Mrs. Twining, was widowed the following year.

[3] Dora Q., who had died the previous July.

lost, etc., She had then been for 3 weeks a close prisoner from the influenza and tho' recovering, said 'she was so weak as that a grasshopper might have thrown her down'. But since that time, I understand, she had gone to Church, taken cold and had a relapse—and from the daily notes from Miss Hoare (who thank God seems to be wonderfully supported) during the last week, we cannot but look for what will be such a general grief. Even at her great age, a year older than our selves, there was so much youthful energy about her, that one could not but hope she might be spared to brighten and dispense blessing and happiness a while longer to the large family of relatives and friends of which she was the centre. Not to *speak* of her charity: both from her purse and in her personal exertion she was indefatigable. But God's will be done—she goes to her great reward. And my beloved friend, we shall soon follow—and O that we could but feel *as* ready for the change, as we cannot but feel, unpresumptuously I hope, Her Spirit is ripe for.

Our friend Mr Robinson is in his usual redundant Spirits—he is now our only guest[1]—and would find his visit very dull, only he is such a welcome and chearful visitor in the neighbourhood—Mrs Davy's, Miss Martineau, Mr Carr, Mr Gregg,[2] etc., etc.,—he has a common interest with them all and he is an active walker. *We* stay quietly at home, but our neighbours come to us—Mrs Fletcher and Mary will be with us this evening. And we have had flying visits, by the rail way, from Mr Carter[3]—and dearest John comes to us whenever he can—but now we shall not see him till after the holidays—he will, poor fellow, have enough to do to keep his undisciplined school boys in order.

W^m and Fanny intend to come to us about the 7th or 8th when W$^{m's}$ office duties will set him at liberty—but their stay will be but short—as they are preparing their new house to enter upon at Candlemas. The necessity for this change is most unlucky—but we must hope that their next settling will be permanent, and that they may enjoy better health. Fanny has returned *for her* well, I suppose, and I have not heard but that she continues so. Poor William still suffers, but I hope not to that degree which he did a while ago, tho' he has not escaped the prevalent cold—they are

---

[1] H. C. R. arrived at Rydal Mount on 17 Dec., and 'remained at Wordsworth's till the 8th of January with very little pleasure on account of the deep sorrow of Wordsworth and Mrs. Wordsworth . . .' (*HCR* ii. 670).

[2] William Rathbone Greg, the political writer (see *LY* pt. iv, L. 1632).

[3] W. W.'s clerk, now employed by W. W. jnr. in the Stamp Office at Carlisle.

still staying with their Friends in Abbey Street where they will remain till they come to us.

We had much pleasure and comfort from the visit of Dr C. Wordsworth and his excellent wife.[1] You will be glad to hear what I think I have not mentioned to you before, that Chris undertook to prepare, after his Uncle's day, some biographical notices,[2] which, being understood that such is intended to appear from that quarter, may prevent indifferent persons to take upon them to Publish—as poor Cottle[3] and others have done for Coleridge. Susan took from her Uncle some notes; and they were referred to you, dear friend, for what you could help them to, if in God's goodness it should please him that you survive us—and for those notes regarding the time and circumstance connected with the publication of his several poems: by the bye how far did you get in this work[4] which you so patiently and

[1] C. W. jnr. and his wife Susan had stayed at Rydal Mount the previous month. On 11 July 1850, E. Q. was to note in his Diary (*WL MSS.*): 'Mrs W. told me today that C. W. knew less of W.'s poetry than almost any of her acquaintances, and his wife nothing at all.'

[2] This is the first reference to C. W. jnr.'s *Memoirs of William Wordsworth* which were to find so little favour among those who had known the poet best, when they were published in 1851. W. W. had always been opposed to biographies of poets, believing, as stated in the *Letter to a Friend of Robert Burns*, that 'if their works be good, they contain within themselves all that is necessary to their being comprehended and relished.' (*Prose Works*, iii. 122). But, in dictating to I. F. in the winter of 1842–3 a long series of notes about his published poems, W. W. had apparently envisaged the eventual publication of an illustrative commentary on his works, and it was this task—along with the publication of *The Prelude*—that was to be entrusted after the poet's death to C. W. jnr. Any prior claims of E. Q., as one of W. W.'s executors, 'to be principal in the work' were passed over and he was not consulted at this stage, his relationship with the Wordsworths having deteriorated since the death of Dora Q.

[3] Joseph Cottle's *Early Recollections; Chiefly Relating to the Late Samuel Taylor Coleridge*, had appeared in 1837. It had been preceded in 1836 by Thomas Allsop's *Letters, Conversations, and Recollections of S. T. Coleridge*.

[4] The Fenwick Notes, I. F. had told H. C. R. in Mar. 1843, 'are now written down in a book interleaved with M^r Q's help—so that when they are revised they may be added to—if any other matter should recur to the Poet's mind.' (Morley, i. 479). Dora and E. Q. had made a transcript the following August (*WL MSS.*), and I. F. was now proposing to send her original drafts to him. H. C. R. advised caution, being concerned that E. Q. might not cooperate with C. W. jnr. by making the Notes available to him (see Morley, ii. 656, 660, 665); but in the event his fears proved groundless (see *Mem.* i, 22n.; Morley, ii. 727, 731, and *HCR* ii. 706).

kindly undertook? If I remember rightly Mr Q. transcribed your copy. *He* must be applied to at some proper time to aid Christopher,—perhaps he may be hurt that he was not asked to be principal in the work, (Christopher who had been talking with Willy on the subject offered his service), for you know he is easily offended.

The Q's[1] dined with us on Xtmas day—a melancholy day, but we retired to bed in thankfulness it was past. Mr Q. left us, as he always does, soon after dinner, being fearful of the night air—otherwise he seems to be quite well. He is now busy with Camoens.[2]

From Mathon we have had comfortable tidings. George[3] they tell us becomes more himself every day, and had now, I believe, commenced with the parish duty satisfactorily—at least his Sister Eliz: speaks hopefully—and they were when she wrote looking forward to a happy Christmas—expecting their dear cheerful Uncle,[4] and Thos:[5] and his wife, who seems to have endeared herself very much to the family.

I think dear friend I must have tired you with my details, and did I not know how clever you are at reading bad writing, I should feel that I had written more than you could make out—I must now be done, for my hands are quite benumbed—so in the hope and trust, beloved friend, that you are gaining strength, and with dear love and best wishes from my husband (who, if he could do anything and what he most wishes, would write it himself), *and* with earnest prayers for your everlasting happiness, believe me ever dearest friend to remain lovingly yours

M. Wordsworth.

Should you see, or have any communication with Miss Pollard[6] Pray say all that is kind and that you think will be acceptable

[1] Writing to I. F. on 24 Dec., H. C. R. had referred to W. W.'s reluctance to visit E. Q. at Loughrigg Holme on account of its associations with Dora Q., and E. Q.'s resentment of what he took as a personal affront: 'Q: expresses himself so strongly that I fear the foundation is laid for a lasting estrangement which might widen and lead to an entire alienation.' (Morley, ii. 656).

[2] E. Q.'s translation, 'his laborious work . . . from which he never can gain emolument or fame', according to H. C. R. (Morley, ii. 686), was published in part posthumously in 1853.

[3] M. W.'s nephew George Hutchinson.

[4] John Monkhouse of The Stow. [5] Thomas Hutchinson jnr.

[6] Jane Marshall's sister.

from us to her—had I resolution I would write to her—but alas!—and also to dear Anna Hoskyns[1] from whom we had a kind Christmasday letter—an effort it had been for her to write from her weak state of health—and which *ought* to be an example to me—but I fear it will end in a reproach. Again farewell—here come the Cooksons to spend the day, with their love they bid me say you will hear from them now that they know where to find you.

M. W. to W. W. JNR.

MS. WL.
MW, p. 320 (—).

Monday
[Early Sept. 1850]

My dearest W^m,

Chris: has been reading a letter to me which he has written to you upon the *business* part of his work,[2] which if I understand it right, I think is quite fair, and indeed liberal on his part, bearing in mind, that during the flush of the Sale of Dr Arnold's life Stanley[3] reaped the *whole profits*—afterwards the family allowed

---

[1] Formerly Anna Ricketts, married to Chandos Wren-Hoskyns.

[2] Following W. W.'s death in Apr. 1850, C. W. jnr. was spending some time at Rydal Mount assembling materials for the *Memoirs*. In May M. W. had reluctantly allowed him 'so far to enlarge on the sketch at first contemplated as to give anything, or everything, that may illustrate the Poet in the Man—but to exclude all that is not necessary to that object', thereby increasing the misgivings of H. C. R. who was totally out of sympathy with C. W. jnr.'s high-church principles. 'I fear he will try to make W: appear as a Puseyite', H. C. R. had written to his brother. But E. Q. expressed himself to H. C. R. as satisfied with the arrangements: 'There is no doubt that you and I both knew Wordsworth much better than his nephew knew him: but in some respects he is quite the proper man; and those friends of mine are much mistaken who suppose I much dislike the arrangement for there are many reasons, and one or two of them very weighty ones, why I am well contented not to be saddled with the responsibilities attached to the office of a faithful chronicler.' (Morley, ii. 729, 739–40). For C. W. jnr.'s own conception of his work, see *Mem.* i. 3: 'Regarding the Poems as his Life, the author of these volumes considers it to be his duty to endeavour to supply materials, subordinate and ministerial to the Poems, and illustrative of them; in a word, to write a biographical commentary on the Poet's works.'

[3] A. P. Stanley's *Life and Correspondence of Thomas Arnold* had appeared in 1844.

him to divide with them. The work as far as I have heard it read is admirably executed—and must I feel sure, tend *very much* to encrease the Sale of the works, from the masterly manner in which he has *illustrated* the Poems. This he has in great measure been able to accomplish from the *ample notes* which Miss Fenwick elicited and transcribed from your dear Father's dictation. These notes she intended as a gift to your Sister but after her death she transferred them to her husband, who generously gave the book up to Christopher (into which he and your Sister jointly had made a fair manuscript). I am only sorry that Moxon is not at once to have the offer of the Publication—but Chris: feels himself bound to his own Publisher.[1]

I should like that you could come over for a day even, before they leave us, as I am sure you would be pleased to see how the subject is treated. It will be a most interesting work.

I am glad we have such fine weather—now that their residence here is drawing to a conclusion—and also for John who is stretching his legs, I suppose, for a few days in Ireland. The S. Cooksons[2] are out mounting Scawfell—Mr M. does not reach

---

[1] John Murray.

[2] The Baudouins had made overtures to H. C. R. which suggested that they were seeking money as the price for silence on what Strickland Cookson, W. W.'s solicitor, called 'W. W.'s French entanglement of 1791/2', and H. C. R. had consulted Cookson while he was on holiday in Grasmere. H. C. R.'s reply to the Baudouins and subsequent journey to Paris, seem to have disposed effectively of any claims they may have been pressing on the family, and C. W. jnr. no longer felt it necessary to anticipate their supposed revelations by himself giving a full account in the *Memoirs* of the facts concerning Annette Vallon and W. W.'s French daughter. But what H. C. R. called his 'canting commonplace remark on the perils to which Wordsworth was exposed in his youth at Paris' (*Mem.* i. 74–5) still displeased the family, and H. C. R. tried, unsuccessfully, to get it cut out in proof. (Morley, ii. 756–7; *HCR* ii. 703, 708–9). C. W. jnr. later had second thoughts on the matter, writing to E. Q. on 21 Mar. 1851 that he now doubted 'whether I ought not to have told all the circumstances of the case', but defending what he had said in the *Memoirs*: 'As it is, I have suggested such extenuating circumstances as the case admits of; and thus endeavoured to guard his memory, and to prevent his lapse from being perverted into an example for leading others astray. I believe that David (who was inspired) is a better guide in these matters than any living adviser: and I cannot forget his language in the Penitential Psalms: and I am persuaded that the departed Spirit, if he is cognizant of what is done on earth, would desire that the subject should be so treated, as, under all the circumstances of the case, seems most conducive to the divine honour and the good of men's souls.' (*WL MSS.*)

Rydal. Dear Miss F., Mr Q. writes,[1] seemed no worse for her journey—he saw her into a cab for Mortlake at 3 oc on Sat. even[g]—he was going to see Mr Robinson from whom, on his arrival at Chester asking him to breakfast on Sunday, yester[y] [mg].

I fancy you may have seen Edith[2] ere this, on her way to Morpeth. I trust Fanny and the Babe are well.

God bless you all. Mr Jackson[3] had another stroke last Thursday, and from the report I hear is in an uncertain state.

M. W.

M. W. to W. W. JNR.

MS. WL.
MW, p. 321.

Sat.
[mid-Sept. 1850]

My dearest W[m],

I do think Chris is the most amiable Creature I ever had to deal with.

—Since our last conversation, which ended to my wish—the thoughts of the other part of the Subject, (*the removing the book*[4] from Moxon) has shaken me so much, that I durst not trust myself to talk on the matter; so this morn[g], after my Restless night, I wrote what my opinions and feelings were—and gave the paper to him after breakfast—He came so lovingly to me and met all I had expressed in so straight forward a way, that I feel we are safe in his hands—and that nothing being committed to Murry the thing will be settled to our full approval after his, Christopher's views, are submitted to Mr Carter, Mr Q. and ourselves. The fact is, *in his mind this*, he is in no way satisfied with the *stability* of M. whom he has no objection to, on the contrary likes him; and feels our connexion with him—as much as he respects his own, with the other Publisher etc., etc., I write this to *you* to put aside *in your mind* any unpleasant feelings towards Chris.—for depend upon it he will not act in any way contrary

---

[1] I. F. had left Rydal Mount on 30 Aug. and E. Q. was due back from London on 20 Sept. (Morley, ii. 756, 758): hence the dating of this letter. The syntax of this sentence is somewhat incoherent.

[2] Edith Southey, now Mrs Warter.

[3] Thomas Jackson of Waterhead, agent at Rydal Hall.   [4] The *Memoirs*.

to our wishes and *judgement*—and he has a tender regard for *my* feelings, and for the world will not go contrary to them, when my mind is convinced.—*But* I confess I *have* been harassed by the thoughts of aught being settled contrary to the Will of y^r beloved Father—and as he used to say, the considerations of the 3 last days have *added some* nails to my coffin

God bless you
M. W.

A note from Mr Carter speaking of John's arrival[1] mentions his sorrow that M. is not to be Publisher—tell him what I have written on that Subject and that I should wish he were to be here in the course of next week—to meet you.
—11 oc. I see there is a letter to [?] from you.
I should say if there is any danger—with M.—have as small an Ed: as you like—but do not let us discard him at once—and upon a supposition—

M. W. to W. W. JNR.

Address: The Revd Chris: Wordsworth DD, Cloisters, London.
MS. WL.
MW, p. 325 (—).

30th October 1850

My dear William,
As you request me to give you in writing the circumstances under which your dear Father made the arrangement with Christopher that he should prepare such a brief memoir to be published with his Biographical Poem[2] (after his death) as might be necessary to illustrate his Works, I will endeavour, to the best of my recollection to do so as nearly as I can in the words in which I recalled the circumstance to the mind of Dr W. soon after he had commenced his work—and he observed, what I said, was perfectly correct.
The conversation turned upon the Biography of Authors—and Christopher's opinions seemed to be so perfectly in accord with your Father's (to *you* who have so often heard him speak so strongly on the subject, I need not repeat that he thought an

---

[1] At Carlisle, presumably.   [2] *The Prelude.*

Author's—especially a Poet's works, were the only biography the world had any right to call for) that after C. left the room, I observed to your Father 'you would do well to appoint Chris *your* Biographer'. I well remember his answer was 'Do you think so—he has too much to do to take the trouble' to which I replied 'Let us ask him'. I did so, and he readily agreed, saying he should, if it was his Uncle's wish, have much pleasure in undertaking the office and to be of any use in his power to his family.

So it was settled. And afterwards, the same morning, Dr W. expressed his desire that he should have a written memorandum of what had been settled. Upon my telling y^r Father this—He said 'Well then give him one'—I then wrote the one Ch^r: holds: (you know dear Father, since poor Dora's death, mostly threw these little matters of business upon me), and after he had read and approved what I had written, he signed the Paper, and I took it to Dr Wordsworth, who having read it, said it was all he wanted, to shew what authority was given him—but said he, 'you, Aunt, sign it also'—I did so, and no more was then said.[1]

Some time afterwards, a 2^d Mem: was sent to him, referring him, when the time came, to Miss F. Mr Q. Mr Robinson and Mr Carter, who were best able to be of use to him in the drawing up *such a memoir as was then contemplated*[2]—

---

[1] This memorandum, and the second one quoted below, are printed, in a transcript by H. C. R. from W. W. jnr.'s copies of the original documents, in Morley, ii. 728:

Rydal Mount 16 Novr 47

This morning at my request my nephew Dr Chr Wordsworth has kindly undertaken if he survives me, to prepare for publication any notices of my life that may be deemed necessary to illustrate my writings And by this document I express a wish that my family Executors and Friends may furnish him with any information or memorandums that they may possess which he may think useful to aid him in the Work.

William Wordsworth

Witnessed by Mary Wordsworth.

[2] To Dr Chr Wordsworth. Cloisters Westminster.

My Sons, Son-in-law, dearest Miss Fenwick, Mr Carter and Mr Robinson with whom I have travelled, will I am surely [*Sic*] be kindly disposed to give you any help and information you may require when writing the brief personal notices you dear Christopher undertook to prepare to be attached to my writings

Signed W. Wordsworth.

Rydal Mount
17 Jan: 1848

M. WORDSWORTH

Your Father afterwards, at Susan's request, dictated to her some family historical notices, such as dates, etc.,[1] but I was not aware that this was with a view of publication.

[Written across the top of this letter is a note in W. W. Jnr.'s hand]

Please return this to me. 4th Novr 1850. Wm Wordsworth. Please let this also be returned to me. The originals, of which these are correct copies, were received of me from my mother in the 30th Octr. 1850, and were sent to Dr W. in my letter of the 4th Nov. 50. W. W.

[Enclosure]

[M. W. writes]

Let it in the first instance be understood that I will no longer oppose Dr W's wishes, if the rest of the Parties interested agree with him. He knows all my opinions and feelings which are, I confess, strengthened the more I read of his beautiful Works. Viz that I think it ought not to be separated from the Poems with which it is so closely connected in that in some measure it is like a Paraphrase. Hence (to look at it with regard to Moxon's interest) it may satisfy many (who only read to talk) instead of the Poems. But my chief view of the subject is that it was my husband's desire for *no* separate *Life* (which the work is) so that my feeling was to keep what was done *for him*, as closely connected as possible, with what was done by *himself*.

M. W. Sept. 1st 50.

My dear Chris^r,

When I returned your letter, I omitted to put into the cover the enclosed Mem:, Wm having written about the same time and read to Mr Monkhouse, to whom also you read *your* letter. He suggested to us both to withhold at that time what he had written, but as you have kindly sent me your letter, I think it but fair you should see my Mem:

M. W.

With regard to the proceeds of the Work undertaken by my nephew Dr Christopher Wordsworth in illustration of his Uncle's writings, my wish and hope is as follows.

That after payment of the necessary expenses of my nephew in

[1] Presumably the *Autobiographical Memoranda* (*Mem.* i. 7–17; *Prose Works*, iii. 371–5), referred to above in M. W.'s letter to I. F., 27 Dec. 1847.

connection with the preparation and publication of this work, the profits arising therefrom should be divided into two equal Shares; one share to be assigned to me during my life and to be wholly at my disposal for ever, with reservation of one third part of such share to my Son-in-law Ed: Quillinan during his life, and the other moiety of the profits to be at the disposal of the Author and his representatives.

Sept 5, 1850
Mary Wordsworth

Copy from C. W.

I hereby signify my compliance with this wish of my dear Aunt Mary Wordsworth.

Chris: Wordsworth
Septr 5th, 1850

M. W. to MARY HUTCHINSON

MS. WL.
MW, p. 326.

Monday ½ past 11 oC a.m.
[11 Nov. 1850]

My dearest Sister,

I write a line to put off the time of waiting for the Carriage to take us to the Station—it is a mild but dull day—and with God's blessing the dear Boy,[1] about whom I cannot but be anxious, will take no harm—and change may do good. He does not look better, and Dr Davy thinks it prudent to go on with *small* blisters which shews he is not quite at ease about him, dear good Man that he is. Thank yr dear Br[2] for his interesting letter recd yesterday, and dear Sarah[3] for her legible writing. Ask the Girls if they ever began to copy the Green's Narrative[4] and if so what they did with it. Fanny[5] says Eliz was about it when she was at Carlisle, and Sarah talked of doing it at the Cooksons, but I cannot understand it was done. The family have applied again for it, and Mr Carter is ready to make them a Copy, if he hears one is

---

[1] John W.'s son William, had been at Rydal Mount recovering from bronchitis, and was now returning to Brigham by way of Carlisle.

[2] John Monkhouse of The Stow.

[3] Sarah and Elizabeth (mentioned below), Mary Hutchinson's daughters.

[4] D. W.'s *Narrative Concerning George and Sarah Green*, written in 1808.

[5] W. W. jnr.'s wife.

not in forwardness.

It will please Aunty[1] if one of you will write to her—for she often tells us 'nobody takes notice of her'. She has been very cross lately.

Tell John—we hope Mr Moxon will be the Man after all—He came down for a few hours one day last week and has since had 2 interviews with D[r] W.[2]—and he, Moxon, says Murray's is 'a flat proposal'—

God bless you all lovingly yours
M. Wordsworth

M. W. to SUSAN WORDSWORTH

MS. British Library.
MW, p. 329 (—).

14th April [1851] Rydal Mt.

My dearest Susan,

I will not trouble dear Christopher by my thanks, otherwise than thro' you, for his very kind letter received yesterday, knowing how much his valuable time is occupied. You must therefore, for me, congratulate him upon the completion of his labour of love, and say to him that I quite agree with him in thinking the Agreement was a most unnecessary expence, but Men of business will have their way, and having to do with them, we must submit to their arrangements.

[1] i.e. D. W.

[2] Moxon's proposals for publishing the *Memoirs* were finally accepted in December (see *HCR* ii. 705–6).

[3] C. W. jnr.'s *Memoirs of William Wordsworth*, published under the shadow of the 'Papal Aggression', had a mixed reception within the family circle. In a letter to M. W., written while he was overseeing the proofs, E. Q. deplored the author's polemical stance: 'Dr W., just as I feared he would, is (as I have told him, though I do not expect him to take the smallest notice of my remonstrance) turning sweet to sour, making his Memoir serve as a medium for party polemics—enlisting the name and fame of the poet on the side of Lord Littlejohn and the treacherous Whigs, and in short, while serving also Dr. C. W.'s High Church Dogmatism, and the zealotry of all bigotted parties, Dissenters of all kinds, is putting the Poet . . . in a very unworthy . . . harness with Lord John Russell with his letter to the Bp of Durham.—To me this turn . . . has poisoned the whole Memoir. My sympathies with Dr C. W. and his compilation are all gone; and as the proofs are going through my hands, it wd be disingenuous in me not to declare my opinion at once.—There is no help for it, I suppose: but it

We have not seen the Memoir,[3] which has already reached the Stow, and my dear Sister expresses great pleasure and gratification as far as they had time to read,—the Book had only arrived the morning upon which she wrote. I suppose those Copies intended to be sent to Rydal Mount are waiting to be brought by Mr Quillinan, who is expected at home this Evening.

This evening I am also looking for my Grandaughter Jane. You know Fanny and her sweet little Darling[1] are already here—and William, who is now in London, will we hope join them—(as Mr Carter kindly goes to day to supply his place at Carlisle) about the middle of next week. So that my considerate Children have contrived that I should not be left to brood over Sad thoughts during the return of this blessed Season, to me so blended with sad and sorrowful remembrances.[2]

Eliz[th] Hutchinson, I regret to say, does not as I had hoped she might have done get rid of her unmanageable complaints, which even D[r] Davy, with all his attention to her, cannot discover whence they proceed. We have therefore determined that she should try the effect of a more complete change; and as Mr and Mrs Harrison,[3] *she* having the like motive for leaving home, have kindly admitted Eliz to go with them to Kissingen (some famous unexpensive and very salutary Baths in Germany—not far from Frankfurt), I shall have my dear Winter's Companion for a short time in the course of a Fortnight. She is to join Mr and Mrs H., who are now in London, there, and will return with them about the end of June I believe. I much hope this Excursion will quite renovate poor Eliz. Her Mother and Uncle are both sanguine in their expectations and she goes under the tender care of Mr and Mrs H.—so that none of us will have anxiety on that account.

Mr Monkhouse is going on with great spirit in the course you so kindly put him upon,[4] and for doing so he and all of us are so

will do much harm; and draw on much anger towards that venerated man . . . If I had seen Dr C. W.'s MS . . . I would have declined having anything to do with it.' (*MS. Mr. Jonathan Wordsworth*). In spite of his earlier misgivings, H. C. R.'s estimate was more moderate: 'If not the whole man is given, portions are faithfully, though inevitably in magnitude disproportioned to the other portions of his character' (*HCR* ii. 709). But in writing thus, he was acknowledging the omissions and imbalances in W. W.'s biography which were not to be corrected for more than half a century.

[1] Her daughter Mary Louisa.
[2] They were approaching the first anniversary of W. W.'s death.
[3] Of Green Bank.   [4] The nature of this project is unexplained.

grateful to you. My Sister mentioned in one of her letters that they had left him at his Studies one night—and found him at work when they arose in the morning. I fancy he is now making progress in writing—and his having (from you I suppose) received copies of the Gospels he had been waiting for, has lately made him very happy. Nevertheless he is not one bit less enthusiastic in bringing his Animals to, what I call, *Unperfection*. He is even preparing specimens for the Monster Exhibition—and my Sister thinks he intends, tho' he does not venture to tell them so, to go to Town and trust himself among the senseless hubbub that will be there assembled.

I have been, dear Susan, sorry to think of your separation from all the dear Children, and that your entry upon your parochial duties[1] should have been so trying—it will be a blessing if you escape infection. I do pray that you may, and that the village may soon be purified so that the Darlings may be able to join you safely. We promise ourselves the pleasure of hearing much that will interest us of you all, from Mr. Quillinan.

It is long since I have heard aught of dear Charles[2] and his Belongings, I trust they are all well and going on satisfactorily. And your own family also.

Your dear Aunt Dorothy continues in her usual state—she gets out several times most days, for short intervals, for she is I think somewhat more restless—and less *under restraint* than when you were with us: Otherwise there appears no change in her general health.

Of dear Miss Fenwick and other matters you have heard from Mr. Quillinan so that dear Susan, I need only add my tenderest love to you all, and beg you believe me ever to be affectionately

Yours
M Wordsworth

Your Aunt, joins with Fanny and Elizabeth in love to you and all.

[1] C. W. jnr. had been appointed to the living of Stanford-in-the-Vale, Berks.
[2] C. W. jnr.'s brother, now Warden of Trinity College, Glenalmond.

Addenda and Corrigenda
to
The Letters of William and Dorothy Wordsworth

The Early Years

L. 43	MS. now in *WL* (Moorsom Papers).
L. 79	MS. now at Rosenbach Foundation, Philadelphia.
L. 84	MS. now in Princeton University Library.
L. 101	MS. now in *WL*. Postmark: 17 Oct. 1798. Stamp: Foreign Office.
L. 119	MS. now at Rosenbach Foundation.
L. 120	MS. now at Rosenbach Foundation.
L. 122	MS. now at Rosenbach Foundation.
L. 146	MS. now at Rosenbach Foundation.
L. 206	MS. now in *WL*.
L. 210	MS. now in *WL*.

The Middle Years

L. 104	MS. in Colgate University Library.
L. 125	MS. in Sharpe Collection, University College, London.
L. 131	MS. in John Rylands Library, Manchester.
L. 144	MS. now in *WL*.
L. 159	MS. now in *WL*.
L. 163	MS. now in *WL*.
L. 169	MS. now in *WL*.
L. 233	MS. in *WL*.
L. 244	MS. formerly in the possession of Dr. E. L. McAdam, jnr., present location unknown.
L. 276	MS. in Sharpe Collection, University College, London.
L. 294	MS. in *Cornell*.
L. 361	MS. in Hyde Collection, Yale University Library.
L. 388	MS. in St. John's College, Cambridge.
L. 398	MS. in Yale University Library.
L. 432	MS. in *WL*.
L. 450	MS. in Sharpe Collection, University College, London.
L. 571	MS. in Keats House, Hampstead.
L. 571a	MS. in Sheffield University Library.
L. 579	The reference is not to Juan Fernandez Navarrete, the Spanish painter, but to D. Martin

The Middle Years cont.

L. 579 *cont.* Fernandez Navarrete, the biographer and editor of Cervantes, and to his *Life* of Cervantes, Madrid, 1819.

L. 585　　Also published in *Certificates in favour of Mr. John Wilson, Advocate*, [Edinburgh, 1820], p. 36.

L. 598　　MS. in St. John's College, Cambridge.

The Later Years

L. 403　　MS. now in *WL* (Moorsom Papers).

L. 560　　MS. now in *WL* (Moorsom Papers). The postmark is 15 July 1830, which establishes the date of the letter more accurately. It should follow L. 554.

L. 689　　MS. now in *WL* (Moorsom Papers). The letter, in M. W.'s hand and signed by W. W., is dated April 13th, and so it should follow L. 692.

L. 1380　　The reference is probably not to Robert Weaver's *Monumenta Antiqua*, which had only just appeared, but to *Ancient Funeral Monuments . . .* 1631, by John Weever (1576–1632), the poet and antiquarian. W. W. drew on the work extensively in his *Essays upon Epitaphs*.

L. 1773　　The quotation, which should read 'Stanemoor's wintry waste', is from l. 513 of the expanded manuscript version (1794) of *An Evening Walk*. See *PW* i. 28, and *An Evening Walk* (*The Cornell Wordsworth*), ed. James Averill, 1984, p. 147. Stanemoor (or Stainmore), a wild and solitary waste near Brough, is discussed in the *Guide to the Lakes* as one of the three approaches to the Lakes through Yorkshire (see *Prose Works*, ii. 155, 287–9). W. W. and S. T. C. had crossed it on their way to the Lakes in Nov. 1799 (see *EY*, L.124). Why W. W. and M. W. should apparently assume that I. F. would respond to the quotation here is not entirely clear, as the line had no place in any published version of the poem. Presumably she was acquainted with the 1794 revisions.

L. 1835　　MS. formerly in the possession of Dr. E. L. McAdam, jnr., present location unknown.

INDEX

Index

Index

Low Wood, 206.
Lowther, Viscount, M.P., *Letter to*: 170.
Lowther, 190, 213, 214. *See also* W.W.,
  Visits and journeys.
Lucerne, Lake of, 216.
Ludlow, 24, 116, 134.
Luff, Capt. Charles, 51, 54, 65, 98, 110,
  111, 118, 121, 126, 131, 133.
— Mrs., 171, 187.
Lyme, 245.
Lynedoch, 147.

Machiavelli, Niccolò, *Art of War*, 264n.
Mackintosh, Sir James, 56, 60, 86.
— Lady, 60, 86.
Mackareth, George, his son, 74; 170.
— Lucy, 172.
— Mary, 172.
Mackereth, Gawen, 33.
the Mackereths, 118.
MacVickar, Revd. John, at Rydal
  Mount, 206.
Malham Tarn, 103.
Maling, Mrs., 60–1.
Malkin, Benjamin Heath, translation of
  Le Sage's *Gil Blas*, 42.
Malvern, 220.
Malvern Hills, 28, 108.
Manchester, 21.
Mansfield, Lord, *see* Murray, David
  William.
Marsh, Anne, *Letter to*: 254; *Emilia
  Wyndham*, dedicated to W.W., 254.
Marsh, Peggy, 198.
Martineau, Harriet, *Letter to*: 256; 254n,
  262, 280.
Marylebone, 53, 95, 113.
Masterman and Co. (bankers), 210.
Mathon (nr. Malvern), 282.
Matthews, Mr., *Letter to*: 204.
May, John, *Letter to*: 164.
Melrose, 152.
Merewether, Revd. Francis, *Letter to*: 222.
— Mrs., 223.
Merrit, Mr. (bookseller), 130.
Middlesex Hospital, 158.
Militia Laws, 263–5.
Miller, Revd. John, *Letter to*: 19.
Milton, John, *Paradise Lost*, quoted 66,
  209; portrait, 159; *Works*, 197;
  Digression to History of Britain, 272–3.

Monckton, Mary, Lady Cork, 86.
Money, Robert Cotton, *Letter to*: 194.
Monkhouse, Elizabeth (M.W.'s aunt),
  Letter to: 140; 16, 100, 134.
— John (of The Stow, M.W.'s cousin),
  Letter to: 15; 12, 34, 66, 123, 124, 131,
  282, 288, 289, 290, 291.
— Thomas (M,W.'s cousin), 55, 61, 74,
  77, 79, 93, 107, 111, 116, 117, 118,
  119, 122, 133, 140, 157, 183, 187.
— Mrs., 183, 187, 189.
— William (M.W.'s uncle), 17.
Montagu, Alfred, 50.
— Algernon, 136.
— Basil, *Letters to*: 10, 248; 32–3, 49, 50,
  51, 52, 54, 58, 59, 65, 68, 69–70,
  75–6, 118, 119.
— Mrs., 32–3, 63, 66, 119, 120, 248, 249.
— Charles, 50.
— William, 50.
Montagus, the, 40, 49, 61, 81, 112, 129.
Montgomery, James, 74, 81, 157.
Moresby, 206, 207.
Morgan, John James, 72, 81, 90, 105,
  121.
— Mrs. Mary, 72, 121.
Morgans, the, 93, 95.
Morghen, Rafaello, engraving, 242.
Morpeth, 285.
Mortlake, 285.
Moryer and Co., *Letter to*: 209.
Moxon, Edward, *Letters to*: 248, 253;
  284, 285, 286, 288; publisher of
  Memoirs of W.W., 290.
Muirhead, James Patrick, 258n.
Mulgrave, Lord, *see*, Phipps, Henry.
Munich, 216, 237.
Murray, David William, 3rd Earl of
  Mansfield, 97.
— John, 4th Duke of Atholl, 148.
— — (publisher), 284, 285, 290.

Naples, 235.
National Debt, 269–72.
Nelson, Lord, death of, 257.
New York, 169, 206.
Newcastle upon Tyne, 28.
Newgate, prison, 82.
Norris, Revd. Henry Handley, *Letter to*:
  181.
— Mrs., 181.

301

Index

Wilkinson, Revd. Joseph, *Letter to*: 20; *Select Views in Cumberland, etc.* 20, 25.

Willes, Miss Anne (Lady Beaumont's sister), 109.

Williamson, Mary (servant), 127, 128; her mother, 126.

— Revd. William, *Letter to*: 193.

Wilson, John ('Christopher North'), 14; his poem, 91; 164, 195.

Winchester, 245.

Windsor, 40, 48; Castle, 43.

Wolverhampton, 44.

Wood, William (attorney), 232.

Woodruff, Thomas, 52, 65, 81, 111, 118, 119, 124, 126.

Woodstock, Blenheim Palace, 45, 122.

Worcester, 28, 29, 85, 108, 114, 122, 125.

Wordsworth, Caroline (W.W.'s 'French' daughter, later Mme. Baudouin), 62n., 111, 118n.; her financial expectations, 133; learning English, 133; 204n.; her marriage settlement, 275 and n.

— Catharine (W.W.'s daughter), lameness, 21; 25, 31, 37, 68, 75, 84, 87; death of, 116, 123, 124, 126, 127–8, 134; burial, 116, 126, 131; medical condition, 137–8, 140.

— Charles (C.W.'s son), 28, 292.

— — (W.W.'s grandson), 255.

— Dr. Christopher (W.W.'s brother), *Letter to*: 206; 3, 11, 20, 27; his family cares, 28, 41; 31, 40, 45, 49, 64, 69, 72, 81, 88, 108, 109, 110, 112, 118, 125, 173, 175; illness, 177–81; his pamphlet, 194; seeks property at Bowness, 208; his epitaph, 255; his portrait at Trinity, 255.

— Dr. Christopher (C.W.'s son), *Letters to*: 246, 255; 28, 192, 206; sermon and translation, 246; church building activities, 256; undertakes *Memoirs* of W.W., 281, 283–4, 285–8, 290–1; appointed to living, 292.

— Mrs. (*née* Susan Frere), *Letter to*: 290; 246, 247, 256, 281, 288; son John born, 246; daugher Susanna born, 255.

— Dorothy (W.W.'s sister), *Letters to*: 11, 43, 69, 71, 84, 113, 130, 147.

Family and friends: at Saville Green, 1, 4, 11; at Coleorton, 21–3; on S.T.C., 68, 78; impression of Lady Scott, 106; attitude towards Luff, 110; writes to Annette, 119; on death of Catharine W., 125, 127–9, 132; on John W., 125; on the Wordsworth children, 139; her nephews, 179; sending letters abroad, 204.

Visits and journeys: journey to Racedown (1795), 28; at Bury, 32, 39–42; at Binfield, 40n.; at Calais with W.W. (1802), 62; up Usk valley with W.W. (1798), 120; Scottish tour (1803), 147; in Wales, 156; at Lambeth rectory, 175, 177–81; at Birmingham, 178–9; at Coleorton, Birmingham, Oxford, London, 185–7; at Hallsteads and Patterdale, 208.

Interests: abridges W.W.'s sheets for Wilkinson, 25; in court at Bury, 40; Bury gateway and ruins, 40; country round Bury, 41; reads Malkin's *Gil Blas*, 42; her French, 119; on misuse of private letters, 179–81; asks for books, 217; taste in reading, 217.

Health: 5, 13, 22, 34, 40, 77; limited activities, 198; re-established health, 207; weakness, 214; an invalid, 217; confined to her room, 223; a 'wreck', 235; 'struggling', 255; comes down every evening, 279; 'very cross lately', 290; out most days, 292.

Writings: 'Christmas Day', 229–30; *Narrative Concerning George and Sarah Green*, 289.

— Dorothy ('Dora', W.W.'s daughter, later Mrs. Quillinan), *Letter to*: 238; 4, 16, 31, 37, 106, 125, 130, 131, 134, 139, 140, 187, 192, 193, 198, 206, 207, 211; at Dover, 236, 238; wishes to marry E.Q., 239n.; illness, 242–3; death of, 284, 287.

— Fanny Eliza (*née* Graham), 280, 285, 289, 291.

— Henry (W.W.'s grandson), 279.

— Jane (W.W.'s granddaughter), 278–9, 291.

— John (W.W.'s brother), 4, 5; shipwrecked, 104, 105.

plans house at Rydal, 191–2; sends autograph, 203, 208; receives Welsh dictionary, 211; picnic in Grasmere Vale, 213; on childhood power, 214–15; on Malvern, 220; proposes joint venture on mineral rights, 224; subscribes to restoration fund, 228; on the English Lakes, 237; receives engraving, 242; on Rydal Mount in spring, 243; Poet Laureateship, 245; spectacles, 248; objects to publication of private letters, 248; presented at Court, 250; accepts drawing of Rydal, 256; accepts presents, 257; agrees to subscribe to volume, 261.

Visits and journeys: in London, 9, 11; at Coleorton, 9, 21–3; at Dunmow, 11; at Hindwell, 26, 32–4; at Windsor, 43, 48; at Birmingham, 27–8, 44; at Oxford, 44–6; in London, 48 ff.; at Hampstead, 94, 95–8, 106, 107, 113, 114, 117; at Greenwich, 105, 113, 114; at Penrith with M.W. (1788–9), 110; up Usk valley (1793 and 1798), 120; at Bocking, 123; at Hindwell, 123, 125, 131–2, 134; Scottish tour (1803), 147; Scottish tour (1814), 147–53; at Edinburgh, 152; on the Yarrow, 152n.; at Birmingham, 180; at Lambeth rectory, 181; on the Continent (1820), 181; in London, 181; at Coleorton, Birmingham, Oxford, London, Lee Priory, 185–7; at Harrogate, 193; at Walham Green, 193; in Ireland, 198; in Duddon valley, 199; at Moresby, 207; at Cambridge, 207; at Lowther, 213, 214, 236; at Workington, 220; in London, 226, 234–5; Continental tour (1837), 234–5, 237, 252; at Bath, 241; at Bagborough, 244; at Alfoxden (1841), 244; at Brinsop, 246; at Stockton, 246; in London and Brinsop, 250.

Current affairs and politics: at the House of Commons debate on barracks, 53; on the fashionable world, 62; on industrial unrest, 63, 66; on Bellingham and criminal justice, 82; no faith in Ministers, 89; on growth of manufactures and changes in national

character, 92; on the Prince Regent, 96; on Wellington and his wife, 99, 115; on General Fitzpatrick, 102, 115; country in a deplorable state, 103; on the Princess Regent, 104, 115; promotes new paper for Kendal, 166; Westmorland politics (1818), 166–7; on America, 169–70; on freedom of the press, 171; on the Slavery question, 186; on Grasmere enclosures, 188–9; on concession, 202–3; Westmorland politics (1832), 215; on the Kendal and Windermere Railway, 249–50; on Corn Laws and Protectionists, 256; visits to France during Revolution, 259.

Religion and Church affairs: reliance on God's goodness, 141; at Kirk, 149–50; on Romaine's preaching, 150; the Litany, 161; religious art in churches, 166–7; on Christianity in India, 196; on the assurance of personal immortality, 200; on belief in Providence, 201–2; on Church of England, 202; stands sponsor, 219; promotes new church at Cockermouth, 228–9, 230–3; opposition, 232; on Italian religion and morals, 253.

Views on literature: on the written language, 3; on Lope de Vega, 6; loathes publication, 11; on Sotheby, 56; on Bowles, 65, 76; on Byron, 149, 155, 168n., 177, *Childe Harold*, 65, 80; on James Montgomery, 74; 'foolish and stupid novels', 77; on Blake, 80n.; on S.T.C.'s unpopularity, 83; on his habits and genius, 83; on Thurlow's poems, 83; on S.T.C.'s lectures, 85; on John Wilson, 91; on Leigh Hunt, 144–5; on Gillies's *Egbert*, 155; on Hogg's *Queen's Wake*, 155–6; on poetic vocabulary, 156; on Hazlitt, 161–2; on Southey's industry, 163; on Money's poems, 194–5; on workmanship in poetry, 196; on the circulation of periodicals, 201; on Hare's publications, 199–202; on Niebuhr, 200–1; on Lady Northampton's poems, 225; on *The Tribute*, 237–8; on W. R. Hamilton's verses, 239–40; on Allston's portrait of S.T.C., 241; advises Boner to delay